Young Arthur

A six weeks tour, through the southern counties of England and Wales

By the author of the Farmer's letters

Young Arthur

A six weeks tour, through the southern counties of England and Wales
By the author of the Farmer's letters

ISBN/EAN: 9783337184919

Printed in Europe, USA, Canada, Australia, Japan

Cover: Foto ©Andreas Hilbeck / pixelio.de

More available books at **www.hansebooks.com**

THE PRESIDENT'S REPORT.

To the Honorable Board of Regents:

I have the honor to present to you my Annual Report for the year ending September 30, 1893.

The following is a list of appointments made and of resignations accepted:

In October, 1892, F. R. Mechem, was appointed Tappan Professor of Law; and Assistant Professor J. E. Reighard, Professor of Animal Morphology.

In November, 1892, George F. Metzler, Ph. D., Instructor in Mathematics: E. W. Dow, A. B., Instructor in History, each for one year; Carl W. Belser, Ph. D., (reappointed for three years), Assistant Professor of Oriental Languages; Judge Samuel Maxwell, Lecturer on Code Pleading, (one year); William G. Hammond, LL. D., Lecturer on History of Common Law (one year).

In December, 1892, Assistant Professor T. C. Trueblood was made Professor of Elocution and Oratory, from January 1, 1893.

In February, 1893, the resignations of Assistant Professor Belser, Ph. D., Arthur G. Hall, B. S., Instructor in Mathematics, and Moritz Levi, A. B., Instructor in French, were accepted, and Pomeroy Ladue, B. S., was appointed Instructor in Mathematics, and Eugene Leser, Ph. D., Instructor in French, each for the second semester.

The President was authorized to fill the vacancy in the chair of Oriental Languages. He afterwards appointed W. Muss-Arnolt, Ph. D., Acting Assistant Professor for the second semester.

In May, F. C. Newcombe, B. S., was appointed Acting Assistant Professor of Botany, for the next year, to take the work of Professor Spalding, who was granted permission to spend the coming year in Europe. Professor McLaughlin was also granted leave of absence for a year, to pursue studies in Europe. The resignation of Professor John J. Abel, Ph. D., was accepted.

In June the following appointments were made:

IN THE LAW DEPARTMENT,

(for one year).

Andrew C. McLaughlin, A. B., LL. B., Advanced Course in Constitutional Law and Constitutional History.

Thomas M. Cooley, LL. D., Lecturer on Interstate Commerce.

Henry B. Brown, LL. D., Lecturer on Admiralty.

Victor C. Vaughan, Ph. D., M. D., Lecturer on Toxicology in its Legal Relations.

Marshall D. Ewell, LL. D., Lecturer on Medical Jurisprudence.

Samuel Maxwell, Lecturer on Code Pleading.

James L. High, LL. D., Lecturer on Injunctions and Receivers.

Melville M. Bigelow, Ph. D., Lecturer on Insurance.

John B. Clayberg, LL. B., Lecturer on Mining Law.

Richard Hudson, A. M., Lecturer on Comparative Constitutional Law.

George H. Lothrop, Ph. B., Lecturer on Patent Law.

Henry C. Adams, Ph. D., Lecturer on the Railroad Problem.

William G. Hammond, LL. D., Lecturer on History of Common Law.

Elias Finley Johnson, B. S., LL. M., Instructor in Law.

IN BOTH THE MEDICAL AND LITERARY DEPARTMENTS.

Warren P. Lombard, A. B., M. D., permanent appointment as Professor of Physiology and Histology.

Frederick G. Novy, Sc. D., M. D., Junior Professor of Hygiene and Physiological Chemistry, to act under the direction of Professor Vaughan.

IN THE LITERARY DEPARTMENT.

John C. Rolfe, Ph. D., Junior Professor of Latin.

George Hempl, Ph. D., Junior Professor of English.

Edward D. Campbell, B. S., Junior Professor of Metallurgy and Metallurgical Chemistry (he to provide his own assistant).

Each of the above three persons is required to work under the direction of the Senior Professor in his branch (Professor Campbell under Professor Prescott).

Fred N. Scott, Ph. D., reappointed Assistant Professor of Rhetoric, for three years.

Frank N. Cole, Ph. D., reappointed Assistant Professor of Mathematics, for three years.

George H. Mead, A. B., appointed Assistant Professor of Philosophy, for three years.

Joseph L. Markley, Ph. D., reappointed Instructor in Mathematics, for three years.

Moritz Levi, A. B., reappointed Instructor in French, for three years.

Fred Morley, C. E., reappointed Instructor in Descriptive Geometry and Drawing, for three years.

Elmer A. Lyman, A. B., reappointed Instructor in Mathematics, for three years.

The following reappointments and new appointments were made for one year·

Dr. James A. Craig, appointed Professor of Oriental Languages.

Herman V. Ames, Ph. D., Acting Assistant Professor of American History.

Hiram A. Sober, A. B., Instructor in Latin.

George O. Higley, B. S., Instructor in General Chemistry.

Alfred H. Lloyd, A. M., Instructor in Philosophy.

Jonathan A. C. Hildner, A. M., Instructor in German.

Ernst Voss, Instructor in German.

David M. Lichty, M. S., Instructor in General Chemistry.

John O. Reed, Ph. M., Instructor in Physics.

Benjamin P. Bourland, A. M., Instructor in French.

John R. Effinger, Ph. B., Instructor in French.

Lorenzo N. Johnson, A. M., Instructor in Botany.

Herbert F. DeCou, A. M., Instructor in Greek.

Henry B. Ward, Ph. D., Instructor in Morphology.

Ernst H. Mensel, A. M., Instructor in German.

Lawrence McLouth, A. B., Instructor in German.

Earle W. Dow, A. B., Instructor in History.

Pomeroy Ladue, B. S., Instructor in Mathematics.

Eugene Leser, Ph. D., Instructor in French.

George E. Dawson, A. B., Instructor in English.

Moses Gomberg, M. S., Instructor in Organic Chemistry.

Clarence G. Wrentmore, B. S., Instructor in Descriptive Geometry and Drawing.

Eric Doolittle, B. S., Instructor in Astronomy.

Karl E. Guthe, Ph. D., Instructor in Physics.

Tobias Diekhoff, A. B., Instructor in German.

George A. Miller, A. M., Instructor in Mathematics.

Marshall S. Brown, A. M., Instructor in History.

The following assistants were reappointed for one year:

Charles H. Cooley, A. B., in Political Economy.
Frank H. Dixon, Ph. B., in Political Economy.
Alice L. Hunt, in Drawing.
William F. Edwards, B. S., Instructor and Accountant in the Chemical Laboratory.

DEPARTMENT OF MEDICINE AND SURGERY,
(for one year).

William F. Breakey, M. D., Lecturer on Dermatology.
Martin L. Belser, M. D., Instructor in Pathology.
Simon M. Yutzy, M. D., Instructor in Osteology, Assistant Demonstrator of Anatomy.

SCHOOL OF PHARMACY.

Julius O. Schlotterbeck, B. S., Instructor in Pharmacognosy and Botany, (for one year).

THE GENERAL LIBRARY.

Fred P. Jordan, A. B., Assistant in charge of catalogue.
Byron A. Finney, A. B., Assistant in charge of circulation.
Anderson H. Hopkins, Ph. B., General Assistant.

The following appointment was made at the August meeting:

Arthur R. Cushny, A. M., M. D., Professor of Materia Medica and Therapeutics, for one year, in the Department of Medicine and Surgery.

Dr. J. C. Wood resigned the Professorship of the Diseases of Women and Children in the Homœopathic Medical College.

At the meeting on September 1st, Charles Gatchell, M. D., resigned the chair of Theory and Practice in the Homœopathic Medical College.

The following appointments were made:

S. D. Townley, M. S., Instructor in Astronomy, in place of Eric Doolittle, appointed in June, who declined.

D. C. Worcester, A. B., Instructor in Animal Morphology, in place of Dr. H. B. Ward, resigned.

H. S. Jennings, B. S., Assistant in Vertebrate Morphology.

C. G. Darling, M. D., Clinical Lecturer on Oral Pathology in the Dental College.

At the meeting on September 20th, the following appointments were made:

F. M. Taylor, Ph. D., Assistant Professor, was made Junior Professor of Political Economy and Finance.

Maurice P. Hunt, M. D., Professor of Gynecology and Obstetrics in the Homœopathic Medical College.

E. R. Eggleston, M. D., Professor of Theory and Practice in the same department.

Louis P. Hall, D. D. S., Instructor in Dental Anatomy and Operative Dentistry.

J. B. Johnston, Ph. B., Assistant in Invertebrate Morphology.

Max Winkler, Ph. D., Instructor in German.

Degrees were conferred as follows, during the year:

DEGREES ON EXAMINATION.

Bachelor of Letters	29
Bachelor of Science (in Biology)	8
Bachelor of Science (in Chemistry)	5
Bachelor of Science (in Electrical Engineering)	13
Bachelor of Science (in Mining Engineering)	2
Bachelor of Science (in Mechanical Engineering)	13
Bachelor of Science (in Civil Engineering)	15
Bachelor of Science	15
Bachelor of Philosophy	53
Bachelor of Arts	73
Master of Letters	2
Civil Engineer	1
Master of Science	4
Master of Philosophy	5
Master of Arts	12
Doctor of Philosophy	1
Doctor of Medicine (Department of Medicine and Surgery)	49
Bachelor of Laws	330
Master of Laws	18
Pharmaceutical Chemist	20
Master of Pharmacy	1
Doctor of Medicine (Homœopathic Medical College)	20
Doctor of Dental Surgery	53
	742

HONORARY DEGREES.

Master of Science	1
Master of Arts	2
	745

Last year the number of degrees conferred, 699, was

the largest recorded in the history of any American University. But that number is now exceeded by 46. This is the more noteworthy, because owing to the transition in Medical Schools from a three years' course to a four years' course, the number graduating in the Department of Medicine and Surgery was only about half as large as usual. The coming year the graduating class in that Department will be about as large as it was in former years. If the increase in the number of graduates were occasioned by a lowering of the standard of graduation, it would afford no ground for satisfaction. But it has come in the face of an advance in the requirements of graduation, and is, therefore, gratifying.

The attendance has been as follows:

SUMMARY OF STUDENTS.

DEPARTMENT OF LITERATURE, SCIENCE, AND THE ARTS.

Holder of the Elisha Jones Classical Fellowship	1	
Resident Graduates	65	
Candidates for an Advanced Degree, Enrolled in Other Departments	6	
Graduates Studying *in Absentia*	44	
Undergraduates:		
Candidates for a Degree	1131	
Students not Candidates for a Degree	244	1491

DEPARTMENT OF MEDICINE AND SURGERY.

Resident Graduates	3	
Fourth Year Students	46	
Third Year Students	76	
Second Year Students	91	
First Year Students	128	344

DEPARTMENT OF LAW.

Resident Graduates	24	
Seniors	319	
Juniors	270	
Special Students	12	
Students enrolled in the Department of Literature, Science, and the Arts	14	639

SCHOOL OF PHARMACY.

Resident Graduates	2	
Second Year Students	33	
First Year Students	47—	82

HOMŒOPATHIC MEDICAL COLLEGE.

Resident Graduate	1	
Fourth Year Students	21	
Third Year Students	13	
Second Year Students	10	
First Year Students	18—	63

COLLEGE OF DENTAL SURGERY.

Resident Graduates	7	
Seniors	52	
Juniors	76	
Freshmen	54—	189
		2808
Deduct for names counted more than once		30
Total		2778

The number of students was larger than in the year preceding by 86. By far the largest increase was in the Literary Department, 161. The School of Pharmacy and the Dental College had each one more student than in the preceding year, while the attendance fell off a little in each of the other Professional Schools. We regard the growth of the Literary Department as the surest proof of the prosperity of the University. There was a gratifying increase in the attendance of most of the stronger colleges and universities of the country last year. But though this growth of the western institutions might have been expected to reduce our numbers, such did not prove to be the fact. The students from other States than Michigan were even more than in 1891–2. But the aggregate increase of 86 was chiefly due to the increased number from Michigan, which was 79 greater than in the previous year. For the first time in many years Michigan furnished a fraction of one per cent. more than one-half of all our students. This evinced a gratifying appreciation by the State of the advantages the University offers to her children, and also of the value of a higher education.

Forty-four of our States and Territories were represented in our students, Illinois sending 310, Ohio 217, Indiana 114, Iowa 71, Pennsylvania 72, New York 67, Missouri 55, Kansas 38, Wisconsin 38, Nebraska 33, Minnesota 30, Utah 29, California 27, Massachusetts 24, Colorado 23, Kentucky 21, Oregon 15, Washington 15, Tennessee 12, Maryland 9, Montana 9, Texas 9, New Hampshire 8. Every New England State was represented. Students were present from the following foreign States and Provinces: Ontario (29), Japan, England, Germany, China, New Brunswick, Hawaiian Islands, Italy, Barbadoes, Bermuda, Bulgaria, Costa Rica, Manitoba, Porto Rico, Quebec, Scotland, South Africa. It is a fact of special interest that two women from China are in attendance on the Medical Department. They are under the care of American missionaries, who are here with them. So far as I know they are, with a single exception, the first Chinese women who have ever left their native land for the purpose of study. The importance of such an experiment can hardly be overestimated.

The attendance of women was as follows:

Department of Literature, Science, and the Arts	514
Department of Medicine and Surgery	71
Department of Law	2
School of Pharmacy	6
Homœopathic Medical College	14
College of Dental Surgery	7
Total	614

Compared with the previous year, there was an increased attendance of women: in the aggregate, 83, or 15.6 per cent.; in the Literary Department, 77, or 17.6 per cent.; in the Medical Department, 12, or 20 per cent.; in the Pharmacy Department of 2. There was a decrease in the Law Department of 1, in the Homœopathic College of 6, in the Dental College of 1. The women now constitute nearly 37 per cent. of the attendance in the Literary Department. Last year they formed 33 per cent. Whether one observes the high schools or the colleges of the country, one cannot but be struck with the increase in the number of women, compared with that of the men, who are obtaining an academic or collegiate education. In many of the Michigan high schools the graduating classes are made up almost wholly of girls. The boys are drawn off to wage-earning pursuits before they have completed the school course. It is no longer an exceptional thing for the girl in the family to go to college. She looks forward, if her father's means permit the anticipation, from the high school to the college as she looked forward from the grammar school to the high school. So it has come to pass that the number of young women not only in the colleges which are intended for their sex alone, but also in the colleges and universities, which receive students of both sexes, is rapidly increasing. It is indeed becoming a question whether a generation hence there will be as many college-trained men as college trained women in this country. The educational, intellectual, and social consequences of this forward movement in the training of women we may not be able to foresee fully, but that they must be very important no one can doubt. I cannot but think that they will be very beneficent. Just now, however, the stimulus to obtain collegiate education needs to be given to the boys more than to the girls, at least in the west.

One cannot but be struck with the rapidly increasing favor with which the policy of opening universities and colleges to women is received in Europe as well as in America. The success of women in all branches of university study, and the wise use which they are making of their attainments in life, are fast overcoming the objections long held to offering them the opportunities for higher education, while the experience of the institutions which are educating men and women together is rapidly conquering the theoretical objections to coeducation of the sexes. The benefits of this rational policy of opening to women the advantages of education long offered to men are not to be measured by the blessings thus conferred personally upon the women, who enjoy those advantages, but account must be taken of the vast improvement thus secured to the schools in which these women are teaching. A new inspiration has been carried into the seminaries, high schools and colleges, in which women, graduates of good colleges, are now giving instruction. Few agencies have been more potent in lifting the grade of secondary education in the west in the last few years than the thorough collegiate training of the women who have been charged with the duty of teaching in the secondary schools.

The subscriptions for the Waterman Gymnasium, though insufficient for the completion of the building, have enabled us to put up the walls of the main structure, to roof it, and to lay the principal floors. We need about $18,000 to finish the building which is now enclosed, and we should have about $20,000 more to complete the wing for the women. The severity of the financial crisis in the country has rendered it useless to attempt to secure these sums during the months just past. We trust that when business prosperity returns we may receive the needed help. It seems due to the benefactors who have already contributed that we should push the building to completion at the earliest date possible.

Some of our Professors have continued what is known as the University Extension work during the past winter, at Detroit, Grand Rapids, East Saginaw, Toledo and Cadillac. Professor Demmon gave courses on English Literature, Professor Adams on Problems of Transportation, Professor Vaughan on Hygiene and Sanitation, Professor Carhart on Electricity, and Professor Scott on Art.

Classes of good size were organized, and work was successfully accomplished. It is still too early to say whether the popular interest in this work is to grow or to decline. But it is already very clear that the draught which the lecturing makes on the Professors, when added to their regular work, is heavy, and if it is thought to be the duty of the University to provide much instruction of this kind as a part of its regular work, than we shall be obliged to appoint, as some universities have appointed, men to give most of their time and strength to lecturing to Extension classes. If the means are available, something can be said for doing so. But I am not convinced that in our circumstances we are yet called to make special appointment of Extension lecturers. We may however, give the subject further consideration.

In my last report I called attention to the importance of giving more attention to the work of graduate students in the Literary Department. The Faculty of that Department had then been for a year carefully considering how we could increase the efficiency of our instruction of the graduates. They decided to commit the direction of the work to an Administrative Council, composed of the Senior Professors in the various branches taught. That body has devoted much labor and thought to the best mode of conducting the graduate work, and it is believed that during the year considerable improvement has been made. More careful supervision of the students has been made practicable, and certain important principles in respect to graduate study and the conditions of attaining Master's and Doctor's degrees have been agreed upon.

It has been decided to discontinue giving degrees for study *in absentia*. The object sought in offering Master's degrees to graduates who could not come here to study has been accomplished in much smaller measure than was expected. It was believed that it would stimulate teachers especially to continue advanced work while engaged in their schools. Though to a certain extent this proved to be a result, yet it has been found that the duties of teachers in the high schools are so exacting that prolonged and sequent study of the grade required for the attainment of a degree is practicable in fewer cases than we had supposed. Of all of our graduates who have made the attempt *in absentia* to win the Master's degree, only about 15 per cent. have succeeded in accomplishing it. The contrast between the work of most of these candidates and that of graduates in residence was very marked. Therefore, while we regard it as possible for some to deserve the second degree by studies pursued *in absentia*, we have reluctantly come to the conclusion that in the interests of sound learning it is wise to ask all candidates for it to reside here during their term of study. It is believed that nearly every one who has the strength of purpose needed to complete his studies while engaged in teaching can find a way to return here for a year.

The candidates for a Doctor's degree have always been required to reside here for at least a year. They will now be required to reside here at least two years, and are given especially to understand that more time than that may be necessary. They are henceforth to have a reading knowledge of two modern languages when they are received as candidates. Much stress will be laid on the preparation of an acceptable dissertation, which must be a positive contribution to scholarship or to scientific knowledge. In thus establishing a high standard of work for the attainment of the Doctorate, we are acting in harmony with the better American Universities, which are aiming to give significance and value to that degree.

It is certainly one of the functions of a university like this to furnish the higher training which our graduate school is attempting to provide. It must be understood that it is costly to provide it. Much of the time of our most experienced Professors must be given to a comparatively few students. Special means of illustration are often required. Especially are books needed. The Faculty are very grateful that an unusually generous appropriation has been made by the Board this year for the purchase of books. It will enable us to fill many bad gaps in our Library. If we can attract and teach a large body of gifted and aspiring graduate students, their presence will have a strong lifting and inspiring influence on the undergraduates, and their achievements in various spheres of intellectual activity after they leave us will be of immense service to the University. Perhaps nothing would benefit the graduate school more just now than the establishment of fellowships in it, such as several of the stronger American Universities now have. Friends of the University who wish to aid it by gifts could do nothing more helpful than to establish such fellowships, yielding, say, five hundred dollars a year each. It is matter of congratulation that, although we have only one such fellowship, we have been able to hold so large a number of graduates as we have had in recent years.

The Literary Faculty have decided with your approbation to ask in 1895, and thereafter, for certain preparation in French or German or Latin of the students who are to enter on engineering courses. The requirements for admission to those courses omitted all foreign languages, mainly because in our section of the country for many years a considerable number of men of mature years, who had grown up in offices of engineers without much opportunity for training in languages, came here to prepare themselves for engineering work. But under the stimulus given in recent years to engineering study, especially to the preparation for mechanical and for electrical engineering, by far the larger number of matriculants in these courses are young men prepared in our High Schools, where the languages are well taught. A good knowledge of French and German is so helpful to the accomplished engineer of our time that it is wise to encourage the student to get a good reading knowledge of these tongues early in his course.

The literary Faculty have been much engaged during the year in the consideration of requirements for admission and for graduation. There is a wide-spread belief, which is probably well founded, that in this country an unnecessary amount of time is consumed in carrying the student from his primary studies to graduation from college. Many of our best educational experts are convinced that a better adjustment and distribution of studies in the preparatory schools are possible, and are seeking improvement in the present scheme of work. It is thought by some of our Professors that too many hours are required for graduation in some of our courses. While the Faculty are not yet prepared to make specific recommendations to you on these subjects, it is proper that you should know that with a vigilant regard for the interests of the University and for the utmost efficiency of our system of secondary and higher education, they are carefully studying the problems which are now engaging the attention of our best guides in educational policy.

The increasing interest in the study of the Oriental Languages has seemed to justify the appointment of a professor of those tongues. The new interest throughout the country in Biblical Literature and in the studies which serve to illustrate it must have struck every one. Courses of lectures on these subjects have attracted large assemblies. Our Students' Christian Association has had a large voluntary attendance on its Biblical Institutes. It is natural, therefore, that a new interest in Hebrew, Assyrian and Semitic studies generally should have manifested itself in colleges and universities. It is not improbable that the existence of the various guilds which churches in this city have established may make a Professorship of Oriental Languages especially useful here. One communion represented here is already making arrangements to give a certain amount of theological instruction to its candidates for the ministry, who may matriculate in the University and pursue such linguistic and philosophical studies as they desire. We cannot have a theological department. But if the guilds or other societies assemble theological students here for instruction, we may, with propriety, and with satisfaction, receive such students to our classes.

The extension of the medical course to four years and the establishment of a requirement for admission substantially like that for admission to the scientific course in American colleges have proved wise. These measures have not caused the diminution in attendance which might have been feared, while they have brought us a class of students better prepared for medical study than we used to receive. It was a gratifying fact that of the class which might have been graduated in three years, the large number of 44 decided to remain and complete the four years' course. The number of new students admitted was 128, a large class for us. These are proofs that the profession and the students are quite ready for the steps which we have taken to raise the standard of medical education. Indeed for years we have taken no forward steps, which has not been justified by the results.

Our instruction in medicine is every year taking on more completely a genuinely scientific form. The laboratories furnish a larger and larger proportion of the teaching. The special advanced or "practical" courses established here last year before they had been introduced in any other medical school, have proved of the greatest service, and have attracted much attention. The representatives of European medical schools, who have visited us this year on their way to the Columbian Exposition, have warmly commended these courses. One of the most distinguished French Professors declared to us that there was nothing like them elsewhere, and that he should seek to have them established in France on his return home. The Hospital has been crowded to repletion with patients, and many have been quartered in private houses. The need of another ward is very pressing.

The institution of a preparatory course for medical studies in our Literary Department is proving helpful. By judicious elections students may pursue the sciences which they especially need as a preparation for the medical course, and thus shorten by a year the time required to complete both the work needed for the degree of Bachelor in the Literary Department, and that needed for the degree of Doctor of Medicine. Students are now coming to us with the definite purpose of completing both courses on this plan.

The attendance upon the Law School, though slightly smaller than in the year preceding, was still larger than that in any other Law School in the country. The demands upon the students for work have been made more stringent than ever before. Plans have been matured for the establishment of a practice court, in which students shall be thoroughly trained in all the details of procedure, both by common law pleading and by code pleading.

The Homœopathic Medical College has been somewhat disturbed by differences of opinion in the Faculty concerning the policy to be pursued in conducting it. Some homœopathic physicians both in the State and out of it have been needlessly agitated by reports that the regents were likely to adopt statutes injurious to it. Professors Wood and Gatchell have resigned their chairs to accept appointments elsewhere. Professors Eggleston and Hunt have been appointed in their places. It is superfluous to say that the Board are seeking, as they have in years past sought, the best interests of the college. Unhappily differences and parties in the profession embarrass the Board in some degree in achieving such success for the college as they earnestly desire.

The School of Pharmacy continues to do its work with its usual thoroughness. The number of its students is somewhat falling off. This is due to three causes. First, a considerable number of Pharmacy Schools have been established, and the requirements for admission and for graduation, in most of them, are much lower than ours. Secondly, the temporary effect of the laws of Michigan for examinations in pharmacy is to send many students to the short-term schools. Thirdly, since in the Literary Department we have offered a four years' course, leading to the degree of Bachelor of Science in Chemistry, a certain number of the more aspiring students, who would formerly have contented themselves with the Pharmacy course, now prefer the longer and richer course.

The elevation of the standard of admission to the Dental College and the extension of its course of instruction to three years, did not reduce the total number of students, though the number in the Freshman class was smaller by 31 than it was in the previous year. But with our present accommodations and teaching force, it is perhaps well that the classes should not be much larger. The wisdom of raising the standard of admission and of graduation cannot be questioned.

We have continued the publication of the University Record. It contains much matter of interest to those who wish to understand the details of the work of the University and the aims of its Faculties. It is a valuable medium of communication with the schools. It is to be regretted that more of our alumni do not subscribe for it. We should be gratified if our friends would aid us in enlarging its circulation.

The following data are taken from the Librarian's report:

Number of volumes in all the libraries, Sep., 1893 ———— 85,781
  "   " unbound pamphlets   "   " ———— 16,000
  "   " maps   "   " ————   800
Increase of volumes from Oct. 1, 1892, to Sept. 30, 1893 —— 3,434
  "   " unbound pamphlets ————————————————————   70
  "   " maps ————————————————————————————————   74

Recorded use of books in reading rooms for the above twelve months ———————————————————————————————— 131,130

Number of volumes drawn from the library by Professors
    for the same time------------------------------------- 4,800
                                                         ———————
                                                         135,939

We have received and placed in our Art Gallery the final installment of the Randolph Rogers collection. It was the cast of the Columbus Doors of the Capitol at Washington. It was a happy coincidence that it arrived in this year of the Columbian Exposition. It is, perhaps, Rogers's most original and successful work. The entire collection consists of ninety-six pieces and is the most valuable gift, except the Lewis collection of works of art, ever made by any person to this University. The new catalogue of the Art collection, prepared with great care by Professor D'Ooge, gives 205 titles in sculpture, 36 in architectural ornaments and models of antique remains, 175 in paintings, and 1789 in gems and medallions. The Lewis collection is not included in this enumeration.

We sent as full a University exhibit to the Columbian Exposition at Chicago as the means at our disposal would enable us to make. We aimed to show as far as possible the methods and the results of our work in various departments. Of course, a large part of the best work of a university cannot be exhibited in a visible form. But we have reason to be satisfied with the attention which our exhibit received and with the commendations which it elicited. Our thanks are due to the Committee of the Faculties who had it in charge, and who bestowed so much labor on the preparation of it.* Professor Steere with his assistants in the Museum prepared a representative collection of the fauna of the state for the Michigan Building. The specimens in our Museum were supplemented by the purchase of such as we did not possess.

Representatives from the University took an important part in many of the congresses which were held in

---

*The committee consisted of Professors Cooley, Prescott, Greene, Steere, and Kelsey.

connection with the Exposition, and on the Boards of Judges.

In my last Report I called attention to the desirableness and importance of making an addition to the salaries of our teachers. It was a source of gratification that the Board found themselves able during this year to increase somewhat the salaries of the Professors. I am sure they regretted their inability to recognize in the same way the value of the services of the Assistant Professors and the Instructors. It is to be hoped that at no distant day the condition of our treasury may make this possible. Otherwise we shall be in danger of losing some of our more promising young men, whom we much desire to retain. Our scale of compensation is below that of the institutions with which we are ranked.

We desire to acknowledge with gratitude the generous consideration which we received at the hands of the Legislature last winter. With a hearty appreciation of our needs they voted to raise the tax which is levied for our support from one-twentieth to one-sixth of a mill.* They require by the terms of the act that we shall maintain all the present Departments of the University, and that we shall not run in debt for buildings. On the present valuation of the taxable property of the state, this tax will yield $188,300 a year. It is, of course, understood that the appropriation of this sum will obviate the necessity of our going to the Legislature at each session for a number of specific appropriations. But it will enable us to make little, if any, enlargement of our work. Yet the bestowal of aid in this way gives us ground to hope that we can surely depend on it for an indefinite period in the future. It promises stability in the support of the Institution so that we can with reasonable safety plan for the future. That is the reason why we are so much gratified at this action of the Legislature. We believe also that we can

---

*See Act in Appendix A.

Disbursements.

None
Balance in Treasury, June 30th, 1893 . . . . 1,381 93

ART FUND.
Receipts.

Balance in Treasury, July 1st, 1893	80 82	
Donations	15 00	
Interest	1 79	97 61

Disbursements.

Paid Vouchers for Expenses	81 48	
Balance in Treasury, June 30th, 1893	16 13	97 61

APPENDIX B.

AN ACT.

To amend section one of act number thirty-two of the public acts of eighteen hundred and seventy-three, entitled "An act to extend aid to the University of Michigan, and to repeal an act entitled 'An act to extend aid to the University of Michigan' approved March fifteenth, eighteen hundred and sixty-seven, being sections three thousand five hundred and six and three thousand five hundred and seven of the compiled laws of eighteen hundred and seventy-one," the same being section four thousand nine hundred and forty-four of Howell's annotated statutes.

SECTION 1. *The People of the State of Michigan enact*, That section one of act thirty-two of the public acts of eighteen hundred and seventy-three, entitled "An act to extend aid to the University of Michigan, and to repeal ah act entitled 'An act to extend aid to the University of Michigan' approved March fifteenth, eighteen hundred and sixty-seven, being sections three thousand five hundred and six and sections three thousand five hundred and seven of the compiled laws of eighteen hundred and seventy-one," the same being section four thousand nine hundred and forty-four of Howell's annotated statutes, be and the same is hereby amended so as to read as follows:

SECTION 1. *The People of the State of Michigan enact:* That there shall be assessed upon the taxable property of the State, as fixed by the State board of equalization, in the year one thousand eight hundred and seventy-three and in each year thereafter, for the use and maintenance of the University of Michigan, the sum of one-sixth of a mill on each dollar of said taxable property, to be assessed and paid in to the treasury of the State in like manner as other State taxes are by law levied, assessed and paid; which tax, when collected, shall be paid by the State treasurer to the board of regents of the University, in a like manner as the interest on the University fund is paid to the treasurer of said board. And the regents of the University shall make an annual report to the Governor of the State of all the receipts and expenditures of the University. Provided, that the board of regents shall not authorize the building or the commencement of any additional building or buildings, or other extraordinary repairs, until the accumulations of savings from this fund shall be sufficient to complete such building or extraordinary expense.

Also provided; That the Board of Regents of the University shall maintain at all times a sufficient corps of instructors, in all departments of said University, as at present constituted, shall afford proper means and facilities for instruction and graduation in each department of said University; shall make a fair and equitable division of the funds provided for the support of the University, in accord with the wants and needs of said departments as they shall become apparent, said departments being known as, Department of Literature, Science, and The Arts, Department of Medicine and Surgery, the Department of Law, the School of Pharmacy, the Homœopathic Medical College, and the Department of Dental Surgery.

Should the Board of Regents fail to maintain any of said departments as herein provided, then at such time shall only one-twentieth of a mill be so assessed.

Approved March 23d, 1893.

AN ACT.

Making the mill tax available for the use and maintenance of the University of Michigan, for the year eighteen hundred and ninety-three, and every year thereafter.

SECTION 1. *The People of the State of Michigan enact:* That the State Treasurer be and is hereby authorized and directed to pay to the Regents of the University, in the year eighteen hundred and ninety-three, and each year thereafter, in quarterly installments, upon the warrant of the Auditor General, the amount of the mill tax provided for by law to extend aid to the University of Michigan; and that said treasury be reimbursed out of the taxes annually received from said mill tax when collected; and said Auditor General shall issue said warrants as in the case of special appropriations: Provided, that in the year eighteen hundred and ninety-three the first and second installments shall be paid together on the first day of July.

This act is ordered to take immediate effect.

Approved May 4th, 1893.

APPENDIX C.

EXAMINATIONS FOR DEGREES.

The following examinations were held in 1893:

CANDIDATE FOR THE DEGREE OF DOCTOR OF PHILOSOPHY.

ALDRED SCOTT WARTHIN, A. M., 1890.

Candidate for the degree of PH.D.

THESIS.—The Value of Music as a Dramatic Element. Subjects for examination: Major.—English Literature. Minors.—German. Music.

CANDIDATES FOR THE DEGREE OF MASTER OF ARTS.

ALLISON WIX AUGIR, A.B., *Hillsdale College*, 1890.

Subjects for examination: Major.—Organic Chemistry.—Minors.—Physics. General Chemistry.

WILLIAM WARNER BISHOP, A.B., 1892.

Subjects for examination: Major.—Greek. Minors.—Latin. Pedagogy.

MAMAH BOUTON BORTHWICK, A.B., 1892.

Subjects for examination: Major.—English Literature. Minors.—Philosophy. French.

CHARLES AMBROSE BOWEN, A.B., 1892.

Subjects for examination: Major.—Philosophy. Minors.—Hellenistic Greek. Hebrew.

HEBER DOUST CURTIS, A.B., 1892.

Subjects for examination: Major.—Greek. Minors.—Latin. Classical Archæology.

JOHN PATTERSON DAVIS, A.B., 1885.

THESIS.—The Union Pacific Railway to the Year 1865. Subjects for examination: Major.—Political Economy. Minors.—English History. American History.

ELLEN ELIZABETH GARRIGUES, A.B., 1889.

THESIS.—The Beginnings of Satire in England. Subjects for examination: Major.—English Literature. Minors.—French. Philosophy.

JONATHAN AUGUST CHARLES HILDNER, A.B., 1890.

THESIS.—Influence of the Romantic School upon Heinrich Heine. Subjects for examination: Major.—German Literature. Minors.—Middle High German. English Literature.

ELLEN CLARINDA HINSDALE, A.B., *Adelbert College*, 1885.

Subjects for examination: Major.—German. Minors.—French. Pedagogy.

GEORGE FREDERICK RUSH, A.B., 1889.

Subjects for examination: Major.—History. Minors.—Political Economy. American Literature.

THOMAS CHALKLEY SEVERANCE, A.B., 1889.

Subjects for examination: Major.—English Literature. Minors.—Ethics. American History.

ALBERT BOYNTON STORMS, A.B., 1884.

THESIS.—The Kantian and Cartesian Ideas of God. Subjects for examination: Major.—Philosophy. Minors.—History. English.

CANDIDATES FOR THE DEGREE OF MASTER OF PHILOSOPHY.

AUGUSTA LEE GIDDINGS, B.L., *University of Wisconsin*, 1890.

Subjects for examination: Major.—French. Minors.—English. Æsthetics.

TOYOGIRO KOTEGAWA.

Subjects for examination: Major.—Political Economy. Minors.—Philosophy. History.

JOHN OREN REED, PH.B., 1885.

Subjects for examination: Major.—Physics. Minors.—Mathematics. Mechanics.

EUGENE HERBERT ROBERTSON, Ph.B., 1891.

Thesis.—Ferments in the Urine. Subjects for examination: Major.—Physiological Chemistry. Minors.—Physiology. Bacteriology.

MARILLA CAROLINE WOOSTER, B.S., *Hillsdale College*, 1875.

Subjects for examination: Major.—English Literature. Minors.—Philosophy. Pedagogy.

CANDIDATES FOR THE DEGREE OF MASTER OF SCIENCE.

IDA MAY CLENDENIN, B.S., *University of Missouri*, 1886.

Subjects for examination: Major.—Vegetable Physiology. Minors.—Cryptogamic Botany. Organic Chemistry.

GEORGE OSWIN HIGLEY, B.S., 1891.

Thesis.—On the Reduction of Nitric Acid by Copper. Subjects for examination: Major.—General Chemistry. Minors.—Physiology. Physiological Chemistry.

ABRAHAM LINCOLN KNISELY, B.S., 1891.

Thesis.—The Nitrogen Compounds of Milk. Subjects for examination: Major.—Organic Chemistry. Minors.—Physiological Chemistry. Botany.

PAUL HENRY SEYMOUR, B.S., 1892.

Subjects for examination: Major.—General Chemistry. Minors.—Metallurgy. Astronomy.

CANDIDATES FOR THE DEGREE OF MASTER OF LETTERS.

BLANCHE KINGSBURY BARNEY, B.L., 1889.

Subjects for examination: Major.—American Literature. Minors.—American History. Pedagogy.

HELEN LOUISE HATCH, B.L., 1891.

Subjects for examination: Major.—Philosophy. Minors.—German. American Literature.

CANDIDATE FOR THE DEGREE OF CIVIL ENGINEER.

JAMES ALLEN LEWIS, B.S., C.E.

UNIVERSITY OF MICHIGAN.

THE
PRESIDENT'S REPORT

TO THE

BOARD OF REGENTS

FOR THE

YEAR ENDING SEPT. 30,

1894.

ANN ARBOR, MICH.:
PUBLISHED BY THE UNIVERSITY.
1894.

THE REGISTER PUBLISHING COMPANY
ENGRAVERS AND PRINTERS
ANN ARBOR.   MICHIGAN

PRESIDENT'S REPORT.

UNIVERSITY OF MICHIGAN,
ANN ARBOR, Oct. 24, 1894.

To the Honorable Board of Regents:

I present to you my Annual Report for the year ending September 30, 1894.

The University has been called to mourn the loss of several men who had rendered her valuable service.

Hon. Lyman Decatur Norris, who was appointed Regent in 1883 to fill a vacancy, and who served one year, died at Grand Rapids January 7, 1894, aged seventy years. He was the first student matriculated in this University. He was a man of high intelligence, pure character, and a worthy reputation as a lawyer. He always cherished a deep interest in the University.

On May 25 Regent Henry Howard died at Port Huron, aged sixty-six. Mr. Howard was elected Regent in 1890. He was a man of marked ability for business, of the highest integrity, and of a strong sense of private and public duty. Until fatal illness seized him, he devoted himself to the interests of the University with the greatest fidelity.

On August 6 ex-Regent Austin Blair, after a prolonged illness, died at his home in Jackson. He served the full term of eight years as Regent from 1882 to 1890. A graduate of Union College, a man of large experience in public life, a lawyer of acuteness and learning, a leader with high intellectual and moral ideals and with the most fearless spirit, he was able to render the University large service by his wise counsels and by his addresses to the legislature. He was Governor of this State from 1861 to 1865, and a

Representative in Congress from 1867 to 1873. He filled both offices with conspicuous ability. Few men, if any, have done more for the State of Michigan than Austin Blair. This University in recognition of his worth conferred on him the degree of Doctor of Laws in 1890.

On September 29, 1894, Professor Joseph Estabrook, D. D., died at Olivet, at the age of seventy-four years. As a High School teacher, Principal of the State Normal School, Professor in Olivet College, State Superintendent of Public Instruction, and Regent of the University (from 1870 to 1878), his services to education in Michigan had been eminently conspicuous. As a preacher his influence had been large and most beneficent.

On June 29, 1894, Henry D. Bennett, who was Secretary and Steward from 1866 to 1883, died at Pasadena, Cal. His service fell in a period of signal development of the University. He is remembered with respect and affection by the many teachers and students who were brought into relations with him.

On April 14, Corydon L. Ford, the senior Professor in the Department of Medicine and Surgery in the University, died suddenly at his residence in this city. He had just completed his fortieth course of lectures to our students, and was to retire as Professor Emeritus. He had reached his eightieth year. Having obtained his general and medical education in the face of great obstacles, he began teaching as early as 1830, and devoted his whole life to the profession. He lectured in Medical Schools at Buffalo, Castleton, Vt., Brunswick, Me., Brooklyn, N. Y., as well as in our school. In clearness and aptness of statement, in the arrangement of his matter, in his power to illustrate by dissection while he lectured, he has probaby not been surpassed by any teacher of Anatomy in this country. The simplicity and purity of his character and the earnestness of his religious spirit, left a deep impress on the thousands of his pupils. He testified his devotion to the University not only by his long and useful life in her service, but by a generous bequest to the library, the largest in fact which it has ever received.

The following is a list of appointments and reappointments of Professors, Assistant Professors and Instructors, and of resignations accepted. The Instructors were appointed for a term of one year, except as otherwise indicated.

In October, 1893, Henry A. Sanders, A. B., Instructor in Latin, in place of Hiram A. Sober, A. B., resigned.

Clarence L. Meader, A. B., Instructor in Latin.

Edwin F. Conely, Professor of Law, resigned.

Alexis C. Angell, A. B., LL. B., appointed Professor of Law.

Otto Kirchner, appointed Professor of Law.

In November, 1893, Judge Henry H. Swan, A. M., was appointed Lecturer on Admiralty Law for one year, in place of Justice Henry B. Brown, LL. D.

In April, 1893, Dr. James B. Fitzgerald was appointed Director of the Gymnasium for one year.

In May, Instructor John O. Reed, Ph. M., was appointed Assistant Professor of Physics for three years, from October, 1894.

Dean C. Worcester, A. B., Acting Assistant Professor of Animal Morphology, in charge of the Laboratory for one year during the absence of Professor Reighard in Europe.

Charles A. Kofoid, Ph. D., Instructor in Vertebrate Morphology.

Frederick C. Newcombe, Ph. D., reappointed Acting Assistant Professor of Botany, for one year, discharging the duties of Professor Spalding, absent in Europe.

Lorenzo N. Johnson, A. M., reappointed Instructor in Botany.

Wallace S. Elden, A. M., Instructor in French.

Arthur G. Hall, B. S., Instructor in Mathematics.

The resignation of John Dewey, Ph. D., Professor of Philosophy, was accepted.

On June 11, the resignation of George H. Mead, A. B., Assistant Professor of Philosophy, was accepted.

Maurice P. Hunt, M. D., received the permanent appointment of Professor of Gynæcology and Obstetrics, and Eugene R. Eggleston, M. D., that of Professor of the Theory and Practice of Medicine in the Homœopathic Medical College. Oscar R. Long, M.

D., was appointed Lecturer on Mental Diseases for one year in the same College.

J. Playfair McMurrich, Ph. D., was appointed Professor of Anatomy in the Department of Medicine and Surgery.

John W. Dwyer, LL. M., was appointed Instructor in Law.

Thomas W. Hughes, LL. M., was appointed Instructor in Law.

At the meeting of the Board, June 25-27, the following appointments were made:

Thomas A. Bogle, LL. B., Professor of Law for one year.

Elias F. Johnson, B. S., LL. M., Instructor in Law.

Walter D. Smith, LL. B., Instructor in Law for one year.

James A. Craig, Ph. D., Professor of Semitic Languages and Literature and Hellenistic Greek.

Alexander Ziwet, C. E., Assistant Professor of Mathematics, three years.

George W. Patterson, Jr., A. M., S. B., Assistant Professor of Physics, three years.

George A. Hench, Ph. D., Assistant Professor of German, three years.

George O. Higley, M. S., Instructor in General Chemistry three years.

David M. Lichty, M. S., Instructor in General Chemistry, three years.

Max Winkler, Ph. D., Instructor in German, three years.

The following were appointed Instructors for one year:

Jonathan A. C. Hildner, A. M., German.

Benjamin P. Bourland, A. M., French.

John R. Effinger, Jr., Ph. M., French.

Julius O. Schlotterbeck, Ph. C., B. S., Pharmacognosy and Botany.

Herbert F. DeCou, A. M., Greek and Sanskrit.

Ernest H. Mensel, A. M., German.

Lawrence A. McLouth, A. B., German.

Earle W. Dow, A. B., History.

George E. Dawson, A. B., English.

Moses Gomberg, Sc. D., Organic Chemistry.

Clarence G. Wrentmore, B. S., Descriptive Geometry and Drawing.

Karl E. Guthe, Ph. D., Physics.

Tobias Diekhoff, A. B., German.

George A. Miller, Ph. D., Mathematics.

William F. Edwards, B. S., Organic Chemistry, and Accountant in the Chemical Laboratory.
Sidney D. Townley, M. S., Astronomy.
Henry A. Sanders, A. M., Latin.
Clarence L. Meader, A. B., Latin, and Lecturer on Roman Law in the Law Department.
William D. Johnston, A. M., History.
Simon M. Yutzy, M. D., Instructor in Osteology and Assistant Demonstrator of Anatomy.
Frank W. Nagler, B. S, Instructor in Electro-Therapeutics.
William F. Breakey, M. D., Lecturer on Dermatology (permanent appointment).
Martin L. Belser, M. D., Instructor in Pathology and Autopsies.
Thomas M. Cooley, LL. D., Lecturer on Interstate Commerce
Marshall D. Ewell, LL. D., Lecturer on Medical Jurisprudence.
James L. High, LL. D., Lecturer on Injunctions and Receivers.
John B Clayberg, LL. B., Lecturer on Mining Law.
Melville M. Bigelow, Ph. D., Lecturer on Insurance.
George H. Lothrop, Ph. B., Lecturer on Patent Law.
Henry H. Swan, A. M., Lecturer on Admiralty Law.
Andrew C. McLaughlin, A. B., LL. B., Lecturer on Constitutional Law and Cons itutional History.
Victor C. Vaughan, Ph. D., M. D., Lecturer on Toxicology in its Legal Relations.
Henry C. Adams, Ph. D., Lecturer on the Railroad Problem.
Richard Hudson, A. M., Lecturer on Comparative Constitutional Law.

On September 19, the following appointments for one year were made:

George Rebec, Ph. B., Instructor in Philosophy.
Frank R. Lillie, Ph. D, Instructor in Zöology.
Daniel B. Luten, B. S., Instructor in Engineering.
John Bigham, Ph. D., Instructor in Philosophy.
The Chair of Zöology was declared vacant.

Professor H. B. Hutchins. Ph. B., was appointed Professor of Law and Dean of the Law Department, with the understanding that he would enter upon his duties next year.
I regret to say, that John Dewey, Ph. D., who was Instructor

in Philosophy here from 1884 to 1886, and Assistant Professor from 1886 to 1888, and who succeeded the late Professor Morris as Professor of Philosophy in 1889, has resigned to take the position of Head Professor of Philosophy in the University of Chicago. He has added new honor to the Chair, which his illustrious predecessors here have filled with so eminent success.

The number of degrees conferred was as follows:

DEGREES ON EXAMINATION.

Bachelor of Letters	22
Bachelor of Science (in Biology)	5
Bachelor of Science (in Chemistry)	10
Bachelor of Science (in Electrical Engineering)	6
Bachelor of Science (in Mechanical Engineering)	15
Bachelor of Science (in Civil Engineering)	11
Bachelor of Science	19
Bachelor of Philosophy	45
Bachelor of Arts	60
Master of Letters	3
Mining Engineer	1
Civil Engineer	2
Master of Science	4
Master of Philosophy	9
Master of Arts	16
Doctor of Philosophy	5
Doctor of Science	1
Doctor of Medicine (Department of Medicine and Surgery)	65
Bachelor of Laws	275
Master of Laws	21
Pharmaceutical Chemist	23
Master of Pharmacy	1
Doctor of Medicine (Homoeopathic Medical College)	9
Doctor of Dental Surgery	64
Doctor of Dental Science	1
	703

HONORARY DEGREES.

Master of Arts	3
Doctor of Laws	3
	709

The attendance of students has been as follows:

SUMMARY OF STUDENTS.

DEPARTMENT OF LITERATURE, SCIENCE, AND THE ARTS.

Holder of the Elisha Jones Classical Fellowship	1	
Resident Graduates	77	
Candidates for an Advanced Degree, enrolled in other Departments	7	
Graduates Studying *in Absentia*	32	
Undergraduates:		
Candidates for a degree	1079	
Students not Candidates for a Degree	231—	1427

DEPARTMENT OF MEDICINE AND SURGERY.

Resident Graduates	2	
Fourth Year Students	64	
Third Year Students	88	
Second Year Students	94	
First Year Students	134—	382

DEPARTMENT OF LAW.

Resident Graduates	20	
Seniors	273	
Juniors	283	
Special Students	21	
Students enrolled in the Department of Literature, Science, and the Arts	10—	607

SCHOOL OF PHARMACY.

Resident Graduates	1	
Second Year Students	29	
First Year Students	30—	60

HOMŒOPATHIC MEDICAL COLLEGE.

Fourth Year Students	10	
Third Year Students	3	
Second Year Students	8	
First Year Students	6—	27

COLLEGE OF DENTAL SURGERY.

Seniors	66	
Juniors	52	
Freshmen	67—	185
		2688
Deduct for names counted more than once		29
Total		2659

The number of students was less by 119 than in the previous year. There was a decline in the Literary Department of 74, in the Law Department of 34, in the School of Pharmacy of 22, in the Homœopathic Medical College of 36, in the Dental College of 4. On the other hand in the Department of Medicine and Surgery there was a gain of 38. We believe that the falling off in aggregate attendance was due mainly, if not wholly, to the business depression of the country. The western institutions suffered more from this cause than the eastern. A larger number of the western than of the eastern college students are possessed of so small means that a general financial stringency calls them back from study to some bread-winning pursuit. We should not have been surprised if the same cause which was operative last year had held down our numbers for another year. But it is apparent that such is not to be the case. Michigan continues to gain relatively to other states in the percentage of our students. She sent last year 1,400, or 52.6 per cent. of the total number, which is two per cent. more than in the previous year.

Nineteen foreign states and provinces were represented: Ontario (28), Germany (5), China (3), England, Japan, New Brunswick, Bulgaria, Hawaiian Islands, Quebec, Baden, Barbadoes, Bermuda, Costa Rica, Italy, Manitoba, Porto Rico, Scotland, South Africa and Sweden.

Of the States of our Union Illinois sending 304, Ohio 173 and Indiana 115, furnish us after Michigan by far the largest number. However, Pennsylvania sends us 79, New York 74, and Iowa 65. Forty-five of our states and territories are represented in our company of students. It may be doubted whether a more cosmopolitan group of students is found in any University.

The number of women in attendance last year was as follows:

Department of Literature, Science and the Arts............ 461
Department of Medicine and Surgery........................... 71

Department of Law............	5
School of Pharmacy............	2
Homœopathic Medical College............	5
College of Dental Surgery............	8
	552

The decline in the attendance of women as compared with that of the previous year was ten per cent., while the decline in total attendance was only four per cent. In the Literary Department, where by far the largest number of women are found, they constituted last year 37 per cent., this year 32 per cent. Two years ago they constituted 33 per cent. It would seem therefore that for the present the proportion of women to men in collegiate work is not likely to exceed the figure reached last year. The indication seems to be that the hard times have interfered more with the collegiate attendance of women than of men. The proportion of women to men in the total attendance is 21 per cent. The proportion in all the professional schools is a little more than seven per cent., last year it was a little less than eight per cent. The falling off has been chiefly in the Literary Department.

Meanwhile it is noticeable how, both in the universities of this country and in many of the old and conservative universities of Europe, the doors are opening to women. Even our universities which have relegated women to annexes or separate colleges for education, are beginning to admit women for graduate work, and in some cases to permit undergraduate women to attend the lectures given to the men. It needs no prophet to predict that they will before long find it safe and wise to go yet further in providing for the joint education of men and women.

The building operations have been important. A tasteful and commodious building, containing class-rooms for the Literary Department has been completed, and appropriately named Tappan Hall, in honor of that distinguished man, the first President, Dr. Tappan.

The increase during the last few years in the number of students in the Literary Department, and the multiplication of classes, caused by the introduction of the elective system, rendered absolutely necessary these additional accommodations. The cost of the building and furniture is about thirty thousand dollars.

The main building of the Gymnasium has been completed. The delay in finishing this building has been very unwillingly assented to by the Regents. The financial stringency of the last two years prevented us from receiving contributions which we had good reason to expect when the erection of the building was begun, and which would have sufficed for its completion. But in view of the continued business depression, which cut off all hope of further gifts at this time, the Regents felt that it was due to the generous subscribers to the Gymnasium fund, who had enabled us to rear the walls of the building, and to the students who need the facilities for gymnastic training, to take from our treasury the sum required to prepare the Gymnasium for use this autumn. Fortunately, a fund which students and other friends of the University began to collect nearly twenty years ago, was in the hands of Trustees, who were authorized to turn it over to the Regents for aiding in completing and equipping the Gymnasium. This fund yielded $6,095.03. The sum received from subscribers to the fund for erecting the Gymnasium since January, 1891, including the initial gift of $20,000 by Mr. Joshua W. Waterman, is $42,705. Adding this to the older fund, we have $48,800.03 as the amount contributed by private generosity. The amount which the Regents will have to expend from the University treasury in order to complete the building cannot now be stated, though in a few days the Gymnasium will be opened for use.

It should be remembered that we have been unable to begin the erection of the contemplated wing for the use of the women. This must be built. We have about two thousand dollars in hand for that purpose. But we need about twenty thousand dollars. Will not some generous person provide us the means of erecting this much needed building? The men with their out-door games have, even without the Gymnasium, larger facilities for healthful exercise than the women. Of course for the present the building now completed will be given up at certain times to the women. But separate provision should be made for the latter.

It has unhappily been found necessary to put a new roof on the Museum and repair the walls at an expense of $4,750. That building was so ill-constructed that it has been a constant source of expense and solicitude to us. It is believed, however, that it was never before in so good a condition as it is at present.

The very serious, but necessary, task of reconstructing on a new plan our heating apparatus for all the buildings on the campus, has been undertaken during the past summer. It was found that under our old system there was great loss in the transmission and distribution of heat, and that our outfit was inadequate to meet the additional drafts to be made on it by Tappan Hall and the Gymnasium. It was wisely decided by the Regents to attempt, in making indispensable changes, to adopt a system which should be equal to the demands to be made on it for years to come, or which could easily be enlarged to meet all such demands. The boilers were, therefore, all collected in one boiler house, much larger than either of the old boiler houses, a brick conduit, $6\frac{1}{2}$ feet high by $5\frac{1}{2}$ broad, was made, easily connecting with every building on the campus, and fitted to carry not only steam pipes, but also the electric wires, which it is intended to employ at an early day in lighting our buildings. This work has been accomplished with great expedition by Messrs. Harvey & Sons, of Detroit. The cost according to the contract has been $14,150. It is predicted that the saving in fuel will be important. It is certain that this connection of all the buildings with the central heating plant by conduits will be most serviceable.

In the Literary Department the work of the Graduate School has, as in the previous year, received special attention, under the direction of the Administrative Council, which is composed of the heads of departments. The students, including seven candidates for higher degrees, who were enrolled in the professional schools, numbered 117. The instruction of them makes heavy drafts on our professors, all of whom are also engaged in teaching undergraduates, but the uplifting effect of such a body of graduate students as we have on the spirit of undergraduate work is most inspiring. These students have organized a Graduate School Club, which seeks by the aid of the Faculty to promote the interests of the school by social meetings, by discussions of methods of graduate work, and by securing addresses from eminent graduates. Their zeal and *esprit de corps* are most commendable and most helpful. I cannot but repeat with emphasis the expression of the opinion that in no other way could the gift of moderate sums be more useful to the University and to the promotion of sound learning than by the endowment of fellowships, yielding to graduate students four hundred or five hundred dollars annually. By the aid of such fellowships Harvard, Cornell and Chicago are constantly drawing some of our most promising graduates to their halls.

It gives me great pleasure to acknowledge the generosity of the last graduating class of the Literary Department in presenting to the University a subscription of two thousand dollars, to be known as the "Scholarship Fund of the Class of '94." By the provisions of the gift the income is to be annually loaned to some student who may be studying here as a candidate for a Bachelor's degree.

It is to be hoped that additions may be made to this loan fund by other contributors.

The Faculty have for the last few years been slowly coming to the opinion that there is no good ground for requiring more hours of work for graduation in some courses than in others. We have heretofore asked one-twelfth more hours of work in the University for graduation in other courses than in the classical. The reason given for this was that the preparation for entering upon the classical course called for more work in school than the preparation for the other courses. Practically the plan probably furnished a certain special encouragement to pursue the study of Greek. It has been decided now by the Faculty that this discrimination shall be abandoned. It is believed that in the present circumstances no harm will come to classical studies by this step.

The Faculty have also been brought to the conclusion that many of our students were taking too many hours weekly in the class-room, that there would be less cramming and more faithful study, if the hours of attendance on class-room instruction were diminished, and more time was afforded for reading and writing and reflection. They have therefore fixed the maximum number of hours which a student may take in class-room without special permission of the Faculty at sixteen. The requirements for graduation are such that a course may be completed within the usual time, if no more than sixteen hours are taken at any period. With the spirit of study prevalent among our students, the pressure upon the Faculty has always been not for permission to reduce, but for permission to increase, the number of hours of work beyond the normal number.

The Faculty have given prolonged consideration during the year to the important subject now so generally under discussion through the country of the proper requirements for admission to the University. Probably at no previous period have the problems of secondary education so earnestly engaged the attention of the nation as they do now. The Report of the Committee of Ten appointed by the American Educational Association upon the subject has evoked a general discussion, which should be fruitful of some good results. One Faculty, ever keenly alive to the importance of securing the most helpful relations between the school and the college, are diligently seeking in co-operation with the High School teachers of the state to determine what changes, if any, should be made in the courses of the secondary schools or in the collegiate courses, to lend the highest efficiency to our system of education. They have already decided to ask on and after the beginning of the next academic year preparation in French or German or Latin for admission to the Engineering courses.

The Faculty has so arranged the work for the coming year that there will be no regular meeting of classes after four o'clock in the afternoon. Heretofore appointments have been made for classes up to six o'clock. But both teachers and students have felt the need of the late hours of the afternoon for exercise, whether out of doors or in the gymnasium. We shall be under the necessity of beginning work at eight in the morning, a quarter of an hour earlier than formerly, and also of using Saturday forenoon for class work. We have reason to think that the change will be acceptable to all.

In obedience to what seemed a public demand, we have, during the past summer, tried the experiment of organizing a summer school of instruction. Several colleges and universities have established such schools during the last few years. The attendance in some of them has been large. The persons, who resort to them are chiefly teachers, who wish to enlarge their attainments in branches which they are called to teach in school or college. We formed our plans too late in the year to give as widespread notice of them as was desirable. We have reason to be satisfied with the attendance, as eighty-eight students were present. About half of them were teachers. Most of them were from Michigan, but some came from other states. They gave themselves with great assiduity to their work. There seems every reason to believe that a larger number may be expected next year, if the school is continued, as we expect it will be.

Some of our Professors have, during the past year, continued to give courses of what are called University Extension Lectures, and have been satisfied with the results. But the task of giving such courses is a heavy addition to the duties of the Professor, who is charged with the full work of a chair. I think it is not yet determined whether the demand for such lectures is to be permanent. But if it is, and if the demand is to be met by the University, provision will ultimately have to be made for it by the appointment of special lecturers, who will give their time largely to the work.

The Department of Medicine and Surgery has had a year of exceptional prosperity. Notwithstanding the increased requirements for admission and for graduation, perhaps because of these, that Department, alone of all the Departments of the University, had a decided gain in attendance. The work is organised according to the best methods of scientific instruction. In no other Department is more strenuous work exacted of the student, and in none is the spirit of work among the students more earnest and enthusiastic.

The hospital connected with this school has been crowded to repletion with patients, and is far too small to accommodate those who apply for treatment. The report of the Hospital Boards show that in the University Hospital (open twelve months) 1502 patients received treatment at an average cost to them of $7.82. The Homœopathic Hospital (in nine months) had 297 patients, who were cared for at an average cost to the patients of $8.57. Thus 1799 patients were cared for in the two Hospitals at an average cost to the patients of a little over eight dollars each. Of these many were relieved from a condition of disability, in which they were a charge to their friends or to the county, and were restored to lives of productive activity. Had the University Hospital another ward, a larger number of sufferers could be relieved.

The State Board of Health, holding the view now generally entertained by the best informed physicians that consumption is a contagious disease, has recommended to the legislature to establish a hospital here for patients, suffering from that disease, and to place it under the charge of our medical professors. We shall be very willing to take charge of such an institution, if the State sees fit to establish it.

Our School for Nurses, carried on by the Medical Department, has had the pleasure of seeing its first class, numbering ten, complete their course of study. That study is now attracting a large number of intelligent and devoted women, who render a service to the sick, hardly inferior to that of the physician. Their calling is a most honorable one, and it is a cause of congratulation that the medical school is now regularly preparing women for it.

Those charged with the conduct of the Law School have been of late giving much attention to the problems of legal education, and considering the means of giving more efficiency to our course of instruction. They have organized a Practice Court, in which trials are conducted with all the formalities of a regular court of justice. It has also been decided to extend the course for graduation to three years, beginning with the next academic year. The Faculty has been enlarged by the addition of a Professor. Some modifications of the methods of instruction are going on.

These steps are all in keeping with the spirit which has been awakened in all the better Law Schools of the country for improving the education of lawyers. Since the old method of pursuing the study of law in offices has so largely gone out of vogue, the Law Schools very properly feel the responsibility which is laid on them of giving the best possible preparation for the profession to the students who are crowding their halls. There are still differences of opinion concerning the methods of instruction, but there seems to be a very general agreement among the prominent members of the American bar, that a more prolonged course of study than has generally been taken, even in law schools, has become necessary. It hardly need be remarked that one of the greatest obstacles which Law Schools, especially in the west, encounter in insisting on a high standard of education, is found in the extremely easy conditions on which admission to the bar is secured in some states. It is within the power of the bar to remove this obstacle, and it is to be hoped that they will co-operate with the schools in securing a larger preparation of all who are to assume the responsibile and important duties of lawyers.

The Homœopathic Medical College has had a trying year. Unfounded alarms of some of the profession concerning the plans of the Regents and the Faculty for the conduct of the college, and criticisms of Professors which certain practitioners allow themselves to indulge in, have obviously diverted students to other medical schools, and especially to those which have much briefer courses and less stringent requirements for admission. The Regents have tried for nearly twenty years in good faith to administer this college with efficiency, and have always found one of the chief obstacles to success in the hypercritical spirit of certain members of the homœopathic profession. Whether it is possible for the Board to establish a policy and appoint a Faculty, which the homœopathic physicians can unite in approving is a question which in the light of experience is not easy to answer. Meantime the Board must continue to use its best judgment in deciding how to accomplish the object for which the school was founded, the thorough education of physicians.

The work of the School of Pharmacy and that of the Dental College have been carried on with the usual success. Nothing in their history for the year calls for special remark.

At the Observatory Professor Hall has undertaken with the meridian circle the determination of the positions of the stars now being observed with reference to the question of the variation of latitude at the Army Engineer Observatory, Sault Ste. Marie, Michigan, and the Georgetown College Observatory, D. C. Also, it is planned to make observations here with regard to the variation of latitude, using pole stars above and below the pole, direct and reflected. With the 13 inch equatorial Mr. Townley has followed a list of variable stars, and has observed a number of comets and asteroids.

It is very much to be desired that endowment enough may be secured for the Observatory to obtain the services of at least one assistant who shall have no duties of instruction, but all of whose time may be given to computing and making astronomical observations. Such help is needed even more than additional instrumental equipment.

For the Library the year has been one of unprecedented good fortune. Never before has it received such gifts. By a request of Dr. Ford, as has before been stated, the sum of twenty thousand dollars, and by a bequest of Miss Jean L. Coyl, of Detroit, the sum of ten thousand dollars have been bestowed on the General Library, and by a bequest of Mr. Christian H. Buhl, of Detroit, the sum of ten thousand dollars has been given to the Law Library. Miss Coyl's bequest is made as a memorial of her deceased brother, Col. W. H. Coyl.* Mr. Buhl had in 1885 given

---

*Col. Coyl died in Paris, France. The following is an extract from an article published in Galignani's *Messenger*:

"Col. W. H. Coyl, of the United States army, who has just died in Paris, has left behind him a record to be envied among veterans. It will be remembered by those who are familiar with the details of the battle of Pea Ridge, in Arkansas,

some five thousand volumes to the Law Library. It is to be hoped that these generous examples may be imitated by others, who appreciate the fact that the endowment of the Library opens a fountain of perpetual blessing to the generations of students who are to seek culture at this University.

The following figures are drawn from the Librarian's report:

Number of volumes in all the libraries, Sept. 30, 1894	92,228
Number of unbound pamphlets, Sept. 30, 1894	16,337
Number of maps, Sept. 30, 1894	1,000
Increase from Oct. 1, 1893, to Sept. 30, 1894, volumes	6,447
Increase from Oct. 1, 1893, to Sept. 30, 1894, pamphlets	347
Increase from Oct. 1, 1893, to Sept. 30, 1894, maps	200
Recorded use for the twelve months in Reading Room, volumes	120,420
Number of volumes drawn by Professors for the same time	5,400

We have received important additions to our Museum, among them a considerable collection of minerals from the World's Fair, a choice specimen of polished agatized wood, presented by Regent Hebard, two large models from the Calumet and Hecla Mining Company, one showing a section of the mine with shaft-house and crushers, the other showing a section of the stamp-mill, collections of pre-historic specimens from New Mexico, Arizona and Florida, and a valuable collection (exhibited at the World's

---

March 7, 1862, how desperate was the struggle. It was there that Choctaw, Chickasaw and Cherokee Indian regiments were brigaded with white troops on the side of the confederates. Col. Coyl commanded an Iowa regiment (the famous ninth) during the battle, and every field officer being either killed or wounded, was called by Gen. Curtis to command a brigade. Early in the fight his horse was killed under him, and Col. Coyl led his brigade on foot. During one of the terrible confederate charges Col. Coyl was shot through the lungs. He was taken from the field, and for a long time lingered between life and death. His wound at last healed, and he was appointed judge advocate of the State of Kentucky. It was through his energy that many of the guerillas who then infested that State were brought to justice. The war being ended, Col Coyl resumed the practice of his profession—the law; but his wound having greatly impaired his health, he was induced to visit Europe to consult a physician eminent for the treatment of diseases of the lungs. He left New York in October on board the French steamer Ville de Paris, and, the trip being an exceedingly tempestuous one, he was greatly fatigued on his arrival. He was at once taken to the house of an American gentleman residing in Paris, who had made his acquaintance on board the steamer, and tenderly cared for. But it was too late; he lingered for two weeks, when death relieved him of his sufferings."

Fair) of ores and rocks belonging to the geological cross-sections through the Ishpeming and Dead River ore basins.

Last autumn Mr. Frederick Stearns, of Detroit, who has more than once evinced his generosity to the University, offered to present to us on certain conditions a very valuable collection of fishes from the waters of Japan and of the Bonin Islands, and a lesser collection from the Hawaiian Islands, with paintings of fishes in water colors, mostly of the size of the original, executed by a well known Japanese artist, S. Okubo. The Regents gladly accepted this handsome gift on the conditions named. Unfortunately it was found on opening the cases that the packing of the fishes had not been done with sufficient care to ensure their preservation. But the paintings are in fine condition, and are of much value both from a scientific and an artistic point of view.

Ever since the completion of University Hall we have greatly desired to have a large organ placed in our spacious auditorium to assist in the fine musical entertainments which are now so often given there. At last our desires are met. The University Musical Society, which under the efficient and inspiring leadership of Professor Stanley, has done so much to cultivate in this community the love of the best music, has purchased the organ, which in Festival Hall at the Columbian Exposition attracted much attention, and has placed it, by consent of the Regents, in University Hall. The organ was built by Farrand & Votey, of Detroit, and is valued at twenty-five thousand dollars.

We are trying an interesting, and we believe a promising experiment in the administration of our finances this year. Heretofore appropriations for various purposes have been made at all the meetings of the Board. It has been decided to make up a budget in the spring for the fiscal year. Each Professor in charge of a department is asked to present an estimate of the needs of his department for the year. The Finance Committee gives these careful consideration, and then recommends to the Board specific appropriations and also the salaries to be paid, and the Board takes action, with the distinct understanding that no addition is to be made to the appropriations and salaries thus voted, except in case of unforeseen or extraordinary emergencies.

It will be remembered that the last Legislature voted us the proceeds of a tax of a sixth of a mill, with the provision that we must incur no debt for the erection of buildings. We had asked for a tax of one-fifth of a mill. That would have enabled us to provide pretty well for our current expenses and for most of the buildings we are likely to need soon. Though we are very grateful for the proceeds of the one-sixth mill tax, we have found ourselves unable to meet some very pressing wants. We very much need an electric light plant. But we have had to forego that for the present. Another hospital ward, an enlargement of the Library building, an addition to the engineering workshops, an addition to the chemical laboratory, an addition to the anatomical laboratory, and the woman's wing to the gymnasium are urgently needed. Probably an enlargement of the physical laboratory must soon be made, either by adding to the present building or still better by erecting a hygienic laboratory and surrendering to the physical department the rooms now occupied by the bacteriological and hygienic department. Of course the long wished for Art Building is always desired. We gratefully acknowledge the gift to the University by Hon. Levi L. Barbour of a lot in Detroit valued at twenty-five thousand dollars as a donation towards the erection of such a building, which shall cost not less than a hundred thousand dollars. It will readily be seen that for some years to come the drafts upon our treasury for building purposes must be heavy.

We have long been hoping that private beneficence would supplement the gifts of the State to the University. Now that it seems well settled that the State is ready to make permanent provision for the substantial support of the Institution, we are justified in expecting that the graduates and other friends of the University will testify their interest in it by appropriate donations. Never before in any one year have we received so many gifts as have come to us during the past twelve months. Though these are small compared with the hundreds of thousand of dollars which are annually poured into the treasuries of some of our American universities, they afford us cheering evidence that our friends are remembering us, and they awaken in us the hope that others will imitate them. Where can persons of generous purpose, whether of limited or of ample means, better bestow their gifts than upon a University like this, where those gifts will confer blessings upon unnumbered generations of earnest and aspiring students?

JAMES B. ANGELL.

APPENDIX A.

TREASURER'S REPORT.

To the Finance Committee, Board of Regents, University of Michigan:

GENTLEMEN: Herewith I submit my annual report for the year ending June 30th, 1894.   Respectfully,

H. SOULE, Treasurer.

RECEIPTS.

Miscellaneous Sources, Special Accounts	$ 10 14	
From State Treasurer, Acct. Special Appropriations	6,000 00	
" " " " Current Expenses	302,183 91	
" Miscellaneous Sources	137,610 96	$445,805 01

DISBURSEMENTS.

Balance Overdrawn July 1st, 1893	13,284 56	
From Special Funds, Legislative Appropriations, and Earnings	19,463 59	
From General Fund Account	368,325 52	
Balance in Treasury June 30th, 1894	44,731 34	445,805 01

GENERAL FUND.

RECEIPTS TO THE GENERAL FUND.

From State Treasurer, Account 1-20 Mill Tax		28,250 00	
" " " " 1-6 Mill Tax		235,416 65	
" " " " University Interest		38,517 26	302,183 91
" Interest on Deposits	$3,530 88		
" University Record	106 87		
" University Hospital, Balance for 1892-3, as per last report	266 13		
" University Hospital for 1893-4	3,000 00		
" General Library (Duplicate Books Sold)	4 00		
" Dental Supplies	5,983 84		
" Anatomical Supplies	324 48		
" Sales of General Catalogue	13 00		
" Miscellaneous Sources	1,854 18		15,083 38
" Key Deposits		171 00	
" Medical Department		13,280 00	
" Literary "		41,365 00	
" Law "		26,015 00	
" Dental "		6,920 00	
" Homœopathic "		925 00	
" Pharmacy "		2,335 00	
" Chemical Laboratory		8,615 00	
" Zoological "		474 00	
" Mechanical "		1,627 00	
" Hygienic "		2,332 00	
" Botanical "		368 00	

From Pathological Laboratory	950 00	
" Physical "	500 00	
" General Chemistry Laboratory	784 58	
" Electro-therapeutical "	848 00	
" Histological "	920 00	
" Physiological "	75 00	
" Practical Anatomy "	2,825 00	
" Medical (Demonstration)	4,140 00	
" Photography	8 00	
" Diploma Fees	7,050 00	122,527 58
Balance Overdrawn June 30, 1894		5,477 59
		$445,272 46

Students' Fees, Total	$122,527 58
" " Refunded	5,371 69
" " Net	$117,155 89

DISBURSEMENTS FROM THE GENERAL FUND.

General Pay Roll of Officers, Professors, and Employees	$225,843 00	
University Hospital Pay Roll	4,105 50	
Homœopathic " "	1,117 50	
Homœopathic College " (Deficiency)	2,787 50	
Dental College "	11,150 00	$245,003 50
Vouchers Paid, Students' Fees Refunded	5,371 69	
" " Fuel and Lights	11,431 33	
" " General Library (Books)	11,232 87	
" " General Library (Expenses)	391 69	
" " Museum	726 71	
" " Civil Engineering	221 16	
" " Chemical Laboratory	6,625 94	
" " Histological "	276 57	
" " Botanical "	525 73	
" " Physical "	275 45	
" " Physiological "	1,162 47	
" " Mechanical "	1,341 68	
" " Zoological "	1,904 00	
" " Pathological "	422 20	
" " Hygienic "	3,089 96	
" " Anatomical "	3,225 18	
" " Electro-therapeutical Laboratory	400 30	
" " General Chemistry "	1,560 46	
" " Materia Medica "	466 56	
" " Astronomical Observatory	1,334 44	
" " Dental Supplies	3,316 05	
" " Postage	1,378 34	
" " Calendar	2,065 32	
" " Contingent	8,680 40	
" " Construction (Hospitals)	4,260 00	
" " Dental College (Running Expenses)	917 02	
" " School Inspection	553 11	
" " Advertising Medical Dept.	580 79	

Vouchers Paid, Advertising Law Dept.			391 95	
"	"	Advertising Pharmacy Dept.	193 35	
"	"	Miscellaneous Printing	2,168 77	
"	"	University Hospital, Running Expenses	8,003 17	
"	"	Publishing University Record	503 95	
"	"	Law Library	2,190 13	
"	"	Medical Library	1,130 02	
"	"	Administration Building	21 84	
"	"	Repairs	5,098 33	
"	"	Homœopathic College (Expenses)	394 26	
"	"	Gymnasium Building	710 97	
"	"	Psychology	271 29	
"	"	Homœopathic Hospital (Running Expenses)	1,500 61	
"	"	Medical Demonstration Courses (Running Expenses)	108 19	
"	"	Recitation Building	26,917 77	$368,325 52
Amount Overdrawn July 1, 1893				22,624 71
Amount Transferred to Special Building Account				54,289 03
Amount Transferred to General Library Account				15 82
Amount Transferred to Repairs Account				17 38
				$445,272 46

SPECIAL FUND ACCOUNTS.

HOMŒOPATHIC MEDICAL COLLEGE.

Receipts.

Balance in Treasury July 1st, 1893	$ 2,224 09	
From State Treasurer	6,000 00	
Balance Overdrawn June 30, 1894	1,467 96	9,692 05

Disbursements.

Paid Salaries of Professors and Employees	8,100 00	
Paid Vouchers for Expenses	1,592 05	9,692 05

GENERAL LIBRARY.

Receipts.

From Transfer from General Fund to Balance	15 82	
From Sale of Duplicate Books	5 45	21 27

Disbursements.

Balance Overdrawn July 1st, 1893	15 82	
Paid Vouchers	5 45	21 27

CONTINGENT.

Receipts.

Balance in Treasury July 1st, 1893	3,776 02	3,776 02

Disbursements.

Paid Vouchers for Expenses	3,776 02	3,776 02

REPAIRS.

Receipts.

Balance in Treasury July 1st, 1893	162 87	
Transfer from General Fund Account	17 38	180 25

Disbursements.

Paid Vouchers for Expenses	180 25	180 25

PHYSICAL LABORATORY.
Receipts.
Balance in Treasury July 1st, 1893	1,410 31	1,410 31

Disbursements.
Paid Vouchers for Expenses	974 59	
Balance in Treasury June 30, 1894	435 72	1,410 31

DENTAL SURGERY.
Receipts.
Balance in Treasury July 1st, 1893	1 93	1 93

Disbursements.
Paid Vouchers for Expenses	1 93	1 93

EQUIPMENT OF ENGINEERING LABORATORY.
Receipts.
Balance in Treasury July 1st, 1893	302 60	302 60

Disbursements.
Paid Vouchers for Expenses	152 35	
Balance in Treasury June 30, 1894	150 25	302

CIVIL ENGINEERING.
Receipts.
Balance in Treasury July 1st, 1893	99 40	99 40

Disbursements.
Paid Vouchers for Expenses	29 30	
Balance in Treasury June 30, 1894	70 10	99 40

BOTANICAL AND ZOOLOGICAL LABORATORIES.
Receipts.
Balance in Treasury July 1st, 1893	194 25	
Received for material sold	4 69	198 94

Disbursements.
Paid Vouchers for Expenses	198 94	198 94

INSURANCE.
Receipts.
Balance in Treasury July 1st, 1893	1,184 50	1,184 50

Disbursements.
Paid Vouchers for Expenses	1,184 50	1,184 50

BUILDING FUND.
Receipts.
From General Fund (Transfer)	54,289 03	54,289 03

Disbursements.
Paid Vouchers for Expenses (Gymnasium)	3,268 21	
Balance in Treasury June 30, 1894	51,020 82	54,289 03

SPECIAL FUNDS.
Balances in Treasury June 30, 1894.
Physical Laboratory	435 72	
Civil Engineering	70 10	
Equipment of Engineering Laboratory	150 25	
Building Fund	51,020 82	51,676 89
Less Homœopathic College, Overdrawn		1,467 96
Total		$50,208 39

AFFAIRS OF THE HOSPITALS.

The Superintendent of the Hospitals reports to the Auditing Board the following as all the business done by him during the year. This embraces the running expenses only and does not include the maintenance or permanent expenses which are met from the General Fund of the University.

UNIVERSITY HOSPITAL.

This Hospital was again opened during the vacation months, July, August, and September, 1893, with the following results:

Receipts from Patients		$3,260 02
Disbursements for Extra Salaries, Maintenance, and Refunding to Patients		$4,498 93
Deficiency Paid from General Fund of the University		1,238 91

UNIVERSITY HOSPITAL.

Receipts.

For the College Year, October to June, inclusive, Receipts from Patients		20,774 95

Disbursements.

Amounts Refunded to Patients by Joseph Clark, Superintendent	6,372 45	
Expenses Paid by Joseph Clark, Superintendent	9,026 44	
Cash to Treasurer by Joseph Clark, Superintendent	3,000 00	
Due to Treasurer from Joseph Clark, Superintendent	1,476 06	20,774 95

HOMŒOPATHIC HOSPITAL.

Receipts.

From Collections and Earnings		3,688 14

Disbursements.

Amounts Refunded to Patients by Joseph Clark, Superintendent	1,133 32	
Expenses Paid by Joseph Clark	3,810 06	$4,943 38
Deficiency Paid from General Fund of the University		1,255 24

GIFTS.

Under this head are included gifts which the Regents have received from time to time from benefactors for general purposes, or for stated special purposes. The accounts are as follows:

PHILO PARSONS FUND.

Receipts.

Balance in Treasury July 1st, 1893	$ 78 95	
From Interest	3 21	$82 16

Disbursements.

Balance in Treasury June 30, 1894	82 16	82 16

MARY JANE PORTER FUND.

Receipts.

Balance in Treasury July 1st, 1893	628 47	
From Interest	27 51	655 98

Disbursements.

Balance in Treasury June 30, 1894	655 98	655 98

GŒTHE FUND.
Receipts.
Balance in Treasury July 1st, 1893	310 22	
From Interest	11 73	321 95

Disbursements
Paid Vouchers	20 94	
Balance in Treasury June 30, 1894	301 01	321 95

ELISHA JONES CLASSICAL FELLOWSHIP
Receipts.
Balance in Treasury July 1st, 1893	2 18	
From Mrs. Elisha Jones	500 00	
Interest	.08	502 26

Disbursements.
Paid Vouchers	500 00	
Balance in Treasury June 30, 1894	2 26	502 26

CONTINGENT.
Receipts.
Balance in Treasury July 1st, 1893	2,822 36	
From Interest	114 55	2,936 91

Disbursements.
Balance in Treasury June 30, 1894	2,936 91	2,936 91

GYMNASIUM FUND.
Receipts.
Balance in Treasury July 1st, 1893	5,392 37	
From Interest	158 51	
From John W. Knight, Treasurer Athletic Association, Cash	2,795 03	
From John W. Knight, Treasurer Athletic Association, Bonds $3,300.00.		
From John W. Knight, Treasurer Athletic Association, Interest on Bonds	33 00	
From Donations, Miscellaneous Sources	30 00	8,408 91

Disbursements.
Paid Vouchers	5,581 94	
Balance in Treasury June 30, 1894	2,826 97	8,408 91

WOMAN'S GYMNASIUM.
Receipts.
Balance in Treasury July 1st, 1893	1,381 93	
From Interest	58 07	1,440 00

Disbursements.
Balance in Treasury June 30, 1894	1,440 00	1,440 00

ART FUND.
Receipts.
Balance in Treasury July 1st, 1893	16 13	
From Donations	1 87	18 00

Disbursements.
Paid Vouchers	18 00	18 00

FRIEZE MEMORIAL ORGAN FUND.

Receipts.

From Donation 1 50

Disbursements.

Balance in Treasury June 30, 1894 . . . . 1 50

GIFT FUND BALANCES.

Philo Parsons Fund	82 16
Mary Jane Porter Fund	655 98
Goethe Fund	301 01
Elisha Jones Classical Fellowship Fund	2 26
Contingent Fund	2,936 91
Gymnasium Fund	2,826 97
Woman's Gymnasium Fund	1,440 00
Frieze Memorial Organ Fund	1 50
	$8,246 79

APPENDIX B.

EXAMINATIONS FOR DEGREES.

The following examinations were held in 1894:

CANDIDATES FOR THE DEGREE OF DOCTOR OF PHILOSOPHY.

KENNEDY BROOKS, A. B., *University of Wooster*, 1878, A. M., *ibid.*, 1881.

THESIS.—Taxation in Illinois. Subjects for examination: Major.—Political Economy. Minors.—American History. Political Philosophy.

BENJAMIN CHAPMAN BURT, A.B., 1875, A. M., 1879.

THESIS.—The Logical Idea and Divisions of the History of Philosophy. Subjects for examination: Major.—History of Philosophy. Minors.—History of Education. English Drama.

CHARLES HORTON COOLEY, A.B., 1887.

THESIS.—A Theory of Transportation. Subjects for examination: Major.—Political Economy. Minors.—Sociology. Statistics.

JOHN PATTERSON DAVIS, A.B., 1885, A.M., 1893.

THESIS.—The Industrial Significance of Corporations. Subjects for examination: Major.—Political Economy. Minors.—Constitutional Law. Administrative Law.

JAMES ALLEN SMITH, A. B., *University of Missouri*, 1886, LL.B., *ibid*, 1887.

THESIS.—The multiple Money Standard. Subjects for examination: Major.—Political economy. Minors.—Finance. Comparative Constitutional Law.

CANDIDATE FOR THE DEGREE OF DOCTOR OF SCIENCE.

MOSES GOMBERG, B.S., 1890, M S., 1892.

THESIS.—Trimethylxanthin and some of its Derivatives. Subjects for examination: Major.—Organic Chemistry. Minors.—Physiology. Histology.

CANDIDATES FOR THE DEGREE OF MASTER OF ARTS.

WARREN DWIGHT BAKER, A.B., 1893.
Subjects for examination: Major.—Latin. Minors.—Greek. Roman Antiquities.

VIRGINIA BEAUCHAMP, A.B., 1889.
THESIS.—The Religious Views of Seneca. Subjects for examination: Major.—Latin. Minors.—German. French.

WALTER DENNISON, A.B., 1893.
Subjects for examination: Major.—Latin. Minors.—Greek. Classical Archæology.

GENEVIEVE KATHARINE DUFFY. A.B., 1893.
Subjects for examination: Major.—Greek. Minors. Philosophy. English Literature.

CEYLON SAMUEL KINGSTON, *St. Lawrence Univ.*, 1892.
Subjects for examination: Major.- Psychology. Minors.—American Literature. Pedagogy.

NEWTON D. MERENESS, A.B., 1892.
Subjects for examination: Major.—History. Minors.—Political Economy. American Literature.

WILLIAM HENRY MERNER, A.B., 1892.
Subjects for examination: Major.—Political Economy. Minors.—Philosophy. American History.

JOHN AUGUSTUS MUNSON, A.B., *Central University of Iowa*, 1891.
Subjects for examination: Major.—German. Minors.—French. Philosophy.

MELVIN PARK PORTER, A.B., 1893.
Subjects for examination: Major.—Philosophy. Minors.—Political Economy. Physiology.

HENRY LEWIS FREDERICK REICHLE, A.B., 1893.
Subjects for examination: Major.—Latin. Minors.—Greek. Classical Archæology.

EDWIN CARL ROEDDER, A.B., 1893.
Subjects for examination: Major.—German. Minors.—Rhetoric. Anglo-Saxon.

HENRY ARTHUR SANDERS, A.B., 1890.

Subjects for examination: Major.—Greek. Minors.—Latin Sanskrit.

JOHN HENRY SCHAFFNER, A.B., *Baker University*, 1893.

THESIS.—The Nature and Distribution of Centrosomes and Attraction-Spheres in Vegetable Cells. Subjects for examination: Major.—Botany. Minors.—Animal Morphology. Geology.

JESSIE LOUISE VAN VLIET, A.B., *Wellesley College*.

Subjects for examination. Major.—Latin. Minors.— History of Philosophy. Ethics.

LOUIS GRANT WHITEHEAD, A.B.; 1893.

Subjects for examination: Major.—Ethics. Minors.—Political Economy. Comparative Constitutional Law.

HARRY DALE WRIGHT, A B., 1893.

Subjects for examination: Major.—Greek. Minors.—Latin. Greek History.

CANDIDATES FOR THE DEGREE OF MASTER OF PHILOSOPHY.

WIRT McGREGOR AUSTIN, PH. B., 1887.

THESIS.—The Fall of the Federalists. Subjects for examination: Major—American History. Minors.—Political Economy. American History.

FLORA GALE BARNES, PH.B., *Albion College*, 1893.

Subjects for examination: Major.—English Literature. Minors. —French. Anglo-Saxon.

JOHN ROBERT EFFINGER, JR., PH.B., 1891.

Subjects for examination: Major.—French. Minors.—German. History.

IDA BERTHA PAULINA FLEISCHER, PH.B., 1892.

Subjects for examination: Major.—German. Minors.—Philosophy. Pedagogy.

HARRISON McALLESTER RANDALL, PH.B., 1893.

Subjects for examination: Major.—Physics. Minors.—Organic Chemistry. Quantitative Analysis.

CLARA FRANCES STEVENS, *Mount Holyoke College*.

Subjects for examination: Major.—Rhetoric. Minors.—English Literature. Aesthetics.

LOUIS A. STRAUSS, B.L., 1893.

Subjects for examination: Major.—Rhetoric. Minors.—Philosophy. English Literature.

IRA DUDLEY TRAVIS, Ph.B., *Albion College*, 1889.

Subjects for examination: Major.—European History. Minors. Pedagogy. American History.

PAULINE ELIZABETH WIES, Ph.B., 1892.

Subjects for examination: Major.—German. Minors.—Gothic. French.

CANDIDATES FOR THE DEGREE OF MASTER OF SCIENCE.

ELMER ELLSWORTH BARTLETT, B.S., *Iowa College*, 1887.

Subjects for examination: Major.—European History. Minors.—American History. English.

BENJAMIN CLUFF, Jr., B.S., 1890.

Subjects for examination: Major.—Pedagogy. Minors.—Mathematics. Philosophy.

EDWIN RAYMOND COLE, B.S., 1892.

Subjects for examination: Major.—Physics. Minors.—Mathematics. Music.

JAMES C. GRAVES, B.S., *Albion College*, 1893.

Subjects for examination: Major.—Organic Chemistry. Minors—Analytical Chemistry. Mineralogy.

CANDIDATES FOR THE DEGREE OF MASTER OF LETTERS.

MABEL CRABBE, B.L., 1893.

Subjects for examination: Major.—English Literature. Minors.—History. German.

ELSPA MILLICENT DOPP, B.L., 1893.

Subjects for examination: Major.—History. Minors.—Philosophy. Political Economy.

WALTER JOHN HAMMILL, B.L., 1893.

Subjects for examination: Major.—Political Economy. Minors.—History. Pedagogy.

CANDIDATES FOR THE DEGREE OF CIVIL ENGINEER.

JOSEPH KENDALL FREITAG, B.S. (C.E.)
LOUIS CARLTON SABIN, B.S. (C.E.)

CANDIDATE FOR THE DEGREE OF MINING ENGINEER.

WALTER JOHN BALDWIN, B.S. (M.E.)

UNIVERSITY OF MICHIGAN.

THE

PRESIDENT'S REPORT

TO THE

BOARD OF REGENTS

FOR THE

YEAR ENDING SEPT. 30,

1895.

ANN ARBOR, MICH.:
PUBLISHED BY THE UNIVERSITY.
1895.

ANN ARBOR:
THE INLAND PRESS, PRINTERS.
1895.

THE PRESIDENT'S REPORT.

UNIVERSITY OF MICHIGAN,
October 15th, 1895.

To the Honorable Board of Regents:

I beg to present to you my Annual Report for the year ending Sept. 30, 1895.

During the year two men have died, who long served the University most usefully as Regents.

On Nov. 18, 1894, Thomas Dwight Gilbert died at Grand Rapids. He was a member of the Board from 1864 to 1876. During a large part of the period he was chairman of the Finance Committee. It was a period when the institution was growing rapidly and was beginning to receive substantial aid from the state treasury. It is not too much to say that the public confidence in Mr. Gilbert's economy and financial skill was of great service in leading the legislature to appropriate money for the multiplying wants of the University. He was a man of the highest civic virtue, and the city of his residence manifested at his death its sense of its great obligation to him.

On Dec. 28, 1894, Edward Carey Walker died at his home in Detroit. He was for twelve years a colleague of Mr. Gilbert on the Board, but served six years longer. A graduate of Yale College, he was well fitted to consider the problems of internal administration and the scholarly development of the University. He was most unremitting in his attention to the duties of his office, and his services were of the highest value.

I give here a list of appointments and reappointments of Professors, Assistant Professors, Lecturers, and Instructors and of resignations. The Instructors were appointed for one year, unless otherwise stated.

At the meeting in October, 1894.

Arthur R. Cushny, A. M., M. D., permanent appointment, Professor of Materia Medica and Therapeutics, Department of Medicine and Surgery.

C. G. Darling, M. D., Lecturer on Oral Pathology and Surgery, one year.

Louis P. Hall, D. D. S., Instructor in Dental Anatomy, one year.

At the meeting in January, 1895.

Frank F. Reed, A. B., Lecturer in the Law Department on Copyright Law, one year.

The resignations of the members of the Faculty of the Homoeopathic Medical College, Professors Obetz, Mac Lachlan, Mack, Hunt and Eggleston were accepted, to take effect Oct. 1.

At the meeting on Feb. 5, 1895.

Charles H. Cooley, LL. D., was appointed Instructor in Sociology for the year beginning Oct. 1, 1895.

At the meeting on Feb. 21, 1895.

Instructor D. C. Worcester, A. B., was appointed Assistant Professor of Biology and Curator of the Museum from Oct. 1, 1895.

At the meeting in April.

The resignation of Professor F. N. Cole, Ph. D., was accepted, to take effect Oct. 1.

At the meeting in May.

The appointment of T. A. Bogle, LL. B., as Professor of Law, was made permanent.

W. H. Wait, Ph. D., was appointed Instructor in Greek and Sanskrit.

Instructor J. L. Markley, Ph. D., promoted to an Assistant Professorship of Mathematics from Oct. 1, 1896, with leave of absence for one year from Oct. 1, 1895.

A. S. Warthin, M. D., reappointed Instructor in Pathology.

S. M. Yutzey, M. D., reappointed Instructor in Anatomy.

Frank W. Nagler, B. S., reappointed Instructor in Electrotherapeutics.

J. W. Glover, Ph. D., appointed Instructor in Mathematics.

At the meeting in June.

REAPPOINTED FOR THREE YEARS.

Joseph H. Drake, A. B., Assistant Professor of Latin.

Frank C. Wagner, A. M., B. S., Assistant Professor of Mechanical Engineering.

G. Carl Huber, M. D., Assistant Professor of Histology.

APPOINTED FOR THREE YEARS.

Frederick C. Newcombe, B. S. Ph. D., Assistant Professor of Botany.

James B. Fitzgerald, M. D., Director of Gymnasium.

APPOINTED FOR ONE YEAR.

A. H. Lloyd, Ph. D., Acting Professor of Philosophy.

Geo. A. Hench, Ph. D., Acting Professor of German.

Max Winkler, Ph. D., Assistant Professor in German.

APPOINTED INSTRUCTORS FOR THREE YEARS.

Ernst H. Mensel, A. M., Instructor in German.

Earle W. Dow, A. B., Instructor in History.

Arthur G. Hall, B. S., Instructor in Mathematics.

REAPPOINTMENTS FOR 1895–6.

Geo. Rebec, Ph. B., Instructor in Philosophy.

J. A. C. Hildner, A. M., Instructor in German.

Lorenzo N. Johnson, A. M., Instructor in Botany.

Clarence G. Wrentmore, B. S., Instructor in Descriptive Geometry and Drawing.

Karl E. Guthe, Ph. D., Instructor in Physics.

Tobias Diekhoff, A. B., Instructor in German.

Clarence L. Meader, A. B., Instructor in Latin, and Lecturer on Roman Law in the Department of Law.

Wallace S. Elden, A. M., Instructor in French.

Frank R. Lillie, Ph. D. Instructor in Zoology.

Ernst Voss, Ph. D., Instructor in German.

E. F. Johnson, B. S., L.L. M., Instructor in Law Department.

APPOINTED FOR ONE YEAR.

Louis A. Strauss, Ph. M., Instructor in English.

E. C. Goddard, Ph. B. Instructor in Mathematics.

Charles R. Gillis, Ph. B., Instructor in Astronomy.

E. E. Brandon, A. B. Instructor in French.

Henry F. L. Reichle, A. B , Instructor in Latin.

Edgar Pierce, Ph. D., Instructor in Philosophy.

Harvey J. Goulding, B. S., Instructor in Descriptive Geometry and Drawing.
Henry L. Coar, A. M., Instructor in Mathematics.
Victor E. Francois, Instructor in French.
W. D. Johnston, A. M., Instructor in History.
W. C. Gore, Ph. M., Assistant in English.
Keene Fitzpatrick, Instructor in Gymnasium.
Charles H. Gray, B. L., Assistant in English.
E. C. Roedder, A. M., Assistant in German.

REAPPOINTMENTS IN THE SCHOOL OF PHARMACY.

A. B. Stevens, Ph. C., Assistant Professor of Pharmacy for three years.
Moses Gomberg, Sc. D., Instructor in Organic Chemistry.

At the July meeting.

REAPPOINTMENTS IN THE LAW DEPARTMENT FOR ONE YEAR.

Andrew C. McLaughlin, A. B., LL. B. Advanced course in Constitutional Law and Constitutional History.
Thomas M. Cooley, LL. D. Lecturer on Inter-State Commerce.
Marshall D. Ewell, LL. D. Lecturer on Medical Jurisprudence.
James L. High, LL. D. Lecturer on Injunctions and Receivers.
Melville M. Bigelow, Ph. D. Lecturer on Insurance.
Henry H. Swan, A. M. Lecturer on Admiralty Law.
John B. Clayberg, LL. B. Lecturer on Mining Law.
George H. Lothrop, Ph. B. Lecturer on Patent Law.
Victor C. Vaughan, Ph. D., M. D. Lecturer on Toxicology and its Legal Relations.
Richard Hudson, A. M. Lecturer on Comparative Constitutional Law.
Henry C. Adams, Ph. D. Lecturer on the Railroad Problem.
Frank F. Reed. A. B. Lecturer on Copyright Law.

At the September meeting.

John R. Effinger, Jr., Ph. M., Instructor for three years from October 1, 1896, with permission to spend the coming year in Europe.
H. K. Wilgus, B. S., Acting Professor of Law in the Law Department for one year.
John W. Dwyer, LL. M., Instructor in Law.

Thomas W. Hughes, LL. M. Instructor in Law.
Walter Denton Smith, LL. B. Instructor in Law.

IN THE HOMOEOPATHIC COLLEGE.

Wilbert B. Hinsdale, M. S., M. D. Professor of Therapeutics and Materia Medica, and Dean of the Faculty.

Oscar Leseure, M. D. Professor of Surgery and Clinical Surgery.

R. C. Copeland, M. D. Professor of Ophthalmology, Otology, and Paedology.

O. R. Long, M. D. Lecturer on Theory and Practice.

W. N. Fowler, M. D. House Surgeon and Assistant to the Professor of Ophthalmology.

REAPPOINTMENTS IN THE DENTAL COLLEGE FOR ONE YEAR.

C. G. Darling, M. D. Clinical Lecturer on Oral Pathology and Surgery.

Louis P. Hall, D. D. S. Instructor in Dental Anatomy, Operative Technique and Clinical Operative Dentistry.

A. W. Haidle, D. D. S. Demonstrator of Dental Mechanism.

The degrees conferred were as follows:

DEGREES ON EXAMINATION.

Bachelor of Letters	43
Bachelor of Science (in Biology)	7
Bachelor of Science (in Chemistry)	5
Bachelor of Science (in Electrical Engineering)	16
Bachelor of Science (in Mechanical Engineering)	11
Bachelor of Science (in Civil Engineering)	20
Bachelor of Science	17
Bachelor of Philosophy	53
Bachelor of Arts	65
Master of Letters	3
Electrical Engineer	1
Master of Science	8
Master of Philosophy	3
Master of Arts	6
Doctor of Philosophy	1
Doctor of Medicine (Department of Medicine and Surgery)	66
Bachelor of Laws	305
Master of Laws	9
Pharmaceutical Chemist	19

Doctor of Medicine (Homoeopathic Medical College)......... 1
Doctor of Dental Surgery................................. 46
Doctor of Dental Science 2
                                                          ———
                                                          707

HONORARY DEGREES.

Master of Laws... 1
Master of Arts... 4
Doctor of Laws... 2
                                                          ———
                                                          714

The number of students in attendance was as follows:

SUMMARY OF STUDENTS.

DEPARTMENT OF LITERATURE, SCIENCE AND THE ARTS.

Holder of the Elisha Jones Classical Fellowship.......   1
Resident Graduates....................................   63
Candidates for an Advanced Degree, enrolled in other
   departments   5
Graduates Studying *in Absentia*......................   18
Undergraduates:
   Candidates for a Degree 1196
   Students not Candidates for a Degree............... 244—1527

DEPARTMENT OF MEDICINE AND SURGERY.

Resident Graduates....................................   9
Fourth Year Students   70
Third Year Students...................................   71
Second Year Students..................................   98
First Year Students 134
Special Students   2
Students enrolled in the Department of Literature,
   Science and the Arts:
   Second Year Students in Medicine   6
   First Year Students in Medicine ....   4— 394

DEPARTMENT OF LAW.

Resident Graduates   12
Seniors 308
Juniors 322
Special Students   9
Students enrolled in the Department of Literature,
   Science and the Arts..............................   21— 672

SCHOOL OF PHARMACY.

Resident Graduates	3	
Second Year Students	23	
First Year Students	52—	78

HOMOEOPATHIC MEDICAL COLLEGE.

Third Year Students	4	
Second Year Students	4	
First Year Students	11—	19

COLLEGE OF DENTAL SURGERY.

Resident Graduates	2	
Seniors	48	
Juniors		
Freshmen	72—	185
		2875
Deduction for names counted more than once.		47
Total		2828

SUMMER SCHOOL OF 1894.

Total in the School	91	
Deduct for names counted in other departments	45—	46
Grand Total		2874

This is the largest number of students ever in attendance. Compared with last year the aggregate gain was 169. That more than makes good the loss experienced last year as compared with the year before. This fact is the more surprising, because the depression in business which affected us so seriously in 1893-4 had not ended when our year began.

The actual and the relative attendance from Michigan is rather rapidly increasing. It was 1,551 this last year as compared with 1,400 the previous year. It was almost 55 per cent. of the total attendance. The year before it was 52.6 per cent. This increase is due largely to the constant improvement in our high schools, which are so efficiently preparing and stimulating students to take a university training, and partly, we trust, to the increasing excellence, and attractiveness of the instruction given here.

The 45 per cent. of students, not from Michigan, represent a very cosmopolitan constituency. They came from every State in the union except Nevada, from the Territories of Arizona, New Mexico, Utah and Oklahoma, and from the sixteen following foreign States and Provinces, namely: Ontario, Quebec, New Brunswick, England, Scotland, Barbadoes, Mexico, Argentine Republic, Sweden, Switzerland, Germany, Italy, Bulgaria, South Africa, Japan and China.

As usual, Illinois furnished the largest number of students, 309, after Michigan. Ohio came next with 201, Indiana sent 108, Pennsylvania 85, New York 73, Iowa 62, Missouri 55, Massachusetts 23. When we consider the excellence of the universities and colleges in those states, it is gratifying that so many students from these and from other States, 1,267 in all, seek our halls.

The attendance of women was as follows:

Department of Literature, Science and the Arts	494
Department of Medicine and Surgery	72
Department of Law	3
Homoeopathic Medical College	2
College of Dental Surgery	5
	576

As compared with the previous year that is an increase of 24. There was an increase of 33 in the Literary Department, of 1 in the Medical Department, and a slight decrease in the other Departments. Last year there was a marked falling off in the percentage of women in the Literary Department, namely from 37 to 32 per cent. This year the percentage was 32.4, which is 4.6 per cent less than it was two years ago, but nearly a half per cent. greater than last year. The proportion of women to men in all the Departments this year was 20.4 per cent. about a half per cent. less than the previous year. From a study of the figures of the last few years we may perhaps be justified in expecting that for some time to come the proportion of women to men in the Literary Department is likely to be almost 33 per cent. and in the whole University about 21 per cent.

It is interesting to observe how the example set during the last few years by some of the European universities of opening their doors more or less widely to women is being rapidly followed by others in Scotland, Germany, Switzerland, and it is reported even in Spain.

A most important change in the organization of the Literary Department has been decided on by your Board. It took effect on October first. Heretofore the engineering students have formed a part of the Literary Department. So long as the number of those students was small, no special inconvenience resulted. But as the engineering students now usually number about three hundred, and so large a part of their work is distinctly technical, it has seemed unwise to burthen the Literary Faculty with legislating for them. As a matter of fact, that Faculty has for some time left the details of legislation concerning them to the Professors of Engineering. In view of this condition of things, and with the conviction that the engineering work, now so important, will become better known to the public and more highly appreciated, if the students and the teachers of engineering are formed into a separate organization, the Regents have now established the School of Engineering. It will be under the management of a Faculty composed of the teachers of the engineering students, and possessed of the same control over those students that the Literary Faculty exercise over the students of the Literary Department. The work of the Literary Faculty will thus be in some degree lightened, and it is hoped that the task of administration will be made more simple. There is abundant evidence that although we have taught engineering for more than forty years, many persons in Michigan have been unaware that we have engineering courses pursued by hundreds of students. This singular ignorance of what we are doing seems to be due in some degree to the fact that the engineering students have always been catalogued with the students of the Literary Department. The establishment of the separate Department of Engineering, and the special announcement of its existence and its work should certainly attract the attention of our citizens, too many of whom have supposed that they must send their sons out of the state to be trained as Civil, Mechanical or Electrical Engineers.

The year's experience has, we think, shown the wisdom of two changes made by the Literary Faculty last year, namely, that by which the class-room work with few exceptions closes at four o'clock in the afternoon, thus affording opportunity to students and teachers for exercise, either out of doors or in the gymnasium, between the hours of four and six, and that by which the hours of class-room work are limited to sixteen a week, thus avoiding the danger of cramming and leaving more time for reading, reflection and writing.

The Literary Faculty have given much time during the past two years to the subject which has been so largely engaging the attention of preparatory schools and of colleges throughout the country, that is, the proper requirements for admission to an institution like this. Every opportunity to consult with the High School teachers has been improved, since we always desire to act in full harmony with our High Schools. The most important changes that have been adopted consist first in asking more prolonged work in a small number of sciences in the place of brief study in a large number, and secondly, in asking preparation in some foreign language, either Latin or German or French or in any two of these three tongues, for admission to the B. L. course. These changes are not to take effect until the schools have time for complying with our request. As to the first of these changes, the best scientific teachers may be said to be unanimously of the opinion that it will accomplish great good in training the mind in scientific method, and in preparing it to carry on advanced scientific study in college. As to the second, it was ascertained that nearly every school, which prepares students for us, is already equipped to give instruction in one of the languages, and the linguistic knowledge asked will elevate the work of the English course and make it much more valuable to the student. We expect that the schools will experience no serious embarrassment in meeting the requirements which have been announced, and that the courses in the schools will be materially strengthened and enriched by the changes to be made.

The Faculty of the Literary Department have during the year been considering with much care the expediency of asking the Regents to reduce the number of degrees offered in that Department. Prior to 1851 the American colleges with scarcely an exception had one curriculum of study, for the completion of which the old degree of Bachelor of Arts has given. At that time Brown University established a three years' course, of which Greek formed no part, and for the completion of that course offered the degree of Bachelor of Philosophy. Since then many colleges have instituted a variety of courses and a variety of degrees supposed to be indicative of the nature of the courses, such as Bachelor of Science, Bachelor of Letters, Civil Engineer, and so on. The question has arisen whether the difference in the educational value of the courses is not so slight that one degree or at most two degrees might not suffice. Some important institutions give only one degree for courses that differ very widely from each other. Indeed the general introduction of the elective system into colleges has everywhere largely broken up the uniformity of work, which was once prevalent.

On the other hand, the degree of Bachelor of Arts has in this country so long represented the attainment of a certain amount of training in Latin, Greek and Mathematics that it is thought by many to be hardly just to the holders of that degree to confer it on those who have not that training and so to change greatly its significance. It is feared by some of us in this University, which has long been conspicuous in the west for the extent and thoroughness of its classical instruction, and which has exerted a commanding influence in the west in encouraging classical studies, that to confer the degree of A. B., on those who had not received instruction in the ancient classics, would tend to diminish enthusiasm for these studies in the northwest. It was therefore decided to make no change in the requirements for that degree. The Faculty recommended also the retention of the degrees of Ph. B. and B. S., but the substitution of Ph. B. for B. L., since preparation in one of the three languages, Latin, German and French, is to be asked for admission to the so-called English course two years hence. Some of the holders of the B. L. degree represented that this would impair the value of their diplomas, and the Regents did not adopt the recommendation of the Faculty to substitute the title Ph. B. for that of B. L. We therefore retain the degrees of A. B., Ph. B., B. S., and B. L., in addition to the other degrees for the technical studies in Engineering. After all, it is not easy to show that any special inconvenience arises from this variety of degrees.

Every effort possible had been made by the Faculty to emphasize and develop the work of the Graduate School. While other universities are provided with fellowships, offering from three hundred to five hundred dollars a year to graduate students, it is perhaps a matter for congratulation that we are able to attract so many to our halls, where they are obliged to pay full university fees. We have however received some encouragement in respect to fellowships this year. The Clara Harrison Stranahan Fund, to be known hereafter as the Seth Harrison Fund, is available for graduates as well as undergraduates, if they are descendants of Seth Harrison, and may yield five hundred dollars a year or even more to each incumbent of the scholarship or fellowship. Messrs Parke, Davis & Co., of Detroit are also sustaining this year a fellowship in Chemistry with five hundred dollars. And in this connection it may be added that Frederick Stearns of Detroit has endowed a Fellowship for research in the School of Pharmacy with three hundred dollars a year for two years.

We trust these worthy examples may stimulate other friends of the University to establish fellowships. In no way can the interests of higher learning be better promoted.

It is gratifying to observe that of the four Fellowships awarded by the American Archaeological Institute, providing for residence and study at the American School at Athens, or at the American School at Rome, two have been bestowed on our graduates, Herbert De Cou and Walter Dennison. There were some thirty competitors, representing the principal colleges and universities of the country. This certainly speaks well for our classical training.

In this connection I may call attention to the fact that at the instance of the classical department of the University, a conference of some three hundred classical teachers from various parts of the country assembled here last spring and discussed important questions concerning classical training in schools and colleges.

During the second semester, after the Frieze Memorial Organ was placed in University Hall, vesper services were instituted twice a week at four o'clock p. m. The services consisted of brief devotional exercises, reading of the scriptures, and the singing of hymns and anthems by a chorus of a hundred voices, under the direction of Professor Stanley, who presided at the organ. The students of all Departments and the public generally were invited and a good number of persons were present at these edifying services.

During the past year the meridian circle at the Observatory has been employed by Professor Hall for the determination of the places of small stars to be used in latitude work. Some progress has been made with the reduction of these observations.

The number of advanced students in Astronomy has increased a little. Some of these students intend to teach and some propose to enter observatories.

It is rather remarkable how many men, trained in this observatory, have been called to take up important astronomical work in other observatories and universities.

The Department of Medicine and Surgery has had a year of marked prosperity. It is evident that the profession and students intending to enter the profession are ready for the higher standard of admission and the prolonged course of four years which this school adopted a few years ago. The Hospital connected with this Department was not spacious enough to receive the patients who desired treatment.

It was greatly regretted that, mainly for pecuniary reasons, it was deemed necessary to close both hospitals during the summer. Of course the patients began to disperse before the second semester ended, and new patients could not be then received. It was also impracticable to fill the hospitals by the time the first semester of the new university year opened.

There was severe disappointment in many parts of the state, whence patients desired to come during the summer months for treatment. These expressions of disappointment showed how widely the beneficent influence of this charitable institution, for such it is, extends.

The attendance upon the hospitals during the year was as follows: University Hospital, 1611, Homoeopathic Hospital, 284; total 1,895. Of these 1,076 were classed on the books as farmers, laborers or persons engaged in domestic service. A very large proportion of the patients were persons of very limited means, who but for the opportunity to attend these hospitals could not have secured the kind of medical and surgical care they needed.

I desire to call attention to the useful work which our Hygienic Laboratory has done for the people of this State. It makes analyses of water and examination of articles of food for the authorities of cities and towns at a nominal price, while it furnishes instruction to students.

Since its establishment, Dr. Vaughan and his assistants have tested 301 samples of drinking water in cases where typhoid fever or other diseases has been suspected of being due to the water. In nearly one-third of these samples, they have found harmful germs. In every case where a typhoid epidemic was at the time prevailing, and an analysis of the water led to the detection of harmful germs, and the use of the water was discontinued, the typhoid epidemic has disappeared. Health officers and other village and city authorities have taken great interest in this work, and it is quite safe to say that many cases of sickness have been avoided by the results obtained.

During the same time, about 100 samples of food suspected of being poisonous have also been examined. These foods consist of milk, cheese, cream, ice-cream, custard, meats of various kinds, canned fruits, etc. In about one-fourth of these the cause of the poison has been detected.

The attendance upon our Law School continues, I believe, to be larger than that at any other school in the country. During the year plans have been carefully studied and finally adopted to increase the usefulness of the instruction. The course has been extended to three years. Two men have been added to the Faculty, Professor Wilgus, who is to give instruction largely in elementary law, and Professor H. B. Hutchins, who is called to the Deanship. Professor Hutchins was formerly a member of our Law Faculty, and has been for some years a conspicuous member of the Faculty of the Law School of Cornell University. The extension of the course has afforded an opportunity for a better arrangement as well as for a fuller treatment of subjects. We are gratified to see that the presence of a large number of students in the new class indicates that our action in lengthening the course is not premature. However, owing to the transition from the two years' course to the three years' course we must expect a smaller aggregate attendance next year.

The School of Pharmacy has in years past had to contend with the difficulties arising from the existence of a considerable number of schools with short courses and low requirements for admission and graduation. But it has held firmly to high standards and has used its influence to bring the pharmacists of the country to the approval of them. It is encouraging to learn that at the recent national convention of Schools of Pharmacy at Denver a large majority of them were pronounced in their approbation of the policy pursued here.

This school, which has so long been a pioneer in making advance, has now taken another important forward step. It has established a four years' course, leading to the degree of B. S. in Pharmacy. The requirements for admission are the same as those for admission to the B. S. course in the Literary Department. And the requirements in Mathematics, Physics, English, German and French for graduation are also the same as those for graduation in the B. S. course in the Literary Department. Of course a large amount of work in Chemistry is called for.

This provision is intended to meet the demand for a course, which shall train experts in manufacturing pharmacy and teachers for schools of pharmacy.

The Homoeopathic College has had a trying year. Discussions of a policy advocated by the late Dean divided the profession, and excited the earnest opposition of so many physicians in Michigan and throughout the country that only few students remained in the school. The legislature passed a law directing the removal of the school to Detroit. The Regents deemed it necessary to make an entire change in the Faculty. All the Professors consequently resigned at the end of the year.

The Regents deemed it impracticable, even if they had thought it wise, to transfer the College to Detroit at once, on account of the expense involved, and because the conditions to be met in Detroit had not been fulfilled. They have taken the opinion of eminent lawyers on the question which has been raised whether the Act directing the removal to Detroit was passed in such form as to be a law. Judicial determination of the question may be asked.

Meanwhile a new and able Faculty has been appointed and has begun its work. It remains to be seen what attitude the profession will take in respect to the college. Should they act in a friendly and sympathetic spirit toward it, there is no doubt that a good attendance can be secured, and efficient instruction can be given. If they choose, however, to antagonize the present organization, they can doubtless direct students to other and inferior schools, and limit the usefulness of this college. The state has provided most generously for its needs, and the Regents have done and are doing everything in their power to make it useful and successful. If those for whom assistance it was especially organized choose to embarrass rather than to support it, on them must rest the responsibility for the consequences.

The Dental College still maintains its eminence both in respect to its numbers and the excellence of its work. It could profitably use for its outfit a larger sum than we are now able to appropriate to it. The fact that it constantly draws students from Europe shows how high is its reputation.

The Summer School was continued this year with a

degree of success which warrants its permanent organization. Instruction was given not only in the branches taught in the Literary Department, but also in certain branches of Law. Twenty-three teachers took part in the instruction and 191 students were present. A large proportion of these were teachers. It is necessary that during this year arrangements be made for a more complete organization of the school.

The following facts are drawn from the Librarian's Report:

No. of volumes in all of the Libraries, Sept. 30, 1895......	98,707
No. of unbound pamphlets in all of the Libraries, Sept. 30, 1895...	17,241
No. of maps in all of the Libraries, Sept. 30, 1895........	1,151
Of these there were in the General Library, volumes....	79,342
" " " " " pamphlets..	15,759
" " " " " maps.......	1,151
In the Law Library, volumes...........................	11,805
In the Medical Library, volumes.......................	6,815
" " " pamphlets......................	1,482
In the Library of the Dental College, volumes...........	745
Total increase for the year, 1894-'95.	
Volumes......................	6,479
Unbound pamphlets............	904
Maps..........................	151
Increase of General Library, volumes...................	4,987
(Bought 2,817; presented 1,557; bound periodicals 613).	
Pamphlets......................	517
(Bought 101; presented 416).	
Maps...........................	151
(Bought 38; presented 113).	
Increase of the Law Library, volumes...................	340
Increase of the Medical Library, volumes...............	1,041
(Bought 583; presented 297; binding periodicals 161).	
Pamphlets......................	387
(Bought 1; presented 386).	
Increase of Library of Dental College, volumes..........	111
(Bought 73; binding periodicals 38).	

Recorded circulation in the Reading Room	122,352
Drawn by Professors for home use	6,469
Total	128,821

The embarrassment, to which I have called attention in previous reports, arising from the crowded condition of the Library, of course grows more serious every year. A pretty large addition, providing for the storage of books and for seminary rooms should soon be built, unless the Art Gallery in the third story is vacated. That is of course impracticable, unless a new Art Gallery is erected.

In accordance with the provisions of the will of the late Henry C. Lewis, of Coldwater, Mich., his valuable collection of pictures and statuary has now come into the possession of the University. It consists of about six hundred paintings and about one hundred pieces of statuary. It cost Mr. Lewis over two hundred thousand dollars. Several noted artists are represented in the collection by works of a high order of merit. There may be named Bouguereau, Adolph Schreyer, E. J. Verboeckhoven, P. O. J. Coomans, Peralta, G. H. L. DeHaas, Spiridon, Gerome, Szerner and Van Marcke. There are copies of many of the most noted works of the great Italian masters. There are portraits, some of them excellent paintings, of a large number of men and women distinguished in history.

We are placing on the walls of our Museum of Art as many of the best pictures as can be displayed there. The time has come when we greatly need a new Museum of Fine Arts. This Lewis collection, the Rogers collection of statuary, consisting of nearly a hundred pieces, some of them of heroic size, added to the pictures and statuary which we had been collecting for years before these large collections were presented to us, would now fill a pretty large gallery. If our catalogue were completed it would now contain about 1,800 numbers. It addition to these we have about 2,500 photographs, which have been gathered by the classical professors to represent ancient life.

Had we a proper building, we could now with little expense establish a School of Art as a Department of the University. We are hoping that some friend of the Institution will help us to erect a suitable building as a monument of his generosity. It ought to be a structure of stone and of appropriate architecture, costing from $100,000 to $200,000. It is time that in our plannings for the future we began to think of securing buildings of better architecture. The cheap and plain, sometimes tasteless structures, upon our campus may have answered for the earlier days, when collegiate architecture had attracted no attention in the country. But the best interests of the University require that we spare no pains to secure henceforth tasteful and elegant plans for our more important buildings, and above all for an Art Gallery.

The Gymnasium was completed last year so that it has been available for the students. The entire cost of the building with equipment was $65,134.14. The women were allowed the use of the Gymnasium in the forenoon and the men in the afternoon and evening. It was decided not to make attendance on the instruction and exercise compulsory. But very large classes of volunteers were formed, and the interest displayed by them was very great. The beneficial effect upon the health and intellectual vigor of the students was marked.

But it was soon obvious that there is great need of a gymnasium to be used exclusively by the women. One of the Regents, Mr. Hebard, secured ten thousand dollars—a large part his own gift—towards the erection of such a building as a wing of the present gymnasium, and another Regent, Mr. Barbour, gave for the same purpose a lot of land in Detroit valued at twenty-five thousand dollars. The women in the university, including the wives of the professors, set on foot a movement to raise fifteen thousand dollars more, to meet the estimated cost of the building, fifty thousand dollars. Only a portion of that sum has yet been secured. But it is so probable that it will be obtained, that it is hoped that work may be begun upon the foundation at no distant day.

The purpose is not only to provide a gymnasium in this building, but also other rooms which the women much need, such as bath rooms, parlors, and an assembly room, that will accommodate a few hundred persons where lectures especially for the women may be given. We have hoped that some generous woman would give us a good part of the sum yet needed. In no way could money be expended more helpfully to the five hundred women in the university.

The general management of athletic games under the direction of a board, composed of five members of our Faculties chosen by the University Senate and of four members chosen by the Athletic Association of students from their own number, has been fairly satisfactory both to the Faculties and to the students. While intercollegiate games have been permitted, the number allowed is limited by rule. No professional players, and no persons who have "conditions" in their studies standing against them are allowed to play in match games. It is believed that most of the objectionable features of athletic games have been avoided and most of the advantages to be derived from them have been gained during the past year. There is doubtless room for some improvement in the conduct of them, and I think that the students as well as our Faculties are sincerely desirous of securing these improvements.

A great desideratum has long been to awaken in the great body of students the same interest in their own physical training that they feel in the training and success of the athletic teams. Our new gymnasium has done much to accomplish this end. But not a few students who most need its aid neglect the opportunities it affords. Still several hundreds of students, both men and women, took the regular class work in gymnasium last year.

The legislature last winter passed two bills, at the request of the Regents. One empowers the Regents to take and hold in perpetual trust, lands or other property. It was thought that they had this power before. But to remove all shadow of doubt it was deemed expedient to ask for this legislation. The other provides for the payment to the State Treasurer of all moneys given to the Regents in trust to expend the income thereof, and for the payment of interest upon all such moneys by the State to the Regents in furtherance of such trust.

It is well known that the proceeds of the sale of the lands which were given to the State by the United States as an endowment of the University were turned into the State Treasury, and the State arranged to pay the Regents the interest on the sum in perpetuity. It began by paying seven per cent. which was much less than the customary rate of interest in those early years, and has continued to pay that rate until this year. The Auditor General has now assumed to cut the rate down to six per cent., and is remitting to us on that basis. We have been advised by able counsel that he has no authority for this step, and the Regents regard it as their duty to obtain the opinion of the Supreme Court on this important question.

We have been obliged to administer our affairs with most rigid economy. We have denied ourselves many things, which may fairly be called necessities. But we have been determined to keep our expenditures within our income. The Treasurer's Report, appended hereto, will show that we have done so. Only those who are familiar with the legitimate demands which a prosperous and growing Institution like this makes upon its treasury can understand how many painful denials of the laudable requests of zealous teachers it necessitates to accomplish this.

We cannot but hope that with returning business prosperity, which seems to be generally anticipated, some of our generous friends will come to our aid. Pressing and immediate needs are the enlargement of the Law Building, of the Chemical, Physical, Anatomical and Bacteriological Laboratories, of the Library Building and of the Hospital wards, the establishment of an electric light plant, and the erection of an Art Gallery. There is always room for the wise use of funds in the increase of facilities for teaching in additions to our Library Fund, in the endowment of scholarships and fellowships and professorships. All observation shows that generosity can find no more efficient means of doing lasting good to generation after generation than the endowment of schools of learning. We have no doubt that the State of Michigan, for which this University has done so much, will continue to supply many of its most urgent wants. But there is ample room for private beneficence to supplement, as it has already done to some extent, the gifts of the State.

JAMES B. ANGELL.

APPENDIX A.

TREASURER'S REPORT.

To the Finance Committee, Board of Regents, University of Michigan:

GENTLEMEN: Herewith I submit my annual report for the year ending June 30th, 1895. Respectfully,

H. SOULE, Treasurer.

RECEIPTS.

Balance in Treasury July 1st, 1894	$ 44,731 34	
From State Treasurer, Acct. Special Appropriations	6,000 00	
" " " " Current Expenses	225,722 36	
" Earnings, Miscellaneous Sources	163,693 17	$440,146 87

DISBURSEMENTS.

From Special Funds Account	$ 68,692 91	
" General Fund Account	365,539 01	
Balance in Treasury June 30th, 1895	5,914 95	$440,146 87

GENERAL FUND.

RECEIPTS TO THE GENERAL FUND.

From State Treasurer, Account 1-6 Mill Tax	$188,333 31	
" " " " University Interest	37,389 05	$225,722 36
" Interest on Deposits	2,687 06	
" Dental Supplies	5,459 37	
" Miscellaneous Sources	898 26	
" General Catalogues, sold	15 00	
" General Library—duplicate books sold	30 18	
" University Record—subscriptions paid	12 85	
" University Hospital Earnings (Balance for year 1893-94)	1,476 06	
" University Hospital Earnings, for 1894-95	5,000 00	
" Physical Laboratory Earnings	2 50	
" Anatomical Material	566 56	$ 16,147 86

To Students' Fees and Deposits, as follows:

Medical Department	$ 15,620 00
Literary "	51,790 00
Law "	31,305 00
Dental "	7,385 00
Homœopathic Department	890 00
Pharmacy Department	3,840 00
Chemical Laboratory	8,720 00
Hygienic "	2,754 78
Physiological Laboratory	93 00
Botanical Laboratory	797 00

Pathological Laboratory	1,105 00		
Zoological "	533 00		
Electrical Engineering Laboratory	541 00		
General Chemistry "	923 53		
Electrotherapeutical "	840 00		
Pharmacological "	40 00		
Practical Anatomy	2,610 00		
Histological Laboratory	840 00		
Mechanical "	1,620 00		
Medical Demonstration	3,380 00		
Gymnasium Lockers	2,162 00		
Diplomas	7,189 00		
Key Deposits	571 00		
Summer School	2,016 00	147,545 31	147,545 31
			$ 389,415 53
Students' Fees, Total	$147,545 31		
Students' Fees Refunded	5,656 97		
Net	$141,888 34		

DISBURSEMENTS FROM THE GENERAL FUND.

To Balance Overdrawn July 1st, 1894			$ 5,477 59
" Transfer to Special Building Fund			6,303 53
" General Pay Roll	$157,517 85	$157,517 85	157,517 85
" Medical Department, Pay Roll	38,341 00	38,341 00	
" " " Books		2,498 10	
" " " Miscellaneous		278 86	41,117 96
" Law Department, Pay Roll	21,612 50	21,612 50	
" " " Books		1,749 11	
" " " Miscellaneous		417 87	23,779 48
" Pharmacy and Chemistry, Pay Roll	18,696 00	18,696 00	
" " " " Miscellaneous		6,977 22	25,673 22
" University Hospital, Pay Roll	4,569 27	4,569 27	
" " " Miscellaneous		3,504 94	8,074 21
" Homœopathic Hospital, Pay Roll	1,337 50	1,337 50	
" " " Miscellaneous		4,149 32	5,486 82
" Dental College, Pay Roll	11,350 00	11,350 00	
" " " Miscellaneous		4,064 97	15,414 97
Amount of Pay Rolls	$253,424 12		
" Contingent Account			8,034 03
" Repairs			7,440 17
" Fuel and Lights			21,495 86
" General Library, Books			9,792 78
" " " Miscellaneous			1,083 33
" Postage			1,476 50
" Printing and Advertising			3,258 31
" Museum			64 25
" Botanical Laboratory			644 25
" Histological Laboratory			414 92
" Hygienic "			2,785 51
" Mechanical "			1,027 47

" Pathological Laboratory 624 00
" Physiological " 351 84
" General Chemistry Laboratory 1,434 75
" Electrical Engineering Laboratory . . . 864 82
" Practical Anatomy " 1,892 68
" Materia Medica " 419 18
" Zoological " 197 79
" Theory and Practice " 50 22
" Psychological " 302 68
" Geology 427 19
" Ophthalmology 77 05
" Morphology 355 68
" Civil Engineering 1,015 65
" Observatory 1,282 34
" Greek 30 60
" Demonstration Courses 18 50
" Electrotherapeutics 238 88
" Nervous Diseases 65 92
" Dermatology 50 00
" History 140 96
" Diseases of Women and Children . . . 234 25
" Surgical Demonstrations 416 84
" Homœopathic College 150 50
" Recitation Building 2,024 15
" Gymnasium 546 54
" Steam Heating 1,668 95
" Latin Department 152 58
" Museum Roof 3,762 92
" Columbian Organ Account 163 68
" Horse and Cart Expenses 89 68
" Summer School " 1,818 34
" Insurance 272 00
" Oriental Languages 104 11
" University Record 277 49
" Water Supply 1,193 80
" Carpenter Shop Supplies 709 94
" School Inspection 403 55
" Mineralogy 107 62
" Students' Fees Refunded 5,656 97
" Commencement Expenses 733 00
" Lewis Art Collection 620 42
" Balance—Cash in hand 5,914 95
" Cash Loaned to Special Fund Account . . 6,180 45   12,095 40
                                                      ─────────
                                                      $389,415 53

SPECIAL FUND ACCOUNTS.
HOMŒOPATHIC MEDICAL COLLEGE.

Receipts.

From State Treasurer . . . . . $ 6,000 00
Balance Overdrawn June 30th, 1895 . . . 6,273 51 $ 12,273 51

Disbursements.

Balance Overdrawn July 1st, 1894 . . . $ 1,467 96
Paid Salaries to Professors and Employees . . 10,800 00
Paid Vouchers for Expenses . . . . 5 55 $ 12,273 51

PHYSICAL LABORATORY.

Receipts.

Balance in Treasury July 1st, 1894	$ 435 72	$435 72

Disbursements.

Paid Vouchers for Expenses	$ 428 66	
Balance in Treasury June 30th, 1895	7 06	$ 435 72

CIVIL ENGINEERING.

Receipts.

Balance in Treasury July 1st 1894	$ 70 10	$ 70 10

Disbursements.

Paid Vouchers for Expenses	$ 61 00	
Balance in Treasury June 30th, 1895	9 10	$ 70 10

EQUIPMENT OF ENGINEERING LABORATORY.

Receipts.

Balance in Treasury July 1st, 1894	$ 150 25	$ 150 25

Disbursements.

Paid Vouchers for Expenses	$ 73 35	
Balance in Treasury June 30th, 1895	76 90	$ 150 25

BUILDING FUND.

Receipts.

Balance in Treasury July 1st, 1894	$51,020 82	
Transfer from General Fund	6,303 53	$ 57,324 35

Disbursements.

Paid Vouchers for Expenses, Gymnasium Account	$ 11,084 08	
" " " " Steam Heating Account	45,169 12	
" " " " Museum Roof "	1,000 00	
" " " " Organ Account	71 15	$ 57,324 35

SPECIAL FUNDS.

Balances June 30th, 1895.

Equipment of Engineering Laboratory	76 90		
Physical Laboratory	7 06		
Civil Engineering	9 10		
Borrowed from General Fund	6,180 45	$ 6,273 51	
Homœopathic College, Overdrawn			$ 6,273 51

AFFAIRS OF THE HOSPITALS.

The Superintendent of the Hospitals reports to the Auditing Board the following as all the business done by him during the year. This embraces the running expenses only and does not include the maintenance or permanent expenses which are met from the General Fund of the University.

UNIVERSITY HOSPITAL, JULY TO SEPTEMBER, 1894.

This Hospital was again opened during the vacation months, July, August, and September, 1894, with the following results:

Receipts.

Receipts from Patients	$ 3,474 39	
Deficiency	67 28	$ 3,541 67

Disbursements.

Refunded to Patients	884 08		
Paid for Salaries and Maintenance	$ 2,657 59	$ 3,541 67	

UNIVERSITY HOSPITAL, OCTOBER, 1894, TO JUNE, 1895.

Receipts.

For the College Year, October to June, inclusive, Receipts from Patients	$ 20,664 88	$ 20,664 88

Disbursements.

Amount Refunded to Patients by Joseph Clark, Superintendent	$ 5,957 40	
Amount of Expenses Paid by Joseph Clark, Superintendent	9,707 48	
Amount of Cash to Treasurer by Joseph Clark, Superintendent	5,000 00	$ 20,664 88

HOMŒOPATHIC HOSPITAL, JULY TO SEPTEMBER, 1894.

This Hospital was opened during the summer months for the first time and with the following results:

Receipts.

Received from Patients by Joseph Clark, Superintendent.	$ 658 90	
Amount of Deficiency Paid from the University General Fund	579 80	$ 1,238 70

Disbursements.

Amount Refunded to Patients by Joseph Clark, Superintendent	$ 198 89	
Amount of Expenses Paid by Joseph Clark, Superintendent	1,039 81	$ 1,238 70

HOMŒOPATHIC HOSPITAL, OCTOBER, 1894, TO JUNE, 1895.

Receipts.

From Collections and Earnings for the College Year, October to June, inclusive, Receipts from Patients by Joseph Clark, Superintendent	$ 3,351 97	
Deficiency	940 20	$ 4,292 17

Disbursements.

Amount Refunded to Patients by Joseph Clark, Superintendent	$ 1,050 09	
Amount of Expenses Paid by Joseph Clark, Superintendent	3,242 08	$ 4,292 17

GIFTS AND TRUST FUNDS.

Under this head are included gifts and other funds which the Regents have received from time to time from benefactors for general purposes or for stated special purposes, and to which list during the year have been added:

Bequest of Miss Jean L. Coyl of Detroit, Mich., for the Coyl Collection	$ 10,000 00
Bequest of Mr. Christian H. Buhl of Detroit, Mich., for the Buhl Law Library	10,000 00
From Mrs. Clara Harrison Stranahan of Brooklyn, N. Y., for the Seth Harrison Scholarship Fund	25,000 00
Bequest of Dr. Corydon L. Ford, for the Ford-Messer Fund	5,000 00

Contributions to the Class of Ninety-four Scholarship Fund		195 00
Contributions to the Women's Gymnasium Fund		1,240 56

The Accounts are as follows:

PHILO PARSONS FUND.
Receipts

Balance in Treasury July 1st, 1894	$ 82 16	
Interest	3 36	$ 85 52

Disbursements.

Balance in Treasury June 30th, 1895		$ 85 52

MARY JANE PORTER FUND.
Receipts.

Balance in Treasury July 1st, 1894	$ 655 98	
Interest	27 08	$ 683 06

Disbursements.

Balance in Treasury June 30th, 1895		$ 683 06

GOETHE FUND.
Receipts

Balance in Treasury July 1st, 1894	$ 301 01	
Interest	11 06	$ 312 07

Disbursements.

Paid Vouchers for Expenses	$ 50 12	
Balance in Treasury June 30th, 1895	261 95	$ 312 07

ELISHA JONES CLASSICAL FELLOWSHIP.
Receipts.

Balance in Treasury July 1st, 1894	$ 2 26	
Interest	1 09	
From Mrs. Elisha Jones	500 00	$ 503 35

Disbursements.

Paid Vouchers	$ 500 00	
Balance in Treasury June 30th, 1895	3 35	$ 503 35

CONTINGENT.
Receipts.

Balance in Treasury July 1st, 1894	$ 2,936 91	
Interest	127 46	$ 3,064 37

Disbursements.

Balance in Treasury June 30th, 1895		$ 3,064 37

GYMNASIUM FUND.
Receipts.

Balance in Treasury July 1st, 1894	$ 2,826 97	
Interest on Deposits	72 06	
Sale of $3,300 00 U. S. Bonds, Nov. 19th, 1894	3,765 50	
Interest on U. S. Bonds, 2 quarters to Oct. 1st	66 00	
Balance Overdrawn June 30th, 1895	120 75	$ 6,851 28

Disbursements.

Paid Vouchers		$ 6,851 28

WOMEN'S GYMNASIUM FUND.
Receipts.

Balance in Treasury July 1st, 1894	$ 1,440 00	
Interest	61 32	
Gifts	1,240 56	$ 2,741 88

Disbursements.

Balance in Treasury June 30th, 1895	$ 2,741 88

FRIEZE MEMORIAL FUND.
Receipts.

Balance in Treasury July 1st, 1894	$ 1 50	
Interest	02	$ 1 52

Disbursements.

Paid Vouchers	$ 1 52

COYL COLLECTION.
Receipts.

Received from the Estate of Miss Jean L. Coyl	$ 10,000 00	
Interest	286 01	$ 10,286 01

Disbursements.

Balance in Treasury June 30th, 1895	$ 10,286 01

BUHL LAW LIBRARY.
Receipts.

Received from the Estate of Mr. Christian H. Buhl	$ 10,000 00	
Interest	229 48	$ 10,229 48

Disbursements.

Balance in Treasury June 30th, 1895	$ 10,229 48

SETH HARRISON SCHOLARSHIP FUND.
Receipts.

From Mrs. Clara Harrison Stranahan	$ 25,000 00	
Interest	213 89	$ 25,213 89

Disbursements.

Balance in Treasury June 30th, 1895	$ 25,213 89

CLASS OF NINETY-FOUR SCHOLARSHIP FUND.
Receipts.

Subscriptions Paid	$ 195 00	
Interest	10	$ 195 10

Disbursements.

Balance in Treasury June 30th, 1895	$ 195 10

FORD-MESSER FUND.
Receipts.

From the Administrator of the Estate of Dr. Corydon L. Ford—On Account of Bequest	$ 5,000 00

Disbursements.

Balance in Treasury June 30th, 1895	$ 5,000 00

The subscribers who have paid to the Class of 1894 Scholarship Fund are as follows:

Walter P. Martindale	$ 5 00
Dwight O. Miller	5 00
Delia S. Bailey	5 00

Wiley W. Mills	1 00
Jesse C. Moore	5 00
Frederick W. Newton	3 00
Helen A. Rice	5 00
Bernice L. Haug	5 00
William L. Whitney	5 00
Eugene C. Woodruff	5 00
Sarah M. Howard	5 00
Adoniram J. Ladd	5 00
Fannie M. Elliott	5 00
Robert F. Hall	5 00
Jamie Maud Blanchard	5 00
Charles W. Adams	5 00
John Q. Adams	5 00
Barend H. Kroeze	1 00
Sara M. Riggs	5 00
Eugene C. Sullivan	5 00
Robert V. Friedman	5 00
George T. Tremble	5 00
Ralph W. Newton	5 00
James B. Overton	10 00
Clare Briggs	5 00
Jeannette E. Caldwell	5 00
Walter M. Hamilton	5 00
Carrie E. Penfield	5 00
Almira A. Prentice	5 00
Lewis G. Seeley	5 00
Charles J. Harmon	10 00
Delos F. Wilcox	5 00
Oscar Greulich	5 00
Almon H. Demrick	5 00
Anna Trainor	5 00
Daniel B. Luten	5 00
Joseph R. Nelson	5 00
Lucy E. Textor	5 00
Lelia Brouillette	5 00
	$ 195 00

Contributions to the Women's Gymnasium Fund have been received from the following sources during the year:

Mrs. P. B. Loomis,	Jackson.	$ 15 00
Mrs. Dr. Hartley,	Ann Arbor.	10 00
Miss Annah May Soule,	" "	25 00
Gamma Phi Beta,	" "	25 00
Dr. Mary Wood Allen,	" "	10 00
Prof. E. D. Campbell,	" "	5 00
Oratorical Association Depew Reception,		192 95
Women's Literary Club,	Charlotte.	10 00
Rev. Frank O'Brien,	Kalamazoo.	25 00
Miss Elizabeth M. Farrand,	Detroit.	5 00

Mrs. Lucy D. S. Parker,	Ann Arbor.	50 00
Mrs. G. C. Huber,	" "	5 00
Katherine S. Fletcher,	Lake Linden.	10 00
Mrs. N. W. Cheever,	Ann Arbor.	5 00
Mrs. W. H. Nichols,	" "	5 00
Mrs. L. H. Hall,	" "	5 00
Miss Eunice Lambie,	Ypsilanti.	1 00
Ann Arbor Comedy Club,	Ann Arbor.	15 00
Mrs. Abbie H. Bartlett,	Chicago, Ill.	50 00
Miss. Katherine A. Puncheon—Collections,	Ann Arbor.	9 50
Mrs. J. H. Boutell,	Detroit.	10 00
Sarah M. Howard,	Kalamazoo.	10 00
Mrs. Caroline I. Kleinstueck,	"	25 00
M. M. Hoyt,	"	25 00
Ladies' Literary Club,	St. Louis.	5 00
Charles A. Rathbone,	Detroit.	25 00
Margaret E. P. Howard,	Tewksbury, Mass.	5 00
T S. McGraw,	Detroit.	25 00
Miss Winifred Lane,	"	5 00
William J. Cocker,	Adrian.	50 00
Miss Helen P. Lovell,	Flint.	1 00
Prof. Alfred H. Lloyd and wife,	Ann Arbor.	15 00
Detroit Branch of Collegiate Alumnæ,	Detroit.	231 31
Mrs. Walter H. Nichols,	Ann Arbor.	10 00
Women's Glee and Banjo Club,	" "	25 00
Sophomore Class Social Committee of 1895,	" "	10 00
Mrs. C. C. Bloomfield,	Jackson.	25 00
Henrietta P. R. Moore,	Detroit.	3 00
Women's League—Anita's Trial,	Ann Arbor.	1 50
Mrs. Israel Hall,	" "	50 00
Miss Emma E. Bower,	" "	5 00
Women's League—Ice Cream Benefit,	" "	64 05
Mrs. James Shaw,	Detroit.	5 00
Mrs. A. C. Angell,	"	10 00
Prof. Thomas—Proceeds of Ibsen Lectures,	Ann Arbor.	20 00
Miss Hess—Collection,	" "	2 00
Mrs. Alice Freeman Palmer,	Cambridge, Mass.	25 00
Mrs. Zimmerman.	Ann Arbor.	10 00
Miss Schrobel,		2 00
Miss K. A. Puncheon—from College Girls,	Ann Arbor.	12 00
Frank C. Parker,	" "	10 00
Pi Beta Phi,	" "	28 00
Bertha Christy,		1 00
Mrs. F. P. Jordan—from College Girls,	Ann Arbor.	2 00
Ann Arbor High School Seniors,	" "	9 25

Contributed during the year ending June 30th, 1895, $ 1,240 56

APPENDIX B.

EXAMINATIONS FOR DEGREES.

The following examinations were held in 1894:

CANDIDATE FOR THE DEGREE OF DOCTOR OF PHILOSOPHY.

FRANK HAIGH DIXON, Ph.B., 1892.

Thesis.—Railway Control in Iowa. Subjects for examination: Major.—Political Economy. Minors.—Finance. American History.

CANDIDATES FOR THE DEGREE OF MASTER OF ARTS.

ARCHIE ERNEST BARTLETT, A.B, 1894.

Subjects for examination: Major.—Greek. Minors.—Latin. Classical Archæology.

RUDOLPH FREDERICK FLINTERMANN, A.B., 1894.

Subjects for examination: Major.—Organic Chemistry. Minors.—Quantitative Analysis. Mineralogy.

JACOB GEORGE HALAPLIAN, A.B., 1894.

Subjects for examination: Major.—Hebrew. Minors.—Assyrian. Hellenistic Greek.

CYRUS B. NEWCOMER, A.B., *Carthage College*, 1889.

Subjects for examination: Major.—Latin. Minors.—Greek. Sanskrit.

JOSEPHINE ELIZA SONDERICKER, A.B., 1889.

Subjects for examination: Major.—Greek. Minors.—Latin. Classical Archæology.

CARRIE TAYLOR STEWART, A.B., *University of Kansas*, 1892.

Subjects for examination: Major.—German. Minors.—French. Gothic.

DELOS FRANKLIN WILCOX, A.B., 1894.

Subjects for examination: Major.—Comparative Constitutional Law. Minors.—American History. Sociology.

CANDIDATES FOR THE DEGREE OF MASTER OF PHILOSOPHY.

CHARLES FRANKLIN EMERICK, A.B., *Wittenberg College*, 1889, M. S., *Mich. Agr. College*, 1891.

Subjects for examination: Major.—Political Economy. Minors.—History and Pedagogy.

WILLARD CLARK GORE, Ph.B., 1894.

Subjects for examination: Major.–Rhetoric. Minors.—English Literature. Philosophy.

CLARENCE MORTIMER MULHOLLAND, Ph.B., *Albion College*, 1894.

Subjects for examination: Major.—United States History. Minors.—Comparative Constitutional Law. Political Economy.

CANDIDATES FOR THE DEGREE OF MASTER OF SCIENCE.

LYMAN JAMES BRIGGS, B.S., *Michigan Agricultural College*, 1893.

Subjects for examination: Major.–Physics. Minors.—Mathematics. Mechanics.

GERTRUDE BUCK, B.S., 1894.

Subjects for examination: Major.—Rhetoric. Minors.—Psychology. English Literature.

WILBUR OLIN HEDRICK, B.S., *Michigan Agricultural College*, 1891.

Subjects for examination: Major.—Political Economy. Minors.—Finance. History.

ELLEN CLARA HOGEBOOM, B.S., 1877.

Subjects for examination: Major.—General Chemistry. Minors.—Organic Chemistry. Crystallography.

EMERSON ROMEO MILLER, Ph.C., 1892, Ph.M., 1893, B.S., 1894.

Subjects for examination: Major.—General Chemistry. Minors.—Organic Chemistry. Mineralogy.

WILLIAM WALTER PARKER, B.S., *Michigan Agricultural College*, 1893.

Subjects for examination: Major.—Organic Chemistry. Minors.—General Chemistry. Mineralogy.

RAYMOND ELMOINE VAN SYCKLE, B.S, 1891.

Subjects for examination: Major.—Political Economy. Minors.—Political Philosophy. Finance.

NEIL HOOKER WILLIAMS, B.S., 1893.

Subjects for examination: Major.—Physics. Minors.—Chemistry. Mathematics.

CANDIDATES FOR THE DEGREE OF BACHELOR OF LETTERS.

FRANK THOMSON MERRY, B.L., 1890.

Subjects for examination: Major.—History. Minors.—American History. Political Economy.

SARA GENEVIEVE O'BRIEN, B.L., 1894.

Subjects for examination: Major.—European History. Minors.—English Literature. Pedagogy.

ANNAH MAY SOULE, B.L., 1894.

Subjects for examination: Major.—United States History. Minors.--Political Economy. Comparative Constitutional Law.

WM. DEARBORN BALL, B.S., Mech. E., 1890,

Having completed the work required, was recommended for the degree of Electrical Engineer.

ROBERT CAMPBELL GEMMELL, B.S., C.E., 1884,

Having completed the work required, was recommended for the degree of Civil Engineer.

APPENDIX C.

RECENT LEGISLATION CONCERNING THE UNIVERSITY.

AN ACT to enable the Regents of the University to take and hold in perpetual trust land or other property.

SECTION 1. *The People of the State of Michigan enact,* That it shall be competent for the Regents of the University to take, by gift, devise or bequest, and hold in perpetuity any land or other property in trust for any purpose not inconsistent with the objects and purposes of the University.

Approved March 26, 1895.

AN ACT to provide for the payment to the State Treasurer of all moneys given to the Regents of the University in trust to expend the income thereof, and for the payment of interest upon all such moneys by the State to the Regents of the University in furtherance of said trust.

SECTION 1. *The People of the State of Michigan enact,* That whenever any money or other property, of whatever nature and kind, with directions or with power to convert the same into money, is or shall be given to the Regents of the University upon trust to expend the income thereof in furtherance of any of the objects of the University, it shall be the duty of the Regents to pay such money to the State Treasurer, and the Auditor General be and he hereby is required to credit to the University interest fund interest not to exceed the rate of four per cent. per annum upon all such moneys from and after the first day of the month next after such moneys have respectively been received by said State Treasurer, and to draw his warrant upon the State Treasurer for the same. And the State Treasurer is hereby required to pay the same to the treasurer of the University upon his application therefor in the same way and manner as is now provided by law for the payment of the University fund: *Provided*, That said interest shall not be paid from the specific tax fund.

SEC. 2. The interest so paid as provided in the preceding section shall be expended by the Regents in strict accordance with the terms of the trust upon which the money or other property as aforesaid was originally given, and in no other manner.

Approved May 11, 1895.

UNIVERSITY OF MICHIGAN

THE
PRESIDENT'S REPORT

TO THE

BOARD OF REGENTS

FOR THE

YEAR ENDING SEPT. 30,

1896.

ANN ARBOR, MICH.:
PUBLISHED BY THE UNIVERSITY.
1896.

ANN ARBOR:
THE INLAND PRESS, PRINTERS.
1896.

THE PRESIDENT'S REPORT.

To the Honorable the Board of Regents.

I beg leave to present to you my annual report for the year ending September 30, 1896.

The following is a list of the appointments, reappointments and resignations of members of the Faculties. The Instructors were appointed for one year, unless a longer term is mentioned.

At the meeting in October, 1895:

M. H. Parmelee, M. D., Acting Professor of Gynæcology and Obstetrics in the Homœopathic Medical College, for one year.

At the meeting in November, 1895:

Albert H. Walker, LL. B, non-resident Lecturer on Patents in Law Department, for one year.

The titles of the following gentlemen were changed to stand as follows:

Jacob Reighard, Ph. B., Professor of Zoölogy and Director of the Zoölogical Laboratory and Museum.

Dean C. Worcester, A. B., Assistant Professor of Zoölogy and Curator of the Zoölogical Museum.

Frank R. Lillie, Ph. D., Instructor in Zoölogy.

M. L. D'Ooge, Ph. D., LL. D., was reappointed Dean of the Department of Literature, Science and the Arts for one year.

At the January meeting, 1896:

Robert Mark Wenley, D. Sc., Ph. D, Professor of Philosophy.

Eliza M. Mosher, M. D., Professor of Hygiene and Women's Dean in the Department of Literature, Science, and the Arts.

P. L. Sherman, Ph. D., Instructor in General Chemistry, for Second Semester.

L. N. Johnson, A. M, Instructor in Botany, resigned on account of illness

At the February meeting:

J C. Rolfe, Ph. D., Professor of Latin, was granted leave of absence for the next University year.

At the meeting in March:

David C. Davol, Ph. C., was appointed Instructor in Organic Chemistry for one year, in place of Dr. Gomberg, who received leave of absence for one year.

At the meeting in April:

The resignation by Calvin Thomas, A. M., of the Chair of Germanic Languages and Literatures, was presented and accepted.

At the May meeting:

The resignation by John W. Champlin, LL. D., of his Professorship of Law was accepted.

APPOINTED FOR THREE YEARS.

Fred N. Scott, Ph. D., Junior Professor of Rhetoric.
Alex. Ziwet, C. E., Junior Professor of Mathematics.
Max Winkler, Ph. D, Assistant Professor of German.
M. Levi. A. B., Assistant Professor of French.
E. A. Lyman, A. B., Instructor in Mathematics.
C. L. Meader, A. B., Instructor in Latin.
C. H. Cooley, Ph. D., Instructor in Sociology.
Karl Guthe, Ph. D., Instructor in Physics.
C. G. Wrentmore, B. S., Instructor in Descriptive Geometry and Drawing.
Ernst Voss, Ph. D., Instructor in German.

REAPPOINTED FOR THREE YEARS.

F. M. Taylor, Ph. D., Junior Professor of Political Economy.

APPOINTED FOR ONE YEAR.

A. H. Lloyd, Ph. D., Assistant Professor of Philosphy.
E. B. Lease, Ph. D., Assistant Professor of Latin.
C. E. St. John, Ph. D., Instructor in Physics.
Arthur Lachman, Ph. D., Instructor in General Chemistry.

REAPPOINTED FOR ONE YEAR.

George Rebec, Ph. B., Instructor in Philosophy.
J. A. C. Hildner, A. M., Instructor in German.
F. R. Lillie, Ph. D., Instructor in Zoölogy.
W. R. Wait, Ph. D., Instructor in Greek, Latin and Sanskrit.
J. W. Glover, Ph. D., Instructor in Mathematics.
L. A. Strauss, Ph. M., instructor in English.

E. C. Goddard, Ph. B., Instructor in Mathematics.
H. J. Goulding, B. S., Instructor in Descriptive Geometry.
H. L. Coar, A. M., Instructor in Mathematics.

REAPPOINTMENTS IN THE LAW DEPARTMENT FOR ONE YEAR.

INSTRUCTORS.

John W. Dwyer, LL. M., Thomas W. Hughes, LL. M., Walter D. Smith, LL. B.

NON-RESIDENT LECTURERS.

Henry H. Swan, A. M., Lecturer on Admiralty.
James L. High, LL. D., Lecturer on Injunctions and Receivers.
Melville M. Bigelow, Ph. D., Lecturer on Insurance.
John B. Clayberg, LL. B., Lecturer on Mining Law.
Albert H. Walker, LL. B., Lecturer on Patent Law.
Frank F. Reed, A. B., Lecturer on Copyright Law.

SPECIAL LECTURERS.

A. C. McLaughlin, A. B., LL. B., Lecturer on Constitutional Law.
Thomas M. Cooley, LL. D., Lecturer on Interstate Commerce.
Victor C. Vaughan, M. D., Lecturer on Toxicology in its Legal Relations.
Richard Hudson, A. M., Lecturer on Comparative Constitutional Law.
Clarence L. Meader, A. B., Lecturer on Roman Law.

At the June meeting:

The resignation of Ernst Voss, Ph. D., Instructor in German, was accepted.

The following appointments were made:

P. L. Sherman, Ph, D., Instructor in General Chemistry.
T. Diekhoff, A. B., Instructor in German for three years.
Otto E. Lessing, A. B., Instructor in German.
W. E. Johnston, A. M., Instructor in History.
Perry F. Trowbridge, Ph. B., Instructor in Organic Chemistry and Accountant in the Chemical Laboratory.
Julius O. Schlotterbeck, Ph. C., B. S., Assistant Professor of Pharmacognosy and Botany for three years in the School of Pharmacy.
The title of E. D. Campbell, B. S., was changed from Junior Professor of Metallurgy and Metallurgical Chemistry to Junior Professor of Analytical Chemistry.

REAPPOINTMENTS IN THE DENTAL DEPARTMENT FOR ONE YEAR.

C. G. Darling, M. D., Lecturer on Oral Pathology and Surgery.

L. P. Hall, D. D. S., Instructor in Dental Anatomy and Operative Dentistry.

A. W. Haidle, D. D. S., Demonstrator of Dental Mechanism.

IN THE DEPARTMENT OF MEDICINE AND SURGERY.

S. M. Yutzy, M. D., Instructor in Osteology and Assistant Demonstrator of Anatomy.

The title of Dr. Darling was changed to Demonstrator of Surgery and Lecturer on Minor Surgery.

Charles E. Marshall, Ph. B., Instructor in Bacteriology.

IN THE HOMŒOPATHIC MEDICAL COLLEGE.

M. H. Parmelee, M. D., Acting Professor of Gynæcology and Obstetrics.

At the September meeting:

W. A. Dewey, M. D., Professor of Materia Medica and Therapeutics in the Homœopathic Medical College.

John R. Allen, Mech. Eng., Instructor in Mechanical Engineering.

The title of W. B. Hinsdale, M. D., was changed to Professor of Theory and Practice of Medicine, and of Clinical Medicine in the Homœopathic Medical College.

F. C. Wagner, A. M., B. S., resigned the Chair of Assistant Professor of Mechanical Engineering.

Walter Denton Smith, Instructor in Law, died on September 20 at his home in Galesburg, Mich. He was a young man of high intelligence and of large promise.

I have also to record the death of one of our former Regents, James Frederic Joy, LL. D., at his home in Detroit on September 24. He had reached the advanced age of 85 years. He was a member of the Board of Regents from 1882 to 1887, when owing to the press of business cares, to our great regret, he resigned. Those marked characteristics, which made him so conspicuous a figure in the history of Michigan for the last fifty years, rendered his services to the University of the highest value.

DEGREES CONFERRED.

The following degrees were conferred:

DEGREES ON EXAMINATION.

Bachelor of Letters	45
Bachelor of Science (in Biology)	8
Bachelor of Science (in Chemistry)	4

Bachelor of Science (in Electrical Engineering)	26
Bachelor of Science (in Mechanical Engineering)	19
Bachelor of Science (in Civil Engineering)	24
Bachelor of Science in (Mining Engineering)	1
Bachelor of Science	11
Bachelor of Philosophy	51
Bachelor of Arts	55
Master of Letters	3
Mechanical Engineer	2
Civil Engineer	1
Master of Science	5
Master of Philosophy	5
Master of Arts	10
Doctor of Philosophy	1
Doctor of Medicine (Department of Medicine and Surgery)	53
Bachelor of Laws	318
Master of Laws	20
Pharmaceutical Chemist	23
Doctor of Medicine (Homœopathic Medical College)	6
Doctor of Dental Surgery	60
	751

HONORARY DEGREES.

Bachelor of Science (in Pharmacy)	1
Master of Arts	1
Doctor of Laws	4
Total	757

SUMMARY OF STUDENTS.

DEPARTMENT OF LITERATURE, SCIENCE AND THE ARTS.

Holders of Fellowships	2	
Resident Graduates	57	
Candidates for an Advanced Degree, enrolled in other Departments	6	
Graduates studying *in Absentia*	10	
Undergraduates:		
Candidates for a Degree	919	
Students not Candidates for a Degree	211	1205

DEPARTMENT OF ENGINEERING.

Resident Graduates	6	
Graduates studying *in Absentia*	6	
Undergraduates:		
Candidates for a Degree	299	
Students not Candidates for a Degree	20	331

DEPARTMENT OF MEDICINE AND SURGERY.

Resident Graduates	12	
Fourth Year Students	58	
Third Year Students	84	
First Year Students	181	
Students enrolled in the Department of Literature, Science and the Arts:		
Third Year Students in Medicine	1	
Second Year students in Medicine	2	
First Year Students in Medicine	9	
Students enrolled in the School of Pharmacy:		
First Year Students in Medicine	2—	456

DEPARTMENT OF LAW.

Resident Graduates	26	
Seniors	344	
Second Year Students	23	
First Year Students	246	
Special Students	21	
Students enrolled in the Department of Literature, Science and the arts	15—	675

SCHOOL OF PHARMACY.

Holder of Stearns Fellowship	1	
Undergraduates:		
Candidates for a Degree	72	
Students not Candidates for a Degree	10—	83

HOMŒOPATHIC MEDICAL COLLEGE.

Fourth Year Students	6	
Third Year Students	3	
Second Year Students	7	
First Year Students	11—	27

COLLEGE OF DENTAL SURGERY.

Seniors	62	
Juniors	59	
Freshmen	67	
Students enrolled in the Department of Literature, Science and the Arts	1—	189
		2966
Deduct for names counted more than once		44
Total		2922

SUMMER SCHOOL OF 1895.

Total in the School	187	
Deduct for names counted in other departments	90—	97
Grand Total		3019

Again we have to report, as in the remarkable history of our growth we have so generally had occasion to report, that the number of students in attendance exceeded that of any previous year. In 1894-5 we had the unprecedented number of 2828. But that is less by 94 than the number for 1895-96, namely, 2922. If we add the number in attendance on the Summer School in 1895, not counting the regular students who took courses in that school, the grand total is 3019.

It should be borne in mind that we take no special and extraordinary measures, such as are employed by some institutions, to call the attention of students to the advantages of the University. Indeed we often find in Michigan signal proofs of the ignorance of some intelligent citizens concerning the opportunities we offer for the acquisition of a collegiate, technical, or professional education. We cannot but regard it as a proof of the value set by our graduates and the communities in which they dwell on the education imparted here, that in the most quiet and natural way the attendance continues steadily to increase. This is the more noteworthy because in several States from which we draw a large number there are universities of a very high order.

It is true, and we do not regret the fact, that the number of Michigan students has been for some years proportionally gaining on the number from other states. For several years just about half our students came from Michigan and half from elsewhere. Last year the relative proportion was very nearly 55 per cent. and 45 per cent. This year the proportion is very nearly 56 per cent. and 44 per cent. During the years 1893-4, 1894-5, 1895-6, the attendance of Michigan students has been respectively, 1400, 1551, 1632. This is a gratifying proof that Michigan students are more and more appreciating the advantages presented here.

At the same time, the number of non-resident students has not been declining but slowly increasing. In the three years above referred to 1893-4, 1894-5, 1895-6, their number was 1259, 1267, 1290. In 1895-96 they came from forty-one States of the Union, and from the District of Columbia, Oklahoma, New Mexico and Arizona, and from the following foreign states and provinces, Ontario, Quebec, Barbadoes, South Africa, England, Germany, Norway, Austria, Russia, Bulgaria, Hawaiian Islands, Japan and China. From Illinois came 335, Ohio 194, Indiana 109, New York 87, Pennsylvania 85, Iowa 76, Missouri 51, Wisconsin 37, Kansas 23, California 22, Massachusetts 21, Minnesota 21, Nebraska, 20. Every New England State was represented. The total number from that section, so richly supplied with excellent colleges, was 33.

The number of women in attendance was as follows:

Department of Literature, Science and the Arts	513
Department of Medicine and Surgery	68
Department of Law	5
School of Pharmacy	6
Homœopathic Medical College	3
College of Dental Surgery	6
	601

The total number is greater by 25 than last year. The slight increase is mainly in the Literary Department, but the total relative increase of women to men is only one-tenth of one per cent. The proportion of women to men remains with very small modifications from year to year. This last year it was 20.5 per cent.

The separation of the Engineering from the Literary Department proves to have been advantageous to both Departments. They act in entire harmony with each other, and more efficient supervision of the students is practicable than formerly. The Announcement of the Engineering Department contains a most valuable and interesting register of the engineering graduates from 1860. It shows the positions which each graduate has filled. The importance of the work they have accomplished is at once an evidence of their ability and industry and a proof of the excellence of the instruction they received.

There has been no change in the methods of the Literary Department to call for special remark. The modified requirements for admission referred to in my last report go into effect next year. We anticipate that the schools will have no special difficulty in meeting them, and we are confident that the courses indicated will be better both for the schools and for us. We should certainly be unwilling to ask of the schools any change which would not be a real improvement in their work.

Like all the leading universities, we are doing all that our resources will allow, to develop the Graduate School. It would be a great mistake for us to diminish in the least the value of our services to the undergraduates in order to add to the efficiency of instruction for the graduates. Possibly there is a little danger to some institutions or to some professors of committing this error. The day may come when some American university may be able to give its exclusive attention to graduates. But at present our universities must do collegiate work. It would, however, be a grave mistake for the Regents or for the State to fail in appreciation of the great value to us of the vigorous prosecution of the advanced work of graduate students. The presence of such a body of mature and aspiring students is uplifting and inspiring in its influence on the undergraduates. Moreover, if we are really to prepare men and women for conspicuous positions, we must carry them beyond the boundaries of the undergraduate curriculum. Especially is this true of those who are aiming to occupy prominent places as teachers. There is in almost every field of activity a call for a certain number of men so thoroughly trained that they may justly be called experts in their special departments. The institution that is unable to furnish this kind of training can hardly aspire to the name of a University. It is the proper and the necessary function of this University to supply this instruction. Else the sons and the daughters of Michigan must needs go elsewhere to find it. We do not believe that the State desires that they should be compelled to go elsewhere. But it should be understood that this advanced teaching makes great demands on the professors. Each teacher can profitably instruct only a small number. The teaching must be largely personal, that is, specially adapted to the needs of each individual student. It is of course more expensive than undergraduate instruction. The question, therefore, with which this University and the other large State Universities is confronted is this; are the States willing to furnish the means for providing this kind of instruction? Just now, there is no more important questions concerning higher education to be passed on by our western States. Upon the answer to be given to this question it depends whether the State Universities are to have their development arrested at their present stage, and so are to fall behind the universities, which depend for their support on private endowments. When we remember how the western States have so far met the increasing demands which the development and improvement of their common schools, normal schools, agricultural colleges and universities have made on them, we are hopeful that they will be willing, if their universities are economically administered, as they should be, to maintain them at the same level of efficiency as the best universities, which rest on private generosity for their support.

When we consider that we have only a very small number of fellowships available for graduates, while other important institutions have many, we have reason to be gratified at our number of graduate students. It is also interesting to note that about half of them come to us from other institutions, both in the east and in the west.

The Department of Medicine and Surgery has had a very successful year. The raising of the standard of admission has borne excellent fruit. The number of students is about as large as we can accommodate. Indeed, some of the laboratories are too crowded. As a very large part of the instruction is now given by laboratory methods, there is a limit to the number we can properly receive.

Not a few students are availing themselves of the opportunity afforded to abridge the time required for the completion of the literary and medical courses by a judicious election of certain scientific branches, common to the two courses. Though the plan adopted has proved very satisfactory, we are still considering whether some improvement cannot be made in it. The time required for the completion of a four years' collegiate curriculum and then of a four years' professional course is so great that many have been tempted or forced by circumstances to enter upon professional study without having completed or even entered upon the collegiate studies. That is certainly to be regretted. And we regard it as our duty to do all in our power to make it practicable for a student to secure the benefit of both courses, and yet to begin the practice of his profession before he is far into the twenties. We believe that we have done something to accomplish this and hope that we may do yet more.

The most important feature in the work of the Law Department has been the extension of the course to three years. It is clear that the profession is ready for this change. Our action in making it has been warmly approved. Owing to the fact that schools in adjoining states still hold to the shorter course, and to the more deplorable fact that in some states, which furnish us many students, persons are admitted to the bar after very brief terms of study, we had thought it probable that the entering class would be smaller than its predecessors. But the new class has proved to be larger than that of last year. This fact shows conclusively that our change has not been made too soon. During the past year more strenuous labor has been exacted of the law students than ever before, and some valuable modifications have been made in the methods of instruction. Literary students who come to the beginning of their last year with only a small amount of work remaining for the earning of the bachelor's degree are allowed to take work in the Law School, and so shorten by a year the aggregate time required for completing the literary and law courses. A joint committee of the Literary and Law Faculties is now considering whether any better plan for accomplishing this result is practicable. As in the case of medical students, it is deemed very desirable to find some means of making it feasible for a larger proportion of law students to complete the collegiate course.

The most important change in the School of Pharmacy has been the establishment of a four years' course leading to the degree of Bachelor of Science in Pharmacy. The requirements are similar to those for the Bachelor's degree in General Science, but having a special application to pharmaceutical work. It is especially intended for those who are expecting to be professors in schools of pharmacy. It has been the fortune of this school, as one of the earliest and strongest, to furnish teachers for other schools of this kind. And there seems to be a certain limited demand on us for this thorough and complete course of training. We trust we shall thus be able to add another to the services which this school in its quiet and unostentatious way has rendered.

The Homœopathic Medical College has had a year, which is not without promise for the future. The members of the Faculty have worked harmoniously, and more students were present than could be expected, in face of the opposition of so many of the homœopathic physicians, who did not desire that the school should succeed at Ann Arbor. It is perfectly apparent that, if the present Faculty can be reasonably encouraged and sustained by the profession, the college may have a useful career. With the aid of the ample laboratories of the University and with its well-appointed hospital, its students can receive a professional education not surpassed in thoroughness in any homœopathic school in the country.

The Regents regarded it as their duty to ask the Supreme Court to determine whether an Act of the last Legislature requiring them to remove the college to Detroit was mandatory on them. The Court decided that it was not, and established the important principle that the control of the University is left by the Constitution in the hands of the Regents.

The Dental College, like the Department of Medicine and Surgery, has as many students as it can well accommodate, and pursues the even tenor of its way in a very satisfactory manner, though certain desired improvements in its appliances could be secured, if a moderate addition could be made to its resources.

The Summer School has had another successful term. Thirty-seven teachers from the Literary Department and five from the Law Department gave instruction. The number of students under the former was 205, that of the law students was 26. The tentative and temporary arrangement for the appointment and payment of the teachers proved fairly satisfactory. But it deserves consideration whether a better one cannot be devised for permanent use. And it seems expedient to plan for the permanent establishment of the School. It is clear that there is a genuine demand for such a school, especially on the part of teachers, who need to enlarge their preparation for their work. The University in meeting this demand is rendering a substantial service to public education, and is attaching the schools, in which these pupils are giving instruction, more closely to itself.

A valuable service was rendered to us by the State Board of Corrections and Charities in providing gratuitously a course of lectures to our students on practical problems in Sociology. The lecturers were Rev. Wm. Knight of Saginaw, Rev. C. F. Swift of Lansing, and the following gentlemen from Detroit, Rabbi Louis Grossman, Rev. Lee S. McCollester, and H. C. Wyman, M. D. These lectures were largely attended, especially by the students of Political Economy and Sociology. It would be of value to us to have a small fund, as many universities have, with which to bring scholarly lecturers on special topics before our classes.

At the Observatory Professor Hall has been principally engaged in securing with the meridian circle a series of observations for the determination of the variation of terrestial latitudes, taking altitudes of Polaris above and below the pole. Also, observations have been continued of the places of stars to be used at other observations with Talcott's method.

The following summary is taken from the Librarian's report:

Number of volumes in all the libraries Sept. 3, 1896	105,047
Number of unbound pamphlets in all the libraries	17,509
Number of maps in all the libraries	1,197
Of these there were in the General Library, volumes	84,698
" " " " " " " pamphlets	16,020
" " " " " " " maps	1,197
In the Law Library, volumes	12,064
In the Medical Library, volumes	7,510
" " " pamphlets	1,488
In Library of Dental College, volumes	775
Total increase for 1895-96, volumes	6,340
Unbound pamphlets	268
Maps	68

Increase of General Library, volumes, 5,356. (Bought, 3,440; presented, 1,361; bound periodicals, 555). Pamphlets, 261. (Bought, 144; presented, 117). Maps, 68. (Bought, 22; presented, 46).

Increase of Law Library, volumes, 259.

Increase of Medical Library (including Homœopathic books), volumes, 695. (Bought, 486; presented, 49; binding periodicals, 160). Pamphlets, 6. (Bought, —; presented, 6).

Increase of Library of Dental College, volumes, 30. (Bought, 30; presented —). Pamphlets, 1.

Recorded circulation in the Reading Room, volumes......... 126,901
Drawn by Professors for home use, volumes.................... 6,614

Total.. 133,515

We have received two valuable additions to the Library by gift. One is the collection of works on philosophy from the library of the late Professor Morris, which has been presented by his widow, Mrs. Morris. It contains about 1,100 volumes, mainly on ethics and the history of philosophy. The other collection was bequeathed by the late Governor Felch, and comprises the bulk of his valuable library. It consists of about 3,500 volumes, and is especially rich in works on American history. Both these collections are treasured by us, not only on account of their intrinsic value, but also because of their association with men who had in their lives rendered so valuable service to the University.

The ten thousand dollars bequeathed by Mr. Buhl to the University for the Law Library has now become available for the purchase of books, and steps have been taken for its judicious expenditure. The addition which it will secure is greatly needed.

As the number of volumes in our General Library is now about 85,000, I desire to urge the Regents to consider earnestly the feasibility of setting apart a certain number of books, which students may be allowed to draw from the Library and take to their rooms for a limited period. Believing that such use of certain books will be much more advantageous to the readers, I have long looked forward to the time when it would be practicable for us to permit it. I have always thought that when the number of volumes approached 100,000, we might safely give this larger liberty to students under certain restrictions. Of course only certain classes of books could thus be spared from the library. Many copies of certain books will be needed. The expense of service at the desk may be a little increased. The risk of loss is perhaps somewhat enhanced. But after all proper weight is given to these facts, we have to remember that the library is the great central power in the instruction given in the University, and that the books are here not to be locked up and kept away from readers, but to be placed at their disposal with the utmost freedom compatible with safety and with the general and equal convenience of all the students. The Library Committee have given some consideration to the subject, and can doubtless soon furnish you with the essential facts, which you may require in order to determine when, if at all, the change suggested should be made in the administration of the Library.

In this connection I may say that the experiment, we have been trying for some months, of doing our bookbinding ourselves, has proved satisfactory. We did not anticipate much diminution in the cost of the work. But the convenience of having the work done when the Librarian desires it and under his own eyes is very great. The petty repairs can also be much better directed.

A good deal of labor has been expended during the year on the better arrangement of the collections in our Museum, and a definite policy concerning its management has been adopted. The policy is one approved by the best scientific authorities. The aim is to make collections of typical species, to be representative, though not exhaustive, and to exhibit them so as to make them teach as much as possible. The Curator well suggests that the State might wisely undertake, through us, to make here a complete collection of the natural history of Michigan. We have a large amount of material already, and shall always be glad to receive additions to it.

We have during the year taken some further steps in advance in the regulation of athletic games. It was found that the rules, which the Advisory Board on Athletics, a body consisting of five members of the Faculties chosen by the University Senate and of four students chosen by the Athletic Association had made, were hardly stringent enough to prevent some abuses. So more vigorous regulations have been adopted. An unusually severe test in administering them was furnished at the end of the year. On the eve of a baseball game, which was to decide the championship of the West, it was found that three of our most skillful players had hired themselves out for a "professional" game. The Advisory Board immediately dropped them from the team. The team lost the decisive game, as was expected, but the University won a much greater victory than could have been gained by any superiority in playing. I believe too that the students generally approved with heartiness the action of the Board. The sooner all students can understand that what helps the University in athletic games is not so much victory in a contest as clean and honorable conduct on the part of the players, the better it will be for all concerned.

The wholesome rule that no student, who has "conditions" in any study standing against him, can play in a match game of base-ball or foot-ball, has also been applied to students who are members of glee clubs or editors of the University daily paper. They cannot go abroad with any glee club or serve on the paper if their work is in arrears. The principle which governs the action of the authorities in all these cases is that study is the first work of every student, and that no occupation or amusement can be allowed to interfere seriously with that.

The gymnasium is highly appreciated by a large number of our students, and is unquestionably of great service to them. It has, however, become more and more apparent that the completion of the gymnasium for the women is in the highest degree desirable. The structure is now so far advanced that we cannot doubt that means for its completion will soon be forthcoming. The women students have labored with unremitting zeal to secure the needed funds.

The building and the athletic work in it will be placed under the control of Eliza M. Mosher, M. D., who has been appointed Women's Dean and Professor of Hygiene. Dr. Mosher graduated from the Department of Medicine and Surgery, and has held several responsible administration and professional positions. It is expected that by her instruction in hygiene and by her personal relations with the women students she can be of great service to them. Her teaching, however, is not to be confined to women. Her lectures will be open to all students. Her familiarity with the problems of domestic and public sanitation specially fits her for most valuable discussions of them.

Far more pains has been taken than ever before in caring for the campus. The result has been most gratifying to all. It is to be hoped that yet more may be done to beautify our grounds, which have been too long neglected.

A few of the gifts which have been bestowed on us, besides the gifts to the library mentioned above, are worthy of notice here.

The Chicago Alumni Association, which has so frequently testified its interest in us, has sent us two medals of most artistic design and workmanship to be presented as prizes for excellence in oratory. They propose to give such prizes annually. The medals were designed by Mr. Louis H. Sullivan, of Chicago, and executed by Mr. Barber, the chief engraver of the United States mint at Philadelphia. Two copies of the medals were also sent to be deposited permanently with our collection of medals in the Art Gallery.

The Executive Committee of the Field Columbian

Museum have presented us with two of the large pictures of the Michigan artist, Gary Melchers, which formed the tympani of the Manufacturers' Building of the Columbian Exposition. We have placed them on the walls of University Hall. The subjects are, "The Arts of War and the Arts of Peace."

In February last Mrs. Anna E. P. Marsh, M. D., who graduated from the Homœopathic Medical College, died in Golden, Colorado. She bequeathed to the University for the endowment of scholarships bearing her name, most of her estate, subject to certain charges. The property was largely real estate, situated in Colorado and Arizona, and at the time the will was made bore a much higher value than it has now. The gift was intended to be a loving testimonial to the school in which the testator received her professional education. It is doubtful, however, whether the charges with which the gift is burdened are not larger than the probable income of the estate. The University may therefore be compelled to decline it.

The last graduating class of the Literary Department pledged itself to pay for the casts of the sculpture on the Arch of Trajan at Benevento, which are among the most interesting specimens of Roman antiquities.

The Treasurer's report, appended hereto, shows that heavy as have been our expenses, we have kept them within our receipts. In my last report I referred to the action of the Auditor General in assuming to cut from seven per cent. to six per cent. the rate of interest which the State was paying us on the proceeds of the sale of the lands with which the United States endowed the University. The Supreme Court has decided that his action was without authority, and we have therefore received the arrears due us.

In the interests of economy the Regents have diminished somewhat the number of teachers in the Literary Faculty. They have also made a slight increase in the annual fees of students. The fees in the Engineering Department are made the same as those in the professional schools on the theory that the training is as strictly professional as that in law or medicine or dentistry.

In these times of industrial depression the Regents are desirous that the University shall be so administered as not to be burdensome to the State. At the same time they cannot forget that in the sharp competitions of industrial communities, those which are most intelligent and enterprising are sure to be in the lead. They believe that Michigan has heretofore been more prosperous and influential because of the help which the University has afforded to the sons of Michigan. The most short sighted economy for the State would be the curtailment in any degree of the efficiency of its educational institutions. The custodians of the University believe that now is the time when this institution can be of special service to the State by sending out men and women trained for all the duties and exigencies of life. They trust that the people of the State will take the same view of the function of the University, and will continue to uphold it with their generous support.

In conclusion, it is proper and becoming that I should acknowledge, and I desire to acknowledge with all my heart, the kindness, with which the Regents, the Senate, the alumni, and other friends of the University joined in celebrating the completion of my twenty-fifth year of service as President of this institution. Of the many tokens of appreciation of what I have sought to do for the welfare of the University, I can only say that they will, if possible, increase the zeal, with which I shall attempt to serve the University during the years that I may be spared to labor for her prosperity.

JAMES B. ANGELL.

APPENDIX A.

TREASURER'S REPORT.

To the Finance Committee, Board of Regents, University of Michigan,

GENTLEMEN: Herewith I submit my annual report for the year ending June 30th, 1896.

Respectfully,

H. SOULE, Treasurer.

RECEIPTS.

Balance in the Treasury July 1, 1895	$ 5,914 95	
From State Treasurer, Acct. Special Appropriations	6,000 00	
" " " " Current Expenses	210,939 97	
" Miscellaneous Sources and Earnings	180,842 60	$403,697 52

DISBURSEMENTS.

Special Fund Accounts	$ 9,639 16	
General Fund Accounts	372,264 65	
Balance in Treasury June 30, 1896	21,793 71	$403,697 52

GENERAL FUND.

RECEIPTS TO THE GENERAL FUND.

From Balance July 1, 1895		$12,095 40
" State Treasurer, Account 1-6 Mill Tax	$188,333 32	
" " " University Interest	22,606 65	
" Interest on Deposits	3,942 87	
" Sale of Dental Supplies	6,122 25	
" Miscellaneous Sources	1,094 58	
" General Library—duplicate books sold	7 33	
" Rent of Gymnasium	100 00	
" University Hospital	10,125 90	
" Homœopathic Hospital	1,557 68	$233,890 56

From Students' fees and deposits as follows:

Medical Department	$ 18,080 00	
Literary "	41,945 00	
Law "	30,785 00	
Dental "	7,850 00	
Homœopathic Department	1,025 00	
Pharmacy Department	3,805 00	
Engineering Department	10,960 00	
Chemical Laboratory	12,170 00	
Mechanical Laboratory,	1,570 00	
Hygienic "	3,045 00	
Physiological "	108 00	
Botanical "	450 00	
Pathological "	885 00	
Zoological "	860 00	
Electrical Engineering	503 00	
Electrotherapeutics	1,104 00	

Practical Anatomy	1,935 00	
Histological Laboratory	1,075 00	
Medical Demonstration	4,230 00	
Gymnasium Lockers	2,362 00	
Drawing Boards	222 00	
Key Deposits	303 00	
General Chemistry	1 01	
Practical Pharmacology	110 00	
Diplomas	7,800 00	
Summer School	4,709 00	
Students' fees received, total	$157,892 01	$157,892 01
" " refunded	6,650 17	
Net	$151,241 84	
		$403,877 97

DISBURSEMENTS FROM THE GENERAL FUND.

To General Pay Roll	$ 137,814 41	$ 137,814 41
" Medical Department, Pay Roll	35,236 50	35,236 50
" " " Books		1,424 20
" " " Miscellaneous		449 90
" Law " Pay Roll	27,537 50	27,537 50
" " " Books		949 42
" " " Miscellaneous		596 48
" Pharmacy " Pay Roll	18,321 00	18,321 00
" " " Miscellaneous		9,136 49
" Dental College, Pay Roll	11,350 00	11,350 00
" " " Books		143 97
" " " Miscellaneous		4,590 48
" Engineering Department, Pay Roll	23,374 65	23,374 65
" " " Miscellaneous		16 00
" University Hospital, Pay Roll	6,228 48	6,228 48
" " " Miscellaneous		8,880 78
" Homœopathic Hospital, Pay Roll	1,390 71	1,390 71
" " " Miscellaneous		3,036 91
Amount of Pay Rolls	$ 261,253 25	
" Contingent Account		6,621 02
" Repairs		12,131 55
" Fuel and Lights		19,450 24
" General Library, Books		7,656 98
" " " Miscellaneous Expenses		723 16
" Homœopathic College, Books		184 38
" Postage		2,239 79
" Printing and Advertising		2,628 96
" Museum		484 56
" Botanical Laboratory		910 95
" Histological Laboratory		358 72
" Hygienic "		1,483 17
" Mechanical "		1,163 78
" Pathological "		431 57
" Physiological "		146 59
" Electrical Engineering Laboratory		839 37
" Anatomical Laboratory		2,659 89
" Materia Medica Laboratory		375 50
" Zoological Laboratory		476 24
" Philosophy		1 00
" Women's Gymnasium		37 64
" Theory and Practice of Medicine		221 11

To Psychology		403 46
" Geology		65 55
" Ophthalmology		6 25
" Morphology		378 60
" Civil Engineering		507 90
" Observatory		350 82
" Greek		175 00
" Medical Demonstration		174 84
" Electrotherapeutics		245 19
" Nervous Diseases		131 08
" Dermatology		36 99
" English		8 50
" Diseases of Women and Children		87 60
" Homœopathic College		178 50
" Gymnasium		457 10
" " Rent Refunded		100 00
" Latin Department		205 24
" Summer School		4,327 73
" Horse and Cart Expenses		103 63
" Insurance		70 00
" Water Supply		1,396 39
" Carpenter Shop Supplies		415 75
" School Inspection		368 89
" Students' Fees Refunded		6,650 17
" Commencement Expenses		574 19
" Mining Engineering		4 67
" Book Bindery		1,416 16
" Athletic Grounds		600 00
" Diplomas		1,092 25
" Oriental Languages		26 25
		$ 372,264 65
Loan to Special Funds	$ 9,819 61	
Balance in Treasury June 30, 1896	21,793 71	31,613 32
		$ 403,877 97

SPECIAL FUND ACCOUNTS.

HOMŒOPATHIC MEDICAL COLLEGE.

Receipts.

From State Treasurer	$ 6,000 00	
Balance Overdrawn June 30, 1896	9,821 56	$ 15,821 56

Disbursements.

Balance Overdrawn July 1, 1895	$ 6,273 51	
Paid Salaries to Professors and Employees	9,450 00	
" Vouchers for Expenses	98 05	$ 15,821 56

PHYSICAL LABORATORY.

Receipts.

Balance in Treasury July 1, 1895	$ 7 06	$ 7 06

Disbursements.

Paid Vouchers for Expenses	$ 7 06	$ 7 06

CIVIL ENGINEERING.

Receipts.

Balance in Treasury July 1, 1895	$ 9 10	$ 9 10

Disbursements.

Paid Vouchers for Expenses	$ 7 15	
Balance in Treasury June 30, 1896	1 95	$ 9 10

EQUIPMENT OF ENGINEERING LABORATORY.

Receipts.

Balance in Treasury July 1, 1895	$ 76 90	$ 76 90

Disbursements.

Paid Vouchers for Expenses	$ 76 90	$ 76 90

RECAPITULATION.

Balances in Special Funds.

Civil Engineering	$ 1 95	
Loan from General Fund	9,819 61	$ 9,821 56

Overdrawn.

Homœopathic Medical College	$ 9,821 56

GIFTS AND TRUST FUNDS.

Under this head are included gifts and other funds which the Regents have received from time to time from benefactors for general purposes, and to which that during the year have been added:

The Ford-Messer Fund	$ 5,000 00	
Music Hall Fund, Establishment of	1,000 00	
Establishing American School at Rome Fund	125 00	
" Parke-Davis Scholarship Fund	500 00	
" Stearns Pharmacy Fellowship Fund	300 00	
" '96 Class Memorial Fund	217 00	
" Phillips Scholarships Fund	45 93	
Contributions to the '94 Class Scholarship Fund	230 78	
" " Women's Gymnasium Fund	9,379 19	
		$ 16,797 90

PHILO PARSONS FUND.

Receipts.

Balance in Treasury July 1, 1895	$ 85 52	
Interest	3 51	$ 89 03

Disbursements.

Balance in Treasury June 30, 1896	$ 89 03	$ 89 03

MARY JANE PORTER FUND.

Receipts.

Balance in Treasury July 1, 1895	$ 683 03	
Interest	28 17	$ 711 23

Disbursements.

Balance in Treasury June 30, 1896	$ 711 23	$ 711 23

GOETHE FUND.

Receipts.

Balance in Treasury July 1, 1895	$ 261 95	
Interest	10 51	$ 272 46

Disbursements.

Paid Vouchers	$ 6 78	
Balance in Treasury June 30, 1896	265 68	$ 272 46

ELISHA JONES CLASSICAL FELLOWSHIP.

Receipts.

Balance in Treasury July 1, 1895	$ 3 35	
Interest	96	
From Mrs. Elisha Jones	500 00	$ 504 31

Disbursements.

Paid Vouchers	$ 500 00	
Balance in Treasury June 30, 1896	4 31	$ 504 31

CONTINGENT.
Receipts.
Balance in Treasury July 1, 1895	$ 3,064 37	
Interest	124 57	$ 3,188 94

Disbursements.
Balance in Treasury June 30, 1896	$ 3,188 94	$ 3,188 94

WOMEN'S GYMNASIUM.
Receipts.
Balance in Treasury July 1, 1895	$ 2,741 88	
Interest	224 53	
Gifts	9,379 19	$ 12,345 60

Disbursements.
Paid Vouchers	$ 11,169 31	
Balance in Treasury June 30, 1896	1,176 29	$ 12,345 60

WATERMAN GYMNASIUM.
Receipts.
From Earnings	$ 100 00	
Balance Overdrawn June 30, 1896	20 75	$ 120 75

Disbursements.
Balance Overdrawn July 1, 1895	$ 120 75	$ 120 75

COYL COLLECTION.
Receipts.
Balance in Treasury July 1, 1895	$ 10,286 01	
Interest	256 82	$ 10,542 83

Disbursements.
Paid Vouchers	$ 126 02	
Balance in Treasury June 30, 1896	10,416 81	$ 10,542 83

BUHL LAW LIBRARY.
Receipts.
Balance in Treasury July 1, 1895	$ 10,229 48	
Interest	415 29	$ 10,644 77

Disbursements.
Balance in Treasury June 30, 1896	$ 10,644 77	$ 10,644 77

SETH HARRISON SCHOLARSHIP FUND.
Balance in Treasury July 1, 1895	$ 25,213 89	
Interest	789 23	$ 26,003 12

Disbursements.
Paid Vouchers	$ 1,010 50	
Balance in Treasury June 30, 1896	24,992 62	$ 26,003 12

CLASS OF NINETY-FOUR SCHOLARSHIP FUND.
Receipts.
Balance in Treasury July 1, 1895	$ 195 10	
Subscriptions paid	230 78	
Interest	9 93	$ 435 81

Disbursements.
Balance in Treasury June 30, 1896	$ 435 81	$ 435 81

FORD-MESSER FUND.
Receipts.
Balance in Treasury July 1, 1895	$ 5,000 00	
From the Administrator of the Estate of Corydon L. Ford—on account of Bequest	5,000 00	
Interest	167 99	$ 10,167 99

Disbursements.

Paid Vouchers	$ 1 50		
Balance in Treasury June 30, 1896	10,166 40	$ 10,167 99

THE PHILLIPS SCHOLARSHIPS FUND.
Receipts.

From the Estate of Henry Phillips	$ 45 93		
Interest	94	$ 46 87

Disbursements.

Balance in Treasury June 30, 1896	$ 46 87	$ 46 87

AMERICAN SCHOOL AT ROME.
Receipts.

From Donations	$ 125 00	$ 125 00

Disbursements.

Paid Vouchers	$ 125 00	$ 125 00

MUSIC HALL FUND.
Receipts.

From Donations	$ 1,000 00		
Interest	4 16	$1,004 16

Disbursements.

Balance in Treasury June 30, 1896	$ 1,004 16	$ 1,004 16

NINETY-SIX CLASS MEMORIAL.
Receipts.

From Donations	$ 217 00		
Balance Overdrawn June 30, 1896	35 11	$ 252 11

Disbursements.

Paid Vouchers	$ 252 11	$ 252 11

HOMŒOPATHIC HOSPITAL FREE BED.
Receipts.

Donation	$ 61 19		
Interest	82	$ 62 01

Disbursements.

Paid Vouchers	$ 62 01	$ 62 01

PARKE-DAVIS FUND.
Receipts.

Donation	$ 500 00		
Interest	9 25	$ 509 25

Disbursements.

Paid Vouchers	$ 500 00		
Balance in Treasury June 30, 1896	9 25	$ 509 25

STEARNS PHARMACY FELLOWSHIP FUND.
Receipts.

Donations	$ 300 00	$ 300 00

Disbursements.

Paid Vouchers	$ 300 00	$ 300 00

RECAPITULATION.

GIFT FUNDS—BALANCES JUNE 30, 1896.

Philo Parsons Fund	$ 89 03	
Mary Jane Porter Fund	711 23	
Goethe Fund	265 68	
Elisha Jones Classical Fellowship Fund	4 31	
Contingent	3,188 94	
Coyl Collection Fund	10,416 81	
Buhl Law Library Fund	10,644 77	
Seth Harrison Fund	24,992 62	
Ninety-Four Scholarship Fund	435 81	
Ford-Messer Fund	10,166 49	
Phillips Scholarships Fund	46 87	
Music Hall Fund	1,004 16	
Parke-Davis Fund	9 25	
Women's Gymnasium Fund	1,176 29	$ 63,152 26
Deduct for the following overdrawn balances:		
Waterman Gymnasium	$ 20 75	
Ninety-Six Class Memorial	35 11	55 86
Total in Treasury		$ 63,096 40

Contributors to the Ninety-Four Class Scholarship during the year:

Norman W. Price	$ 5 00
Albert R. Crittenden	5 00
Ross C. Whitman	5 00
Elmer J. Ottaway	5 00
Henry O. Chapoton	10 00
Robert E. Jones	5 00
Fred A. Sager	5 00
S. Archibald Smith	3 00
Joseph Weare	5 00
Samuel D. Magers	5 00
Taka Kawada	5 00
George T. Tremble	5 00
Abraham K. Adler	10 30
Daniel F. Lyons	10 30
Dwight O. Miller	5 00
S. Archibald Smith	3 00
Lucy E. Textor	5 00
Oscar Greulich	5 00
Joseph Weare	5 00
Maud Blanchard	5 00
Adrian J. Pieters	10 00
Bernice L. Haug	5 00
Robert V. Vriedman	5 00
Frederick W. Newton	3 00
Adoniram J. Ladd	5 00
John Q. Adams	5 00
Daniel B. Luten	5 00
William L. Whitney	5 00
Sarah M. Howard	5 00
Almira Prentice	5 00
Arthur L. Hubbard	5 00
George Ingersoll, Jr.	6 18
Walter M. Hamilton	5 00
Eugene C. Woodruff	5 00

Delos F. Wilcox	5 00
Charles W. Adams	5 00
Delia S. Bailey	5 00
Sara M. Riggs	5 00
Fannie M. Elliott	5 00
Anna Trainor	5 00
Mrs. Carrie E. Penfield Harvey	5 00
Mrs. Jeannette E. Caldwell Mix	10 00
Total	$ 230 75

APPENDIX B.

EXAMINATIONS FOR DEGREES.

The following examinations were held in 1896:

CANDIDATE FOR THE DEGREE OF DOCTOR OF PHILOSOPHY.

ERNST HEINRICH MENSEL, A.B., *Carthage College*, 1887, A.M., *ibid.*, 1890.

THESIS.—Die langen Flexions-und Ableitungssilben im Althochdeutschen. Subjects for examination: Major.—Germanic Philology. Minors.—German Literature. Old English.

CANDIDATES FOR THE DEGREE OF MASTER OF ARTS.

LAWRENCE THOMAS COLE, A.B., 1892, S.T.B., *General Theological Seminary*, 1895.

THESIS.—The Christian Philosophers of the First and Second Centuries. Subjects for examination: Major.—History of Philosophy. Minors.—Ethics. History.

HUMPHREY SNELL GRAY, A.B., 1893.

THESIS.—The Liability of Administrative Officers. Subjects for examination: Major.—Constitutional Law. Minors.—Political Economy. History.

GEORGE DEPUE HADZSITS, A.B., 1895.

Subjects for examination: Major.—Greek. Minors.—Latin. Music.

WALTER MONROE HAMILTON, A.B., 1894.

Subjects for examination: Major.—Mathematics. Minors.—Physics. Astronomy.

CLEMMA BELLE HAYES, A.B., 1893.

Subjects for examination: Major.—American History. Minors.—European History. Political Economy.

VIOLET DE LILLE JAYNE, A.B., 1887.

Thesis.—Romanticism in English Poetry. Subjects for examination: Major.—English Literature. Minors.—History. German.

FRANK ADDISON MANNY, A.B., 1893.

Thesis.—James Russell Lowell. Subjects for examination: Major.—American Literature. Minors.—European History. Rhetoric.

WALTER THOMSON PEIRCE, A.B., *Ohio Wesleyan University*, 1894.

Subjects for examination: Major.—French. Minors.—English Literature. Italian.

ESTHER LAKIN SANBORN, A.B., 1895.

Thesis.—The Ethical and Religious Teachings of the Plays of Sophocles. Subjects for examination: Major. -Greek. Minors.—German. History.

ORRIN EDWARD TIFFANY, A.B., 1895.

Subjects for examination: Major.—United States History. Minors.—Finance. European History.

CANDIDATES FOR THE DEGREE OF MASTER OF PHILOSOPHY.

DAVID PORTER MAYHEW, Ph.B., 1893.

Thesis.—On the Time of Reflex Winking. Subjects for examination: Major.—Physiology. Minors.—Bacteriology. Physiological Chemistry.

CARLTON RAYMOND ROSE, Ph.B., 1894.

Subjects for examination: Major.—General Chemistry. Minors.—Organic Chemistry. Analytical Chemistry.

FANNIE ELLIS SABIN, Ph.B., 1895.

Subjects for examination: Major.—Latin. Minors.—Classical Archæology. Roman Political Institutions.

KATHARINE ELIZA SUMNER, Ph.B., 1891.

Thesis.—Browning as a Dramatic Writer. Subjects for examination: Major.—English Literature. Minors.—History. Pedagogy.

MARY ETTA TRUEBLOOD, Ph.B., *Earlham College*, 1893.

Subjects for examination: Major. — Mathematics.—Minors.—German. Astronomy.

ROYAL BRUNSON WAY, Ph.B., *Albion College*, 1894.

Subjects for examination: Major.—American History. Minors.—Political Economy. Comparative Constitutional Law.

CANDIDATES FOR THE DEGREE OF MASTER OF SCIENCE.

WILLIAM ELI DAVIS, B.S , *Michigan Agricultural College*, 1889.

Subjects for examination: Major.—Physics. Minors.—Mathematics. General Chemistry.

ALFRED BERTHIER OLSEN, M.D., 1894, B.S., 1895.

Subjects for examination: Major.—Histology. Minors.—Bacteriology. Physiological Chemistry.

HORACE WHITE, B.S., *Swarthmore College*, 1895.

Subjects for examination: Major.—Mathematical Electricity. Minors.—Heat and Light. Mechanical Engineering.

EUGENE CYRUS WOODRUFF, B.S., 1894.

THESIS.—Color Reactions of Nitric and Chloric Acids with Certain Aromatic Bodies. Subjects for examination: Major.—Chemistry. Minors.—Physics. Music.

CANDIDATES FOR THE DEGREE OF MASTER OF LETTERS.

PETER WILLIAM DYKEMA, B.L., 1895.

Subjects for examination: Major.—English Literature. Minors.—French. Rhetoric.

CHARLES HENRY GRAY, B.L., 1895.

Subjects for examination: Major. — English Literature.—Minors.—Pedagogy. Rhetoric.

JOHN EDWARD LAUTNER, B.L., 1895.

Subjects for examination: Major. — American Literature. Minors.—Rhetoric. German.

UNIVERSITY OF MICHIGAN

THE PRESIDENT'S REPORT

TO THE

BOARD OF REGENTS

FOR THE ACADEMIC YEAR

ENDING SEPTEMBER 30, 1897

AND THE

Report of the Treasurer

FOR THE FISCAL

YEAR ENDING JUNE 30, 1897

ANN ARBOR, MICH.:
Published by the University
1897

ANN ARBOR, MICH.:
THE INLAND PRESS, PRINTERS
1897

THE PRESIDENT'S REPORT

FOR YEAR ENDING SEPTEMBER 30, 1897.

To the Honorable, the Board of Regents:

By request of President Angell, I have prepared, and beg leave to present to you, the President's annual report for the year ending September 30, 1897. In the performance of this duty, I have labored under considerable embarrassment by reason of the fact that during the year that the report covers, I was identified with but one department of the University and had only a limited opportunity for observing the work of the University as a whole. For the most of this report I am indebted to the heads of the different departments, who, at my request, have kindly furnished me with necessary information and with suggestions as to pressing needs.

Appended to the report will be found a list of the appointments, reappointments, and resignations of members of the Faculties during the year; a statement of the degrees conferred since the last report; a summary of students in attendance, and a list of the examinations for advanced degrees held during the year.

As will be seen in the summary of students in attendance, the total enrollment of the year, exclusive of Summer School students, was twenty-eight hundred and seventy-eight, a slight falling off from the attendance of the previous year, which was twenty-nine hundred and twenty-two. In most of the Departments, however, the attendance was larger than ever before, the decrease being mainly in the Department of Law. But this was expected, and was due to the change in that

Department from a two to a three years' course. It should be noted in this connection that the attendance of the present year exceeds that of any previous year, it having now reached the unprecedented number of 3,090. It is probable that the total enrollment of the present year, exclusive of Summer School students, will reach 3,150. One fact in connection with the attendance of the last few years must especially challenge attention, namely, that the number of Michigan students has been steadily gaining. During the years 1893-4, 1894-5, 1895-6, and 1896-7, the attendance from Michigan was, respectively, 1,400, 1,551, 1,632, and 1,747. The University of Michigan belongs to the people of the State, and that there is a growing appreciation among the people of the advantages offered here is certainly apparent from the increasing attendance of Michigan students. With over sixty-five per cent. of our students coming from Michigan homes, it cannot be doubted that the influence of the University is rapidly permeating every part of our commonwealth. But while we are gratified with this proof of local appreciation, we should not forget that our non-resident contingent contributes much to the strength and influence of the University. It is certainly a matter of congratulation that the non-resident attendance continues to be so large and that so many States and countries are represented in our student community. During the last year the non-resident students numbered 1,131, coming from forty-four different States and territories and from the following foreign countries and provinces: China, England, Japan, Germany, Hawaiian Islands, Austria, Barbadoes, Bulgaria, Norway, Russia, South Africa, Ontario, and Quebec. Illinois sent us the largest number, 307. The number from Ohio was 199; from Indiana, 102; from Iowa, 82; from New York, 70; from Pennsylvania, 68; from Missouri, 39; from Wisconsin, 33; from Massachusetts, 30; from Kansas, 24; from California and Kentucky, each 23; from Minnesota, 19; from Colorado and Utah, each 17; from Montana and Nebraska, each 13; from Washington, 11. Ontario sent us 16 students, and 63 came from the New England States.

The number of women in attendance was as follows:

Department of Literature, Science, and the Arts	551
Department of Medicine and Surgery	71
Department of Law	6
School of Pharmacy	7
Homœopathic Medical College	7
College of Dental Surgery	5
	647

In the last report of the President, the number of women in attendance was given as 601. The increase of 46 was mainly in the Literary Department, although, with one exception, there was a slight increase in all departments.

The notable event of the year was the appointment of President Angell to the Turkish mission. Three times before during his long and brilliant service as chief executive of the University, he has been summoned by our General Government to public duties of great delicacy and responsibility. And in the discharge of these public trusts he has always brought signal honor to himself and to the University. His learning, his natural temperament and abilities, together with his large experience in public affairs, so eminently fit President Angell for diplomatic service that his selection for further labors in that field met with a generous and universal approval. Although regretting the temporary withdrawal from active duties here that the acceptance of the call would necessitate, and the loss to the University that would inevitably come therefrom, the members of this Board were of the opinion that the wishes of the Administration and the public should be respected. They, therefore, unanimously granted a leave of absence.

In the general work of the Literary Department during the past year there was little that calls for special comment. The different courses were given as announced, and it is the universal feeling that the best of results were realized. In some lines of work the instructors labored under serious embarrassment by reason of the large classes that they were compelled to conduct. In lecture courses, the size of the class is a matter of small importance, but in courses in which the scheme of instruction contemplates that the student shall receive individual attention and drill, if substantial advancement is to be made, it is of the highest importance that the sections be of a size that will admit of personal work with each student at each exercise. My inquiries have led me to the conclusion that in the departments of modern language particularly the classes are over-crowded, and that relief should be afforded by enlarging the instructing force as soon as the necessary funds are available.

The Professorship of Philosophy, which had been vacant for nearly two years, was filled at the January meeting of this Board, in 1896, by the election of Professor Robert M. Wenley. He entered upon his duties October 1, 1896. Under his direction the department was reorganized during the past year and more fully equipped. Provision was made for instruction in physiological psychology, and, by reason of the increase in the instructing force, the department was enabled materially to enlarge its field of work. As a result, a new impetus was given to the study of philosophy and larger numbers were at once attracted to the courses.

During the past year there were eighty-six students doing graduate work in the Literary Department. Five of these were studying *in absentia* for the Master's degree and five, although candidates for an advanced degree, were enrolled in other departments. The enrollment of the previous year in the Graduate School was seventy-four. This slight increase in attendance is encouraging, but the growth and prosperity of the Department are not what they should be, or what they would be if the necessary funds for its development were forthcoming. Our first duty as a State University is undoubtedly to the undergraduates. This is emphatically true so long as the State makes no special appropriation for the equipment and maintenance of a graduate department and the department is without private endowment or support. Under existing circumstances, we can conduct graduate study only in connection with the undergraduate work and as incidental thereto. No professor can give his undivided attention and predominant energies to graduate students, and no professor should, under the present conditions or unless specially engaged for that purpose. In this University graduate instruction should never, in my judgment, be given at the expense of undergraduate instruction. But this advanced work must be done in some way, if we are to retain our place as one of the leading universities of the country. There are other reasons, also, for its encouragement, and not the least of these is the wholesome influence of a graduate department upon undergraduate work. There is, moreover, a demand for advanced instruction, and we should not forget that, in providing for this, we are serving the commonwealth, for we are supplying in some measure the pressing and increasing public necessity for young men and young women who are thoroughly equipped for expert work in the higher departments of activity It is pertinent, I think, that I should quote briefly upon this subject from President Angell's last report: "It would," he says, "be a grave mistake for the Regents or for the State to fail in appreciation of the great value to us of the vigorous prosecution of the advanced work of graduate students. The presence of such a body of mature and aspiring students is uplifting and inspiring in its influence on the undergraduates. Moreover, if we are really to prepare men and women for conspicuous positions, we must carry them beyond the boundaries of the undergraduate curriculum. Especially is this true of those who are aiming to occupy prominent places as teachers. There is in almost every field of activity a call for a certain number of men so thoroughly trained that they may justly be called experts in their special departments. The institution that is unable to furnish this kind of training can hardly aspire to the name of a university. It is the proper and the necessary function of this University to supply this instruction. Else the sons and daughters of Michigan must needs go elsewhere to find it. We do not believe that the State desires that they should be compelled to go elsewhere. But it should be understood that this advanced teaching makes great demands on the professors. Each teacher can profitably instruct only a small number. The teaching must be largely personal, that is, specially adapted to the needs of each individual student. It is, of course, more expensive than undergraduate instruction. The question, therefore, with which this University and the other large State universities is confronted, is this: Are the States willing to furnish the means for providing this kind of instruction? Just now there is no more important question concerning higher education to be passed on by our western States." It is certainly to be hoped that the people of the State of Michigan will in the near future answer this question in the affirmative and come to the aid of the University in its effort to supply the demand for graduate instruction, or that some of our wealthy citizens may liberally endow the department. It is a most worthy object for private benefaction, and a gift for this purpose would be of inestimable value not only to the graduate department but to the University as a whole. It would also be a graceful and enduring testimonial to the cause of advanced scholarship in the west.

At the January meeting of this Board in 1896, Dr. Eliza M. Mosher was elected Professor of Hygiene and Women's Dean in the Department of Literature, Science, and the Arts. This was a step that had been for some time contemplated, and the wisdom of the action was at once recognized. The expected completion at an early date of the Women's Gymnasium emphasized the necessity of provision being made at once for the superintendence and direction of the physical education of the women of the University. Dr. Mosher entered upon her duties October 1, 1896. She at once organized a course in Hygiene. This was made elective but was very generally attended. The first semester was devoted to a consideration of Personal Hygiene; the second, to Domestic and Municipal Hygiene, including School Hygiene. It was the aim of the instructor to make her teaching so practical that it should make its own appeal for adoption into the lives of those taught. Dr. Mosher's duties as Dean include, in addition to those which ordinarily belong to that office, a general physical examination of each new woman student and a registration of her physical history and condition upon beginning her course of study in the University. This examination, in addition to the incidental use that it serves in connection with the granting of excuses for absences, enables the instructor to decide as to the advisability and safety of gymnasium work for each student. It also brings her into close relation with the women of the University in the early months of their student life, thus giving opportunity for personal counsel at a time when it is often much needed. During the year one hundred and fifty-three women were enrolled for gymnasium work. Careful physical measurements of nearly all were made and a chart was prepared for each. In this way the instructor was able to estimate at the close of the year the degree of development attained. As planned, the gymnasium course for women extends over three years, the work of each year being more difficult and demanding greater skill and self-control than that of the previous year. In a communication to me upon the subject, Dr. Mosher states that the gymnasium work was interrupted and made more difficult by reason of irregularity in attendance, and suggests that in her judgment the highest success can be gained only by including the work in that required by the University or by placing it upon the credit basis. The experience of the past year has, in my judgment, demonstrated the necessity for the new chair and the fitness of the incumbent. It is to be hoped that the way will be opened in the near future for completing the women's gymnasium, as in its present unfinished state the work of the department must necessarily be more or less imperfect and incomplete.

The gymnasium work with the men was carried on during the past year without any particular change. But a special effort was made to interest the students more generally in the physical examinations. Improved physical measurements were adopted which show at a glance, by means of a chart, the general condition of the student examined and also his relation to the average student. These charts are furnished the students free of charge, and they are proving quite successful. The total membership of the gymnasium for men, as shown by the lockers rented, was ten hundred and thirty-two, divided among departments as follows: Faculty, six; Literary, three hundred and ninety-seven; Law, two hundred and forty; Engineering, one hundred and fifty; Medical, one hundred and thirty-seven; Dental, seventy-four; Pharmacy, twenty-three; Homœopathic, five. The average daily attendance is reported by the Director as having been about three hundred and fifty. The number of classes daily was three. Many lockers were rented by students simply for the purpose of having access to the baths, and this, I am advised, continues to be the practice. It is a very general feeling among the faculties that some means ought to be devised for awakening a more extended interest in regular gymnasium work. Under the present regulations which leave the taking of the courses and attendance at classes entirely at the option of the student, the Director must necessarily be seriously handicapped in any efforts that he may make to reach large numbers or to bring about regularity in work. In many universities certain classes of students are required to report regularly at the gymnasium for assigned exercises, and in others, when a student has once elected the work, he is required to attend regularly and complete the course unless excused by the proper authority. The matter has been considered by the Literary Faculty and by the Senate at different times, but such consideration has never resulted in the adoption of definite requirements. It is to be hoped that some scheme will be formulated whereby the opportunities offered by the gymnasium may be taken advantage of by larger numbers and particularly by those who are most in need of physical training and development.

The separation of the Department of Engineering, two years ago, from the Department of Literature, Science, and the Arts, of which it had so long been a part, brought the engineering instructors more in touch with the students, and it became possible to look more carefully after matters of administration and discipline. The engineering students still have the same privileges of choice of the different branches given in the Department of Literature, Science, and the Arts so far as is compatible with the amount of required work in their chosen lines; and in social and class matters, they are regarded by the literary students as classmates. As the young men come from the same schools, at the same age, it has been felt desirable to foster and encourage a mutual respect for literary and technical studies.

The revised and moderately increased requirements for admission to the Department of Engineering, already accepted by this Board, go into effect next year. Good results are expected from the change. After a long and careful discussion, and with the approval of the Board, the scheme of required work has been recast, some new subjects added, and the number of hours of work prescribed for a degree increased from *one hundred and twenty* to *one hundred and thirty*. The prescribed work of the first year has been made the same for all students. This change necessitates the postponement by the new student of the definite choice of a particular branch of engineering for a year, when, it is thought, he is better able to select the line of work for which he is suited.

The shops of the Department are now busy and crowded through both semesters, and any material increase in the number of students will necessitate an increase of shop capacity, unless the required work is cut down.

More room is needed in the Department of Electrical Engineering, as it is without a drafting room, and there is but one lecture-room for both Physics and Electrical Engineering. The experimental work in steam and mechanical engineering should also have enlarged quarters. Some of the apparatus has to be set up and taken down each year to make room for other experiments. Consequently the number of students that can work in experimental lines is seriously limited. The quarters occupied by the Electrical Engineering Laboratory are also very restricted. A new building for experimental work in these two departments is very much needed and should, if possible, be provided in the near future.

Some short courses in Electrical Engineering will hereafter be offered to students in Civil and Mechanical Engineering, and some of the courses in drafting and experimental electrical work will be extended. These additions have been made possible by the employment of another instructor. There seems to be a growing disposition for students to extend their course so as to include both Mechanical and Electrical Engineering.

Attention of the Board, I think, should be called to the fact that frequent inquiries are made for a course in Architecture and also for a course in Marine Engineering or Naval Architecture. If facilities in these lines could be offered, they would undoubtedly attract many students.

During the past year the Department of Medicine and Surgery experienced a large degree of success. In 1890 this Department began the first obligatory four years' course demanded by any medical school in the United States. The friends of the Department and of the University in general were very much afraid that the increased requirements for admission and the increased length of the courses of instruction would greatly diminish the number of students. That this fear was altogether groundless, is shown by the fact that the number of students enrolled last year was greater than ever before in the history of the Department, with the exception of a few years directly after the close of the war, when many young men who had been in the hospital service of the army crowded into the Medical schools. While success is not by any means to be measured by the number of students, but rather by the excellence of the work, it is gratifying to know that the men and women who intend to enter the medical profession are willing to spend more time and more money in getting their professional education, provided they feel confident that they are obtaining the best that the country affords.

The number of students in this Department is as large as can be accommodated with the present equipment. In fact, all the laboratories are crowded to their utmost capacity and there is urgent need of liberal appropriations from some source in order to enlarge and improve the facilities. Medical education has made great advances within recent years, and if the University is to maintain the position that it has won among the great medical schools of the world, we must have improved facilities. It is to be hoped that the Legislature and the people will appreciate these facts and that provision for the pressing needs of this Department will be forthcoming.

During the past year only about fifty-six per cent. of the patients applying for admission to the University Hospital were accommodated inside the building. The number of beds should be largely increased. The University Hospital is a great medical charity; it is worthy of the support of the State. The majority of patients coming here are people who can well afford to pay the small fees demanded for board and room, but would not be able to pay for expert medical attention. Hundreds are saved from the pauper classes each year by the work of this institution. An examination of the list of patients for a number of years past shows that the majority come from the rural communities of the State. The farmers, more than any other class, reap the benefits of the hospital facilities given by the University. The last Legislature apparently appreciated these facts, and made an appropriation for keeping the hospitals open during the summer. Two or three bills were also passed which will better provide for those who need the care that can be given here. This Board has done what it could with the limited means at its command, to improve the hospital facilities. Sun-rooms have been added, and a building is now in process of erection for the accommodation of nurses. This building will also furnish dining-room accommodation for patients. But the other improvements indicated are in the nature of pressing needs, and it is hoped that the way for making them will soon be opened.

I am pleased to be able to report that the last year was a successful one in the Department of Law. For the first time the three years' course was in full operation. Its success has now been thoroughly demonstrated. As was expected, there was a slight falling off in attendance last year, but that it was only temporary, and due entirely to the lengthening of the course, is apparent from the fact that this year the attendance is very much larger than ever before in the history of the Department. The increase is particularly significant when we remember that, in addition to the lengthening of the course, the requirements for admission have been materially raised, and that the new requirements went into effect for the first time this year. With three large classes in attendance, the accommodations for this Department, as this Board well understands, are entirely inadequate. The failure of the Legislature at its last session to make an appropriation for an addition to the building, made it necessary for us to resort to some temporary arrangement for the accommodation of the increasing numbers. The old chapel in the central building has been temporarily assigned to this Department, and is now in constant use for law classes. But the expedient is far from satisfactory. The room was not designed for lecture purposes; with reference to the Law Department it is inconveniently located, and it is much needed at times for exercises of the Literary Department. Furthermore the mingling of large classes from different departments in the same building is liable to result in more or less confusion and disorder. With the increased attendance the library accommodations of the Department are far from adequate. I am well aware of the fact that the Board understands fully the necessity for an addition to the building of this Department and that the needed improvement will be made as soon as the means therefor are available.

During the year there were some changes in the Faculty of this Department. These are noted in Appendix A. The practical work of the Department was materially strengthened by the addition of a course in conveyancing and by the provision for a professorship in this subject. As stated by the Librarian in his report, a large part of the Buhl bequest has been expended for additions to the Law Library, principally for foreign reports, in which the collection was noticeably weak. The Library is now one of the best in the country for law school purposes and with a comparatively small additional expenditure could be made practically complete. The expense of keeping it up, however, is considerable, and it is hoped that some friend of the Department will provide a permanent endowment for that purpose.

Under arrangements perfected during the past year, it is now possible for a student to carry on, to some extent and under certain conditions, collegiate studies and studies in law at the same time, and thereby shorten the combined courses by one year. Students taking this combined course are subject to the special direction and control of a joint committee from the Literary and Law Departments. This step, I think, is a most desirable one. Already quite a large number of students are taking advantage of the opportunity, and the result will undoubtedly be that many will be attracted to collegiate work who otherwise would pass directly from the high school to their law studies.

In the School of Pharmacy the course of four years is steadily gaining ground, both in the number of its students and in the opportunities of its graduates. The research work has received, in the past two years, the support of a fellowship granted by the liberality of Messrs. F. Stearns & Co., and now continued for another year. Of still larger advantage has been the employment in the laboratory of the school of graduate workers in research upon the Revision of the Pharmacopœia of the United States. This employment of our graduates, now authorized for another year, embraces both experimentation in the laboratory and compilation in the library, the resources of the latter being fully taxed to meet this demand. The highest awards for investigation have been accorded lately by the American Pharmaceutical Association to work done under the fellowship in this school.

During the past year the laboratories of the Chemical Building provided for an average number of about three hundred and thirty students working at the same time. Of these about one hundred and forty were students of the Departments of Literature and of Engineering, one hundred and twenty were students of the Medical and Dental Schools, and over seventy were students of the School of Pharmacy. The number of different students taking laboratory courses during the year was six hundred and seven. And over seven hundred students of the University were enrolled in the various chemical lecture courses within the year. These numbers, and the advanced character of various parts of the work, make severe demands upon the building and its outfit, as well as upon the teaching force. Many portions of the building are greatly in need of thorough renovation, as well as better lecture room provision. The limited expenditures made for these needs a year ago gave much relief. Until there is permanent renewal of the ceilings, interior walls, and floors, temporary repair is a necessity of common cleanliness.

The Chemical Building, its outfit, and its teaching force are factors in the education of the students of the several departments of the University, as enumerated above. And on these factors will depend almost wholly the graduate work in pure chemistry and the advanced work in chemical technology, interests which together have drawn a fair number of enthusiastic students, and which represent many active chemical alumni. These interests so closely concern the industrial advantage of the State with its great natural chemical resources, and so affect its educational credit in the world, that they may well be commended to the wise judgment and the supporting hand of the State and to the benefaction of private individuals.

The Homœopathic Medical College enjoyed a year of unusual prosperity. The attendance, although small as compared with other Departments, was much larger than the year previous, nearly double in fact. The year gave promise of the increasing prosperity of the present year. The Department is now well under way. It has an able Faculty, is free from internal discords, and with the aid of the extensive laboratories of the University and its well-equipped hospital, it certainly furnishes to its students a professional education that is not second in completeness and thoroughness to that given by any homœopathic school in the country. The books of the superintendent show that the hospital patronage in this Department last year was greater than ever before, and that the hospital came nearer paying running expenses than ever before. The new and increased facilities given by this Board in the way of a pharmacological laboratory for the proving of drugs are fully appreciated by the Department, as are the additional teaching advantages that have been provided for in pathology, clinical dermatology, and obstetrical clinics. The training school for nurses established in connection with the Homœopathic Hospital, had a successful year and is doing a good work.

There was nothing in the affairs of the College of Dental Surgery during the past year that calls for special mention or comment. The attendance was somewhat larger than the year before, and the work was prosecuted with the earnestness and thoroughness that have from the first characterized this Department, and that have gained for it an international reputation in the profession. The largely increased attendance of the present year is taxing to the utmost the accommodations and equipment of the Department.

From the report of the Librarian, already presented to this Board, and which covers the nine months from October 1, 1896, to June 30, 1897, I make the following extracts:

"There were in all the libraries of the University June 30, 1897, 113,990 volumes, 17,555 unbound pamphlets, and 1,275 maps. Of these there were in the General Library, 91,112 volumes, 16,065 unbound pamphlets, and 1,275 maps; in the Law Library, 13,849 volumes; in the Medical Library, 7,762 volumes and 1,490 unbound pamphlets; in the Library of the Dental College, 817 volumes; and in the Library of the Homœopathic Medical College, 450 volumes. During the year 625 periodicals were regularly received as follows: In the General Library, 450; in the Medical Library, 131; in the Law Library, 12; in the Library of the Dental College, 13; and in the Library of the Homœopathic Medical College, 19. Ten daily and fifteen weekly newspapers were also regularly received."

The Librarian reports the following additions during the nine months covered by his report: To the General Library, 6,414 volumes, 45 unbound pamphlets, and 78 maps; to the Medical Library, 577 volumes; to the Law Library, 1,785 volumes. This large increase in the Law Library over the acquisitions of former years was due to purchases made from the Buhl bequest. To the Library of the Dental College, 42 volumes were added, and to the Homœopathic Library 125 volumes.

The Librarian reports the following gifts: "From the Duke of Loubat was received a copy of a Pre-Columbian Mexican Book, known as the Vatican MS., No. 5773. An explanatory treatise accompanies it. It is most interesting as showing the form of book in use on a part of this continent at the time of its discovery. We are under obligations to Mr. Harlan I. Smith, of Washington, for presenting the claims of this University for a copy of the work to the Duke of Loubat.

"From His Highness the Maharajah of Japan, through Col. S. S. Jacob, Superintending Engineer, six portfolios of architectural drawings were received. These drawings were chiefly from old buildings at or near Delhi and Agra. Students of architecture cannot fail to find these inspiring.

"The Government of Her Majesty the Queen of England presented a set of the Report of the Scientific Results of the Challenger Expedition, 44 volumes. These volumes are of first importance for the work in Zoology and the other natural sciences.

"The purchase of a copy of the Third Folio of Shakespeare, 1664, was authorized by the Hon. James McMillan at a cost of $381.75. Mr. McMillan at the same time authorized the expenditure of $100.00 more to make additions to the Shakespeare Library.

"Mr. D. M. Ferry, of Detroit, provided means for making additions to the Library in the specialties of English Literature and the works of the early Christian writers. * * * * * * In all there were added to the Library through Mr. Ferry's generosity 105 volumes and twenty-five pamphlets.

"Mr. James E. Scripps, of Detroit, made provision for the purchase of books illustrative of Roman Archæology for the Department of Latin. Of books of this nature, there have been added at Mr. Scripps's expense 144 volumes. It is a most valuable reinforcement to the art literature of the Library.

"Gifts were also received from President Angell, Dr. Herdman, Dr. S. A. Jones, E. B. Pond, Esq., Mr. H. C. Ryan, a former student, Dr. S. A. Green, of Boston, Dr. L. G. Doane, of New York, Professors Demmon, Hinsdale, Walter, Kelsey, and others."

The following from the Librarian's report in regard to the necessity of increased library facilities is of special importance, and I commend it to the thoughtful consideration of every alumnus and friend of the University:

"An extension of the Library Building has become a necessity, unless we are willing to see its growth and usefulness arrested. I think there is no doubt of this necessity in any quarter. The shelving capacity of the book-room, including all the temporary shelving that it will contain, has been exhausted. To dispose of the overflow outside of the book-room, rooms needed for other purposes have been occupied. If more temporary shelving can be provided, we can better our present condition, but the congested state will still remain, and the conditions for administering the library, which are now hard, will be very hard.

"We already have a good deal of matter that is rare and valuable, and some that is unique. It is impossible under present conditions to guard this against indiscriminate handling, and consequently from injury, or loss. There should be rooms that are of fire proof construction where this can be preserved from danger, and yet made accessible to any who may need to consult it. Having such conveniences for the safe keeping of especially valuable material would greatly increase our chances of securing more of it.

"The present methods of conducting advanced work in literature, art, philosophy, language, and the political sciences have come to be called "laboratory methods." There must be actual contact of the teacher, the student, and the illustrative matter, as books, periodicals, maps, diagrams, models, and pictures. This cannot be done successfully in recitation rooms distant from the place where all this material is housed. The rooms must be a part of the Library Building. These advantages for advanced work are enjoyed in many of the universities now, and all are working in that direction.

"What lies in the way of this enlargement is a lack of funds. The Legislature can be appealed to for help, but can a reasonable hope of timely help from that quarter be entertained?

"If it were to be the sole request made it is not impossible that it might be granted, but, if coupled with others, as it would almost necessarily be, it is *impossible*.

"In going over the possible ways of obtaining help the following has seemed to promise most. That it contemplates several things rather than a single one, increases, it is thought, ather than diminishes, the prospect of success. An appeal to the Alumni is proposed. The several objects are:

1. A practical object, viz., an extension of the bookroom sufficient to relieve the present pressure and provide for the increase of fifteen or twenty years.

2. Another practical object, viz., to erect at the end of the extension, and as a part of it, a building to be known as Alumni Hall. This is to be devoted to the work of the Graduate School, and provide a home for that now, and hitherto, homeless branch of the University.

3. A sentimental object, viz., to make this Alumni Hall a memorial of the students of the University who died in the civil war. This memorial feature may appear in a general way in the architecture of the building, and specifically in some portion of it, open to the public, where the names of the fallen may appear in mural inscriptions and where their devotion to their country may be symbolized in appropriate statuary.

"The probable cost of the whole would be $100,000.

"The propriety of some kind of a memorial has been discussed somewhat among the alumni at various times, and is referred to as something that ought, at some time or other, to be accomplished."

I heartily concur in the foregoing, and I desire to express the hope that some way may be found in the near future for providing for the necessities of this important department of the University.

Several changes were made in the Museum during the past year. The mineralogical collections were removed to

Tappan Hall, and the space thus vacated in the south wing utilized for a museum lecture room for classes in Zoology, Geology, and Botany, thus obviating the necessity for carrying the specimens needed for illustration about the campus. Electricity was brought in for the stereopticon, and the room provided with opaque shades, making a good lantern room with a seating capacity of about a hundred and fifty.

Room 4, in the fourth story, was provided with adjustable shelving for the reception of the collections of alcoholic material formerly scattered in part through the museum and in part stored in the zoological laboratory. Possible danger from fire was guarded against by providing an adequate system of overhead sprays, and a metal covered floor, inclined toward a discharge pipe opening on the outside of the building. The water can be turned on from the outside, and the whole room instantly drenched.

The work of identifying and labelling the bird collection has been completed, and the record reduced to the form of a card catalogue. The specimens are catalogued both under their scientific and their common names, and a system of numbering adopted which shows the exact whereabouts of each individual specimen so that any specimen desired can be found at once. A large number of duplicate specimens have been removed from the exhibition cases, and the space thus gained has been utilized for the installation of a number of bird groups, each of which is intended to illustrate an important fact.

No gifts of importance were received during the past year, but two noteworthy additions were made to the mammal collection by purchase. The Museum has been fortunate enough to secure a fine pair of walruses, collected by Lieutenant Peary, and a group of fur-seals from the Pacific.

At present, work upon the collection of shells is in progress. This valuable collection, which has been long stored away out of sight, is being identified and catalogued and a series of specimens prepared for exhibition.

Reference should be made to the following gifts that were received during the year besides those mentioned in the Librarian's report: The F. D. Bennett Scholarship Fund of $150.00; a contribution from the class of 1896, in the Literary Department, of $200.00 to the Archæological Fund; and a Class Memorial Fund of $135.34 from the Literary Class of 1897.

The electric light plant provided for by the last Legislature has been practically completed, and bids fair to give excellent satisfaction. It was a much needed improvement and is most thoroughly appreciated.

During the past summer arrangements were made with the State Board of Agriculture whereby different professors from the University are to address farmers' institutes in several counties of the State during the present year. They will speak upon practical subjects that will be of special interest to farmers, and it is hoped and expected that mutual benefit will result. Twelve or fifteen men from our different Faculties will engage in this work, but in such a way as not to interfere materially with University duties. The carrying out of the plan will be without expense to the University.

A notable event in the history of the past year at the University which cannot fail, I think, to result in great good to the institution, was the amalgamation of the alumni societies of the different departments into one University Alumni Association. The movement has met with unqualified approval from the alumni and friends of the University in all parts of the country. Already an enthusiasm that is quite unprecedented is manifest, and the outlook is most encouraging. A paid Secretary has been installed in quarters provided by the University, and he is expected to give his entire time and predominant energies to the work of the Association. The plan contemplates among other things the formation of local associations in different parts of the State and country, where they do not now exist, and a continuous attempt to keep the alumni interested in the University by a systematic distribution among them of the journal of the Association and the various University publications. The movement is certainly one of great significance, and it means much, I am sure, to the University.

In gathering the data for this report, I have been impressed, as you doubtless have in listening to it, with the many pressing needs of our great University. From one point of view the conditions may seem discouraging. But they are far from being so; for we should remember that our necessities are a sure indication of our great prosperity. They arise from our remarkable growth and development. To provide for them, is not beyond the power of the people of this great commonwealth, aided, as I am sure they will be, by the generous efforts of our devoted alumni and friends. That they will be fully met and that the University will continue to be in the front rank of our great institutions of learning, I most confidently predict.

In closing, I desire to bear testimony to the high ideals, the unselfish devotion, and the unwearied enthusiasm of the members of our instructing force. Throughout her entire history, Michigan University has been signally fortunate in the many learned and inspiring men that she has had upon her faculties. No more striking illustration of the truth that men and not buildings make a great University, can be found.

Respectfully submitted, for the President, by

HARRY B. HUTCHINS,

Acting President.

APPENDICES.

APPENDIX A.

APPOINTMENTS, REAPPOINTMENTS, RESIGNATIONS, ETC., DURING THE YEAR ENDING SEPTEMBER 30, 1897.

April 28, 1897, President James B. Angell, LL. D., was granted leave of absence until October 1, 1898, to enable him to perform the duties of Envoy Extraordinary and Minister Plenipotentiary from the United States to Turkey.

May 5, 1897, Professor Hutchins was appointed Acting-President during the absence of President Angell.

Resignations:

At the meeting of May 12, 1897, the resignation of Levi T. Griffin, A. M., Fletcher Professor of Law, was presented and accepted.

At the meeting of June 28, 1897, the resignation of Professor Martin L. D'Ooge, LL. D., as Dean of the Department of Literature, Science, and the Arts, was presented and accepted.

Leaves of absence:

At the meeting in February, 1897, Assistant Professor George W. Patterson, A. M., S. B., was granted leave of absence for the academic year, 1897-8; and the leave of absence formerly granted to Earle W. Dow, A. B., Instructor in History, was extended for an additional year.

At the meeting in April, 1897, Tobias Diekhoff, A. B., Instructor in German, was granted leave of absence for the academic year, 1897-8.

At the meeting of June 2, 1897, Professor J. N. Martin, M. D., was granted leave of absence for the academic year, 1897-8; and Clarence L. Meader, A. B., Instructor in Latin, was granted leave of absence for the same term. Professor Henry C. Adams was also granted a leave of absence for one year.

Non-resident Lecturers in the Department of Law were appointed at the meeting of June 2, 1897, as follows:

Henry H. Swan, A. M., Admiralty.
James L. High, LL. D., Injunctions and Receivers.
Melville M. Bigelow, Ph. D., Insurance.
John B. Clayberg, LL. B., Mining Law.
Frank F. Reed, A. B., Copyright Law.
Albert H. Walker, LL. B., Patent Law.

A non-resident Lecturer in the Homœopathic Medical College was appointed at the meeting in November, 1896, as follows:

Oscar R. Long, M. D., Mental Diseases.

Special Lecturers in the Department of Law were appointed as follows:

At the meeting in November, 1896:

Henry C. Adams, Ph. D., The Railroad Problem.

At the meeting of June 2, 1897:

Thomas L. Cooley, LL. D., Interstate Commerce.
Andrew C. McLaughlin, A. B., LL. B., Constitutional Law and Constitutional History.
Victor C. Vaughan, Ph. D., M. D., Toxicology in its Legal Relations.
Richard Hudson, A. M., Comparative Constitutional Law.
Clarence L. Meader, A. B., Roman Law.
Henry C. Adams, Ph. D., The Railroad Problem.

At the meeting of June 28, 1897:

William J. Herdman, Ph. B., M. D., Neurology, Electrology, and Railway Injuries.

The following list comprises other appointments, reappointments, and changes of title of members of the Faculties. The Instructors were appointed for one year, unless a longer term is mentioned. The names of assistants and of others appointed to positions of lower grade than Instructor are not here included.

At the meeting in October, 1896:

John T. Faig, B. M. E., Instructor in Mechanical Engineering.
Frank W. Nagler, B. S., Instructor in Electrotherapeutics.
Charles A. Rabethge, M. D., Instructor in the Gymnasium.

At the meeting in November, 1896:

Horace L. Wilgus, M. S., Acting Professor of Law for one year.
Victor E. François, Instructor in French.
Sidney D. Townley, M. S., Instructor in Astronomy.

At the meeting in February, 1897:

Theodore C. Smith, Ph. D., Instructor in History.

At the meeting in April, 1897:

Frank H. Dixon, Ph. D., Acting Assistant Professor of Political Economy for the year 1897-8.

Warren W. Florer, Ph. D., Instructor in German.
Walter B. Pillsbury, Ph. D., Instructor in Psychology.

At the meeting of May 12, 1897:

The title of Acting Professor George A. Hench, Ph. D., was made to stand Professor of Germanic Languages and Literatures.

At the meeting of June 2, 1897:

James G. Lynds, M. D., Acting Professor of Gynæcology for the year 1897-8.

Cyrenus G. Darling, M. D., Lecturer on Minor Surgery for the year 1897-8.

Simon M. Yutzy, M. D., Instructor in Osteology.

Aldred S. Warthin, Ph. D., M. D., Instructor in Pathology for three years.

Frank W. Nagler, B. S., Instructor in Electrotherapeutics.

Herbert H. Waite, A. B., Instructor in Bacteriology.

The title of Junior Professor George Hempl, Ph. D., was changed to stand Professor of English Philology and General Linguistics.

Victor H. Lane, C. E., LL. B., Fletcher Professor of Law.

James H. Brewster, A. B., Professor of Conveyancing.

The title of Acting Professor Horace L. Wilgus, M. S., was changed to stand Professor of Law.

The title of Assistant Professor Elias F. Johnson, B. S., LL. M., was changed to stand Professor of Law.

Aaron V. McAlvay, A. B., LL. B., Acting Professor of Law for 1897-8.

John W. Dwyer, LL. M., Instructor in Law.

Thomas W. Hughes, LL. M., Instructor in Law.

Albert J. Farrah, LL. B., Instructor in Law.

George W. Patterson, Jr., A. M., S. B., Assistant Professor of Physics for 1897-8; to be Junior Professor from October 1, 1898.

John O. Reed, Ph. M., Assistant Professor of Physics for three years.

Alfred H. Lloyd, Ph. D., Assistant Professor of Philosophy for three years.

George O. Higley, M. S., Instructor in General Chemistry for three years.

David M. Lichty, M. S., Instructor in General Chemistry for three years.

William H. Wait, Ph. D., Instructor in Greek, Latin, and Sanskrit.

James W. Glover, Ph. D., Instructor in Mathematics.

Louis A. Strauss, Ph. M., Instructor in English.

Edwin C. Goddard, Ph. B., Instructor in Mathematics.

Herbert J. Goulding, B. S., Instructor in Descriptive Geometry and Drawing.

Victor E. François, Instructor in French.

Otto E. Lessing, A. B., Instructor in German.

John R. Allen, B. S., M. E., Instructor in Mechanical Engineering.
John T. Faig, M. E., Instructor in Mechanical Engineering.
Sidney D. Townley, M. S., Instructor in Astronomy.
Edwin C. Roedder, A. M., Instructor in German.
Alfred H. White, A. B., Instructor in Chemical Technology.
Walter Dennison, A. M., Instructor in Latin.
Henry F. L. Reichle, A. M., Instructor in Latin.
Carroll D. Jones, B. S., E. E., Instructor in Electrical Engineering.
John S. P. Tatlock, A. B., Instructor in English.
Fanny E. Langdon, B. S., Instructor in Botany.

At the meeting of June 28, 1897:

The appointment of Junior Professor George W. Patterson, Jr., A. M., S. B., was made to take effect from October 1, 1897.

The chair of the Assistant Professor of Anatomy was discontinued.

The title of Simon M. Yutzy, M. D., was changed to stand Demonstrator of Anatomy and Instructor in Anatomy.

Perry F. Trowbridge, Ph. B., Instructor in Organic Chemistry.

Moses Gomberg, Sc. D., Instructor in Organic Chemistry.

Louis P. Hall, D. D. S., Instructor in Dental Anatomy, Operative Technique, and Clinical Operative Dentistry.

Cyrenus G. Darling, M. D., Clinical Lecturer on Oral Pathology and Surgery.

Charles A. Rabethge, M. D., Instructor in the Gymnasium.

George Rebec, Ph. B., Instructor in Philosophy for three years.

Frank R. Lillie, Ph. D., Instructor in Zoology for three years.

Penoyer L. Sherman, Ph. D., Instructor in General Chemistry.

Arthur Lachman, Ph. D., Instructor in General Chemistry.

Edgar E. Brandon, A. B., Instructor in French.

John E. Lautner, M. L., Instructor in German.

John B. Johnston, Ph. B., Instructor in Zoology.

Richard Hudson, A. M., Dean of the Department of Literature, Science, and the Arts.

Alice G. Snyder, Instructor in the Women's Gymnasium.

At the meeting in September, 1897:

Wilbur C. Abbott, B. Litt., Instructor in History.

The title of Clarence G. Taylor, B. S., M. E., was changed to stand Professor of Mechanical Practice and Superintendent of Shops.

Claudius B. Kinyon, M. D., Professor of Obstetrics and Gynæcology in the Homœopathic Medical College.

Albert J. Elliott, M. D., Instructor in Pathology in the Homœopathic Medical College.

APPENDIX B.

DEGREES CONFERRED.

The following degrees were conferred during the year October 1, 1896, to September 30, 1897:

DEGREES ON EXAMINATION.

Bachelor of Letters	40
Bachelor of Science (in Biology)	14
Bachelor of Science (in Chemistry)	9
Bachelor of Science (in Electrical Engineering)	20
Bachelor of Science (in Mechanical Engineering)	17
Bachelor of Science (in Civil Engineering)	9
Bachelor of Science (in Pharmacy)	3
Bachelor of Science	16
Bachelor of Philosophy	51
Bachelor of Arts	62
Master of Letters	1
Electrical Engineer	1
Mechanical Engineer	1
Civil Engineer	2
Master of Science	8
Master of Philosophy	7
Master of Arts	17
Doctor of Science	2
Doctor of Philosophy	2
Doctor of Medicine (Department of Medicine and Surgery)	66
Bachelor of Laws	57
Master of Laws	10
Pharmaceutical Chemist	21
Doctor of Medicine (Homœopathic Medical College)	5
Doctor of Dental Surgery	50
	491

HONORARY DEGREES.

Master of Pharmacy	1
Master of Science	1
Master of Arts	1
Doctor of Science	1
Doctor of Laws	4
Total	499

APPENDIX C.

SUMMARY OF STUDENTS.

DEPARTMENT OF LITERATURE, SCIENCE, AND THE ARTS.

Holders of Fellowships	2	
Resident Graduates	74	
Candidates for an Advanced Degree, enrolled in other departments	5	
Graduates Studying *in Absentia*	5	
Undergraduates:		
Candidates for a Degree	996	
Students not Candidates for a Degree	187—	1269

DEPARTMENT OF ENGINEERING.

Resident Graduates	5	
Graduates Studying *in Absentia*	3	
Undergraduates	276—	284

DEPARTMENT OF MEDICINE AND SURGERY.

Resident Graduates	6	
Fourth Year Students	71	
Third Year Students	93	
Second Year Students	138	
First Year Students	140	
Students enrolled in the Department of Literature, Science, and the Arts:		
Third Year Student in Medicine	1	
Second Year Students in Medicine	11	
First Year Students in Medicine	12	
Students enrolled in the School of Pharmacy:		
First Year Student in Medicine	2	
Students enrolled in the College of Dental Surgery:		
Third Year Student in Medicine	1	
Second Year Students in Medicine	2—	477

DEPARTMENT OF LAW.

Resident Graduates	11	
Third Year Students	51	
Second Year Students	200	
First Year Students	294	
Special Students	19	
Students enrolled in the Department of Literature, Science, and the Arts	9—	584

SCHOOL OF PHARMACY.

Resident Graduates	7	
Undergraduates:		
Candidates for a Degree	63	
Students not Candidates for a Degree	2—	72

HOMŒOPATHIC MEDICAL COLLEGE.

Resident Graduates	3	
Fourth Year Students	5	
Third Year Students	8	
Second Year Students	10	
First Year Students	21—	47

COLLEGE OF DENTAL SURGERY.

Seniors	59	
Juniors	56	
Freshmen	82	
Student enrolled in the Department of Literature, Science, and the Arts	1—	198
		2931
Deduct for names counted more than once		53
Total, exclusive of Summer Schools		2878

SUMMER SCHOOLS OF 1896.

In Department of Literature, Science, and the Arts	199	
In Department of Law	25—	224
Deduct for students enrolled in 1896-7 in some department of the University	127—	97

SUMMER SCHOOLS OF 1897.

In Department of Literature, Science, and the Arts	185	
In Department of Law	40—	225
Deduct for students enrolled in 1896-7 in some department of the University	102—	123

APPENDIX D.

EXAMINATIONS FOR HIGHER DEGREES.

The following examinations for higher degrees were held in 1897:

CANDIDATES FOR THE DEGREE OF DOCTOR OF PHILOSOPHY.

IRA DUDLEY TRAVIS, Ph.B., *Albion College*, 1889, Ph.M., 1894.

THESIS.—The Clayton-Bulwer Treaty: its History and Interpretation. Subjects for examination: Major.—American History. Minors.—Political Economy. European History.

MARY GILMORE WILLIAMS, A.B., 1895.

THESIS.—De Julia Domna. Subjects for examination: Major.—Latin. Minors.—Greek. Political Antiquities.

CANDIDATES FOR THE DEGREE OF DOCTOR OF SCIENCE.

JAMES BARKLEY POLLOCK, B.S., *University of Wisconsin*, 1893, M.S., *ibid.*, 1895.

THESIS.—Mechanism of the Traumatropic Curvature of Roots. Subjects for examination: Major.—Botany. Minors.—Experimental Vegetable Physiology. Organic Chemistry.

SIDNEY DEAN TOWNLEY, B.S., *University of Wisconsin*, 1890, M.S., *ibid.*, 1892.

THESIS.—Investigation of the Orbit of Asteroid No. 16 (Psyche). Subjects for examination: Major.—Practical Astronomy. Minors.—Theoretical Astronomy. Optics.

CANDIDATES FOR THE DEGREE OF MASTER OF ARTS.

CHARLES WALLACE ADAMS, A.B., 1894.

Subjects for examination: Major.—Political Economy. Minors.—American History. Constitutional Law.

ALICE BROWN, A.B., 1896.

THESIS.—The Development of the Cabinet, 1789–1801. Subjects for examination: Major.—American History. Minors.—Constitutional Law. Political Economy.

EMMA JANE CHESNEY, A.B., *Kalamazoo College*, 1892.

Subjects for examination: Major.—Latin. Minors.—Roman Political Antiquities. English Literature.

CHARLES HALL COOK, A.B., 1874.

THESIS.—The Unseen World of the Great Poets. Subjects for examination: Major.—English Literature. Minors.—Ethics. Philosophy.

CHARLES HENRY COLE, A.B., 1882.

Subjects for examination: Major.—Pedagogy. Minors.—History of Philosophy. English Literature.

CARL HERBERT COOPER, A.B., *Upper Iowa University*, 1895.

Subjects for examination: Major.—Political Economy. Minors.—History. Sociology.

CHARLES ALBERT FARNAM, A.B, 1896.

Subjects for examination: Major.—Latin. Minors.—Greek. Roman Political Antiquities.

SAMUEL ALLEN JEFFERS, A.B., *Central Wesleyan College*, 1892.

Subjects for examination: Major.—Latin.; Minors.—Greek. Pedagogy.

ELLEN ANN KENNAN, A.B., 1896.

Subjects for examination: Major.—Greek. Minors.—Latin. Greek Archæology.

FRANK PATTENGILL KNOWLTON, A.B., *Hamilton College*, 1896.

Subjects for examination: Major.—Physiology. Minors.—Experimental Morphology. Physiological Chemistry.

ANNA WILLARD LOCKE, A.B., *Wellesley College*, 1892.

THESIS.—Bacteriological Examination of Drinking Water. Subjects for examination: Major.—Bacteriology. Minors.—Physiological Chemistry. Histology.

AURA MAUD MILLER, B.L., 1890.

Subjects for examination: Major.—English Literature. Minors.—English Language. Pedagogy.

ERASTUS DEVILLO PALMER, A.B., *Hillsdale College*, 1889.

Subjects for examination: Major.—English Literature. Minors.—European History. Pedagogy.

BESSIE BINGHAM STEVENS, A.B., 1896.

Subjects for examination: Major.—Latin. Minors.—Greek. Classical Archæology.

JAMES WELLINGS STURGIS, A.B., 1896.

Subjects for examination: Major.—Latin. Minors.—Roman Political Antiquities. Greek.

LOUISE BRADFORD SWIFT, A.B., *Wellesley College*, 1890.

Subjects for examination: Major.—Latin. Minors.—Greek. Roman Political Antiquities.

ELBERT WOOD, A.B., *Olivet College*, 1888.

Subjects for examination: Major.—English Literature. Minors.—Old English. Pedagogy.

CANDIDATES FOR THE DEGREE OF MASTER OF PHILOSOPHY.

MARY JOICE ADAMS, Ph.B., 1896.

THESIS.—History of the Suffrage in Michigan. Subjects for examination: Major.—American History. Minors.—English History. Latin.

JENNIE CLAIRE ANDERSON, Ph.B., *Oberlin College*, 1894.

Subjects for examination: Major.—Latin. Minors.—Roman Political Antiquities. Pedagogy.

GEORGIANA CLEIS BLUNT, Ph.B., 1896.

Subjects for examination: Major.—American Literature. Minors.—French Literature. History of Philosophy.

ELLA BOURNE, Ph.B., *De Pauw University*, 1893.

Subjects for examination: Major.—Latin. Minors.—German. Roman Political Antiquities.

HARRIETT ELVIRA McKINSTRY, Ph.B., 1896.

Subjects for examination: Major.—Latin. Minors.—Classical Archæology. Roman Political Antiquities.

LOIS AZUBAH McMAHON, Ph.B., 1896.

Subjects for examination: Major.—English Literature. Minors.—English History. Political Economy.

LURA WALLACE TOZER, Ph.B., 1885.

THESIS.—Thoreau's Personality as Deduced from his Writings. Subjects for examination: Major.—American Literature. Minors.—German. French.

CANDIDATES FOR THE DEGREE OF MASTER OF SCIENCE.

LOUIS BEGEMANN, B.S., 1889.

Subjects for examination: Major.—Sound and Light. Minors.—Pedagogy. Electricity.

EDNA DAISY DAY, B.S., 1896.

Subjects for examination: Major.—Botany. Minors.—Embryology. Hygieen.

CHARLES EDWARD EVERETT, B.L., 1889.

Subjects for examination: Major.—Botany. Minors.—Vegetable Physiology. Organic Chemistry.

FANNY ELIZABETH LANGDON, B.S., 1896.

Subjects for examination: Major.—Botany. Minors.—Invertebrate Morphology. Experimental Embryology.

WILLIAM ADAMS LEWIS, B.S., 1896.

THESIS.—Internal Improvements in Michigan. Subjects for examination: Major.—American History. Minors.—Pedagogy. English Literature.

CLAYTON AMOS PETERS, B.S., 1895.

THESIS.—The Embryology of Drosera. Subjects for examination: Major.—Botany. Minors.—Experimental Vegetable Physiology. Animal Embryology.

CANDIDATE FOR THE DEGREE OF MASTER OF LETTERS.

VERDIE JANE BAKER McKEE, B.L., 1893.

Subjects for examination: Major.—American Literature. Minors.—Rhetoric. Pedagogy.

THE TREASURER'S REPORT

FOR YEAR ENDING JUNE 30, 1897.

To the Finance Committee, Board of Regents, University of Michigan,

GENTLEMEN: Herewith I submit my annual report for the fiscal year ending June 30, 1897.

Respectfully,

H. SOULE, Treasurer,

RECEIPTS.

Balance in the Treasury, July 1, 1896	$ 21,793 71	
From State Treasurer, Acct. of Special Appropriations	6,000 00	
" " " " Current Expenses	187,410 18	
" Earnings and Miscellaneous Sources	199,939 48	
" Balance Overdrawn, June 30, 1897	6,492 36	$421,635 73

DISBURSEMENTS.

To Special Fund Accounts	$ 10,570 95	
" General Fund Accounts	411,064 78	$421,635 73

GENERAL FUND.

RECEIPTS TO THE GENERAL FUND.

From Balance, July 1, 1896		$31,613 82
" State Treasurer, Account of 1-6 Mill Tax	$141,249 99	
" " " " University Interest	46,160 19	
" Interest on Bank Deposits	5,006 19	
" Sale of Dental Supplies	5,430 27	
" Miscellaneous Sources	1,565 40	
" General Library—Sale of Duplicate Books	119 80	
" University Hospital	15,176 56	
" Homœopathic Hospital	2,800 34	$217,508 74

From Students' Fees:

Literary Department	$ 49,115 00
Engineering "	12,110 00
Medical "	20,822 50
Law "	30,090 00
Pharmacy "	3,592 50
Dental "	9,010 00
Homœopathic "	2,060 00
Chemical Laboratory	12,309 19
Mechanical "	1,370 00
Hygienic "	2,898 03
Physiological "	144 00
Botanical "	709 00
Pathological "	1,235 00
Zoological "	571 20
Electrical Engineering Laboratory	479 00
Electrotherapeutical "	960 00
Anatomical "	2,090 00
Histological "	1,577 00
Medical Demonstrations	4,580 00
Gymnasium Lockers	2,878 00
Drawing Boards	210 00

Key Deposits	288 00		
Pharmacological Laboratory	70 00		
Summer Schools	6,072 50		
Diplomas	5,100 00		
Students' Fees Received, Total	$169,810 92		$169,810 92
" " Refunded	5,683 33		
" " Net	$164,127 59		
			$418,932 98

DISBURSEMENTS FROM THE GENERAL FUND.

To General Pay Roll		$133,790 34	$133,790 34	$133,790 34
" Engineering Department, Pay Roll		31,366 24	31,366 24	
" " " Expenses			801 63	32,167 87
" Law Department, Pay Roll		28,750 00	28,750 00	
" " " Books			1,189 52	
" " " Expenses			855 53	30,795 05
" Medical " Pay Roll		35,175 00	35,175 00	
" " " Books			2,436 25	
" " " Expenses			530 17	38,141 42
" Pharmacy " Pay Roll		19,487 67	19,487 67	
" " " Expenses			8,265 78	27,778 45
" Dental " Pay Roll		11,500 00	11,500 00	
" " " Books			40 34	
" " " Expenses			4,845 08	16,385 42
" University Hospital, Pay Roll		6,571 26	6,571 26	
" " " Expenses			10,549 98	17,121 24
" Homœopathic Hospital, Pay Roll		1,781 00	1,781 00	
" " " Expenses			5,143 73	6,924 73
		$ 268,421 51		
" University Hospital Office				3,117 14
" Contingent Expenses				9,743 50
" Repairs				5,663 52
" Fuel and Lights				16,387 20
" General Library, Books				11,140 56
" " " Expenses				489 87
" Athletic Grounds				1,102 90
" Tennis Court				196 59
" Homœopathic College, Books				221 87
" " " Expenses				300 73
" Materia Medica				507 18
" Postage				1,955 25
" Advertising and Printing				3,136 76
" Museum				487 23
" Botanical Laboratory				712 12
" Histological "				479 75
" Hygienic "				3,406 89
" Zoological "				1,272 31
" Mechanical "				1,391 41
" Pathological "				859 79
" Physiological "				223 42
" Physical "				404 69
" Anatomical "				2,145 14
" Theory and Practice Laboratory				576 81
" Ophthalmological "				15 65
" Electrotherapeutical "				441 06
" Nervous Diseases				65 27
" Surgical Demonstrations				226 94
" Astronomical Observatory				222 24
" Summer School				5,117 59
" " " of Law				661 06

To Gymnasium	244 39
" Fees Refunded	5,683 83
" Bindery	1,706 18
" School Inspection	710 28
" Insurance	2,980 75
" Horse and Cart	570 07
" Carpenter Shop	796 75
" Lewis Art Collection	447 26
" Women's Gymnasium	18,472 85
" Geology	73 96
" Water Supply	1,438 09
" Commencement Expenses	752 41
" Latin Department	230 13
" Greek "	28 45
" Mineralogy	27 51
" Music	18 75
" Dermatology	7 00
" Oriental Languages	113 61
" Diseases of Women and Children	110 25
" General Catalogue	12 75
" Diplomas	882 05
	$411,064 78
Balance in Treasury, June 30, 1897	7,868 20
	$418,932 98

SPECIAL FUND ACCOUNTS.

HOMŒOPATHIC MEDICAL COLLEGE.

Receipts.

From State Treasurer	$ 6,000 00	
Miscellaneous Earnings	30 00	
Balance Overdrawn, June 30, 1897	14,360 56	$20,390 56

Disbursements.

Balance Overdrawn, July 1, 1896	$ 9,821 56	
Salaries of Professors and Employees	10,500 00	
Vouchers for Expenses	69 00	$20,390 56

CIVIL ENGINEERING.

Receipts.

Balance in Treasury, July 1, 1896	$ 1 95	$ 1 95

Disbursements.

Vouchers for Expenses	$ 1 95	$ 1 95

GIFTS AND TRUST FUNDS.

Under this head are included gifts and other funds which the Regents have received from time to time from benefactors for special purposes, and to which list during the the year have been added:

F. D. Bennett Scholarship Fund	$ 150 00
The Detroit Archæological Fund	200 00
Library of Early Christian Literature Fund, by D. M. Ferry	265 00
James E. Scripps Library Fund	527 90

WATERMAN GYMNASIUM.

Receipts.

Earnings	$ 20 75	$ 20 75

Disbursements.

Balance Overdrawn, July 1, 1896	$ 20 75	$ 20 75

PHILO PARSONS FUND.
Receipts.
Balance in Treasury, July 1, 1896	$ 89 03	
Interest	3 64	$ 92 67

Disbursements.
Balance in Treasury, June 30, 1897	$ 92 67	$ 92 67

MARY JANE PORTER FUND.
Receipts.
Balance in Treasury, July 1, 1896	$ 711 23	$ 711 23

Disbursements.
Transferred to Women's Gymnasium Fund	711 23	$ 711 23

GOETHE FUND.
Receipts.
Balance in Treasury, July 1, 1896	$ 265 68	
Interest	9 53	$ 275 21

Disbursements.
Vouchers	$ 64 21	
Balance in Treasury, June 30, 1897	211 00	$ 275 21

ELISHA JONES CLASSICAL FELLOWSHIP.
Receipts.
Balance in Treasury, July 1, 1896	$ 4 31	
From Mrs. Elisha Jones	500 00	
Interest	1 46	$ 505 77

Disbursements.
Vouchers	$ 500 00	
Balance in Treasury, June 30, 1897	5 77	$ 505 77

CONTINGENT FUND.
Receipts.
Balance in Treasury, July 1, 1896	$ 3,188 94	$ 3,188 94

Disbursements.
Transferred to Women's Gymnasium Fund	[$ 3,188]94	$ 3,188 94

WOMEN'S GYMNASIUM.
Receipts.
Balance in Treasury, July 1, 1896	$ 1,176 29	
Transfer, Mary J. Porter Fund	711 23	
" Contingent Fund	3,188 94	
Gifts	639 57	
Balance Overdrawn, June 30, 1897	1,632 47	$ 7,348 50

Disbursements.
Vouchers	$ 7,348 50	$ 7,348 50

COYL COLLECTION.
Receipts.
Balance in Treasury, July 1, 1896	$10,416 81	
Interest	628 23	$11,045 04

Disbursements.
Vouchers	$ 275 28	
Balance in Treasury, June 30, 1897	10,769 76	$11,045 04

BUHL LAW LIBRARY.
Receipts.
Balance in Treasury, July 1, 1896	$10,644 77	
Interest	249 91	$10,894 68

Disbursements.
Vouchers	$ 8,379 80	
Balance in Treasury, June 30, 1897	2,514 88	$10,894 68

SETH HARRISON SCHOLARSHIP FUND.

Receipts.

Balance in Treasury, July 1, 1896	$24,992 62	
Interest	1,478 78	$26,471 40

Disbursements.

Vouchers	$ 701 50	
Balance in Treasury, June 30, 1897	25,769 90	$26,471 40

CLASS OF NINETY-FOUR SCHOLARSHIP FUND.

Receipts.

Balance in Treasury, July 1, 1896	$ 435 81	
Interest	19 47	
Gifts	158 80	$ 614 08

Disbursements.

Balance in Treasury, June 30, 1897	$ 614 08	$ 614 08

FORD-MESSER FUND.

Receipts.

Balance in Treasury, July 1, 1896	$10,166 49	
From the Administrator of the Estate of Corydon L. Ford on Account of Bequest	2,000 00	
Interest	638 13	$12,804 62

Disbursements.

Balance in Treasury, June 30, 1897	$12,804 62	$12,804 62

THE PHILLIPS SCHOLARSHIPS FUND.

Receipts.

Balance in Treasury, July 1, 1896	$ 46 87	
From the Estate of Henry Phillips	306 43	
Interest	3 57	$ 356 87

Disbursements.

Vouchers	$ 190 75	
Balance in Treasury, June 30, 1897	166 12	$ 356 87

MUSIC HALL FUND.

Receipts.

Balance in Treasury, July 1, 1896	$ 1,004 16	
Interest	40 70	$ 1,044 86

Disbursements.

Balance in Treasury, June 30, 1897	$ 1,044 86	$ 1,044 86

NINETY-SIX CLASS MEMORIAL.

Receipts.

Interest	$ 83	
Subscriptions Paid	59 00	$ 59 83

Disbursements.

Balance Overdrawn, July 1, 1896	$ 35 11	
Vouchers	5 80	
Balance in Treasury, June 30, 1897	18 92	$ 59 83

PARKE-DAVIS FUND.

Receipts.

Balance in Treasury, July 1, 1896	$ 9 25	
Interest	37	$ 9 62

Disbursements.

Balance in Treasury, June 30, 1897	$ 9 62	$ 9 62

STEARNS PHARMACY FELLOWSHIP FUND.

Receipts.

From Frederick Stearns & Co	$ 300 00	
Interest	77	$ 300 77

Disbursements.

Vouchers	$ 300 00	
Balance in Treasury, June 30, 1897	77	$ 300 77

DETROIT ARCHÆOLOGICAL FUND.

Receipts.

Gift	$ 200 00	$ 200 00

Disbursements.

Balance in Treasury, June 30, 1897	$ 200 00	$ 200 00

LIBRARY OF EARLY CHRISTIAN LITERATURE.

Receipts.

Gift from D. M. Ferry	$ 265 00	$ 265 00

Disbursements.

Vouchers	$ 238 10	
Balance in Treasury, June 30, 1897	26 90	$ 265 00

JAMES E. SCRIPPS LIBRARY FUND.

Receipts.

Gift	$ 527 90	$ 527 90

Disbursements.

Vouchers	$ 527 75	
Balance in Treasury, June 30, 1897	15	$ 527 90

F. D. BENNETT SCHOLARSHIP.

Receipts.

Gift	$ 150 00	$ 150 00

Disbursements.

Vouchers	$ 150 00	$ 150 00

RECAPITULATION.

GIFT FUND BALANCES.

Philo Parsons Fund	$ 92 67	
Goethe "	211 00	
Elisha Jones Classical Fellowship Fund	5 77	
Coyl Collection "	10,769 76	
Buhl Law Library "	2,514 88	
Seth Harrison Scholarship "	25,769 90	
The '94 Class Scholarship "	614 08	
The Ford-Messer "	12,804 62	
The Phillips Scholarships "	166 12	
Music Hall "	1,044 86	
'96 Class Memorial "	18 92	
The Parke-Davis "	9 62	
" Frederick Stearns "	77	
" Detroit Archeological "	200 00	
" Early Christian Literature "	26 90	
" J. E. Scripps "	15	$54,250 02
Deduct for Overdrawn Balance, Women's Gymnasium		1,632 47
Total in Gift Funds		$52,617 55

UNIVERSITY OF MICHIGAN

THE PRESIDENT'S REPORT

TO THE

BOARD OF REGENTS

FOR THE ACADEMIC YEAR

ENDING SEPTEMBER 30, 1898

AND THE

REPORT OF THE TREASURER

FOR THE FISCAL YEAR

ENDING JUNE 30, 1898

ANN ARBOR, MICH.:
PUBLISHED BY THE UNIVERSITY
1898

THE COURIER OFFICE, PRINTERS AND BINDERS,
ANN ARBOR, MICHIGAN.

THE PRESIDENT'S REPORT.

To the Regents of the University:

I have the honor to lay before you my Annual Report.

By your permission I was absent during the entire year, engaged in the diplomatic service of the United States. I am, therefore, unable to speak from personal observation of the life of the University during the period under consideration. But I have endeavored to inform myself concerning what has been done, and can, I think, see what are some of our most pressing needs.

First of all, I wish to express my hearty appreciation of the industry, energy and wisdom which Acting President Hutchins brought to his executive duties. At your urgent request he most reluctantly undertook them. But students, Faculties and the public most cordially agree with the warm commendations of his work which you have formally uttered in your resolutions of thanks to him.

The weeks of this last summer vacation have been freighted with heavy personal losses to the University.

Scarcely were the festivities of Commencement week ended, when we were shocked by the terrible news that Professor Walter was lost in the fatal disaster to the steamer Bourgogne on July 4. A graduate of this institution in the class of 1868, Mr. Walter had given his whole life to her service. A scholar of ample and various learning, a faithful and inspiring teacher, a man of the noblest character, he will be remembered with deep affection by his colleagues and with gratitude by his many pupils. He had filled the chairs of Assistant Professor of Ancient Languages, of Professor of Modern

Languages, and, when the duties of this last chair were at his request divided, of Professor of Romance Languages and Literatures.

On September 12, last, after a very prolonged illness, Professor Thomas M. Cooley found a welcome release in death. It may safely be said that no man has contributed more to the fame and prosperity of the University than Judge Cooley. A member of the first Faculty of the Law Department in 1859, he has rendered continuous service of some kind to one or another Department of the University almost to the time of his decease. His writings, especially his treatises on Constitutional Law, made his name and that of the University known wherever English law is read. Students came from afar to sit at his feet, and all went away filled with admiration for the teacher and affection for the man. His administrative services as Dean of the Law Department were of the highest value. By the simplicity, sincerity and integrity of his character, and by his quick sympathies and kindness of heart, he bound us all to him by the closest of ties.

On October 3, James L. High, who has been a lecturer on special topics on law for several years in our Law Department, died after a brief illness at his home in Chicago. Mr. High was a graduate of our Law School. He had not only won a high reputation at the Illinois bar, but was well known both here and abroad through his treatises on Injunctions and on Receivers and on Extraordinary Legal Remedies. He was a man of refined and scholarly culture, and he inspired his pupils with the highest ideals of professional life.

I think that never in so brief a period has the University before been called to suffer so heavy an affliction as the loss of these three eminent teachers has brought to it in the past few months. I am painfully reminded of the rapidity of changes in our Faculties, as I reflect that since the death of Professor Cooley and Professor Walter, of the more than two hundred teachers on our rolls only four were members of our Faculties when I assumed the duties of the Presidency in 1871.

In appendices to this report will be found a list of appointments and resignations in the Faculties during the year, a statement of the attendance in the several Departments, a list of the degrees conferred, a report of the examinations for advanced degrees, and the Treasurer's report.

The attendance last year was the largest in the history of the University. The total number of students, exclusive of those in the Summer Schools, was 3,114, an increase over that of the preceding year of 236. If we include the students of the Summer School of 1897, the attendance was 3,223. The gain was largely in the Law Department, which then fully completed its change of course from two years to three years. It is therefore apparent that the public was fully ready for the extension of the course. The gain in the number of undergraduate candidates for degrees in the Literary Department was considerable, 97. The number of graduate students changes but little from year to year. It is encouraging to observe that we retain and attract so many students for graduate work, when most of the stronger Universities are able by endowments to offer our graduates, and the graduates of other institutions, fellowships and scholarships yielding from $300 to $500 a year, or even more. It is well known that we have only one permanent fellowship, though the generosity of some of our friends is temporarily furnishing us two or three others. In other words, with two or three exceptions, graduates must remain here, if at all, at their own charges, while they are offered a comfortable support if they will accept a fellowship at some one of four or five of the stronger Universities in our country. We ought to be encouraged by the fact that seventy-six persons are pursuing graduate studies with us in these circumstances rather than to be discouraged by the fact that there are not more.

At the same time, as has been intimated in some of my previous Reports, one of the gravest questions now confronting this University and several others, is whether the States or private generosity will furnish them the means for carrying beyond the undergraduate curriculum the considerable number of brilliant and aspiring young scholars who are willing to give the time for two or three years of advanced and specialized study. It is by the training of such men that American scholarship will be carried to the high level which the needs of our country demand. It will be for the good of the State and for the glory of the University, if we can be enabled and permitted to do our full part in this honorable work. We shall certainly suffer in reputation and usefulness and influence, if we are unable to do so.

I give as usual some of the interesting figures concerning the residence of our students. Michigan furnished 1,863, which is 116 more than in the previous year, and the largest number ever sent by this State. Estimating the population at two and a half millions, one person in 1,342 is a student in the University. Illinois, although so well furnished with colleges and universities, sent us 365 students, 58 more than in the year before, Ohio furnished 191, Indiana 98, Iowa 86, New York 71, Pennsylvania 69, Missouri 60, Wisconsin 40, California 34, Massachusetts 30, Colorado 28, Kentucky 26, Kansas 19, Nebraska 19, Utah 16, Montana 15.

Every State in the Union, except Delaware, and every Territory, and Alaska, and the District of Columbia, and the Hawaiian Islands, were represented, as were Germany, England, Russia, Turkey, Mexico, Japan, and the provinces of Ontario and Quebec. It may be doubted whether so cosmopolitan a company of students is assembled at any other university in the country. Not the least of the happy influences of life here is found in the opportunity of associating with students from every part of this land and from several foreign lands. While Michigan may be glad to see that an ever increasing number of her sons and daughters are availing themselves of the privileges which the State furnishes by the support of the University, we trust that she is proud to observe that the Institution has sufficient merit and fame to attract students from all parts of the civilized world. Nor need her joy be tempered by the apprehension that the attendance of these students from afar puts an additional burden on the tax-payers of Michigan. In previous Reports it has been repeatedly demonstrated that their presence is of distinct pecuniary advantage to our treasury, as it is of marked benefit in giving a large catholic spirit to the life of the University and in spreading far and wide its reputation and its influence.

The attendance of women was as follows:

Department of Literature, Science, and the Arts,	589
Department of Engineering,	1
Department of Medicine and Surgery,	59
Department of Law,	5
School of Pharmacy,	3
Homœopathic Medical College,	8
College of Dental Surgery,	8
	673

The preceding year the number was 647. The gain was therefore 26. In the Literary Department there was a gain of 48; in some of the Departments there was a slight loss. The relative attendance of women to the total attendance fell from 22.4 per cent. in the previous year to 21.6 per cent. For several years the proportion of women to the total attendance has not fallen below 20 per cent. nor risen above that of 1896–7, 22.4 per cent.

The work of the various Departments has been carried on smoothly and successfully. It is a cause of satisfaction that the condition of the treasury has made it possible to enlarge somewhat the teaching force in the Literary Department, especially for the classes in the modern languages. It is quite impossible to do good work in teaching those languages to large sections.

The arrangements, by which students are allowed in the latter part of their literary course to combine with it studies in law or in medicine, are proving very satisfactory. By availing themselves of the opportunities offered students are able to abridge by a year the time otherwise needed to complete the collegiate and the professional course. One who is studious may thus graduate from both the Literary and the Law Department in six years, or from both the Literary and the Medical Department in seven years. This is possible, not because any of the work is slighted, but because certain work common to the Literary and the Professional course is credited as fulfilling the requirements for both degrees. For example, certain studies in chemistry are properly credited as meeting the requirements for a bachelor's degree and those for the degree of doctor of medicine. In the same way studies in constitutional history or in international law are treated as meeting the requirements for the bachelor's degree in arts and the bachelor's degree in law. A careful committee considers every application for the privilege of pursuing the joint course, and reports favorably only when it is clear that the privilege can safely be granted to the applicant.

There has been much complaint throughout the country because, since the courses in all the best professional schools have been lengthened to three years in law and four years in medicine, students who complete a full collegiate course and a full professional course get so late to their real work in life. Some have proposed as a remedy reforms in the lower grades of schools which should bring the student to college a year or two earlier than he now comes. If such reforms are feasible, some time seems necessary to accomplish them. And some doubt whether if students could get to college at the age of sixteen, they would derive as much profit from the collegiate course as they do when entering at the age of eighteen, and therefore whether the supposed gain in time might not prove a loss in attainments and mental growth. Without deciding if that doubt is well founded or not, it seems clear to us that having all our Departments on the same grounds we can wisely and without inconvenience to the student or without detracting from the thoroughness of his collegiate or professional training pursue the plan which we have adopted.

At the Observatory Professor Hall has been engaged since April with the meridian circle in observing zenith distances of

Polaris for the purpose of determining the variation of latitude and the aberration constant. The preliminary reductions have been kept up as the observations have been made, and results seem to be very satisfactory. Since the instrument was remounted in the piers, it has been much more steady, and probably a cause of trouble that had existed for many years was thereby removed. With the large equatorial Dr. Townley observed several comets and asteroids.

Certain much needed improvements have just been completed in the Chemical Building, which is used to its utmost capacity by the students of the several departments of the University. An enlargement of the Laboratory of General Chemistry has been made, by elevating a portion of the building on the east, and the interior has been adapted to the best laboratory methods. By this extension provision has been made for teaching Physical Chemistry, a branch of much importance. Room has been secured for Chemical Technology by finishing in a substantial manner the entire south basement. The whole of this space has been very carefully fitted with superior appliances for the principal branches of Chemical Technology. This greatly needed improvement will give added impetus to the work in industrial aids and methods, so much in demand.

Messrs. Parke, Davis & Co., of Detroit, have made a gift in support of a fellowship in research in the Laboratory of General Chemistry for the year 1898-9. We were indebted to the same house for a like gift in 1895.

The work of the Department of Medicine and Surgery has as usual been carried on with great thoroughness. The course at present makes very strenuous demands on the students. The requirements for admission have been somewhat modified in order to secure preparation in scientific studies. The rooms assigned to the Department are seriously overcrowded. A building providing larger laboratory facilities is much desired by the Faculty, and is no doubt much needed.

The hospital connected with the Department has had unusual demands on it. The number of patients from July 1, 1897, to July 1, 1898, was the largest ever known here, being 1,715. Of these 1,072 were in-patients, 643 were out-patients. Seventy-six counties of Michigan were represented among them. The farmers numbered 288, the mechanics 100, housewives 375. Persons of almost every vocation were treated. Many were restored from helpless disability to lives of useful productivity. Of these some had become a charge on the treasuries of the counties. Had the hospital been larger, this beneficent assistance could have been rendered to others.

A neat and convenient building has been completed during the year, which affords pleasant rooms for twenty nurses, and a kitchen and dining room for patients.

The Law Department is now housed in a fine building, fitted with modern conveniencies, and having ample accommodations for one thousand students. In 1892, the growth of the Department had been such that the original building had become inadequate, and a large addition was constructed. In 1895, a third year was added to the course, and soon thereafter the requirements for admission were materially increased. It was thought by some that these changes would result in a decrease in the attendance, but instead of this there has been a marked increase. The enrolment of last year was seven hundred and sixty-seven, an increase of one hundred and eighty-one over the enrolment of the year previous. Enlarged accommodations became a necessity, and during the year the Board discussed and finally adopted plans that involved practically the reconstruction of the old building and an addition thereto that would more than double its capacity. The plans were so made and have been so carried out that the old building is completely lost in the present structure, which presents the appearance of an entirely new edifice. The new building has a frontage of 208 feet, and its extreme width is 120 feet. It is three stories high with a basement. The material of the basement and first story is cut stone and of the other two stories pressed brick with stone trimmings. The building is substantial and dignified in appearance, solid in structure, and gives the department a housing that for commodiousness and convenience is second to that of no law school in the United States. Three large lecture rooms, capable of accommodating upwards of three hundred students each, are provided, while six smaller ones, each of half that capacity, furnish ample room for the sections into which classes are divided for recitation purposes. The office of the Board of Regents, the offices of administration, the offices of the several resident professors and four lecture rooms are upon the first floor. The capacious and well lighted reading room that contains the law library is upon the second floor, and clustered around this are seminary, consultation and private study rooms for the use of the students and the Faculty. Near the library and upon the same floor are the court room and the offices of the practice court. There are also three lecture rooms on the second floor. Upon the third floor are two lecture rooms, ample debating and society rooms and the office of the instructors. The building is provided with a fan system of heating and ventilation and is lighted by electricity. For the money expended, about $65,000 including the furnishing, the results are more than could reasonably have been expected at the time the work was undertaken.

The School of Pharmacy now enters upon its thirty-first year. Its graduates number 765 persons. More than half of its students have entered the University from the high schools of this state, but on going out they have been in demand in all the states, in the east even more than in the west, for various services of skill. As an instance of the part which Michigan has taken in pharmaceutical education it may be mentioned that the present dean of the oldest school of pharmacy in New England graduated in pharmacy here in 1883, and came as a boy from the Jackson high school to the University in 1878. As another instance, a few years ago the Maine State College established a department of pharmacy and called to take charge of it a pharmacist resident in Michigan, who had prepared for college in a Michigan high school and earned our degree in pharmacy in 1887. Again, in Alabama, upon the establishment of pharmacy in the Institute of Technology, it was intrusted to a Michigan man, educated in pharmacy at this University.

For the prosecution of chemical and pharmaceutical research at this University in the year now before us, certain trust funds have been placed in the hands of the Regents, in continuation of gifts for like purposes for several years past. It is proper to acknowledge the trust reposed in this institution by the givers of these annual stipends, in their purpose to sustain scientific investigation. The Committee of Revision and Publication of the Pharmacopœia of the United States, 1890-1900, a body representing the physicians, the pharmacists, and the government of this country, out of the proceeds of publication, have set apart a sum sufficient to support two experienced workers in research at this point. This work is to be upon the quantitative methods establishing the purity and strength of remedial agents, under the direction of the School of Pharmacy. Messrs. Frederick Stearns & Co., of Detroit, this year again, support a fellowship in research in the School of Pharmacy, this annual grant having been continuous since 1895.

The Homœopathic Medical College continues to make a moderate but regular increase in numbers. As it now has a united and efficient Faculty and apparently enjoys the cordial support of the profession in the state and in the whole country, there seems to be every reason to expect a high degree of prosperity for it. In its laboratories and its hospital it has now a good outfit for work of the most thorough character. The report of its hospital shows that from October, 1897, to July 1, 1898, it cared for 315 in-patients and 423 out-patients. Compared with the previous year that is an increase of 98 in the number of in-patients, and of 225 in out-patients. It has nearly doubled the earnings of the previous year. As in the other hospital the farmers, of whom there were 71, and the housewives, 104, exceeded in number those of any other calling in life. More than half the counties in the state were represented in the patients. The hospital is emphatically a most useful public charity.

The Dental College continues its work with increasing usefulness and prosperity. Its graduates are now found in all parts of this country and in foreign lands. It is a noteworthy fact that almost everywhere in the world the superiority of American to European dentists is recognized. This is due to the fact that the training in our best dental schools is better than that of foreign schools. Hence we always have some foreign students in the Department.

The growth of our libraries during the past year has been reasonably gratifying. The appropriations made by the Regents from our General Fund, supplemented by the income from the Coyl and Ford legacies and by generous gifts from many donors has added, as we learn from the Librarian's report, 9,022 volumes, 1,079 pamphlets and 24 maps. Our entire collections now number 122,962 volumes, 18,461 pamphlets, and 1,299 maps; of these the General Library contains 98,222 volumes, 16,952 pamphlets and 1,299 maps. The circulation of books was larger than ever before. The recorded use, which is estimated at about one-half of the whole use, reached 142,167 volumes.

It is well known to the Board that students are not allowed to draw books from the Library and take them to their rooms. They must use them, if at all, in the reading room of the Library, which is kept open every week day from 8 o'clock in the morning to 10 o'clock in the evening. As it has always been our policy to give to our readers the largest use of the Library compatible with the safe administration of it, the question has often arisen whether we could not set aside a certain number of books which students might draw and carry to their rooms for a limited time. I have discussed the subject in some previous Reports. It has seemed to me that when we had collected about 100,000 volumes in the General Library, we might try the experiment. Of course most of our books could not thus be loaned. But a considerable number, many of them duplicates, could be selected for circulation without incommoding the great mass of our students. And the students would, it seems to me, be materially aided in much of their work. Perhaps an incidental advantage would be the relief of our reading room, which at certain seasons does not now furnish accommodations for all the readers. The additional expense of administration would not be large. The enlargement of the Library building and the consequent redistribution of our books seem to make this a suitable time to consider the subject afresh. I respectfully commend it to your attention.

It is a cause of great satisfaction that the Regents have been able to make an addition to the Library Building, doubling the capacity of the book room and of our Art Gallery. This addition is fifty four feet in length and forty feet in width. It contains three stories for iron stacks and one story for the art room. This will provide storage room for about 70,000 volumes. It is proposed to provide on the third floor for the special collections and the rare and valuable books, which should be guarded more carefully. There are now several thousands of this character. Space will also be afforded in this third story for the "Concord Room" for the Thoreau and Emerson collections, presented by Dr. S. A. Jones, and for other rooms of a similar character

We shall also be able to display in a fitting manner our collections of paintings, especially those of the Lewis collection, which in our limited space we were unable to provide for as we desired.

I trust that the day is not distant when we may throw out wings from the new book room to provide seminary rooms, for which there is most urgent need. This can easily be done in keeping with the architectural plan of the building. The seminary method for advanced students has now been so generally adopted that all the best College Libraries recently constructed make generous provision for seminary rooms. Our present number is inadequate to our wants.

The Alumni Association, which now receives to membership the graduates of all Departments, is evincing a most encouraging disposition to aid the University. It employs a paid secretary and clerks who gather information about the alumni, and by various means keep them in touch with the University. It is publishing a monthly magazine, the Alumnus, which contains matter of special interest to graduates. A semi-monthly sheet, the University News Letter, is also published from the office of the Association. It is sent to any who desire it, but especially to the newspapers of the State. It is filled with trustworthy items of news from the University, which are given in brief articles that newspapers are invited to produce without giving credit to the News Letter. It is edited by Professor Scott. Through it the newspaper press of the State has been led to give a large circulation to news of real importance to the citizens of the State, who furnish in large part the support of the University. We desire nothing so much as that they should be kept fully advised of the nature and extent of the work done here, and of the worth and beneficent influence of the University.

X When the recent war with Spain broke out, the patriotic spirit of the University flamed up as it did in 1861. So far as known, about one hundred and twenty-five of our students and as many more of our graduates enlisted, and many others would have willingly gone, if their aid had seemed necessary. Three of our prominent Professors also enlisted, Dr. Nancrede, Professor of Surgery in the Department of Medicine, Dr. Vaughan, Dean of that Department, and M. E. Cooley, Professor of Mechanical Engineering. The two former served on the medical staff with the greatest efficiency. They were present at the fighting before Santiago, and Dr. Vaughan was prostrated with the yellow fever. Mr. Cooley, who is an engineer graduate of the Naval Academy, was Chief Engineer on the United States Steamer Yosemite, which was manned by the Naval Reserves of Michigan, and took an active part in the campaign. Dr. Nancrede, after discharging most difficult and responsible duties, was released from the service, and resumed his work here at the opening of the year. Dr. Vaughan, after his recovery from yellow fever, was detailed to study the causes of typhoid fever in certain camps, and is detained in Washington, completing his report. His return to his post here is expected soon. Professor Cooley's services have been so valuable that the navy department has been unwilling to spare him yet, but we hope he may before long secure his discharge. The Board willingly granted these three officers leave of absence for this patriotic duty, and they have all done marked credit to themselves and to the University. The Board also in June conferred degrees on the men who would have completed their courses at that time, but who left for the front in April.

So far as known to us, seven University men lost their lives in the war.

John Albert Bobb, M.D., 1886, was Assistant Surgeon of the 34th Michigan Infantry. He died Aug. 19, on the voyage form Santiago de Cuba to Montauk Point, and was buried at sea. His last words were, "I die for my country; my only regret is that I have not a hundred lives to offer for her."

Charles August Fred von Walthausen, Ph.C., 1896, a private in the 31st Michigan Infantry, died at Camp Thomas, Chickamauga, Aug. 10, aged 23 years.

William James O'Brien, who was from 1894-7 a member of the last graduating class, was a sergeant in Torrey's Rough Riders, and died at Jacksonville, Fla., Sept. 13, of malarial fever.

Oliver Burleigh Norton, of the medical class of 1901, was one of Roosevelt's Rough Riders, and was killed while bravely charging up the hill of San Juan.

John Oliver, a student in the Law Department, a sergeant in the 34th Michigan Infantry died in the hospital at Siboney, Cuba, on Aug. 21, aged 21 years.

Henry Carlton Gowan of the Literary Department, a private in the 33d Michigan Infantry, died of typhoid fever at Grace Hospital, Detroit, on Sept. 17. He was buried at Sault Ste. Marie.

Elihu Harry Boynton, of St. Clair, a private in the 31st Michigan Infantry, died at Knoxville, Tenn., on November 2. His home was St. Clair, Mich. He had studied in the Literary and Law Departments.

The names of these young men will be cherished with those of the heroic spirits who left these halls for their country's sake in the Civil War and fell on southern fields.

A number of students, who left the University and joined the 31st Michigan regiment asked me, when it was apparent that there was no fighting for them to do, to inquire if the War Department would not discharge them from service in order that they might return to their studies. I therefore requested the Secretary of War to release them, if such action was compatible with public interests. He very promptly granted the request, and most of them are already here at their work.

In 1890 we issued a General Catalogue of all the students who up to that time had been connected with the University. It was prepared with immense labor and scrupulous care by Professors Demmon and Pettee. It gave, so far as then could be learned, the occupations, official positions and addresses of every graduate, and the names of those who had attended, but not graduated. The volume was beautifully printed. It has attracted much attention, and has been imitated by some other Institutions. It was expected at the time of publication that a new edition would be published in 1900. Clearly it is of great importance that we should have another issue ready by Commencement Day of that year. In order to accomplish this, it is necessary that the work should soon be taken in hand. I recommend that the Executive Committee be at once charged with the duty of reporting to the Board a plan for preparing the new edition of the General Catalogue. The last one was so well prepared, and Professor Demmon has so faithfully preserved the material which has come to hand for another edition, that the task will be much less onerous than it was before. I may add that Miss Chase of Detroit has generously placed at our disposal the material gathered by her father, the late Theodore R. Chase, who was so many years the necrologist of the Alumni Association, and who prepared two earlier editions of the catalogue of graduates.

It has been decided to require of the first year students in the literary and engineering departments attendance for two hours a week on instruction in the gymnasium. It has been found that often those who are most in need of physical exercise do not take it. It has therefore been thought wise to insist that those who are beginning college work should take some gymnastic work. It is hoped that they will by trial see the benefits of it and acquire the habit of taking systematic and regular exercise.

The gifts which we have received during the year encourage us to hope that our friends will continue to supplement the state appropriations by generous assistance.

In addition to the fellowships provided by Parke, Davis & Co., and Frederick Stearns & Co., Mr. D. M. Ferry also provided one in Botany for the year.

Hon. James McMillan has continued his contributions for the Shakespeare Library.

The Law Library has been enriched during the past year by the gift from the widow and children of the late Judge Samuel T. Douglass, of Detroit, of the law books that formed his office collection, about 700 volumes. While these are very largely duplicates of books that we already have, they will be very useful to the Department, as with our large number of students, many duplicates are needed. The gift of these books was in accordance with a wish expressed by Judge Douglass not long before his death. It is to be hoped that other members of the bar, when providing for the disposition of their law libraries, will remember that a more useful disposition could not in most cases be made than by placing them in the collection of this Department. All such gifts are kept by themselves, and are known by the name of the donor.

In December last Ex-Regent Levi L. Barbour, who had already displayed his generosity to the University by his liberal contribution towards the erection of the Barbour Gymnasium for Women, proposed to present to the Regents of the University certain premises in Detroit valued at $15,000 or more, as a contribution toward the erection of a building to be devoted to the display and promotion of art in the University. The gift was to be made on the condition that within five years the Regents should secure $85,000 for the erection of the art building, and that within six years they should have begun the building and expended at least $20,000 upon it. Mrs. Barbour joined with her husband in this action.

Of our great need of such a building there can be no question. Since the gift of the Rogers Collection of statuary and of the Lewis Collection of pictures, our Art Gallery has proved much too small for the proper display of our objects of art. It is true the extension of the art gallery soon to be completed will much relieve us. But the day is not distant when the whole of our present art gallery, which occupies the upper story of the Library building will be needed for Library purposes. Besides, if we had an appropriate fire proof building set apart exclusively for a gallery, we should receive many gifts for our collections which are not likely to come to us in our crowded rooms.

On April 6, 1898, Miss Elizabeth Bates, M.D., died at Port Chester, N. Y. By will she bequeathed to the University the bulk of her estate. She directed that, subject to certain charges, the property bequeathed should be "for the use of the Medical Department to found a Professorship to be known and called the Bates Professorship of the Diseases of Women and Children, provided, nevertheless, that said University or College will receive female students to pursue their studies thereat, and give to them the same advantages as male students in the Medical Department thereof."

It does not appear that our benefactor ever visited the University. So far as we can learn, she was moved to remember us in this generous manner by the fact that this University was one of the first to offer medical education to women. She wished to testify her appreciation of the service thus rendered to her sex, and to enlarge our facilities for medical education. There seems good ground to expect that the legacy will yield $100,000 or more.

Such instances as these now named of generous regard for our welfare encourage us to hope that other persons of liberal intent will be found ere long to aid the State in ministering to our many needs. No investments are more productive of permanent good than the endowment of schools of learning. Many of these have survived the greatest political and social changes, and bid fair to remain perpetual fountains of blessing to mankind.

JAMES B. ANGELL.

APPENDICES.

APPENDIX A.

APPOINTMENTS, REAPPOINTMENTS, RESIGNATIONS, ETC., DURING THE YEAR ENDING SEPTEMBER 30, 1898.

Resignations:

At the meeting of June 9, 1898, the resignation of Elmer A. Lyman, A.B., Instructor in Mathematics, was presented and accepted.

At the meeting of June 28, 1898, the resignation of Alexis C. Angell, A.B., LL.B., Professor of Law, was presented and accepted.

At the meeting of September 20, 1898, the resignation of Sidney D. Townley, Sc.D., Instructor in Astronomy, was presented and accepted.

Leaves of Absence:

At the meeting of October 20, 1897, Professor Mortimer E. Cooley, M.E., was granted a short leave of absence, to serve as Chief Engineer of the Michigan State Naval Brigade in aiding to bring the U. S. S. Yantic to Detroit.

At the meeting of January 26, 1898, Assistant Professor Dean C. Worcester, A.B., was granted leave of absence for the academic year 1898–99.

At the meeting of February 18, 1898, Junior Professor George W. Patterson, A.M., S.B., was granted leave of absence for the academic year 1898–99.

At the meeting of March 18, 1898, the leave of absence previously granted to Tobias Diekhoff, A.B., Instructor in German, was extended for the academic year 1898–99.

At the meeting of April 22, 1898, Professor Mortimer E. Cooley, M.E., was granted leave of absence to the first of October, to serve as a volunteer officer in the United States Navy; and Junior Professor Alexander Ziwet, C.E., was granted leave of absence for the academic year 1898–99.

At the meeting of May 13, 1898, Professor Charles B. Nancrede, A.M., M.D., was granted leave of absence to the first of October, to serve as volunteer surgeon in the United States Army; the leave of absence previously granted to Clarence L. Meader, A.B., Instructor in Latin, was extended for the academic year 1898-99; and Professor Volney M. Spalding, Ph.D., was granted leave of absence for the academic year 1898-99.

At the meeting of June 9, 1898, Professor Victor C. Vaughan, Ph.D., Sc.D., M.D., was granted leave of absence to the first of October, to serve as volunteer surgeon in the United States Army.

At the meeting of June 28, 1898, Instructor Perry F. Trowbridge, Ph.B., was granted leave of absence for the academic year 1898-99.

At the meeting of September 20, 1898, the leaves of absence previously granted to Professors Cooley and Vaughan, were extended; and Professor Oscar Leseure. M.D., who was serving as volunteer surgeon in the United States Army, was allowed a similar leave of absence beyond the first of October.

Non-resident Lecturers in the Department of Medicine and Surgery were appointed at the meeting of May 13, 1898 as follows:

William M. Edwards, M.D., Mental Diseases.
Edmund A. Christian, A.B., M.D., Mental Diseases.
James D. Munson, M.D., Mental Diseases.
Samuel Bell, M.D., Mental Diseases.
Henry B. Baker, A.M., M.D., Administration of Health Laws.

Non-resident Lecturers in the Department of Law were appointed at the meeting of May 13, 1898, as follows:

Thomas M. Cooley, LL.D., Interstate Commerce.
James L. High, LL.D., Injunctions and Receivers.
John B. Clayberg, LL.B., Mining Law.
Melville M. Bigelow, Ph.D., Insurance.
Henry H. Swan, A.M., Admiralty.
Frank F. Reed, A.B., Copyright Law.
Albert H. Walker, LL.B., Patent Law.

A non-resident Lecturer in the Homœopathic Medical College was appointed at the meeting of October 30, 1897, as follows:

Oscar R. Long, M.D., Mental Diseases.

At the meeting of May 13, 1898, Special Lecturers in the Department of Law were appointed as follows:

Victor C. Vaughan, Ph.D., Sc.D., M.D., Toxicology in its Legal Relations.
Henry C. Adams, Ph.D., The Railroad Problem.

Andrew C. McLaughlin, A.M., LL.B., Constitutional Law and Constitutional History.
Richard Hudson, A.M., Comparative Constitutional Law.
Joseph H. Drake, A.B., Roman Law.
William J. Herdman, M.D., LL.D., Neurology, Electrology, and Railway Injuries.

The following lists comprise other appointments, reappointments, and changes of title of members of the Faculties. The Instructors were appointed for one year, unless a longer term is mentioned. The names of assistants and of others appointed to positions of lower grade than Instructor are not here included.

At the meeting of October 30, 1897.

The title of Assistant Professor Frederick C. Newcombe, Ph.D., was changed to stand Junior Professor of Botany.

At the meeting of December 22, 1897.

Charles A. Rabethge, M.D., was appointed Instructor in Dermatology in the Homœopathic Medical College.

At the meeting of January 26, 1898.

S. Lawrence Bigelow, Ph.D., was appointed Instructor in General Chemistry.

At the meeting of April 22, 1898.

The title of Professor Warren P. Lombard, A.B., M.D., was changed to stand Professor of Physiology.

The title of Professor J. P. McMurrich, Ph.D., was changed to stand Professor of Anatomy and Director of the Anatomical Laboratory.

The title of Assistant Professor G. C. Huber, M.D., was changed to stand Assistant Professor of Anatomy and Director of the Histological Laboratory.

At the meeting of May 13, 1898.

Appointments were made as follows:

Moses Gomberg, Sc.D., Instructor in Organic Chemistry.
Perry F. Trowbridge, Ph.B., Instructor in Organic Chemistry.
Alfred H. White, A.B., Instructor in Chemical Technology.
Simon M. Yutzy, M.D., Instructor in Anatomy.
Frank W. Nagler, B.S., Instructor in Electrotherapeutics.
Herbert H. Waite, A.B., Instructor in Bacteriology.
Louis A. Strauss, Ph.M., Instructor in English for three years.
John S. P. Tatlock, A.M., Instructor in English.

Penoyer L. Sherman, Ph.D., Instructor in General Chemistry.
James W. Glover, Ph.D., Instructor in Mathematics for three years.
Edwin C. Goddard, Ph.B., Instructor in Mathematics for three years.
James B. Pollock, Sc.D., Instructor in Botany.
Wilbur C. Abbott, B.Litt., Instructor in History.
Walter Dennison, A.M., Instructor in Latin.
John R. Effinger, Ph.M., Instructor in French for three years.
Ewald Boucke, Ph.D., Instructor in German.
Victor E. François, Instructor in French for three years.
Herbert J. Goulding, B.S., Instructor in Descriptive Geometry and Drawing for three years.
John R. Allen, M.E., Instructor in Mechanical Engineering.
John T. Faig, M.E., Instructor in Mechanical Engineering.
Carroll D. Jones, E.E., Instructor in Electrical Engineering.
John W. Dwyer, LL.M., Instructor in Law.
Albert J. Farrah, LL.B., Instructor in Law.
Augustus Trowbridge, Ph.D., Instructor in Physics.

At the meeting of June 9, 1898.

Appointments were made as follows:

Benjamin P. Bourland, Ph.D., Instructor in French.
Colman D. Frank, Ph.B., Instructor in French.
William H. Wait, Ph.D., Instructor in Greek, Latin, and Sanskrit.
William H. Butts, A.M., Instructor in Mathematics.
Albert W. Whitney, A.B., Instructor in Mathematics.
Ernst J. Fluegel, Ph.D., Instructor in German.
Hamilton G. Timberlake, A.B., Instructor in Botany.
Julia W. Snow, Ph.D., Instructor in Botany.
John B. Johnston, Ph.B., Instructor in Zoology.
Fanny E. Langdon, M.S., Instructor in Zoology.
Louis P. Hall, D.D.S., Instructor in Dental Anatomy, Operative Technique, and Clinical Operative Dentistry.

At the meeting of June 28, 1898.

Appointments were made as follows:

Keene Fitzpatrick, Acting Director of the Gymnasium for one year.
Robert C. Stevens, A.B., B.S., Instructor in Mechanical Engineering.
Sidney D. Townley, Sc.D., Instructor in Astronomy.
Archibald Campbell, Ph.B., Instructor in Organic Chemistry.

At the meeting of July 21, 1898.

Appointments were made as follows:

Aaron V. McAlvay, A.B., LL.B., Professor of Law for one year.
John R. Rood, LL.B., Instructor in Law.
Shirley W. Smith, B.L., Instructor in English.

At the meeting of August 17, 1898.

Arthur G. Hall, B.S., Instructor in Mathematics for three years.
Hugo P. Thieme, Ph.D., Instructor in French.
Charles A. Rabethge, M.D., Instructor in the Gymnasium.

APPENDIX B.

The following degrees were conferred during the year October 1, 1897, to September 30, 1898:

ORDINARY DEGREES.

Bachelor of Letters	56
Bachelor of Science (in Biology)	9
Bachelor of Science (in Chemistry)	5
Bachelor of Science (in Electrical Engineering)	22
Bachelor of Science (in Mechanical Engineering)	14
Bachelor of Science (in Civil Engineering)	20
Bachelor of Science (in Pharmacy)	2
Bachelor of Science	25
Bachelor of Philosophy	60
Bachelor of Arts	81
Civil Engineer	2
Master of Letters	3
Master of Science	10
Master of Science (Department of Engineering)	2
Master of Philosophy	4
Master of Arts	15
Doctor of Philosophy	7
Doctor of Medicine (Department of Medicine and Surgery)	72
Bachelor of Laws	200
Master of Laws	4
Pharmaceutical Chemist	20
Doctor of Medicine (Homœopathic Medical College)	9
Doctor of Dental Surgery	59
Doctor of Dental Science	2
	703

HONORARY DEGREES.

Doctor of Medicine	1
Master of Arts	1
Doctor of Laws	2
Total	707

APPENDIX C.

SUMMARY OF STUDENTS.

DEPARTMENT OF LITERATURE, SCIENCE, AND THE ARTS.

Holder of Fellowship	1
Resident Graduates	70
Candidates for an Advanced Degree, enrolled in other Departments	3
Graduates Studying *in Absentia*	2
Undergraduates:	
Candidates for a Degree	1093
Students not Candidates for a Degree	164—1333

DEPARTMENT OF ENGINEERING.

Resident Graduates	3
Undergraduates	274— 277

DEPARTMENT OF MEDICINE AND SURGERY.

Resident Graduates	4
Fourth Year Students	77
Third Year Students	102
Second Year Students	113
First Year Students	113
Students enrolled in other Departments of the University:	
Second Year Students in Medicine	12
First Year Students in Medicine	16— 437

DEPARTMENT OF LAW.

Resident Graduates	4
Third Year Students	213
Second Year Students	244
First Year Students	251
Special Students	31
Students enrolled in other Departments of the University	22— 765

SCHOOL OF PHARMACY.

Resident Graduates	5
Undergraduates:	
Candidates for a Degree	64
Students not Candidates for a Degree	10— 79

HOMŒOPATHIC MEDICAL COLLEGE.

Resident Graduates	2
Fourth Year Students	8
Third Year Students	10
Second Year Students	13
First Year Students	26
Students enrolled in the Department of Literature, Science, and the Arts	2— 61

COLLEGE OF DENTAL SURGERY.

Resident Graduates		4
Seniors		55
Juniors		74
Freshmen		90— 223
		3175
Deduct for names counted more than once		61
Total, exclusive of Summer Schools		3114

SUMMER SCHOOLS OF 1898.

In Department of Literature, Science, and the Arts	204	
In Department of Law	31—235	
Deduct for students enrolled in 1897-8 in some Department of the University	100— 135	
Grand total		3249

APPENDIX D.

Examinations for higher degrees were held as follows during the year 1897-98:

IN THE DEPARTMENT OF LITERATURE, SCIENCE, AND THE ARTS.

CANDIDATES FOR THE DEGREE OF DOCTOR OF PHILOSOPHY.

GERTRUDE BUCK, B.S., 1894, M.S., 1896.

THESIS.—The Metaphor. Subjects for examination: Major.—Rhetoric. Minors.—English Literature. Psychology.

WALTER DENNISON, A.B., 1893, A.M., 1894.

THESIS.—De C. Suetoni Tranquilli Caesarum Vitarum Fontibus Epigraphicis. Subjects for examination: Major.—Latin. Minors.—Greek. Oscan.

JOHN ROBERT EFFINGER, JR., Ph.B., 1891, Ph.M., 1894.

THESIS.—The Dramatic Works of Népomucène Lemercier. Subjects for examination: Major.—French Literature. Minors.—Italian Literature. History.

RIOTARO KODAMA, *Doshisha College.*

THESIS.—The Railway System of Japan. Subjects for examination: Major.—Political Economy. Minors.—Finance. History.

GEORGE REBEC, Ph.B., 1891.

THESIS.—Outlines of a Philosophic Theory of Discourse. Subjects for examination: Major.—Ancient Philosophy. Minors.—Logic. Rhetoric.

EDWIN CARL ROEDDER, A.B., 1893, A.M., 1894.

THESIS.—Syntax und Stilistik des Adjectivs im Altsächischen. Subjects for examination: Major.—German. Minors.—Old English. General Linguistics.

ARLETTA LEORA WARREN, Ph.B., *University of Wooster*, 1889.

THESIS.—L. Annaeus Seneca quid de summo bono censuerit. Subjects for examination: Major.—Latin. Minor.—Greek. Ancient Ethics.

CANDIDATES FOR THE DEGREE OF MASTER OF ARTS.

INEZ LOUISE ABBOTT, A.B., 1895.

Subjects for examination: Major.—Latin. Minors.—Greek. Roman Political Antiquities.

MARY EMMA ARMSTRONG, A.B., *Olivet College*, 1894.

Subjects for examination: Major.—Latin. Minors.—Greek. Roman Political Antiquities.

ALLEN LYSANDER COLTON, Ph.B., 1889, A.B., 1890.

Subjects for examination: Major.—Astronomical Photography. Minors.—Physics. Practical Astronomy.

FREDERIC SAMUEL GOODRICH, A.B., *Wesleyan University*, 1890.

THESIS.—Aristophanes as a Critic of Euripides. Subjects for examination: Major.—Greek. Minors.—Hellenistic Greek. Archæology.

SOPHIE CHANTAL HART, A.B., *Radcliffe College*, 1892.

Subjects for examination: Major.—Rhetoric. Minors.—English Literature. Aesthetics.

GEORGE FREDERICK HEFFELBOWER, A.B., 1897.

Subjects for examination: Major.—Latin. Minors.—Greek. History.

ANNIE LOUISE HILL, A.B., 1897.

Subjects for examination: Major.—Latin. Minors.—Greek. English Literature.

EUGENE LA ROWE, A.B., 1896.

Subjects for examination: Major.—Latin. Minors.—Greek. English Literature.

KATHARYNE GRIFFITH SLENEAU, A.B., 1897.

Subjects for examination: Major.—Rhetoric. Minors.—English Literature. Aesthetics.

EDSON READ SUNDERLAND, A.B., 1897.

Subjects for examination: Major.—Modern Philosophy. Minors.—American Constitutional History. Comparative Constitutional Law.

RUBY WINIFRED SUNDERLIN, A.B., *Olivet College*, 1897.

Subjects for examination: Major.—Latin. Minors.—Greek. Roman Political Antiquities.

FREDERICK TYNDALL SWAN, A.B., 1897.

Subjects for examination;—Major.—Latin. Minors.—Greek. English Literature.

JEREMIAH SIMEON YOUNG, A.B., *Kansas College*, 1890, A.M., *ibid.*, 1894.

THESIS.—The Cumberland Road. Subjects for examination: Major.—American History. Minors.—Pedagogy. English Literature.

CANDIDATES FOR THE DEGREE OF MASTER OF PHILOSOPHY.

ROMANZO COLFAX ADAMS, Ph.B., 1897.

Subjects for Examination: Major.—Political Economy. Minors.—American History. American Literature.

ARCHIBALD CAMPBELL, Ph.B., 1896.

THESIS.—The Hydrazo-and Azo-Derivatives of Triphenylmethane. Major.—Organic Chemistry. Minors.—Analytical Chemistry. Geology.

FLORENCE MABELLE HALLECK, Ph.B., 1896.

Subjects for examination: Major.—American History. Minors.—European History. French Literature.

WILLIS HAMEL WILCOX, Ph.B., 1896.

Subjects for examination: Major.—American Literature. Minors.—American History. Pedagogy.

CANDIDATES FOR THE DEGREE OF MASTER OF SCIENCE.

CLIFTON HENRY BRIGGS, B.S., *Michigan Agricultural College*, 1896.

Subjects for examination: Major.—General Chemistry. Minors.—Physics. Analytical Chemistry.

WILLIAM MORGAN CASE BRYAN, A.B., *Washington University*, 1897.

Subjects for examination: Major.—Botany. Minors.—Physics. Chemistry.

JULIET MORTON BUTLER, B.S., 1897.

Subjects for examination: Major.—Vertebrate Zoology. Minors.—Invertebrate Zoology. Vegetable Physiology.

HOMER REDFIELD FOSTER, Ph.B., 1897.

Subjects for examination: Major.—Botany. Minors.—Vegetable Physiology. Zoology.

OLIVER D. FREDERICK, B.S., *West Chester Normal School*, 1895.

Subjects for examination: Major.—Mathematics. Minors.—Physics. Pedagogy.

WILLIAM MARSHALL, B.S., 1897.

Subjects for examination: Major.—Mathematics. Minors.—Mechanics. Physics.

BERT WILLIAM PEET, B.S., *Michigan Agricultural College*, 1892.

Subjects for examination: Major.—General Chemistry. Minors.—Theoretical Chemistry. Mineralogy.

JESSIE PHELPS, B.S., 1894.

THESIS.—The Adhesive Organ of Amia. Subjects for examination: Major.—Vertebrate Zoology. Minors.—Invertebrate Zoology. Botany.

HAMILTON GREENWOOD TIMBERLAKE, A.B., *Lake Forest University*, 1897.

Subjects for examination: Major.—Botany. Minors.—Vegetable Physiology. Zoology.

CHARLES EDWIN VAN ORSTRAND, B.S. (C.E.), *University of Illinois*, 1896, B.S., *ibid.*, 1897.

Subjects for examination: Major.—Theoretical Astronomy. Minors.—Practical Astronomy. Mechanics.

HUGH ELMER WARD, B.S., *Michigan Agricultural College*, 1895.

THESIS.—The Effect of Temperature upon Muscular Contraction. Subjects for examination: Major.—Bacteriology. Minors.—Physiology. Organic Chemistry.

CANDIDATES FOR THE DEGREE OF MASTER OF LETTERS.

ANNIE LOUISE BACORN, B.L., 1896.

Subjects for examination: Major.—Rhetoric. Minors.—English Literature. Philosophy.

WALTER CHARLES HAIGHT, B.L., 1896.

THESIS.—The Binding Effect of the Ordinance of 1787. Subjects for examination: Major.—American History. Minors.—Political Economy. European History.

GRACE LORD LAMB, B.L., 1897.

Subjects for examination: Major.—History of Philosophy. Minors.—History. English Literature.

IN THE DEPARTMENT OF ENGINEERING.

THE DEGREE OF MASTER OF SCIENCE.
JOHN HAROLD MONTGOMERY, B.S., 1897.
CLARENCE GEORGE WRENTMORE, B.S., 1893.

THE DEGREE OF CIVIL ENGINEER.
WILL HAZEN BOUGHTON, B.S., 1893.
MINOTT EUGENE PORTER, B.S., 1893.

IN THE DEPARTMENT OF LAW.

THE DEGREE OF MASTER OF LAWS.
CLARENCE WILLIAM AIRD, LL.B., 1897.
THOMAS ALBERT BERKEBILE, LL.B., 1897.
HARRY YERSHELLE FREEDMAN, LL.B., 1897.
BERTRAN EDWARD NUSSBAUM, LL.B., 1896.

IN THE COLLEGE OF DENTAL SURGERY.

THE DEGREE OF DOCTOR OF DENTAL SURGERY.
THOMAS EDWARD CARMODY, D.D.S., 1897.
DESSIE BROWN ROBERTSON, D.D.S., 1897.

The Treasurer's Report

FOR THE FISCAL YEAR ENDING JUNE 30, 1898.

To the Finance Committee, Board of Regents, University of Michigan.

    GENTLEMEN: Herewith I submit my annual report for the fiscal year ending June 30, 1898.   Respectfully,   H. SOULE, Treasurer.

RECEIPTS.

From State Treasurer, acct. General Expenses	$279,406 39	
" " " " Special Appropriations	29,000 00	
" " " " " Accumulation, 1-6 Mill	20,000 00	
" Earnings and Miscellaneous Sources	213,265 81	
" Balance Overdrawn, June 30, 1898	9,799 52	$551,471 72

DISBURSEMENTS.

To Special Fund Accounts, acct. Legislative Appropriations	$ 32,755 68	
" " " " " Accumulation, 1-6 Mill	24,745 18	
" General Fund, acct. General Expenses	487,478 50	
" Balance Overdrawn, July 1, 1897	6,492 36	$551,471 72

GENERAL FUND.

RECEIPTS TO THE GENERAL FUND.

From Balance, July 1, 1897		$ 7,868 20
" State Treasurer, acct. 1-6 Mill Tax	221,020 46	
" " " " University Interest	58,385 93	
" Interest on Deposits	1,700 20	
" University Hospital Earnings	18,016 24	
" Homœopathic Hospital Earnings	4,025 50	
" Dental College Operating Room Earnings	4,223 37	
" Botanical Laboratory (Sale of Microscopes)	59 85	
" General Library (Sale of Books)	12 45	
" Electric Lighting Plant (Sale of Material)	159 35	
" Mechanical Laboratory (Earnings in Shops)	164 02	
" Miscellaneous Sources	1,580 67	$309,348 04
From Students' Fees:—		
Literary Department	$ 51,965 00	
" " Summer School	4,845 00	
Medical "	19,415 00	
Engineering "	11,885 00	
Law "	36,130 00	
" " Summer School	931 00	
Dental "	10,595 00	

Pharmacy " . .	.	3,945 00	
Homœopathic Department	.	2,875 00	
Chemical Laboratory .	.	12,181 08	
Hygienic " .	.	7,557 08	
Botanical " .	.	468 00	
Zoological " .	.	817 00	
Physiological " .	,	81 00	
Pathological " .	.	1,470 00	
Histological " .	.	1,653 00	
Anatomical " .	.	2,455 00	
Mechanical " .	.	1,525 00	
Dental " . .	.	781 00	
Electric Engineering Laboratory	.	511 00	
Electrotherapeutical "	.	968 00	
Medical Demonstrations	.	4,960 00	
Pharmacology . .	.	35 00	
Gymnasium Lockers .	.	2,330 00	
Women's Gymnasium .	.	412 00	
Law Lockers . .	.	24 00	
Diplomas . .	.	6,995 00	
Key Deposits . .	.	225 00	
Drawing Boards .	.	204 00	$183,324 16 $183,324 16

Total . .	$183,324 16	
Fees Refunded	5,950 54	
Net . . .	$177,373 62	
Balance Overdrawn, June 30, 1898		$ 6,248 66
		506,789 06

DISBURSEMENTS FROM THE GENERAL FUND.

To General Pay Roll . . .	$159,025 11		
" " " " Summer School .	4,365 62	163,390 73	
" " Expenses " " .		325 78	
" Engineering Department Pay Roll .	37,897 04	37,897 04	
" " " Expenses		193 60	
" Law Department Pay Roll . .	37,522 52		
" " " " " Summer School	850 35	38,372 87	
" " " Expenses " "		71 25	
" " " Expenses . .		351 95	
" " " Books . . .		2,413 41	
" Medical " Pay Roll . .	41,006 70	41,006 70	
" " " Expenses . .		192 95	
" " " Books . . .		2,019 77	
" Pharmacy and Chemical Department Pay Roll	24,845 42	24,845 42	
" " " " " Expenses		8,957 89	
" Dental Department Pay Roll . .	12,849 96	12,849 96	
" " " Expenses . .		4,904 18	
" " " Books . .		87 30	
" Homœopathic College Pay Roll .	3,300 00	3,300 00	
" " " Expenses . .		395 29	
" " " Books . .		251 90	
" " " Transfer to Special Fund		19,310 56	
" University Hospital Pay Roll .	6,780 75	6,780 75	
" " " Expenses . .		12,369 37	
" Homœopathic Hospital Pay Roll .	2,707 08	2,707 08	
" " " Expenses .		7,165 49	390,161 24
Pay Rolls Total .	$331,150 55		

To Contingent Account	$ 11,277 24
" Repairs	15,381 68
" Fuel	13,972 18
" Lighting	4,703 56
" Books for General Library	10,122 33
" Expenses for General Library	640 35
" Materia Medica	330 73
" Theory and Practice	99 19
" Postage	2,562 83
" Book Bindery	1,745 38
" Advertising and Printing	2,478 29
" Museum	524 50
" Botany	785 16
" Histology	544 14
" Hygiene	1,886 83
" Zoology	997 56
" Engineering Shops	795 62
" Civil Engineering	732 96
" Astronomical Observatory	377 48
" School Inspection	624 02
" Practical Anatomy	1,886 87
" Electrical Engineering (Physics)	687 06
" Physiology	282 40
" Pathology	458 74
" Electrotherapeutics	474 05
" Nervous Diseases	121 07
" Insurance	346 00
" Waterman Gymnasium	448 95
" Teams	535 52
" Carpenter Shop	118 57
" Women's Gymnasium	2,121 09
" Diplomas	1,077 80
" Geology	187 84
" Surgical Demonstrations	135 54
" Latin	510 50
" Ophthalmology	80 30
" General Chemistry	2 59
" Dermatology	30 95
" University Hospital Dormitory	16,838 14
" Diseases of Women and Children	102 14
" Water Supply	1,587 59
" Psychology	268 50
" Philosophy	114 20
" Semitic Languages	18 52
" Students' Fees refunded	5,950 54
" Electric Lighting Plant	7,125 94
" Hospital Lighting Plant	2,448 42
" University News Letter	67 76
" Alumni Association	380 51
" New Law Building	20 64
" Electrical Supplies	149 93
" Engineering Laboratory	410 05
" English	32 20
" Music	206 06
" State Pathologist	168 56
" Commencement Expenses	641 40
" General Catalogue	5 62
" Addition to General Library	3 24
	$506,789 06

SPECIAL FUND ACCOUNTS.

HOMŒOPATHIC COLLEGE.
Receipts.

From State Treasurer	$ 6,000 00	
Transfer from General Fund	19,310 56	$ 25,310 56

Disbursements.

Balance Overdrawn, July 1, 1897	$ 14,360 56	
Vouchers	9,350 00	
Balance in Treasury, June 30, 1898	1,600 00	$ 25,310 56

ELECTRIC LIGHT PLANT.
Receipts.

From State Treasurer	$ 20,000 00	
Balance Overdrawn, June 30, 1898	405 68	$ 20,405 68

Disbursements.

Vouchers	$ 20,405 68	$ 20,405 68

SUMMER HOSPITALS.
Receipts.

From State Treasurer	$ 3,000 00	$ 3,000 00

Disbursements.

Vouchers	$ 3,000 00	$ 3,000 00

ACCUMULATION OF SAVINGS, LAW BUILDING.
Receipts.

From State Treasurer	$ 20,000 00	
Balance Overdrawn, June 30, 1898	4,745 18	$ 24,745 18

Disbursements.

Vouchers	$ 24,745 18	$ 24,745 18

GIFTS AND TRUST FUNDS.

Under this head are included gifts and other funds which the Regents have received from time to time from benefactors for special purposes, and to which additional amounts have come into the hands of your treasurer during the year as follows:

By the Alumni a fund to be called Frieze Memorial Fund; by the Graduating Class of 1898 a Scholarship Fund; and the Alumni Society have turned over the Williams Fund and the Morris Alumni Fund, which funds are detailed fully in this report.

WOMEN'S GYMNASIUM.
Receipts.

Gifts	$ 1,967 34	
Interest	3 78	$ 1,971 12

Disbursements.

Balance Overdrawn, July 1, 1897	$ 1,632 47	
Vouchers	8 00	
Balance in Treasury, June 30, 1898	330 65	$ 1,971 12

PHILO PARSONS FUND.
Receipts.

Balance in Treasury, July 1, 1897	$ 92 67	
Interest	3 54	$ 96 21

Disbursements.

Balance in Treasury, June 30, 1898	96 21	$ 96 21

GOETHE FUND.
Receipts.

Balance in Treasury, July 1, 1897	$ 211 00	
Interest	8 05	$ 219 05

Disbursements.

Vouchers	$ 14 60	
Balance in Treasury, June 30, 1898	$ 204 45	$ 219 05

ELISHA JONES CLASSICAL FELLOWSHIP FUND.
Receipts.

Balance in Treasury, July 1, 1897	$ 5 77	
Interest	2 30	
From Mrs. Elisha Jones	500 00	$ 508 07

Disbursements.

Vouchers	$ 500 00	
Balance in Treasury, June 30, 1898	8 07	$ 508 07

DETROIT ARCHÆOLOGICAL FUND.
Receipts.

Balance in Treasury, July 1, 1897	$ 200 00	
Gifts	902 28	
Transfer from '96 Class Memorial Fund	7 52	$ 1,109 80

Disbursements.

Vouchers	$ 1,109 80	$ 1,109 80

COYL COLLECTION.
Receipts.

Balance in Treasury, July 1, 1897	$ 10,769 76	
Interest	636 39	$ 11,406 15

Disbursements.

Vouchers	$ 415 23	
Balance in Treasury, June 30, 1898	10,990 92	$ 11,406 15

BUHL LAW LIBRARY.
Receipts.

Balance in Treasury, July 1, 1897	$ 2,514 88	
Interest	70 30	$ 2,585 18

Disbursements.

Vouchers	$ 322 65	
Balance in Treasury, June 30, 1898	2,262 53	$ 2,585 18

SETH HARRISON SCHOLARSHIP FUND.
Receipts.

Balance in Treasury, June 30, 1897	$ 25,769 90	
Interest	1,393 69	$ 27,163 59

Disbursements.

Vouchers	$ 1,000 00	
Balance in Treasury, June 30, 1898	26,163 59	$ 27,163 59

CLASS OF NINETY-FOUR SCHOLARSHIP FUND.
Receipts.

Balance in Treasury, July 1, 1897	$ 614 08	
Interest	25 92	
Subscriptions Paid	292 70	$ 932 70

Disbursements.

Balance in Treasury, June 30, 1898	$ 932 70	$ 932 70

FORD-MESSER FUND.
Receipts.

Balance in Treasury, July 1, 1897	$ 12,804 62	
Interest	696 66	
Bryant Walker, Administrator of Estate Corydon L. Ford	1,500 00	$ 15,001 28

Disbursements.

Balance in Treasury, June 30, 1898	$ 15,001 28	$ 15,001 28

THE PHILLIPS SCHOLARSHIPS FUND.
Receipts.

Balance in Treasury, July 1, 1897	$ 166 12	
Interest	5 85	$ 171 97

Disbursements.

Vouchers	$ 9 20	
Balance in Treasury, June 30, 1898	162 77	$ 171 97

MUSIC HALL FUND.
Receipts.

Balance in Treasury, July 1, 1897	$ 1,044 86	
Interest	40 11	$ 1,084 97

Disbursements.

Balance in Treasury, June 30, 1898	1,084 97	$ 1,084 97

CLASS OF NINETY-SIX MEMORIAL.
Receipts.

Balance in Treasury, July 1, 1897	$ 18 92	
Interest	35	
Gifts	152 33	$ 171 60

Disbursements.

Vouchers	$ 145 08	
Transfer to Detroit Archæological Fund	7 52	
Balance in Treasury, June 30, 1898	19 00	$ 171 60

PARKE, DAVIS & CO. FUND.
Receipts.

Balance in Treasury, July 1, 1897	$ 9 62	
Interest	38	$ 10 00

Disbursements.

Balance in Treasury, June 30, 1898	10 00	$ 10 00

STEARNS PHARMACY FELLOWSHIP FUND.
Receipts.

Balance in Treasury, July 1, 1897	$ 77	
From Frederick Stearns & Co.	350 00	
Interest	01	$ 350 78

Disbursements.

Vouchers	$ 350 00	
Balance in Treasury, June 30, 1898	78	$ 350 78

LIBRARY OF EARLY CHRISTIAN LITERATURE.
Receipts.

Balance in Treasury, July 1, 1897	$ 26 90	
Interest	26	$ 27 16

Disbursements.

Vouchers	$ 20 66	
Balance in Treasury, June 30, 1898	6 50	$ 27 16

JAMES E. SCRIPPS LIBRARY FUND.
Receipts.
Balance in Treasury, July 1, 1897	$ 15	$	15

Disbursements.
Balance in Treasury, June 30, 1898	$ 15	$	15

FRIEZE MEMORIAL FUND.
Receipts.
From L. P. Jocelyn, Secretary, Collections from Graduates	$ 491 50		
Interest on Deposits	3 66	$	495 16

Disbursements.
Vouchers	$ 98 50		
Balance in Treasury, June 30, 1898	396 66	$	495 16

CLASS OF NINETY-EIGHT SCHOLARSHIP FUND.
Receipts.
From Marvin W. Turner, Collections	$ 253 30	$	253 30

Disbursements.
Balance in Treasury, June 30, 1898	$ 253 30	$	253 30

WILLIAMS FUND.
Receipts.
From J. M. Crosby, Treasurer	$ 793 14		
" " " "	14 00		
Interest	920 59		
Loans Paid	3,290 00		
Rent Collected	37 40	$	5,055 13

Disbursements.
Vouchers	$ 327 90		
Cash Balance in Treasury June 30, 1898	4,727 23	$	5,055 13

Invoice of Loans on Mortgages	$ 7,077 44	
" " Property	3,153 68	
	$10,231 12	

CLASS OF NINETY-SEVEN SCHOLARSHIP FUND.
Receipts.
Subscriptions	$ 134 00		
Interest	4 43	$	138 43

Disbursements.
Balance in Treasury, June 30, 1898	$ 138 43	$	138 43

MORRIS ALUMNI FUND.
Receipts.
Cash from Former Treasurer	$ 1,090 74		
Securities " "	1,150 00		
Interest on Deposits	5 09	$	2,245 83

Disbursements.
Balance in Treasury, June 30, 1898	2,245 83	$	2,245 83

D. M. FERRY BOTANICAL FUND.
Receipts.
From D. M. Ferry	$ 250 00	$	250 00

Disbursements.
Vouchers	$ 200 00		
Balance in Treasury, June 30, 1898	50 00	$	250 00

RECAPITULATION OF TRUST FUND BALANCES.

Fund		Type	Amount	Total
Women's Gymnasium Fund		Cash	$ 330 65	$ 330 65
Philo Parsons	"	"	96 21	96 21
Goethe	"	"	204 45	204 45
Elisha Jones Fellowship Fund		"	8 07	8 07
Coyl Collection	"	"	990 92	
" "	"	Securities	10,000 00	10,990 92
Buhl Law Library	"	Cash	2,262 53	2,262 53
Seth Harrison Scholarship "		"	5,663 59	
" " "		Securities	20,500 00	26,163 59
Ninety-Four Class Scholarship Fund		Cash	932 70	932 70
Ford-Messer	"	"	5,001 28	
"	"	Securities	10 000 00	15,001 28
Phillips Scholarships	"	Cash	162 77	162 77
Music Hall	"	"	1,084 97	1,084 97
Class of Ninety-Six Memorial	"	"	19 00	19 00
Parke, Davis & Co	"	"	10 00	10 00
Stearns Pharmacy Fellowship	"	"	78	78
Library of Early Christian Literature Fund		"	6 50	6 50
James E. Scripps Library	"	"	15	15
Frieze Memorial	"	"	396 66	396 66
Class of Ninety-Seven Scholarship	"	"	63 43	
" " "	"	Securities	75 00	138 43
Class of Ninety-Eight Scholarship	"	Cash	253 30	253 30
Williams	"	"	4,727 23	
"	"	Securities	7,077 44	
"	"	Property	3,153 68	14,958 35
Morris Alumni	"	Cash	1,095 83	
" "	"	Securities	1,150 00	2,245 83
D. M. Ferry Botanical	"	Cash	50 00	50 00
				$75,417 14

Aggregate:
    Cash . . . $23,461 02
    Securities . . 44,802 44
    Property at cost . 3,153 68—75,417 14

APPENDIX TO TREASURER'S REPORT.

1. Contributors to the Ninety-Four Class Scholarship Fund during the year 1897-1898:

B. L. Haug, Battle Creek .... $	5 00
F. A. Sager, Urbana, Ill	5 00
Delia S. Bailey, Detroit	5 00
Jamie Maud Blanchard, Los Angeles, Cal.	5 00
Oscar Greulich, Milwaukee, Wis	5 00
Delos F. Wilcox, New York, N. Y.	5 00
J. R. Nelson	5 00
Joseph Weare, Hamilton, Ont	5 00
R. W. Newton, Pittsburg, Pa	5 00
Geo. T. Tremble, Ellsworth, Kansas	5 00
D. F. Lyons, Fenton	5 00
S. A. Smith, Wilton, N. H.	3 00
B. H. Kroeze	2 00
W. M. Hamilton, Ann Arbor	5 00
A. A. Prentice, Kalamazoo	5 00
W. L. Whitney, Moline, Ill.	10 00
Clare Briggs, Battle Creek	5 00
A. J. Ladd, Shabbona, Ill	5 00
F. M. Elliott, Pontiac	10 30
Oscar Greulich, Milwaukee, Wis	5 00
Sara M. Riggs, Cedar Falls, Ia	5 00
F. L. Osenburg, Elsinore, Cal	21 80
Delos F. Wilcox, Cleveland, O	5 00
Anna Trainor, Iron River, ...	10 30
G. L. Davison, South Chicago, Ill.	26 80
F. W. Newton, Ann Arbor	3 00
A. R. Crittenden, Ypsilanti	5 00
D. O. Miller, Greenfield, Ohio	5 00
R. E. Jones, Webster City, Iowa	10 00
D. F. Lyons, Knapp, Wis	5 00
G. T. Tremble, Ellsworth, Kansas	5 00
Sarah M. Howard, Kalamazoo, ...	5 00
Joseph Weare, Hamilton, Ont.	5 00
E. C. Woodruff, Chicago, Ill	5 00
B. L. Haug, Battle Creek	5 00
Lucy E. Textor, Grand Haven, ...	5 00
Jesse C. Moore	15 90
A. J. Pieters, Washington, D. C.	10 00
W. W. Mills, Chicago, Ill.	4 00

Delia S. Bailey Cobb, Detroit	5	00
Jeannette Caldwell Mix, Chicago, Ill.	5	00
H. O. Chapoton	20	60
Total	$ 292	70

2. Contributors to the Women's Gymnasium from July 1, 1897, to June 30, 1898:

Hypatia Club, Detroit	$ 14	00
G. Teckor	5	00
Wixom Club, Caro	5	00
Women's Club, Detroit	35	00
A. Lovell	50	00
Saginaw Tourist Club	4	25
Mrs. E. J. Weeks, Jackson		50
Mrs. C. C. Bloomfield, Jackson	1	00
Mrs. J. M. Root, Jackson		75
Mrs. P. B. Loomis, Jackson	1	00
Women's Historical Club, Detroit	8	00
Women's Club, Saginaw	10	00
Catherine Coman, Wellesley College	1	00
Mrs. J. A. Watling	1	00
Women's League, Battle Creek	43	77
Women's Club, Battle Creek	10	70
Ladies' Tuesday Club, Saginaw	7	21
D. M. Ferry, Detroit	1,000	00
Women's Tourist Club, Jackson	1	00
Zetama Club, Detroit	5	00
Women's Club, Dowagiac	10	00
Wednesday History Club, Detroit	6	00
Alice Snyder, Collections	44	75
Detroit Review Club	12	75
Clio Club, Detroit	2	69
Ladies' Literary Club, Ypsilanti	10	00
Oratorical Association	17	75
Saginaw Reading Club	50	00
Study Club, Ypsilanti	5	00
Winter Club, Saginaw, E. S.	4	50
Mosaic Club, Jackson	3	82
Twentieth Century Club, Detroit	77	50
Mrs. H. Pilcher		50
Ypsilanti Ladies' Literary Society	5	25
Monday Club, St. Louis	7	15
Clara A. Avery	500	00
Women's Club, Howell	5	00
Twentieth Century Club, Detroit		50
Total	$1,967	34

UNIVERSITY OF MICHIGAN.

THE PRESIDENT'S REPORT

TO THE

BOARD OF REGENTS

FOR THE ACADEMIC YEAR

ENDING SEPTEMBER 30, 1899

AND THE

REPORT OF THE TREASURER

FOR THE FISCAL YEAR

ENDING JUNE 30, 1899

ANN ARBOR, MICH.:
PUBLISHED BY THE UNIVERSITY
1899

57317

THE COURIER OFFICE, PRINTERS AND BINDERS,
ANN ARBOR, MICHIGAN.

THE PRESIDENT'S REPORT
TO THE BOARD OF REGENTS.

I have the honor to present to you my annual report for the last academic year.

I regret that I have to announce the death by accident of one of the most useful and promising of our younger professors, George A. Hench, Ph.D. He was Professor of Germanic Languages and Literatures, and was temporarily charged with the supervision of the department of Romance Languages. He left Ann Arbor, after completing his work in the summer school, to seek in the White Mountains the rest of which he was much in need. Scarcely had he arrived at his destination when by a fall from his bicycle on a steep hill he received injuries which soon proved fatal. He died in a hospital at Boston, August 21.

Professor Hench was a graduate of Lafayette College. He pursued extensive studies in Germanic philology in the Johns Hopkins University and in German universities. Though only thirty-two years of age at the time of his death, he was already well known in this country and in Germany as one of the most accomplished of American scholars in the history and development of the German language. He was also deeply interested in the study of the best methods of teaching the German language and literature in American colleges, and was most efficient in the administration of his department. In his death the University has sustained a most serious loss.

The past year has been one of that earnest, quiet, and successful work in the University, which is perhaps the best indication of healthy life. No very important changes have been made in the methods or range of instruction. It is not easy to see how more could have been accomplished with the means at our command.

The attendance did not quite equal that of the preceding year. Not including the summer school it was 3,059, a shrinkage of 55 compared with 1897-98. Counting the attendance in the summer school of 1898, the figures stand 3,192 for the past year, 31 less than the preceding year. The falling off was in the Literary and Engineering Departments. There was a small gain in each of the professional schools, except in the Law Department, where the number in attendance was exactly the same as in 1897-98. That there is no permanent cause of decline is obvious from the fact that at the time of this writing the number in attendance is larger than in 1897-98.

It is interesting to observe that there was a small increase in the number of Michigan students last year, the attendance of these being 1,874, which is 11 more than in 1897-98. The small decline was in the attendance from other states. Still, the number of students from abroad, in spite of the discriminating fee against them, continues very large. It is 41 per cent. of the total number. Illinois sends 328; Ohio 199; Indiana 113; Pennsylvania 86; New York 85; Iowa 84; Missouri 57; Wisconsin 39; California 31. Every state but Delaware is represented. There are 44 students from foreign countries. Notwithstanding the improvement in colleges and universities in all sections of the country, this University continues to draw students from all parts of the land and from other lands.

The number of women in attendance was as follows:

Department of Literature, Science, and the Arts	594
Department of Medicine and Surgery	51
Department of Law	4
Department of Pharmacy	6
Homœopathic Medical College	9
College of Dental Surgery	10
Total	674

The previous year the attendance was 673. It is surprising to see how slight was the change in numbers. There was a gain of 6 in the Literary Department. The difference between the two years in the other departments was trifling and unimportant. The ratio between the number of men and the number of women in the University remains singularly steady. It varies but little from five to one.

In the Literary Department, however, 44 per cent. of the students are women. It may interest those who have feared that women would not desire the old collegiate courses to observe that a trifle more than 50 per cent. of those who graduated last year with the degree of Bachelor of Arts (for which work in both Latin and Greek is required), and of those who graduated with the degree of Bachelor of Philosophy (for which work in Latin is required) were women. On the other hand, of the fifty-three who graduated with the degree of Bachelor of Letters, for which neither Latin nor Greek is asked, only twenty-two were women. Of the twenty-one who earned the Master's degree, six were women. Of the four who took the degree of Doctor of Philosophy, one was a woman.

The large majority of women, who come to the University, are preparing themselves for teaching, though there is an increase in the number of those who are simply seeking culture without the intention of entering the ranks of the teachers. Few factors have been more instrumental in the improvement in our public schools, especially in the west, than the opening to women of the doors of the colleges and universities, in which men are trained. Both they and the public have come to have confidence in their fitness to give instruction in secondary schools. When we remember how largely the teaching in our high schools is given by women, the importance of this fact is apparent to us all.

While the primary duty of the University as at present organized is and must continue to be the instruction of undergraduates, one who watches the development of education in this country must be continually more and more impressed with the desirableness and the necessity of furnishing more advanced instruction to the many aspiring students who wish to carry their studies beyond the undergraduate curriculum. I have so fully presented the subject in previous reports that I do not need to dwell upon it now. I will simply say that no endowment would just now be of more service than one which should provide us with the means for conducting graduate work on a more liberal scale than is possible to us now or for establishing a considerable number of fellowships. The Literary Faculty have during the year made a complete study of the subject of fellowships, and have laid before you a most cogent statement, in which the disadvantages, under which we are laboring from the lack of fellowships, and the great importance of securing them, are clearly set forth. A considerable number of copies of this statement have been circulated, and we trust that the attention of our friends will be directed to it.

At the Observatory Professor Hall has continued his observations of meridian zenith distances of Polaris with the idea of obtaining the variation of latitude at Ann Arbor, as well as the aberration constant. The measures from May, 1898, to July 1899, have been reduced roughly and furnish the value $20''.58$ for the aberration constant, rather large apparently, but the same as those obtained lately by different methods at the observatories of the University of Pennsylvania and the Cape of Good Hope. The observations are to be continued for another year.

For several years the Board have desired to make provision for instruction in marine architecture, but for want of means have been unable to do so. The great development of ship building on our lakes, and the still greater development promised by our present ability to compete with European builders of steel ships, seem to lay on us a command to train young men for the profession of constructors of vessels. Indeed, not a few of our engineer graduates have already been called into important service in our great shipyards. But with special training for the work, a useful career must be open to many men who have aptitude for the profession of designing ships. It is therefore with great satisfaction that the Board has found itself able to provide for a special teacher in marine architecture to be added to our engineering corps. It is hoped that during the year such an addition may be made to our force, and a new service rendered by the University to the State of Michigan.

During the past year we have made attendance on the instruction in gymnastics compulsory on the first year's students of the Literary and Engineering Departments. We found that although we had large and well appointed gymnasiums for both sexes and good instructors, a considerable number of the new students took no advantage of the opportunities offered for physical training. Many of these were persons who most needed to profit by them. It is believed that by a year's training most of the students will have acquired a taste for gymnastic work, or will have learned to appreciate the value of systematic and regular exercise. The absorbing interest in athletic contests on the ball ground by no means leads the great mass of students to secure the exercise which is essential to the preservation of health and to the best success in study.

The Summer School, which has heretofore been conducted by permission of the Board under a voluntary organization of such members of the literary and law faculties as chose to teach, was during the past year, so far as the Literary and Engineering Departments were concerned, placed on a different basis. The Board assumed the direct charge of the school and appointed the instructors. This action was taken at the request of the Literary Faculty. The pecuniary risk, if any, was thus assumed by the Board. Some advantages were gained by this change, and the fees received exceeded by a small sum the expense incurred. The number in attendance was as follows: Literary and Engineering Departments, 219; Law Department, 45; total, 264. Of the 45 in the Law Department 27 have remained to take up the regular work.

The Summer School seems to have become a necessary adjunct to most of the principal colleges and universities and to many normal schools. It is chiefly resorted to by teachers, who wish to prepare themselves for some special work, though the collegiate and normal students furnish a considerable contingent. Of its utility, both to those who attend them, and to the institutions that maintain them, there can be no doubt. The summer vacation of school and college in this country is so long that one-half of it can be given to study by many teachers without serious harm. Access to college libraries, and to laboratories, where the best methods of teaching are found, and association with inspiring teachers for a few weeks, refresh and stimulate them and prepare them to return to their work with new zeal and with better outfit for their duties. On the other hand the college makes a distinct gain by establishing during this summer residence of teachers a closer relation with them and by making apparent to them the advantages which their pupils may find in entering on collegiate work. Everything which draws our schools and the University closer to each other, and enables each to gain a better understanding of the other, is a positive advantage to education in general. I therefore deem it wise for the Board to do whatever is practicable to promote the interests of our Summer School. A subject which deserves careful consideration is whether we can not safely make some reduction in the fees. The sum now asked is rather a heavy tax on many teachers, who receive only very modest salaries. There is good reason to believe that a reduction of one-third in the fees would so largely increase our numbers that possibly our total receipts would not be diminished. If this should prove to be the fact, we should be making the school much more useful by a wider diffusion of its blessings. As our aim is to reach and help as many as possible by the school, I trust the Board may give careful consideration to the question whether the fees may not be safely reduced. But this result should not be sought by any diminution in the compensation of the instructors. Indeed it is to be hoped that such increase can be offered as will induce more of the older professors to take part in the instruction. In that case, a larger number of graduate students would probably attend the summer session. The large attendance of graduates at the summer term of the universities which induce the leading professors to teach in them indicates a real demand on their part for such instruction.

The Department of Medicine and Surgery has about as many students as with its present buildings it can well accommodate. It holds its high standard of work with much strenuousness. But it greatly needs more and better rooms. The methods of medical instruction have been almost totally changed in recent years. Teaching by means of lectures has largely given way to teaching by laboratory methods, to the great advantage of the students. This University was, I think, the very first to provide laboratory instruction in chemistry for its Medical Department. For its other medical laboratories, except the bacteriological. it has been obliged to make use of rooms not originally constructed for the purpose. Some of them indeed were very ill-suited for the work. It is, therefore, with much gratification that we find ourselves, as we hope, about to be provided with the means of beginning the erection of a building specially adapted for the laboratories of the department, and for the biological and botanical laboratories of the Literary Department, which are now very poorly housed in rooms originally constructed for other purposes.

It is gratifying to observe that our graduates are much sought as internes in hospitals and asylums. Twenty-four members of the last graduating class are thus placed in thirteen prominent institutions.

A valuable connection with the four Michigan asylums for the insane has been established. In each of them one of our recent graduates has been appointed as resident pathologist and assistant to a chief pathologist, who has a central laboratory here. Monthly meetings of his staff are held. The result cannot but be beneficial to the state and to the University.

The number of patients treated in the University Hospital continues to increase. From July 1, 1898, to July 1, 1899, the number admitted was 1788. The great majority of these patients were persons who earn their living by manual toil. For instance there were, farmers, 293; farmers' wives, 103; housewives, 325; laborers, 73; domestics, 35. Not a few of these were sent by the counties, and were cured of ailments which had made them a public charge, and were thus made capable of self-support. It should be understood that in both our hospitals medical and surgical aid is furnished gratuitously. A moderate charge is made for the board of the patient while he is receiving treatment.

The Law Department finds its convenience admirably subserved by its new and spacious building. Its beautiful, well lighted, and well ventilated library room is in striking and welcome contrast to the old overcrowded room. The lecture rooms are in every way attractive and commodious. In fact, no other department is now so well provided with needed accommodations. Its work is so efficient and so well known that in spite of the multiplication of law schools in the west its members continue to increase, and it attracts students from all parts of the country. The building, spacious as it is, is by no means too large. But the staff of instruction will probably have to be enlarged.

The Department of Pharmacy so commends itself by its genuine work to the profession which it represents, that it enjoys the favor of prominent pharmacists and the Committee of Revision and Publication of the Pharmacopœia of the United States, who have furnished grants and fellowships for special research by its advanced students.

Certain new industries which have been recently introduced into Michigan are making large demands on the resources of our chemical laboratory. I refer to the alkali plants, the manufacture of Portland cement, and the beet sugar factories. A large amount of capital has been invested in them, and they are all calling for thoroughly trained young men. The natural advantages in this state for all these industries are found to be unsurpassed. Our chemical staff has deemed it their duty to furnish whatever aid science has to offer to those who are conducting them. Professor E. D. Campbell has employed a force of advanced students during the year in investigating the Michigan marls and clays and in determining the best method of handling them. Dr. Freer has given to farmers' clubs the benefits of German scientific investigation on the beet sugar problem, and the manufacturing companies are consulting others of our teachers who have studied the processes of manufacture in Germany for guidance. Courses of instruction on the subject are open to students. Some of our graduates are already holding important posts in these new industries.

Through the generosity of Doctor Brush, an alumnus of the University, we are soon to have a liquid air plant in the laboratory of Dr. Freer, and the use of it is expected to yield most interesting and important scientific results.

The increasing demands which are made upon the chemical laboratory are calling loudly for an enlargement of it and for ample provision for lecture rooms.

The Homœopathic Medical College, in spite of all the difficulties which beset it, has had a fairly successful year.

The attendance, when compared with that of other homœopathic schools which maintain standards comparable to ours, if not entirely satisfactory, is not discouraging. It is clear that some of the adherents of homœopathy have over-estimated the number of persons who desire to prepare themselves for homœopathic practice. The entire number reported a year ago in twenty American homœopathic colleges, including all the large ones, was only 1,740. Some of them had as few as eighteen students. Our college, after all the attacks made upon it, stood eighth in size.

In the Homœopathic Hospital 1,218 patients were treated in the public clinics. Of these 1,113 were from Michigan, and the largest number from any one class of persons came from the farm. According to the report of the Dean, the registration of patients for the year equals that for the five years from 1889-90 to 1893-94.

The Dental Department has as usual had as many students as it could accommodate, and is steadily growing. It has received official information that its diploma is recognized in Holland, as it is in some other European countries. The Faculty are giving careful consideration to the question whether it is not expedient to extend the course to four years. The variety and amount of work required to meet the standard of training desired by the Faculty are so great that in the opinion of some three years hardly suffice. Apparently we must soon choose between raising the requirements for admission, the extension of the course, the refusal of applicants for admission, and the enlargement of our building. It seems impossible to find proper accommodations for larger classes in the present quarters.

No less than 8,000 persons were treated in the dental clinics of the year.

During the year our libraries have been increased by the addition of 10,254 volumes. The total number of bound volumes in all our libraries on June 30 last was 133,206. The recorded circulation of books was 145,565. The unrecorded circulation is believed to be greater.

The addition to the library building, which has doubled the space available for the storage of books, affords a welcome and much needed relief in the administration of the library. But we still greatly need additional seminary rooms in connection with the building. The alternative seems to be the distribution of department libraries in the lecture rooms of various buildings. There are serious objections to distribution among all departments. The principal one is, perhaps, the danger from fire.

The enlargement of the library building has furnished us an additional room for our gallery of art and has enabled us to display the collections more advantageously. We are still waiting for the generous benefactor who will erect for us a suitable art gallery. The rooms now occupied by our collections could be most wisely used for the purposes of the library or for seminary rooms.

All visitors observe with pleasure the improvement in the appearance of our campus. The care which the superintendent of buildings and grounds has given to it for the last few years, with the assistance of the professors in the botanical departments, has been well rewarded by the results. It is gratifying to observe that the plants and shrubs, though within reach of the public, are so seldom disturbed or robbed of their flowers, even by children, who have free access to the grounds.

The occupancy of so large a part of the campus by our present buildings and by those which are soon to be added compels attention to the importance of securing lots adjacent to our present property. It is much to be regretted that purchases were not made years ago. But no one then foresaw the present development of the University. We should avoid the mistakes of our predecessors, and as soon as our means will permit us, should procure suitable property near us. We should act with a wise regard to the future needs of the institution.

In recent years there has been a great revival of interest in the art of public debate in several universities, and especially in this University. Formerly the debating or so-called literary societies of the leading American colleges were a conspicuous feature in their life. Many men, who became eminent as orators or debaters, looked back on the training they received in those societies as the most valuable help they obtained in their undergraduate experience. But about thirty years ago, whether, as many think, owing to the rise of secret fraternities among students or to some other cause, the interest in the old debating societies began to decline. In some colleges the societies expired, and valuable libraries which they had built up were scattered or sold. It became the fashion to speak slightingly of the art of public speaking. At one commencement of a large university the speeches of the graduating class were read from manuscript.

But it soon became clear that the colleges which were neglecting the art of public speaking were making a grave mistake. For the time had not come when the public did not desire to listen to the man who has something interesting to say, and has the faculty of saying it well. It is safe to say the time never will come, when men will be indifferent to good utterance of good thought. There arose among students themselves a healthy reaction against the neglect of practice in effective speaking, whether in formal discourse or in extemporaneous debate. It has resulted in the custom of competitive trials in the preparation and delivery of set speeches or in debates on questions of current interest. Sometimes these trials are between students in the same institution and sometimes between students of different institutions. These contests have greatly deepened the interest in public speaking in most of our universities. Incidentally they have served to correct the false impression of many that athletic contests absorb the entire attention of the American student, to the exclusion of interest in any kind of intellectual achievements. I am happy to say that this University has made an honorable record in both the oratorical and the debating contests, in which our students have been engaged. In seven of the nine oratorical contests with western institutions its representatives have taken the first place. Of nine debates with the University of Wisconsin, the Northwestern University, the University of Chicago, and the University of Pennsylvania it has been successful in six.

Eminent citizens of our country are manifesting a desire that some of our stronger universities should provide courses of instruction more especially fitted than those which are now established to prepare men, so far as education can prepare them, for engaging in international commerce, for responsible positions in banking and other financial pursuits, for careers in our consular and diplomatic service. The primary object which the fathers had in view in founding the first New England colleges, was the education of the ministry. Then it was perceived that the college training was a good preparation for the study of law and medicine. It was much later that it was seen to be of service to men who were to follow a business life. But now a considerable percentage of the men who go to college expect to take up some business pursuit. Many of them ultimately come to posts of great responsibility in the conduct of industrial or commercial enterprises. There is a general and apparently a justifiable expectation that a large expansion awaits our commerce. We are able to produce under conditions which enable us to export freely, and to compete successfully with other great nations in the markets of the world. We should rear a generation of merchants and bankers equipped by intelligence and training to be the peers of any in the world. They need not only the technical training of the counting room, but also a familiarity with the laws of international trade and exchange, and with the languages and economic conditions of the principal commercial nations of the world.

Furthermore, it is generally recognized that our consular system needs much improvement, if it is to render us the service it ought in promoting our foreign trade. It is admitted that we ought to secure special training for the men who are to hold the consular office, and even for those who are to become interpreters at our consulates and legations and embassies.

Of course every strong university now gives a portion of the instruction required for special preparation in the pursuits named. But most probably all American universities would have to add, or at any rate enlarge, work in commercial geography or commercial history, pay attention to some departments of finance and political economy not now usually treated, and give more time than is now devoted to international law, both private and public, and to the mastery of at least German, French, and Spanish for commercial intercourse.

For us to meet those requirements would call for some additions to our teaching force. But such enlargement of our work would render a most valuable service to our country. And the desire for something of the kind is becoming so strong that probably some public spirited merchants or manufacturers may be willing to endow chairs. I regard it my duty to call your attention and that of the public to the subject. I trust that we may at no distant day be able to give the instruction whose general character I have indicated.

I conclude this report by expressing our gratitude for the considerate treatment accorded us by the Legislature at its session last winter. Almost unanimously it raised the appropriation for our aid from the tax of one-sixth of a mill to that of one-fourth of a mill. It thus increased our annual income by about $92,500. This addition to our resources was imperatively needed to keep the University in the position it had so long held among the strong universities of the land. With our great number of students we were in sore need of some new and commodious buildings and also of additions to our faculties. The institution has been maintained with the utmost economy, at an expense not exceeding one-half or two-thirds of that of even smaller universities. The hearty support given us by the Legislature furnishes us the gratifying evidence that the commonwealth which we are striving to serve believes that we are really conferring substantial benefits upon her and upon the nation. That is our sufficient reward and the stimulus to renewed energy in the future.

JAMES B. ANGELL.

APPENDICES.

APPENDIX A.

APPOINTMENTS, REAPPOINTMENTS, RESIGNATIONS, ETC., DURING THE YEAR ENDING SEPTEMBER 30, 1899.

Resignations:

At the meeting of October 18, 1898, the resignation of John T. Faig, M.E., Instructor in Mechanical Engineering, was reported.

At the meeting of April 25, 1899, the resignation of Clarence G. Taylor, B.S., M.E., Professor of Mechanical Practice and Superintendent of Shops, was presented and accepted.

At the meeting of June 20, 1899, the resignation of Frank R. Lillie, Ph.D., Instructor in Zoology, was presented and accepted.

Leaves of Absence:

At the meeting of January 17, 1899, Professor Henry S. Carhart, LL.D., was granted leave of absence for the academic year 1899-1900.

At the meeting of February 16, 1899, Assistant Professor Joseph H. Drake, A.B., was granted leave of absence from the spring recess until the end of the current academic year; Instructor Victor E. François was granted leave of absence for the academic year 1899-1900; and Instructor Penoyer L. Sherman, Ph.D., was granted leave of absence for the remainder of the current academic year.

At the meeting of March 29, 1899, Professor Albert A. Stanley, A.M., was granted leave of absence for the remainder of the current academic year; the leave of absence previously granted to Assistant Professor Dean C. Worcester, A.B., was extended to the first of October, 1899; and Instructor John R. Allen, M. E., was granted leave of absence for the remainder of the current academic year.

At the meeting of May 11, 1899, Professor Martin L. D'Ooge, LL. D., was granted leave of absence for the academic year 1899-1900.

At the meeting of July 26, 1899, the leave of absence previously granted to Assistant Professor Dean C. Worcester, A.B., was still further extended.

Non-resident Lecturers in the Department of Medicine and Surgery were appointed at the meeting of July 11, 1899, as follows:

>William M. Edwards, M.D., Mental Diseases.
>Edmund A. Christian, A.B., M.D., Mental Diseases.
>James D. Munson, M.D., Mental Diseases.
>Henry B. Baker, A.M., M.D., Administration of Health Laws.
>Colonel B. Burr, M.D., Mental Diseases.

Non-resident Lecturers in the Department of Law were appointed as follows:

>*At the meeting of July 26, 1899.*
>
>John B. Clayberg, LL.B., Mining Law.
>Melville M. Bigelow, Ph.D., Insurance.
>Henry H. Swan, A.M., Admiralty.
>Frank F. Reed, A.B., Copyright Law.
>Albert H. Walker, LL.B., Patent Law.
>
>*At the meeting of August 12, 1899.*
>
>Dallas Boudeman, M.S., Michigan Statutes.

Non-resident Lecturers in the Homœopathic Medical College were appointed as follows:

>*At the meeting of October 18, 1898.*
>
>Oscar R. Long, M.D., Mental and Nervous Diseases.
>
>*At the meeting of August 12, 1899.*
>
>Oscar R. Long, M.D., Mental Diseases.
>William A. Polglase, M.D., Theory and Practice of Medicine and Nervous Diseases.

At the meeting of July 26, 1899, Special Lecturers in the Department of Law were appointed as follows:

>Victor C. Vaughan, Ph.D., Sc.D., M.D., Toxicology in its Legal Relations.
>Henry C. Adams, Ph.D., The Railroad Problem.
>Andrew C. McLaughlin, A.M., LL.B., Constitutional Law and Constitutional History.
>Richard Hudson, A.M., Comparative Constitutional Law.
>Joseph H. Drake, A.B., Roman Law.
>William J. Herdman, M.D., LL.D., Neurology, Electrology, and Railway Injuries.

The following lists comprise other appointments, reappointments, and changes of title of members of the Faculties. Junior Professors and Assistant Professors were appointed for three years, and Instructors for one year, unless a different term is mentioned. The names of assistants and of others appointed to positions of lower grade than Instructor are not here included.

At the meeting of October 18, 1898.

The tittle of Professor William J. Herdman, M.D. LL.D., was changed to stand Professor of Diseases of the Mind and Nervous Diseases, and Electrotherapeutics.

Appointments were made as follows:

George L. Grimes, B.S., Instructor in Mechanical Engineering.
Carl V. Tower, Ph.D., Instructor in Philosophy.
Alice G. Snyder, Instructor in the Women's Gymnasium.
Walter B. Pillsbury, Ph.D., Instructor in Psychology.
Earle W. Dow, A.B., Instructor in History for three years.
Joseph H. Drake, A.B., Assistant Professor of Latin.
Dean C. Worcester, A.B., Assistant Professor of Biology and Curator of the Museum.
G. Carl Huber, M.D., Assistant Professor of Anatomy and Director of the Histological Laboratory.
Alviso B. Stevens, Ph.C., Assistant Professor of Pharmacy.
Ernst H. Mensel, Ph.D., Instructor in German for three years.
Warren W. Florer, Ph.D., Instructor in German.
Edwin C. Roedder, Ph.D., Instructor in German.
John E. Lautner, M.L., Instructor in German.

At the meeting of December 21, 1898.

John E. Granrud, Ph.D., was appointed Instructor in Latin.

At the meeting of February 16, 1899.

Clifton H. Briggs, M.S., was appointed Instructor in General Chemistry during the absence of Instructor P. L. Sherman.

At the meeting of March 29, 1899.

Hermann A. Zeitz was appointed Instructor in Music for the remainder of the year.

At the meeting of June 20, 1899.

The following appointments were made:

Allen S. Whitney, A.B., Junior Professor of the Science and Art of Teaching, and Inspector of Schools.

Herbert S. Jennings, Ph.D., Instructor in Zoology.
Thomas E. Oliver, Ph.D., Instructor in French.
Herbert F. DeCou, A.M., Instructor in Greek.
Christian F. Gauss, A.M., Instructor in French.

At the meeting of July 11, 1899.

The following appointments were made:

Keene Fitzpatrick, Director of the Gymnasium for one year.
Fred L. Ingraham, LL.B., Instructor in Elocution.
G. Carl Huber, M.D., Junior Professor of Anatomy, and Director of the Histological Laboratory.
John O. Reed, Ph.D., Junior Professor of Physics.
Alfred H. Lloyd, Ph.D., Junior Professor of Philosophy.
Ernst H. Mensel, Ph.D., Assistant Professor of German.
Earle W. Dow, A.B., Assistant Professor of History.
Charles H. Cooley, Ph.D., Assistant Professor of Sociology.
Aldred S. Warthin, Ph.D., M.D., Assistant Professor of Pathology.
Louis P. Hall, D.D.S., Assistant Professor of Dental Anatomy, Operative Technique, and Clinical Operative Dentistry.
Moses Gomberg, Sc.D., Assistant Professor of Organic Chemistry.
John R. Allen, M.E., Assistant Professor of Mechanical Engineering for one year.
Benjamin P. Bourland, Ph.D., Assistant Professor of French for one year.
Archibald Campbell, Ph.M., Instructor in Organic Chemistry.
Fred M. Taylor, Ph.D., Junior Professor of Political Economy.
Fred N. Scott, Ph.D., Junior Professor of Rhetoric.
Alexander Ziwet, C.E., Junior Professor of Mathematics.
Joseph L. Markley, Ph.D., Assistant Professor of Mathematics.
Max Winkler, Ph.D., Assistant Professor of German.
Moritz Levi, A.B., Assistant Professor of French.
Julius O. Schlotterbeck, Ph.C., Ph.D., Assistant Professor of Pharmacognosy and Botany.
Clarence G. Wrentmore, M.S., Instructor in Descriptive Geometry and Drawing for three years.
Karl E. Guthe, Ph.D., Instructor in Physics for three years.
Tobias Diekhoff, Ph.D., Instructor in German for three years.
Clarence L. Meader, A.B., Instructor in Latin for three years.
James W. Glover, Ph.D., Instructor in Mathematics for three years.
Louis A. Strauss, Ph.M., Instructor in English for three years.
Edwin C. Goddard, Ph.B., LL.B., Instructor in Mathematics for three years.
Herbert J. Goulding, B.S., Instructor in Descriptive Geometry for three years.
William H. Wait, Ph.D., Instructor in Greek, Latin, and Sanskrit.
Walter B. Pillsbury, Ph.D., Instructor in Psychology.

Warren W. Florer, Ph.D., Instructor in German.
Edwin C. Roedder, Ph.D., Instructor in German.
Alfred H. White, A.B., Instructor in Chemical Technology.
Carroll D. Jones, E.E., Instructor in Electrical Engineering.
John S. P. Tatlock, A.M., Instructor in English.
Fanny E. Langdon, M.S., Instructor in Zoology.
Alice G. Snyder, Instructor in the Women's Gymnasium.
Wilbur C. Abbott, B.Litt., Instructor in History.
S. Lawrence Bigelow, Ph.D., Instructor in General Chemistry.
James B. Pollock, Sc.D., Instructor in Botany.
Ewald Boucke, Ph.D., Instructor in German.
Augustus Trowbridge, Ph.D., Instructor in Physics.
Colman D. Frank, Ph.B., Instructor in French.
William H. Butts, A.M., Instructor in Mathematics.
Henry A. Sanders, Ph.D., Instructor in Latin.
Shirley W. Smith, B.L., Instructor in English.
Hugo P. Thieme, Ph.D., Instructor in French.
George L. Grimes, B.S., Instructor in Mechanical Engineering.
Carl V. Tower, Ph.D., Instructor in Philosophy.
William L. Miggett, B.S., Superintendent of Engineering Shops for one year.
Simon M. Yutzy, M.D., Instructor in Anatomy.
Benjamin F. Bailey, B.S., Instructor in Electrotherapeutics.
Herbert H. Waite, A.B., Instructor in Bacteriology.
James R. Arneill, A.B., M.D., Instructor in Clinical Medicine.
Robert C. Bourland, A.B., M.D., Instructor in Anatomy.
Professor Victor H. Lane, C.E., LL.B., was appointed Law Librarian.

At the meeting of July 26, 1899.

The following appointments were made:

John W. Dwyer, LL.M., Instructor in Law.
Albert J. Farrah, LL.B., Instructor in Law.
John R. Rood, LL.B., Instructor in Law.

At the meeting of August 12, 1899.

The following appointments were made:

Eugene C. Sullivan, Ph.D., Instructor in Analytical Chemistry.
Julia W. Snow, Ph.D., Instructor in Botany.

At the meeting of September 21, 1899.

The Chair of Obstetrics and Diseases of Women in the Department of Medicine and Surgery was abolished, and Professor James N. Martin, Ph.M., M.D., was appointed to the Bates Professorship of the Diseases of Women and Children.

The following appointments were made:

Henry C. Anderson, M.E., Instructor in Mechanical Engineering.
Arthur L. Cross, Ph.D., Instructor in History.
George A. Hulett, Ph.D., Instructor in General Chemistry.
Sammel J. Holmes, Ph.D., Instructor in Zoology.
Jonathan A. C. Hildner, Ph.D., Instructor in German.
John Dieterle, A.B., Instructor in German.

APPENDIX B.

The following degrees were conferred during the year October 1, 1898, to September 30, 1899:

ORDINARY DEGREES.

Bachelor of Letters	54
Bachelor of Science (in Biology)	6
Bachelor of Science (in Chemistry)	8
Bachelor of Science (in Electrical Engineering)	23
Bachelor of Science (in Mechanical Engineering)	17
Bachelor of Science (in Civil Engineering)	9
Bachelor of Science	39
Bachelor of Philosophy	64
Bachelor of Arts	65
Civil Engineer	3
Master of Letters	2
Master of Science	5
Master of Science (Department of Engineering)	1
Master of Philosophy	1
Master of Arts	14
Doctor of Philosophy	4
Doctor of Medicine (Department of Medicine and Surgery)	89
Bachelor of Laws	224
Master of Laws	2
Pharmaceutical Chemist	22
Doctor of Medicine (Homœopathic Medical College)	8
Doctor of Dental Surgery	61
Doctor of Dental Science	2
	723

HONORARY DEGREES.

Master of Science	2
Master of Arts	1
Doctor of Laws	1
Total	727

APPENDIX C.
SUMMARY OF STUDENTS.

DEPARTMENT OF LITERATURE, SCIENCE, AND THE ARTS.

Holder of Fellowship		1
Resident Graduates		70
Candidates for an Advanced Degree, enrolled in the Department of Medicine and Surgery		2
Graduates Studying *in Absentia*		2
Undergraduates:		
Candidates for a Degree	1065	
Students not Candidates for a Degree	145	—1285

DEPARTMENT OF ENGINEERING.

Resident Graduates		2
Graduates Studying *in Absentia*		3
Undergraduates	240	— 245

DEPARTMENT OF MEDICINE AND SURGERY.

Resident Graduates		2
Fourth Year Students		88
Third Year Students		102
Second Year Students		86
First Year Students		138
Special Students		2
Students enrolled in other Departments of the University:		
Fourth Year Student in Medicine	1	
Third Year Students in Medicine	4	
Second Year Students in Medicine	8	
First Year Students in Medicine	14	— 445

DEPARTMENT OF LAW.

Resident Graduates		3
Third Year Students		233
Second Year Students		229
First Year Students		244
Special Students		29
Students enrolled in the Department of Literature, Science, and the Arts	27	— 765

SCHOOL OF PHARMACY.

Holders of Fellowships and of Grants for Research		2
Resident Graduates		7
Undergraduates:		
Candidates for a Degree	59	
Students not Candidates for a Degree	13	— 81

HOMŒOPATHIC MEDICAL COLLEGE.

Resident Graduates	11
Fourth Year Students	9
Third Year Students	14
Second Year Students	19
First Year Students	13
Students enrolled in the Department of Literature, Science, and the arts	2— 68

COLLEGE OF DENTAL SURGERY.

Resident Graduates	3
Seniors	69
Juniors	76
Freshmen	86— 234
	3123
Deduct for names counted more than once	64
Total, exclusive of Summer Schools	3059

SUMMER SCHOOLS OF 1899.

In Department of Literature, Science, and the Arts	219
In Department of Law	45—264
Deduct for students enrolled in 1898–9 in some department of the University	100—154
Grand total	3213

APPENDIX D.

Examinations for higher degrees were held as follows during the year 1898–99:

IN THE DEPARTMENT OF LITERATURE, SCIENCE, AND THE ARTS.

CANDIDATES FOR THE DEGREE OF DOCTOR OF PHILOSOPHY.

EDWIN DeBARR, Ph.B., 1892.

THESIS.—The Decomposition of Alpha, Beta, and Gamma Halogen-substituted Acids by Water. Subjects for examination: Major.—General Chemistry. Minors.—Organic Chemistry. Physical Chemistry.

JOHN BLACK JOHNSTON, Ph.B., 1893.

THESIS.—The Structure of the Brain of Acipenser Rubicundns. Subjects for examination: Major.—Zoology. Minors.—Physiological Psychology. Physiology.

ELLA ADELAIDE KNAPP, A.B., *Kalamazoo College*, 1888, A.M., 1890.

THESIS.—A Study of Thoreau. Subjects for examination: Major.—English Literature. Minors.—Old English. American History.

PAUL INGOLD MURRILL, B.S., *State College of Kentucky*, 1895, M.S., *ibid*, 1896.

THESIS.—Halides and Perhalides of the Picolines. Subjects for examination: Major.—Organic Chemistry. Minors.—General Chemistry. Bacteriology.

CANDIDATES FOR THE DEGREE OF MASTER OF ARTS.

GEORGE HENRY ALLEN, A.B., 1898.

Subjects for examination: Major.—History. Minors.—Greek. Latin.

LEWIS CLINTON CARSON, A.B., 1892, A.B., *Harvard*, 1893.

THESIS.—The Relation of the First and the Second Editions of Kant's Critique of Pure Reason. Subjects for examination: Major.—History of Philosophy. Minors.—Philosophy of Religion. Sociology.

CHRISTIAN FREDERICK GAUSS, A.B., 1898.

Subjects for examination: Major.—French. Minors.—Spanish. Aesthetics.

WALTER DAVID HADZSITS, A.B., 1898.

Subjects for examination: Major.—Latin. Minors.—Greek. Sanskrit.

ALICE SARAH HUSSEY, A.B., *Vassar College*, 1894.

Subjects for examination: Major.—Rhetoric. Minors.—Aesthetics. English Literature.

LAMBERT LINCOLN JACKSON, A.B., 1897.

Subjects for examination: Major.—Mathematics. Minors.—Mechanics. Pedagogy.

STEPHEN HERBERT LANGDON, A.B., 1898.

Subjects for examination: Major.—Hebrew. Minors.—Assyrian. Greek.

CLEMENT CHARLES LEMON, A.B., *Indiana University*, 1894.

THESIS.—Death of Plants by Asphyxia. Subjects for examination: Major.—Botany. Minors.—Vegetable Morphology. Zoology.

JOHN HANCOCK McCLELLAN, A.B., 1897.

THESIS.—The Development of the Pronephros of Amia. Subjects for examination: Major.—Vertebrate Zoology. Minors.—Experimental Morphology. Physiology.

NORMAN KING McINNIS, A.B., 1898.

Subjects for examination: Major.—English Literature. Minors.—Rhetoric. Aesthetics.

MAY CECIL RYAN, A.B., 1895.
Subjects for examination: Major.—Latin. Minors.—Greek. Roman Political Antiquities.

HENRY ORMAL SEVERANCE, A.B., 1897.
THESIS.—A Study of Hamlet. Subjects for examination: Major.—English Literature. Minors.—Bibliography. Pedagogy.

HUDSON SHELDON, A.B., 1891.
Subjects for examination: Major.—General Chemistry. Minors.—Physics. Mathematics.

LOURA BAYNE WOODRUFF, A.B., 1895.
Subjects for examination: Major.—Greek. Minors.—Latin. German.

CANDIDATE FOR THE DEGREE OF MASTER OF PHILOSOPHY.
OSCAR REIFF MYERS, Ph.B., 1898.
Subjects for examination: Major.—Rhetoric. Minors.—Pedagogy. English Literature.

CANDIDATES FOR THE DEGREE OF MASTER OF SCIENCE.
LEWIS OLIVER ATHERTON, B.S., *Albion College*, 1895.
THESIS.—The Epidermis of Tubifex. Subjects for examination: Major.—Zoology. Minors.—Experimental Morphology. Botany.

HENRY WILLIAM HESS, B.S., 1898.
Subjects for examination: Major.—Analytical Chemistry. Minors.—Organic Chemistry. Economic Geology.

WILLIAM HUGH HESS, B.S., 1898.
Subjects for examination: Major.—Organic Chemistry. Minors.—Analytical Chemistry. Geology.

FRANCES HINKLEY, B.S., 1890.
Subjects for examination: Major.—Organic Chemistry. Minors.—Analytical Chemistry. International Law.

CANDIDATES FOR THE DEGREE OF MASTER OF LETTERS.
ANNA MARY BAKER, B.L., 1898.
Subjects for examination: Major.—American History. Minors.—Rhetoric. Political Economy.

HANNAH EMILY KEITH, B.L., 1898.
Subjects for examination: Major.—American History. Minors.—German. Political Economy.

IN THE DEPARTMENT OF ENGINEERING.
MASTER OF SCIENCE.
FRANK NOBLE SAVAGE, B.S.
CIVIL ENGINEER.
JULIUS KAHN, B.S.
GARDNER STEWART WILLIAMS, B.S.
SILAS HIRAM WOODARD, B.S.

IN THE DEPARTMENT OF LAW.

THE DEGREE OF MASTER OF LAWS.

COLIN PERCY CAMPBELL, LL.B.
GEORGE KINGSLEY, Jr., LL.B.

IN THE DEPARTMENT OF DENTAL SURGERY.

THE DEGREE OF DOCTOR OF DENTAL SCIENCE.

JAMES ROY DAVIS, D.D.S.
OLIVER WILSON WHITE, D.D.S.

APPENDIX E.

THE ONE-FOURTH MILL ACT.

AN ACT to amend section one of act number thirty-two of the public acts of eighteen hundred seventy-three, entitled "An act to extend aid to the University of Michigan, and to repeal an act entitled 'An act to extend aid to the University of Michigan, approved March fifteenth, eighteen hundred sixty-seven, being sections three thousand five hundred six and three thousand five hundred seven of the Compiled Laws of eighteen hundred seventy-one," as amended by act number nineteen of the Public Acts of eighteen hundred ninety-three, entitled " An act to amend section one of act number thirty-two of the Public Acts of eighteen hundred seventy-three, entitled 'An act to extend aid to the University of Michigan,' and repeal an act entitled 'An act to extend aid to the University of Michigan,' approved March fifteenth, eighteen hundred sixty-seven," the same being compiler's section eighteen hundred seven of the Compiled Laws of eighteen hundred ninety-seven.

The People of the State of Michigan enact:

Section 1. That section one of act number thirty-two of the Public Acts of eighteen hundred seventy-three, entitled "An act to extend aid to the University of Michigan, and to repeal an act entitled 'An act to extend aid to the University of Michigan,' approved March fifteenth, eighteen hundred sixty-seven, being sections three thousand five hundred six and three thousand five hundred seven of the Compiled Laws of eighteen hundred seventy-one," as amended by act number nineteen of the Public Acts of eigteen hundred ninety-three, entitled " An act to amend section one of act number thirty-two of the Public Acts of eighteen hundred seventy-three, entitled 'An act to extend aid to the University of Michigan, and repeal an act entitled 'An act to extend aid to the University of Michigan,' approved March fifteenth, eighteen hundred sixty-seven," the same being compiler's section eighteen hundred seven of the Compiled Laws of eighteen hundred ninety-seven, be and the same is hereby amended so as to read as follows:

Section 1. There shall be assessed upon the taxable property of the State as fixed by the State Board of Equalization, in the year eighteen hundred ninety-nine and in each year thereafter, for the use and maintenance of the University of Michigan, the sum of one-fourth of a mill on each dollar of said taxable property, to be assessed and paid into the State Treasury of the State in like manner as other State taxes are by law levied, assessed and paid; which tax, when collected, shall be paid by the State Treasurer to the Board of Regents of the University, in like manner as the interest on the University fund is paid to the treasurer of said board; and the regents of the University shall make an annual report to the Governor of the State of all the receipts and expenditures of the University: Provided, that the Board of Regents shall not authorize the building or the commencement of any additional building or buildings, or other extraordinary repairs, until the accumulation of savings from this fund shall be sufficient to complete such building or other extraordinary expense. Also provided, that the Board of Regents of the University shall maintain at all times a sufficient corps of instructors in all the departments of said University, as at present constituted, shall afford proper means and facilities for instruction and graduation in each department of said University, and shall make a fair and equitable division of the funds provided for the support of the University, in accord with the wants and needs of said departments as they shall become apparent; said departments being known as the Department of Literature, Science, and Art, Department of Medicine and Surgery, Department of Law, School of Pharmacy, Homœopathic Medical College, and the Department of Dental Surgery. Should the Board of Regents fail to maintain any of said departments herein provided, then at such time shall only one-twentieth of a mill be so assessed. Provided further, that the State Treasurer be and is hereby authorized and directed to pay to the Regents of the University, in the year eighteen hundred ninety-nine and each year thereafter, in such manner as is now provided by law, upon the warrant of the Auditor General, the amount of the mill tax provided for by this act; and that the State Treasury be reimbursed out of the taxes annually received from said mill tax when collected; and said Auditor General shall issue his warrants therefor as in the case of special appropriations.

This act is ordered to take immediate effect.

The Treasurer's Report

FOR THE FISCAL YEAR ENDING JUNE 30, 1899.

To the Finance Committee, Board of Regents, University of Michigan,

GENTLEMEN: Herewith I submit my annual report for the fiscal year ending June 30, 1899. Respectfully, H. SOULE, Treasurer.

RECEIPTS.

From State Treasurer, acct. ⅙ Mill Tax	$147,346 67	
" " " University Interest	38,529 91	
" " " Special Appropriations	9,000 00	
" " " Accumulation ⅙ mill	88,364 40	
" Earnings and Miscellaneous Sources	228,605 62	
" Balance Overdrawn, June 30, 1899	18,764 53	$530,611 13

DISBURSEMENTS.

Balance Overdrawn, July 1, 1898	$ 9,799 52	
Special Fund Accounts, Legislative Appropriations	10,718 27	
" from Accumulation ⅙ mill	81,188 05	
General Fund, Account of General Expenses	428,905 29	$530,611 13

GENERAL FUND.

RECEIPTS TO THE GENERAL FUND.

From State Treasurer, acct. University Interest		$ 38,529 91	
" " " " ⅙ Mill Tax		147,346 67	
" Interest on Deposits		582 02	
" University Hospital Earnings		28,387 01	
" Homœopathic Hospital Earnings		9,014 46	
" Dental College Operating Room Earnings		4,411 03	
" Mechanical Laboratory (Earnings in Shops)		197 43	
" Miscellaneous Sources		1,597 19	
" General Library (Sale of Duplicate Books)		3 45	$230,069 17
From Students' Fees:—			
Literary Department	$49,070 00		
" " Summer School	8,890 00		
Engineering Department	10,505 00		
Medical "	19,170 00		
Law "	35,887 50		
" " Summer School	1,802 00		
Dental "	11,040 00		
Homœopathic "	2,475 00		
Pharmacy "	3,530 00		
Chemical Laboratory	13,149 64		
Hygienic "	2,732 39		
Botanical "	705 00		
Zoological "	347 00		
Physiological "	87 00		
Pathological "	1,550 00		
Histological "	1,372 00		
Anatomical "	2,365 00		
Mechanical "	1,805 00		
Dental "	627 00		
Pharmacological Laboratory	45 00		
Electrotherapeutical "	792 00		
Medical Demonstrations	5,150 00		
Key Deposits	215 00		
Electrical Engineering (Physics)	517 00		

— 29 —

Drawing Boards	171 00		
Waterman Gymnasium Lockers	2,384 00		
Women's Gymnasium Lockers	558 00		
Diplomas	7,320 00	$184,261 53	$184,261 53
Fees, Total	$184,261 53		
Fees Refunded	6,009 23		
Net	$178,252 30		
Balance Overdrawn, June 30, 1898			20,823 25
			$435,153 95

DISBURSEMENTS FROM THE GENERAL FUND.

Balance Overdrawn, July 1, 1898,			$6,248 66
General Pay Roll	$147,798 95		
" " " Summer School	4,551 75	$152,350 70	
Current Expenses " "		607 91	
Engineering Department Pay Roll	30,630 58	30,630 58	
" " Expenses		302 92	
Law Department Pay Roll	32,985 04		
" " " " Summer School	731 23	33,716 27	
" " Expenses " "		108 40	
" " Expenses		596 12	
" " Books		1,578 50	
Medical Department Pay Roll	36,715 10	36,715 10	
" " Expenses		552 27	
" " Books		1,777 73	
School of Pharmacy and Chemical Department Pay Roll	22,879 64	22,879 64	
" Expenses		8,745 64	
Homœopathic College Pay Roll	3,500 00	3,500 00	
" " Expenses		135 80	
" " Books		223 65	
University Hospital Pay Roll	6,309 54	6,309 54	
" " Expenses		16,180 75	
Homœopathic Hospital Pay Roll	2,639 38	2,639 38	
" " Expenses		10,749 80	
Dental College Pay Roll	11,512 42	11,512 42	
" " Expenses		5,581 53	
" " Books		123 27	
Amount of Salaries Paid from General Fund	$300,253 63		
Contingent Account		$ 5,164 61	
Repairs		11,412 63	
Fuel		14,070 83	
Light		2,341 98	
Books for General Library		9,384 26	
Current Expenses for General Library		519 87	
Bindery		2,237 69	
Postage		2,353 94	
Advertising and Printing		2,408 61	
Theory and Practice of Medicine		133 92	
Materia Medica		223 92	
Museum		708 85	
Mineralogy		2 00	
Histology		703 61	
Hygiene		1,894 73	
Botanical Gardens		99 64	
Botany		861 42	
Zoology		858 84	
Engineering Shops		679 90	
Civil Engineering		398 19	
Astronomical Observatory		324 17	
School Inspection		605 63	
Practical Anatomy		1,984 52	
Electrical Engineering (Physics)		1,482 41	
Physiology		760 62	
Pathology		980 89	
Electrotherapeutics		440 17	
Nervous Diseases		82 10	
Student's Fees Refunded		6,009 23	
Hospital Lighting Plant		101 48	
Waterman Gymnasium		176 78	
Hospital Dormitory		765 71	
Teams		1,116 55	
News Letter		104 21	

Carpenter Shop	374 81	
Alumni Association	600 00	
Women's Gymnasium	621 45	
Diplomas	1,140 40	
Geology	226 17	
Surgical Demonstrations	211 65	
Surgical Clinic	312 73	
Latin	255 90	
Gynæcology	273 31	
Ophthalmology	39 45	
Philology	13 92	
General Chemistry	348 95	
Dermatology	5 05	
Diseases of Women and Children	1 95	
Psychology	69 56	
Philosophy	300 45	
German	54 08	
General Catalogue	409 15	
Electric Supplies	1,085 96	
Engineering Laboratory	504 34	
Greek	452 65	
Music	181 95	
Water Supply	1,689 86	
Commencement Expenses	819 73	$428,905 29
		$435,153 95

SPECIAL FUND ACCOUNTS.

HOMŒOPATHIC COLLEGE.
Receipts.

Balance in Treasury, July 1, 1898	$1,600 00	
From State Treasurer	6,000 00	$7,600 00

Disbursements.

Salaries	$7,500 00	
General Expenses	90 52	
Balance in Treasury, June 30, 1899	9 48	$7,600 00

ELECTRIC LIGHT PLANT.
Receipts.

Material Sold	$151 50	
Balance Overdrawn, June 30, 1899	381 93	$533 43

Disbursements.

Balance Overdrawn, July 1, 1898	$405 68	
Vouchers	127 75	$533 43

SUMMER HOSPITALS.
Receipts.

From State Treasurer	$3,000 00	$3,000 00

Disbursements.

Vouchers	$3,000 00	$3,000 00

ACCUMULATION OF SAVINGS, LAW BUILDING.
Receipts.

From State Treasurer	$49,000 00	$49,000 00

Disbursements.

Balance Overdrawn, July 1, 1898	$ 4,745 18	
Vouchers	43,756 43	
Balance in Treasury, June 30, 1899	498 39	$49,000 00

ACCUMULATION OF SAVINGS, EXTENSION TO FOUNDRY.
Receipts.

From State Treasurer	$1,500 00	$1,500 00

Disbursements.

Vouchers	$1,457 45	
Balance in Treasury, June 30, 1899	42 55	$1,500 00

ACCUMULATION OF SAVINGS, EXTENSION TO CHEMICAL LABORATORY.

Receipts.

From State Treasurer	$1,571 14	$1,571 14

Disbursements.

Vouchers	$1,571 14	$1,571 14

ACCUMULATION OF SAVINGS, REPAIRS ON UNIVERSITY HOSPITAL.

Receipts.

From State Treasurer	$2,000 00	$2,000 00

Disbursements.

Vouchers	$1,701 00	
Balance in Treasury, June 30, 1899	299 00	$2,000 00

ACCUMULATION OF SAVINGS, ADDITION TO GENERAL LIBRARY.

Receipts.

From State Treasurer	$15,000 00	$15,000 00

Disbursements.

Vouchers	$14,011 27	
Balance in Treasury, June 30, 1899	988 73	$15,000 00

ACCUMULATION OF SAVINGS, ADDITION TO HOMŒOPATHIC HOSPITAL.

Receipts.

From State Treasurer	$1,500 00	$1,500 00

Disbursements.

Vouchers	$948 64	
Balance in Treasury, June 30, 1899	551 36	$1,500 00

ACCUMULATION OF SAVINGS, ADDITION TO HEATING PLANT.

Receipts.

From State Treasurer	$1,250 00	$1,250 00

Disbursements.

Vouchers	$1,231 52	
Balance in Treasury, June 30, 1899	18 48	$1,250 00

ACCUMULATION OF SAVINGS, ROOF ON MAIN BUILDING.

Receipts.

From State Treasurer	$13,664 26	$13,664 26

Disbursements.

Vouchers	$13,664 26	$13,664 26

ACCUMULATION OF SAVINGS, UNIVERSITY HOSPITAL LAUNDRY.

Receipts.

From State Treasurer	$2,879 00	$2,879 00

Disbursements.

Vouchers	$2,846 34	
Balance in Treasury, June 30, 1899	32 66	$2,879 00

SUMMARY OF BALANCES, JUNE 30, 1899.

Overdrafts.

General Fund	$20,823 25
Electric Light Plant	381 93
	$21,205 18

Balances in Treasury.

Homœopathic College	$ 9 48	
Law Building	498 39	
Extension to Foundry	42 55	
Repairs on University Hospital	299 00	
Addition to General Library	988 73	
Addition to Homœopathic Hospital	551 36	
Addition to Heating Plant	18 48	
University Hospital Laundry	32 66	2,440 65
Net Overdraft, as previously stated		$18,764 53

GIFTS AND TRUST FUNDS.

Under this head are included gifts and other funds which the Regents have received from time to time from benefactors for special purposes. The new accounts which have been opened by your Treasurer during the year are as follows: Special Latin Fund; United States Pharmacopœia Fund; Good Government Club Fund; Peter White Fellowship Fund; '99 Law Class Scholarship Fund; Biological Laboratory Fund; Woman's Professorship Fund; Bates Professorship Fund; all of which are fully detailed below.

PHILO PARSONS FUND.
Receipts.

Balance in Treasury, July 1, 1898	$96 21	
Interest	2 93	$99 14

Disbursements.

Balance in Treasury, June 30, 1899	$99 14	$99 14

GOETHE FUND.
Receipts.

Balance in Treasury, July 1, 1898	$204 45	
Interest	6 23	$210 68

Disbursements.

Vouchers	$ 7 58	
Balance in Treasury, June 30, 1899	203 10	$210 68

ELISHA JONES CLASSICAL FELLOWSHIP FUND.
Receipts.

Balance in Treasury, July 1, 1898	$8 07	
Interest	22	$8 29

Disbursements

Balance in Treasury, June 30, 1899	$8 29	$8 29

WOMEN'S GYMNASIUM.
Receipts.

Balance in Treasury, July 1, 1898	$ 330 65	
John Canfield, Manistee	5,000 00	
Interest	140 37	$5,471 02

Disbursements.

Vouchers	$1,100 48	
Balance in Treasury, June 30, 1899	4,370 54	$5,471 02

COYL COLLECTION.
Receipts.

Balance in Treasury, July 1, 1898	$10,990 92	
Interest	531 65	$11,522 57

Disbursements.

Vouchers	$ 335 33	
Balance in Treasury, June 30, 1899	11,187 24	$11,522 57

BUHL LAW LIBRARY.
Receipts.

Balance in Treasury, July 1, 1898,	$2,262 53	
Interest	63 39	$2,325 92

Disbursements.

Vouchers	$ 744 50	
Balance in Treasury, June 30, 1899	1,581 42	$2,325 92

SETH HARRISON SCHOLARSHIP FUND.
Receipts.

Balance in Treasury, June 30, 1898	$26,163 59	
Interest	1,580 87	$27,750 46

Disbursements.

Vouchers	$ 705 50	
Balance in Treasury, June 30, 1899	27,044 96	$27,750 46

CLASS OF NINETY-FOUR SCHOLARSHIP FUND.
Receipts.

Balance in Treasury, July 1, 1898	$932 70	
Interest	28 02	
Subscriptions paid	268 40	$1,229 12

Disbursements.

Balance in Treasury, June 30, 1899	$1,229 12	$1,229 12

— 33 —

FORD-MESSER FUND.
Receipts.

Balance in Treasury, July 1, 1898	$15,001 28	
Bryant Walker, Administrator of Estate Corydon L. Ford	6,400 00	
Interest	1,598 85	$23,000 13

Disbursements.

Vouchers	$ 374 10	
Balance in Treasury, June 30, 1899	22,626 03	$23,000 13

THE PHILLIPS SCHOLARSHIPS FUND.
Receipts.

Balance in Treasury, July 1, 1898	$162 77	
From Samuel Fox & Co., for the Estate	214 03	
Interest	7 75	$384 55

Disbursements.

Balance in Treasury, June 30, 1899	$384 55	$384 55

MUSIC HALL FUND.
Receipts.

Balance in Treasury, July 1, 1898	$1,084 97	
Interest	8 23	
Contributions	100 00	$1,193 20

Disbursements.

Balance in Treasury, June 30, 1899	$1,193 20	$1,193 20

CLASS OF NINETY-SIX MEMORIAL.
Receipts.

Balance in Treasury, July 1, 1898	$10 00	
Subscriptions	6 00	
Interest	12	$25 12

Disbursements.

Vouchers	$19 00	
Balance in Treasury, June 30, 1899	6 12	$25 12

CLASS OF NINETY-SEVEN SCHOLARSHIP FUND.
Receipts.

Balance in Treasury, July 1, 1898	$138 43	
Interest	3 48	$141 91

Disbursements.

Balance in Treasury, June 30, 1899	$141 91	$141 91

CLASS OF NINETY-EIGHT SCHOLARSHIP FUND.
Receipts.

Balance in Treasury, July 1, 1898	$253 30	
Subscriptions	4 00	
Interest	5 55	$262 85

Disbursements.

Balance in Treasury, June 30, 1899	$262 85	$262 85

PARKE, DAVIS & CO. FUND.
Receipts.

Balance in Treasury, July 1, 1898	$ 10 00	
Parke, Davis & Co.	500 00	
Interest	2 12	$512 12

Disbursements.

Vouchers	$500 00	
Balance in Treasury, June 30, 1899	12 12	$512 12

STEARNS PHARMACY FELLOWSHIP FUND.
Receipts.

Balance in Treasury, July 1, 1898	$ 78	
Stearns & Co.	350 00	$350 78

Disbursements

Vouchers	$350 00	
Balance in Treasury, June 30, 1899	78	350 78

LIBRARY OF EARLY CHRISTIAN LITERATURE FUND.

Receipts.

Balance in Treasury, July 1, 1898	$6 50	
Transfer from Special Latin Fund	71	
Transfer from James E. Scripps Library Fund	15	$7 36

Disbursements.

Vouchers	$7 36	$7 36

JAMES E. SCRIPPS LIBRARY FUND.

Receipts.

Balance in Treasury, July 1, 1898	$ 15	$ 15

Disbursements.

Transfer to Library of Early Christian Literature Fund	$ 15	$ 15

FRIEZE MEMORIAL FUND.

Receipts.

Balance in Treasury, July 1, 1898	$396 66	
Collections to the Fund	703 37	$1,100 03

Disbursements.

Vouchers	$742 90	
Balance in Treasury, June 30, 1899	357 13	$1,100 03

UNITED STATES PHARMACOPŒIA FUND.

Receipts.

Appropriation by Committee on Publication	$815 00	$815 00

Disbursements.

Vouchers	$765 00	
Balance in Treasury, June 30, 1899	50 00	$815 00

SPECIAL LATIN FUND.

Receipts.

From Contributor to the Fund	$200 00	$200 00

Disbursements.

Vouchers	$48 78	
Transfer to Library of Early Christian Literature Fund	71	
Balance in Treasury, June 30, 1899	150 51	$200 00

GOOD GOVERNMENT CLUB.

Receipts.

From Contributor to the Fund	$500 00	$500 00

Disbursements.

Balance in Treasury, June 30, 1899	$500 00	$500 00

PETER WHITE FELLOWSHIP.

Receipts.

From Peter White	$400 00	$400 00

Disbursements.

Balance in Treasury, June 30, 1899	$400 00	$400 00

WOMAN'S PROFESSORSHIP FUND.

Receipts.

From the Donor	$10,000 00	$10,000 00

Disbursements.

Balance in Treasury, June 30, 1899	$10,000 00	$10,000 00

NINETY-NINE LAW CLASS SCHOLARSHIP FUND.

Receipts.

From Subscriptions	$25 00	$25 00

Disbursements.

Balance in Treasury June 30, 1899	$25 00	$25 00

BIOLOGICAL LABORATORY FUND.

Receipts.

From the Donor, D. M. Ferry	$50 00	$50 00

Disbursements.

Vouchers	$50 00	$50 00

WILLIAMS PROFESSORSHIP FUND—PROPERTY.

The property fund of this account was by order of the Board of Regents under date July 21, 1898, placed in the hands of Hon. Levi L. Barbour, of Detroit, and for this I hold his acknowledgment as follows:

Mortgage Securities, Value	$7,077 44	
Other Property "	3,153 68	$10,231 12

The same being in his hands for future management.

WILLIAMS PROFESSORSHIP FUND—CASH.

Balance in Treasury, July 1, 1898,	$4,727 23	
Subscription (H. B. Hutchins)	50 00	
Interest	151 35	$4,928 58

Disbursements.

Vouchers	$ 29 20	
Balance in Treasury, June 30, 1899	4,899 38	$4,928 58

MORRIS ALUMNI FUND.

Balance in Treasury, July 1, 1898, Securities	$1,150 00	
" " " " " " Cash	1,095 83	
Interest	131 18	$2,377 01

Disbursements.

Balance in Treasury, June 30, 1899	$2,377 01	$2,377 01

BATES PROFESSORSHIP.

Receipts.

Balance Overdrawn, June 30, 1899	$1,177 10	$1,177 10

Disbursements.

Vouchers	$1,177 10	$1,177 10

D. M. FERRY BOTANICAL FUND.

Receipts.

Balance in Treasury, July 1, 1898	$50 00	$50 00

Disbursements.

Vouchers	$50 00	$50 00

SUMMARY OF GIFT FUND BALANCES.

	CASH.	LOANED.	TOTAL.
Philo Parsons Fund	$ 99 14		$ 99 14
Goethe "	203 10		203 10
Elisha Jones Classical Fellowship Fund	8 29		8 29
Women's Gymnasium "	4,370 54		4,370 54
Coyl Collection "	1,187 24	$10,000 00	11,187 24
Buhl Law Library "	1,581 42		1,581 42
Seth Harrison Scholarship "	5,544 96	21,500 00	27,044 96
94 Scholarship "	1,229 12		1,229 12
Ford-Messer Library "	15,876 03	6,750 00	22,626 03
Phillips Scholarships "	384 55		384 55
Music Hall "	193 20	1,000 00	1,193 20
96 Class Memorial "	6 12		6 12
97 Class Scholarship "	1 91	140 00	141 91
98 Class Scholarship "	262 85		262 85
Parke, Davis & Co. "	12 12		12 12
Stearns Pharmacy Fellowship "	78		78
Frieze Memorial "	357 13		357 13
U. S Pharmacopœia "	50 00		50 00
Special Latin "	150 51		150 51
Good Government Club "	500 00		500 00
Peter White Fellowship "	400 00		400 00
Woman's Professorship "		10,000 00	10,000 00
99 Law Class Scholarship "		25 00	25 00
Williams "	4,899 38		4,899 38
Morris Alumni "	1,227 01	1,150 00	2,377 01
	$38,545 40	$50,565 00	$89,110 40
Bates Professorship Fund, Overdrawn			$1,177 10
Net Balance in Gift Funds			$87,933 30

APPENDIX TO TREASURER'S REPORT.

Contributors to the Ninety-Four Class Scholarship Fund during the year ending June 30, 1899:

Jamie Maud Blanchard	$ 5 00
Lelia Brouillette	5 00
Ralph Winthrop Newton	5 00
Walter Park Martindale	10 00
Charles Frederick Weller	5 00
Arthur Lucius Hubbard	5 00
John Quincy Adams	10 30
Charles Wallace Adams	10 30
Robert Victor Friedman	15 90
Sara May Riggs	5 00
Dwight Otis Miller	5 00
Eugene Cyrus Woodruff	5 00
Herbert Ephraim French	25 00
Adoniram Judson Ladd	5 00
Samuel Denis Magers	21 80
Frederic Leigh Osenburg	5 00
Abraham Kohn Adler	10 30
Sarah May Howard	5 00
Walter Monroe Hamilton	5 00
Almira Ann Prentice	5 00
Delos Franklin Wilcox	5 00
Clare Briggs	5 00
Fannie Mabel Elliott	5 00
Robert Emmons Jones	5 00
Oscar Greulich	5 00
Carrie Eleanor Penfield Harvey	15 90
Joseph Raleigh Nelson	10 90
Lucy Elizabeth Textor	5 00
George T. Tremble	5 00
Daniel Franklin Lyons	5 00
Frederick Whittlesey Newton	3 00
Jamie Maud Blanchard	5 00
Bernice Lena Haug	5 00
Samuel Archibald Smith	15 00
Joseph Weare	5 00
	$268 40

UNIVERSITY OF MICHIGAN.

THE PRESIDENT'S REPORT

TO THE

BOARD OF REGENTS

FOR THE ACADEMIC YEAR

ENDING SEPTEMBER 30, 1900

AND THE

REPORT OF THE TREASURER

FOR THE FISCAL YEAR

ENDING JUNE 30, 1900.

ANN ARBOR, MICH.,
PUBLISHED BY THE UNIVERSITY
1900

THE PRESIDENT'S REPORT

To the Honorable Board of Regents:

I beg to present to you my report for the year ending June 30, 1900.

The year has been one of marked prosperity. A spirit of earnestness and industry has prevailed throughout the University; the number of students has been greater than ever before; the addition to our resources furnished by the generosity of the Legislature has enabled us to begin the construction of some much-needed buildings, and to prepare for the organization of some new departments of work.

The total attendance exclusive of the Summer School was 3,303, which was 244 more than in the previous year. Including the Summer School of 1899, the total number was 3,441, which was 249 more than in the preceding year. Omitting the students in the Summer School, there was a gain in every department except the School of Pharmacy, in which there was a loss of five.

A noteworthy fact is the marked increase in the number of students from our own State, 2,006, an increase of 132 over the figures for the previous year. They constitute nearly 54 per cent of the whole. The great States near to us, although they are so richly supplied with excellent colleges and universities, still send their sons and daughters to us in increasing numbers. Illinois has enlarged its representation from 328 last year to 354, Ohio from 199 to 215, Indiana from 113 to 129, New York from 85 to 97, Iowa from 84 to 94, and several other States proportionally. The confidence thus shown by our neighbors in the value of our work is encouraging and gratifying. Forty-seven of our States and Territories and our new possessions, the Hawaiian Islands and Porto Rico, were represented in our classes. So were Japan, China, Egypt, Turkey,

South Africa, Germany, Mexico, Ontario, and New Brunswick. Our student population retains its cosmopolitan character in a remarkable degree. The educational value of this fact should not be overlooked. Not the least important contribution to the training of many a student is the knowledge of men gained in this microcosm. It tends to cure him of narrow provincialism and to comprehend in some measure the complex life into which he is soon to be ushered.

The women in the University were as follows:—

Department of Literature, Science, and the Arts	634
Department of Medicine and Surgery	49
Department of Law	5
School of Pharmacy	10
Homœopathic Medical College	7
College of Dental Surgery	9
	714

This is forty more than in the preceding year. The whole of the gain is in the Literary Department. The aggregate attendance in the professional schools is exactly the same as it was in 1898-99. The ratio of men to women in the University still remains as it has been for some years, about five to one. But in the Literary Department the women are about 47 per cent of the students.

The rapid increase in the number of women who are obtaining collegiate training is one of the most striking educational facts of our time. Not only is the proportion of women to men in all of the so-called coeducational institutions growing, but the attendance upon the "annexes" such as Radcliffe and Barnard, and upon the colleges established exclusively for women, like Wellesley and Vassar and Smith and Bryn Mawr, is swelling so rapidly as to test the capacity of those institutions to care for them. It is no longer the case, as in large degree it was twenty years ago, that nearly all the women in college are preparing themselves for teaching or for some form of professional life. A considerable proportion of them are studying merely for the sake of culture, which may enrich and adorn their lives, whatever may prove to be their sphere of activity. It seems not improbable that before many years the number of college-bred women in this country will equal that of the college-bred men. The intellectual and social results of this fact must be of no little importance.

Thus far the theory that women ought to have or would desire an intellectual training essentially different from that usually presented for men has found but slender support. The elasticity afforded by the modern elective system introduced into most American colleges and universities seems to furnish a sufficient range for a wide diversity of choice. When left to themselves, the women manifest the same variety of taste in their election of studies as the men. They have certainly shown no disposition to avoid what has been usually considered the most exacting and difficult branches, and no lack of ability to master them. It appears therefore in the highest degree improbable that any fixed course which educational theorists may attempt to prescribe as the one course for women will be adopted in the better colleges and universities.

Our thirty years' experience in training women for professional work and our observation of their careers in life should fit us in some degree to judge of the inducements which certain professions offer to them.

It is clear that a good number of women achieve success in the practice of medicine and a few in surgery. We could point to some excellent illustrations among our graduates. They have in this country generally overcome the opposition of medical societies to their entrance into the profession, and often take a creditable part in the proceedings of such bodies. They have also gained the confidence of a respectable constituency. Some of them who have gone as medical missionaries to oriental lands where women could not with propriety be ministered to by male physicians, have rendered services of inestimable value to their sex. Others have filled with great usefulness responsible positions in prisons and reformatories for women.

A certain number of women have also succeeded well in the profession of dentistry, both in this country and in Germany. Especially has this been true of those who have made a specialty of caring for children during the periods of their first and second dentition, and also of caring for mothers in times of special need.

Some women who have graduated from the School of Pharmacy have found a congenial and remunerative career as pharmacists, but whether owing to the disinclination of men in the business to employ them, or to the fatigue of the continuous labor in the office, not many remain in the occupation. Some enter the services of manufacturing chemists, or are employed as pharmacists in hospitals or other charitable institutions.

The number of women in the Law School is always small. Of those who graduate only a few engage much in practice in court. Some study the profession for the express purpose of assisting their fathers in office work. A few have taken the course in whole or in part with a belief that a knowledge of law would enable them to be more efficient teachers of political economy, civil government, and history in academies, high schools, or colleges. It seems improbable that any considerable number of women will find it congenial or remunerative to follow the profession of the law.

Undoubtedly it will be true in the future as it has been in the past that the great majority of women graduates, who pursue any profession, will choose that of teaching. They will, of course, avail themselves of the pedagogical instruction which is offered to all who desire it. The employment in recent years of many college-bred women in our high schools has been an important factor in elevating the grade of work in those schools.

During the year some changes have been made in the requirements for admission to the Literary Department. These changes are in the direction of greater flexibility. The only demand absolutely insisted on for all students is preparation in English, Mathematics, and Physics. The remaining requirements, which call in the aggregate for a little more than the amount of study bestowed on those three branches, must be furnished from some of the following branches: Greek, Latin, French, German, English Literature, History, Chemistry, Botany, Zoology, Biology (comprising half a year each of Botany and of Zoology), and Physiography. In each of the sciences (with the exception just named in Botany and Zoology) a full year's study is asked, and it is encouraged in those two sciences. It is deemed better that an entire year should be given to one science than half a year to each of two sciences. Those who intend to go on with Greek or Latin must present adequate preparation in those tongues. Elementary instruction in those languages is not given in the University.

There was a decided gain in the attendance in the Department of Engineering. The marked revival of business all over the country has made a great demand for engineers. We have been unable to meet the calls made upon us for men who have completed some one of our courses.

At the Observatory Professor Hall has continued during the year observations of Polaris with the meridian circle for the determination of the aberration constant. It is intended to continue the series through January next. The observations have been reduced through June, 1900.

It was announced in my last report that we hoped to make provision for establishing a course in marine architecture in order to prepare men for the important work of designing vessels for service on the Great Lakes. The development of commerce on these lakes goes by leaps and bounds. The transportation of agricultural and mineral products of the northwest and of the coal of Ohio and Pennsylvania to the northwest calls for an immense fleet. Great shipyards have of necessity sprung up on the shores of our lakes. Men who are capable of applying the best results of modern science to the construction of vessels are in great demand. It has seemed our plain duty to train men for this service. We have now added to our force of instruction in civil, electrical, and mechanical engineering Mr. Herbert C. Sadler, who in connection with the renowned school of Marine Engineering in Glasgow University, and under guidance of that distinguished expert and teacher, Professor Biles, has won a high reputation. We trust that we shall soon be able to send out young men who will be of great service to the shipbuilders of Michigan and the adjoining States.

Attention was also called in my last report to the desirableness of organizing and enlarging our instruction in some branches so as to furnish better preparation for higher commercial education and certain public administrative duties. A committee of the Faculty made a very careful study of the subject, and have co-ordinated our work in History, Constitutional Law, Politics, Political Economy and Finance, Sociology and Statistics, International Law, Administrative and Municipal Law, Roman Law and Roman Institutions, so as to make special Courses in Higher Commercial Education and Public Administration. Several of the leading universities are providing instruction of a similar scope. We have appointed Dr. John A. Fairlie Assistant Professor of Administrative Law, and have called in several special Lecturers to discuss such subjects as the Industrial Resources of this Country, the International Division of Labor, the Industrial Significance of the West Indies to us, the Function of the Financier in Industrial Organizations, the Industrial Significance of Deep Waterways, and the Function of Trades Unions in Industrial Organizations. The committee particularly charged with this range of studies hope to advise students in selecting courses now offered so as to be of service to them in preparing for the political and social side of newspaper work, for the teaching of History and Political Science and for the conduct of philanthropic and charitable organizations. If Congress shall pass laws which give more assurance than we can now have that appointments in the consular service will be made on the grounds of suitable training rather than on merely partisan grounds, we shall expect to offer larger opportunity than we now do for preparation for entrance on such grades of consular and diplomatic work as are befitting young graduates. Closely and naturally connected with that would be preparation for administrative duties in our new insular possessions.

The number of graduate students in the Literary Department was 90, which is fifteen more than in the previous year. As we had only three Fellowships in the Literary Department to offer, and all the principal Universities have a considerable number, it is perhaps satisfactory to find so many pursuing graduate studies here, when there are so strong pecuniary inducements to them to go elsewhere. We do not abandon the hope that some generous benefactor will yet see how signal a service he may render to sound learning by endowing Fellowships in the Literary Department, and will secure for himself the satisfaction to be derived from making so wise a foundation in the University. We have received encouragement by the endowment of certain Fellowships from year to year by Parke, Davis & Co., of Detroit, in chemical research, by Frederick Stearns & Co. in pharmaceutical research, by Hon. D. M. Ferry in botanical investigation, by Nelson, Baker & Co., in pharmaceutical research, and by Hon. Peter White in American History. All these are available for the coming year.

It is interesting to note that during the past eight years we have received graduate students from seventy-nine colleges and Universities besides our own. About two-thirds of these graduate students, however, received their first degrees here.

The Regents, at the request of the Administrative Council of the Graduate School, have abolished the degrees of Master of Philosophy and Master of Letters, and will confer on all Bachelors who may earn a Master's degree, that of Master of Arts, though, if any of the Masters have pursued their studies along scientific lines, they may at their option receive the degree of Master of Science. It was thought that we had an unnecessary variety of Master's degrees to designate kinds of work which often did not differ much in character or in value.

The Department of Medicine and Surgery continues to increase its numbers by a healthy growth. The severe and strenuous course of instruction, which makes very heavy demands on the students, attracts rather than repels industrious and aspiring persons. The attendance at this time is larger than ever before, not excepting the year after the close of the Civil War, when so many who had been serving as nurses in the hospitals flocked to the school. The Department is waiting anxiously for the day when ampler laboratory facilities can be furnished.

The Law Department has been growing at so rapid a rate that the capacity of the new building is already found not to be in excess of the demands. Increased requirements for admission at the beginning of the year 1900-01 were announced last year. It was supposed that this step would lead temporarily to a diminution in the number of applicants. But it is already obvious that this result will not follow, and that the public were ready for the change. All matriculants in the Department are now asked to have such a preparation as will admit them to some one of the courses in the Literary Department. During the year the Law Library has been carefully re-arranged and catalogued.

The most important event in the history of the Homœopathic Medical College for the year has been the erection of its new Hospital. The site, near the Campus and yet comparatively removed from the noises of the streets, is most eligible. The mansion which was purchased with the lot is well suited for the Nurses' Home. The Hospital Building, while simple in architecture, is tasteful. It is commodious in its arrangements, and is furnished with the most suitable appliances of every kind for hospital service. It is expected to accommodate about seventy-five patients.

The Dental College has been filled to overflowing with students. The progress of this Department both in numbers and in the range of its work since its establishment in 1875 has been very noteworthy. Like other Dental Schools, at that date it asked rather slender preparation and it limited its course of instruction to two terms of six months each. The requirements for admission have been raised repeatedly. It has been decided that after this year the requirement for admission shall be the same as for entrance into the Literary or Medical Department, namely, the completion of a good High School course, or its equivalent.

The length of the course for graduation was extended many years ago from two terms of six months each to two terms of nine months each. Later it was again extended to three years' work of nine months each. It is now decided to require all who enter after this year to complete four years' work of nine months each for graduation. This change may perhaps reduce our numbers for a time, but we are indifferent on that score. We have reasons to suppose that other strong schools will follow our example now as they have done on the occasion of previous extensions of our course.

It is obvious that at no distant day the area of our Campus, though it comprises about forty acres, will prove too limited for the buildings which we must have. We have therefore been watching for some time for a good opportunity to procure land adjacent to it. We count ourselves fortunate in having secured a few months ago the fine lot occupied by the residence of the late Professor Winchell. It is immediately opposite the site selected for the new Science Building, which we hope to begin before long, and is itself an admirable site for some University building. It will be prudent to secure other eligible lots as they come into the market. The value of those contiguous to the Campus must continue to rise. Some of the older Universities, Harvard and Yale for example, find it very expensive now to make the necessary purchases of land adjacent to their grounds. There is true economy in practicing wise foresight in providing for future growth. It is said that in the fifties two hundred acres just east of our Campus, and now entirely covered with houses, could have been bought for ten thousand dollars, and that President Tappan with his prevision strongly urged the Regents to make the purchase, but unhappily his counsel was not followed.

The last year has also witnessed the completion of the Barbour Gymnasium. A more beautiful and commodious building of the kind for women students is found at none of our Universities. In addition to the large hall for gymnastic exercises, there are spacious parlors, and also a hall fitted with a stage for lectures, concerts, or plays, and seating four hundred persons. The gifts of many persons from various parts of the State, of students of several classes, of professors' wives, and of women's societies in our principal cities, have helped to erect and furnish the building, while the name it bears commemorates the gift of the principal donor, Hon. Levi L. Barbour, of Detroit. It is the commodious and congenial meeting place for the women of the University, not only for exercise, but for literary or social gatherings.

It was a source of great satisfaction to us to find at the close of the year that we were in a condition to contract for an addition to the building which contains our engineering shops and the work in Mechanical Engineering. Under increasing demands recently made upon our Department of Engineering, Civil, Electrical, and Mechanical, the space allotted to that work was altogether inadequate. Especially was the provision for instruction in the testing of machines insufficient. Now that we were intending to set up the new work in Marine Engineering, it became indispensable to have more room. The structure will be completed at an early day.

The completion of the addition to the book room in the General Library has enabled us, and in fact compelled us, to make a new arrangement of the books. The labor involved in this and in making the necessary change in our card catalogue has been very great. But our accommodations will suffice for some years. We must, however, keep ever in mind the need of repeated enlargements of the building in the future, and especially the need which we feel keenly even now of additional seminary rooms.

According to the Librarian's Report, the increase in our libraries has been 12,273 volumes; the total number of volumes is 145,479; the recorded circulation, which is estimated as about one half of the whole use, is 152,956 volumes, an increase of 7,391 volumes over that of last year.

The circulation of the University News Letter, which is published under the editorial direction of Professor F. N. Scott, has been of much value to the University. It is filled with information about the work of the Institution, and is widely disseminated among newspapers, schools, newspaper correspondents, and news agencies. Its concise paragraphs and even its more extended articles are widely copied.

Through the energetic action of Professor Kelsey, we have received two valuable additions to the resources of the Latin department. One is the de Criscio Collection of Latin inscriptions. These number more than two hundred and fifty. Most of them are upon slabs of marble. They are of various dates from the age of Augustus to the fifth century, A. D. They were gathered at and near Pozzuoli. They have attracted the attention of German scholars, and a large number of them have been published in the German journals devoted to epigraphy, and others in the American Journal of Archæology. They are for the most part sepulchral inscriptions. They are of great value to the advanced student in Latin. They were presented to the University by Mr. Henry P. Glover, of Ypsilanti.

The other accession consists of the casts of the figures on the renowned arch of Trajan at Benevento. The initial step in securing these was taken by the graduating class of 1898 of the Literary Department, who contributed a handsome sum as a memorial gift. It proved that the cost of bringing the casts was considerably greater than was expected, whereupon a number of Detroit friends of the University furnished the additional sum needed. The value of these figures as specimens of the art of the period to which they belong is well known.

The lack of room in our Art Gallery to display more than a few of these figures emphasizes anew our urgent need of a separate building for our large and constantly increasing collections of statuary and pictures.

I am happy to say that the property bequeathed to the University by the late Elizabeth H. Bates, M. D., has come into our possession, and that the value proves to be about $130,000.

The arrangement of the unique collection of musical instruments presented by Frederick Stearns, Esq., in cases in the museum has been completed. Mr. Stearns is making further purchases for the collection during his visit in Europe.

His son, Mr. Frederick Kimball Stearns, has happily supplemented the father's gift by presenting us with a large collection, numbering 1551 titles, of musical scores and books on music. Some of these works are of great rarity. We are also indebted to Mr. F. K. Stearns for a portrait of his father, which is to be placed in the hall with the collection of musical instruments.

The University has also received a legacy of $2,054.05 from Hannah E. Davis, of Newcastle, Indiana, for the benefit of the University Hospital. She was prompted to this act by witnessing the humane and beneficent work of the hospital while she was on a visit to this city a few months ago. Could more of our citizens see the relief which is afforded in our hospitals, almost without money and without price, to the sufferers who crowd the wards, we should have to record more instances of generous assistance furnished by those whose hearts have been touched by the spectacle of men and women and children restored from helplessness and pain to activity and health and joy.

The Summer School had the most successful session ever held. Several of the full-Professors remained here to teach. This fact together with the reduction in the fees contributed to attract not only a larger number, but a more mature company of students than have before been in attendance. Among them were Principals and Superintendents of Schools. Some students came from States remote from us. The spirit of the School was excellent.

Eighty-seven courses were offered in the Literary Department. Instruction was given by 38 instructors. There was a wholesome tendency on the part of the students to concentrate their work. Of the 351 in attendance, 132 devoted their entire time to a single subject. About one half of the students were teachers, chiefly from the High Schools. The increase in the number of graduates was striking, more than twice as many were present as attended last year. There were 57 graduates of this University, 64 graduates of other colleges and Universities, and 24 graduates of the Michigan Normal College. A course in Nature Study was given gratuitously to the school teachers of the State and was largely attended and warmly appreciated.

The attendance in the Summer Law School was 53. Thus the total attendance, exclusive of the class in Nature Study, was 404. That is an increase of fifty per cent compared with the previous year. There seems good ground for expecting a steady and rapid growth of the Summer School. Of its usefulness to the State and to the University there can be no doubt.   JAMES B. ANGELL.

APPENDICES.

APPENDIX A.

APPOINTMENTS, REAPPOINTMENTS, RESIGNATIONS, ETC., DURING THE YEAR ENDING SEPTEMBER 30, 1900.

Resignations:

At the meeting of February 14, 1900, the resignation of Harry W. Clark, B. S., Superintendent of the University Hospital, was presented and accepted to take effect March 15.

At the meeting of March 14, 1900, the resignation of Dean C. Worcester, A. B., Assistant Professor of Zoology, was presented and accepted.

At the meeting of July 18, 1900, the resignation of Oscar Le Seure, M. D., Professor of Surgery and Clinical Surgery in the Homœopathic Medical College was presented and accepted.

Leave of Absence:

At the meeting of February 14, 1900, Professor Francis W. Kelsey, Ph. D., was granted leave of absence for the academic year 1900-01.

At the meeting of April 18, 1900, Professor Royal S. Copeland, A. M., M. D., was granted a leave of absence for two weeks; Instructor Karl E. Guthe, Ph. D., was granted leave of absence from May 16 to the end of the academic year; Professor Albert B. Prescott, M. D., LL. D., Assistant Professor Alviso B. Stevens, Ph. C., and Assistant Professor Julius O. Schlotterbeck, Ph. D., were granted leave of absence for two weeks; and Professor Arthur R. Cushny, A. M., M. D., was granted leave of absence from May 31 to the end of the academic year.

At the meeting of May 17, 1900, Instructor George O. Higley, M. S., was granted leave of absence for the academic year 1900-01.

At the meeting of June 19, 1900, Assistant Professor Karl E. Guthe, Ph. D., and Instructor Arthur G. Hall, B. S., were granted leave of absence for the academic year 1900-01.

Change of Title, etc.:

At the meeting of October 11, 1899, the title of Joseph H. Vance, LL.B., was changed to Assistant Law Librarian; the appointment of Aaron V. McAlvay, A. B., LL.B., as Professor of Law, was made permanent; and the title of Herbert F. De Cou, A. B., was made Instructor in Greek.

At the meeting of May 17, 1900, Assistant Professor Max Winkler, Ph. D., was asked to take temporary charge of the Department of Germanic Languages and Literatures.

At the meeting of June 19, 1900, the title of Lecturer on Roman Law in the Department of Law was added to the previous title of Assistant Professor Joseph H. Drake, A. B.; and the title of Acting Professor was given to Assistant Professor Max Winkler, Ph. D., while in temporary charge of the German Department.

Special Resident Lecturers and Instructors:

In the Department of Literature, Science, and the Arts, Resident Instructors were appointed for the Summer Session of the year 1900 as follows:

At the meeting of February 14, 1900.

Isaac N. Demmon, LL.D., English and American Literature.
Wooster W. Beman, A. M., Mathematics.
Burke A. Hinsdale, LL.D., The Science and the Art of Teaching.
Thomas C. Trueblood, A. M., Elocution.
John C. Rolfe, Ph. D., Latin.
Robert M. Wenley, Sc. D., D. Phil., Philosophy.
George Hempl, Ph. D., English Philology, General Linguistics, German.
Fred M. Taylor, Ph. D., Political Economy.
Fred N. Scott, Ph. D., Rhetoric.
Allen S. Whitney, A. B., The Science and the Art of Teaching.
John O. Reed, Ph. D., Physics. Chairman of Executive Committee.
Joseph H. Drake, A. B., Latin.
Joseph L. Markley, Ph. D., Mathematics.
Moritz Levi, A. B., Spanish and Italian.
Ernst H. Mensel, Ph. D., German. Secretary of the Executive Committee.
Moses Gomberg, Sc. D., Chemistry.
George O. Higley, M. S., Chemistry.
David M. Lichty, M. S., Chemistry.
John R. Effinger, Jr., Ph. D., French.
Karl E. Guthe, Ph. D., Physics.
Clarence A. Meader, A. B., Latin.
Arthur G. Hall, B. S., Mathematics.
Herbert J. Goulding, B. S., Drawing.
Perry F. Trowbridge, Ph. B., Chemistry.
Herbert H. Waite, A. B., Bacteriology.
Edwin C. Roedder, Ph. D., German.
James B. Pollock, Sc. D., Botany.
Shirley W. Smith, B. L., English.
Eugene C. Sullivan, Ph. D., Chemistry.

Jonathan A. C. Hildner, Ph. D., German.
Charles M. Williams, Physical Training.
Charles L. Bliss, B. S., Physiological Chemistry.
John W. Slaughter, A. B., B. D., Philosophy.

At the meeting of June 19, 1900.
Norman K. McInnis, A. M., English.

At the meeting of July 18, 1900.
George W. Patterson, Jr., Ph. D., Electrical Physics.

In the Department of Law Special Lecturers were appointed for the year 1900-01 as follows:

At the meeting of June 19, 1900.
Victor C. Vaughan, Ph. D., Sc. D., M. D., Toxicology in its Legal Relations.
Henry C. Adams, LL.D., The Railroad Problem.
Andrew C. Mc Laughlin, A. M., LL.B., Constitutional Law and Constitutional History.
Richard Hudson, A. M., Comparative Constitutional Law.
William J. Herdman, M. D., LL.D., Neurology, Electrology, and Railway Injuries.

Non-resident Lecturers and Instructors:

In the Department of Literature, Science, and the Arts, Non-resident Instructors were appointed for the Summer Session of the year 1900, as follows:

At the meeting of February 14, 1900.
Duane R. Stuart, A. B., Greek.
Charles A. Davis, A. M., Geology.
William H. Munson, B. S., Zoology.

At the meeting of September 5, 1900.
Wilbur C. Abbott, B. Litt., History.
Charles B. Scott, A. M., Nature Study.

In the Department of Literature, Science, and the Arts, Non-resident Lecturers in the Commercial Courses were appointed for the year 1900-01 as follows:

At the meeting of May 17, 1900.
Lyman E. Cooley, C. E., Industrial Significance of Ship Canals.
Robert T. Hill, B. S., Commercial Significance of the West Indies for the United States.
Edward D. Jones, Ph. D., Industrial Resources of the United States.
Oliver M. W. Sprague, Ph. D., International Division of Labor.
Thomas L. Greene, Function of Finance in Industrial Organization.

William F. Willoughby, A. B., Function of Trades' Unions in Industrial Organization.

In the Department of Medicine and Surgery, Non-resident Lecturers were appointed for the year 1900-01 as follows:

At the meeting of June 19, 1900.
William M. Edwards, M. D., Insanity.
Edmund A. Christian, A. B., M. D., Insanity.
James D. Munson, M. D., Insanity.
Henry B. Baker, A. M., M. D., Administration of Health Laws.
George L. Chamberlain, M. D., Insanity.

In the Department of Law, Non-resident Lecturers were appointed for the year 1900-01 as follows:

At the meeting of June 19, 1900.
John B. Clayberg, LL.B., Mining Law.
Melville M. Bigelow, Ph. D., Insurance.
Henry H. Swan, A. M., Admiralty.
Frank F. Reed, A. B., Copyright Law and Law of Trademarks.
Albert H. Walker, LL.B., Patent Law.

Other Appointments and Reappointments:

Appointments and reappointments were made in the several departments as indicated in the lists given below. The names of persons appointed as Assistants or, with a few exceptions, to other positions of lower grade than Instructor are not included. Professors and Junior Professors were appointed for unlimited time, Assistant Professors for three years, and Instructors for one year, except in cases where a different period of service is mentioned.

At the meeting of October 11, 1899.
Perry F. Trowbridge, Ph. B., Instructor in Organic Chemistry for three years.
Charles M. Williams, Instructor in the Waterman Gymnasium.
Alice L. Hunt, Instructor in Drawing.
Karl W. Genthe, Ph. D., Instructor in Zoology.

At the meeting of November 17, 1899.
Charles Baird, A. B., Director of Outdoor Athletics from January 1, 1900.

At the meeting of March 14, 1900.
Eugene S. Gilmore, Superintendent of the University Hospital.

At the meeting of April 18, 1900.
Arthur G. Canfield, A. M., Professor of Romance Languages.
Duane Reed Stuart, A. B., Instructor in Latin.

At the meeting of May 17, 1900.

John A. Fairlie, Ph. D., Assistant Professor of Administrative Law for one year.

George O. Higley, M. S., Instructor in General Chemistry for three years.

David M. Lichty, M. S., Instructor in General Chemistry for three years.

Frederick L. Dunlap, Ph. D., Instructor in General Chemistry.

Russell E. Atchison (erroneously printed Hutchins in the Proceedings of the May meeting), Superintendent of the University Hospital (Homœopathic).

At the meeting of June 19, 1900.

Herbert C. Sadler, B. S., Junior Professor of Naval Architecture.
Keene Fitzpatrick, Director of the Gymnasium for three years.
Karl E. Guthe, Ph. D., Assistant Professor of Physics.
John R. Allen, M. E., Assistant Professor of Mechanical Engineering.
Benjamin P. Bourland, Ph. D., Assistant Professor of French.
George Rebec, Ph. D., Assistant Professor of Philosophy.
Walter B. Pillsbury, Ph. D., Assistant Professor of Philosophy and Director of the Psychological Laboratory.
Edwin C. Goddard, Ph. B., LL.B., Assistant Professor of Law.
Cyrenus G. Darling, M. D., Lecturer on Genito-urinary and Minor Surgery in the Department of Medicine and Surgery, and Clinical Lecturer on Oral Pathology and Surgery in the College of Dental Surgery for one year.
Simon M. Yutzy, M. D., Instructor in Osteology and Demonstrator of Anatomy for three years.
William H. Butts, A. M., Instructor in Mathematics for three years.
Henry A. Sanders, Ph. D., Instructor in Latin for three years.
Victor E. François, Instructor in French for three years.
Herbert H. Waite, A. B., Instructor in Bacteriology.
James R. Arneill, A. B., M. D., Instructor in Internal Medicine.
Robert C. Bourland, A. B., M. D., Instructor in Anatomy.
Benjamin F. Bailey, A. M., Instructor in Electrotherapeutics.
Warren W. Florer, Ph. D., Instructor in German.
Alfred H. White, A. B., Instructor in Chemical Technology.
Carroll D. Jones, E. E., Instructor in Electrical Engineering.
John S. P. Tatlock, A. M., Instructor in English.
Alice G. Snyder, M. D., Instructor in the Women's Gymnasium.
S. Lawrence Bigelow, Ph. D., Instructor in General Chemistry.
James B. Pollock, Sc. D., Instructor in Botany.
Ewald Boucke, Ph. D., Instructor in German.
Shirley W. Smith, A. M., Instructor in English.
Hugo P. Thieme, Ph. D., Instructor in French.

George L. Grimes, B. S., Instructor in Mechanical Engineering.
Herbert S. Jennings, Ph. D., Instructor in Zoology.
Christian F. Gauss, A. M., Instructor in French.
Edward B. Escott, B. S., Instructor in Mathematics.
William Marshall, M. S., Instructor in Mathematics.
Eugene C. Sullivan, Ph. D., Instructor in Analytical Chemistry.
Henry C. Anderson, M. E., Instructor in Mechanical Engineering.
Arthur L. Cross, Ph. D., Instructor in History.
George A. Hulett, Ph. D., Instructor in General Chemistry.
Samuel J. Holmes, Ph. D., Instructor in Zoology.
Jonathan A. C. Hildner, Ph. D., Instructor in German.
John Dieterle, A. B., Instructor in German.
Charles M. Williams, Instructor in the Waterman Gymnasium.
Karl W. Genthe, Ph. D., Instructor in Zoology.
Alice L. Hunt, Instructor in Drawing.
John W. Dwyer, LL.M., Instructor in Law.
John R. Rood, LL.B., Instructor in Law.
Charles Baird, A. B., Director of Outdoor Athletics for one year.
Eugene S. Gilmore, Superintendent of the University Hospital.

At the meeting of July 18, 1900.

Herbert D. Carrington, Ph. D., Instructor in German.

At the meeting of September 5, 1900.

Perry W. Cornue, M. D., Acting Professor of Surgery in the Homœopathic Medical College for the first semester of the year 1900-01.
William H. Wait, Ph. D., Instructor in Greek, Latin, and Sanskrit.
George K. Burgess, B. S., Instructor in Physics.
William L. Miggett, B. S., Superintendent of Engineering Shops.

APPENDIX B.

Degrees were conferred as follows during the year from October 1, 1899, to September 30, 1900:

ORDINARY DEGREES.

Bachelor of Letters	59
Bachelor of Science	51
Bachelor of Science (in Electrical Engineering)	9
Bachelor of Science (in Mechanical Engineering)	21
Bachelor of Science (in Civil Engineering)	13
Bachelor of Science (in (Pharmacy)	3
Bachelor of Philosophy	77
Bachelor of Arts	62
Master of Science	4

Master of Arts.. 30
Doctor of Philosophy... 4
Civil Engineer.. 2
Doctor of Medicine (Department of Medicine and Surgery)...... 91
Bachelor of Laws.. 219
Master of Laws.. 1
Pharmaceutical Chemist... 26
Doctor of Medicine (Homœopathic Medical College)............. 14
Doctor of Dental Surgery....................................... 68

                                                              754

HONORARY DEGREES.

Master of Arts.. 7
Doctor of Laws... 5

Total... 766

APPENDIX C.
SUMMARY OF STUDENTS
For the Academic Year, September 25, 1899, to September 24, 1900.

DEPARTMENT OF LITERATURE, SCIENCE, AND THE ARTS.

Holders of Fellowships 3
Resident Graduates 83
Candidate for an Advanced Degree, enrolled in the Department of Law 1
Graduates Studying *in Absentia* 3
Undergraduates:
  Candidates for a Degree 1101
  Students not Candidates for a Degree . 152—1343

DEPARTMENT OF ENGINEERING.

Resident Graduates 4
Graduates Studying *in Absentia* . . . 3
Undergraduates . . . . . . 273— 280

DEPARTMENT OF MEDICINE AND SURGERY.

Resident Graduates 7
Fourth Year Students 96
Third Year Students 90
Second Year Students 124
First Year Students 161
Students enrolled in other Departments of the University:
  Second Year Students in Medicine 12
  First Year Students in Medicine . . . . 10— 500

DEPARTMENT OF LAW.

Resident Graduate		1
Third Year Students		231
Second Year Students		220
First Year Students		326
Special Students		39
Students enrolled in the Department of Literature, Science, and the Arts	20—	837

SCHOOL OF PHARMACY.

Resident Graduates		4
Undergraduates:		
Candidates for a Degree		63
Students not Candidates for a Degree		8
Enrolled in the Department of Literature, Science, and the Arts	1—	76

HOMŒOPATHIC MEDICAL COLLEGE.

Resident Graduates		5
Fourth Year Students		15
Third Year Students		19
Second Year Students		8
First Year Students	23—	70

COLLEGE OF DENTAL SURGERY.

Seniors		72
Juniors		81
Freshmen	94—	247
		3353
Deduct for names counted more than once		50
Total, exclusive of Summer Session		3303

SUMMER SESSION OF 1900.

In Department of Literature, Science, and the Arts	351	
In Department of Law	53—404	
Deduct for students enrolled in 1899-1900 in some department of the University	154—250	
Grand total		3553

APPENDIX D.

Examinations for higher degrees were held as follows during the year 1899-1900:

IN THE DEPARTMENT OF LITERATURE, SCIENCE, AND THE ARTS.

CANDIDATES FOR THE DEGREE OF DOCTOR OF PHILOSOPHY.

JOSEPH HORACE DRAKE, A. B., 1885.

Thesis.—The Relation of the Subordinate Members of the Roman Military Service to the Members of the Civil Service in the Age of Diocletian. Subjects for examination: Major.— Roman History. Minors.— Latin. Jurisprudence.

WALLACE STEDMAN ELDEN, A. B., *Bowdoin College*, 1889, A. M., *ibid.*, 1892.

Thesis.— The Conditional Period of Horace. Subjects for examination: Major.—Latin. Minors.— French Philology. French Literature.

SAMUEL ALLEN JEFFERS, A. B., *Central Wesleyan College*, 1892, A. M., 1897.

Thesis.— The Philosophical Vocabulary of Lucretius. Subjects for examination: Major.— Latin. Minors.— Greek. Ancient Ethics.

CLARENCE LINTON MEADER, A. B., 1891.

Thesis.— A Semasiological Study of the Pronouns *hic* and *iste*. Subjects for examination: Major.— Latin. Minors.— Greek. Greek Archæology.

ITSUO TOKUNAGA, *Doshisha College*, 1894, 1896.

Thesis.— The Bank of Japan. Subjects for examination: Major. — Political Economy. Minors.— Finance. History.

EUGENE CYRUS WOODRUFF, B. S., 1894; M. S., 1896.

Thesis.— The Effects of Temperature on the Tuning Fork. Subjects for examination: Major.— Physics. Minors.— Mathematics. Organic Chemistry.

CANDIDATES FOR THE DEGREE OF MASTER OF ARTS.

BENJAMIN FRANKLIN BAILEY, B. S., 1898.

Thesis.— Electrolytic Interrupters. Subjects for examination: Major.— Physics. Minors.— General Chemistry. Mathematics.

EDNA LENORE BALLARD, A. B., 1898.

Subjects for examination: Major.— Latin. Minors.— Greek. Philosophy.

KENDALL PAGE BROOKS, A. B., *Alma College*, 1897.

Subjects for examination: Major.— Mathematics. Minors. — Physics. Pedagogy.

ALFRED LA RUE DAVENPORT, B. S., *Pomona College*, 1897.
Subjects for examination: Major.— Physics. Minors.— Chemistry. Mathematics.

RACHEL ELLA DAWSON, Ph. B., 1888.
Subjects for examination: Major.— English Literature. Minors.— Philosophy. English Philology.

CHARLES EDMUND FILKINS, B. L., 1891.
Subjects for examination: Major.— English Literature. Minors.— French. Pedagogy.

JAMES LESLIE FRENCH, A. B., 1899.
Subjects for examination: Major.— Hebrew. Minors.— Philosophy of Religion. Modern Ethics.

MAUDE ETHEL FULLER, A. B., 1895.
Subjects for examination: Major.— Latin. Minors.— Greek. English Literature.

ANNA BORDWELL GELSTON, Ph. B., 1881.
Subjects for examination: Major.— English Literature. Minors.— Italian Literature. Rhetoric.

ALICE CLARISSA JOY, Ph. B., *Albion College*, 1898.
Subjects for examination: Major.— American History. Minors.— European History. Political Economy.

FLORENCE BINGHAM KINNE, A. B., 1887.
Subjects for examination: Major.— American Literature. Minors.— Latin. Roman Political Antiquities.

ADONIRAM JUDSON LADD, A. B., 1894.
Subjects for examination: Major.— Pedagogy. Minors.— English Literature. Rhetoric.

RUTH ALBERTA LUDLOW, A. B., *Albion College*, 1898.
Subjects for examination: Major.— English Literature. Minors.— American Literature. Rhetoric.

EDWARD CLARK MARSH, A. B., *Alma College*, 1896.
Subjects for examination: Major.— English Literature. Minors.— Old English. Philosophy.

LOUALLEN FREDERICK MILLER, B. S., 1899.
Thesis.— Electrolytic Interrupters. Subjects for examination: Major.— Physics. Minors.— Analytical Chemistry. Mathematics.

CHARLES RUFUS MOREY, A. B., 1899.
Subjects for examination: Major.— Archæology. Minors.— Greek. Latin.

MARQUIS JOSEPH NEWELL, A. B., *Kalamazoo College;* 1896; A. B., *University of Chicago*, 1899.
Subjects for examination: Major.— Mathematics. Minors.— Pedagogy. Physics.

HARLOW STAFFORD PERSON, Ph. B., 1899.
Subjects for examination: Major.— American History. Minors.
— Political Economy. Sociology.

CARLOTTA EMMA POPE, Ph. B., 1895.
Subjects for examination: Major.— American History. Minors.—
Latin. English Literature.

HELEN FRANCES SAGE, B. L., *University of Cincinnati*, 1899.
Subjects for examination: Major.— American History. Minors.—
English Literature. Pedagogy.

MARTIN SIMPSON, B. S., *Olivet College*, 1899.
Subjects for examination: Major.— Pedagogy. Minors.— History of Education. Philosophy.

SHIRLEY WHEELER SMITH, B. L., 1897.
THESIS.— The Short Story in America. Subjects for examination: Major.— American Literature. Minors.— American History. Rhetoric.

CARRIE MAY SPERRY, A. B., 1893.
Subjects for examination: Major — Latin. Minors.— English Literature. Hygiene.

RALPH WENDELL TAYLOR, A. B., *Albion College*, 1896.
Subjects for examination: Major.— Philosophy. Minors.— Pedagogy. Rhetoric.

MARY MACLEAN THOMPSON, B. L., 1897.
Subjects for examination: Major.— English Literature. Minors.— Rhetoric. American History.

LILA TURNER, A. B., 1899.
Subjects for examination: Major.— American History. Minors.— European History. English Literature.

MAY WALMSLEY, Ph. B., 1899.
Subjects for examination: Major.— European History. Minors.— American History. Sociology.

FREDERICK HENRY WENG, Ph. B., 1898.
Subjects for examination: Major.— German. Minors.— Latin. English Philology.

ETTA RHODA WILBUR, B. S., 1895.
Subjects for examination: Major.— American History. Minors.— German. English Literature.

CANDIDATES FOR THE DEGREE OF MASTER OF SCIENCE.

EDMUND CLAUDE CHAMPION, B. S., 1899.
Subjects for examination: Major.— Analytical Chemistry. Minors.— Chemical Technology. Geology.

HENRY HALL PARKE, B. L., 1898.
THESIS.— Regeneration and Regulation in Hydra. Subjects for

examination: Major.— Experimental Zoology. Minors.— Vertebrate Zoology. Botany.

GEORGE FLETCHER RICHMOND, B. S., *Michigan Agricultural College*, 1898.

Subjects for examination: Major.— General Chemistry. Minors.— Analytical Chemistry. Physics.

HERMAN RUSSELL, B. S., 1898.

Subjects for examination: Major.— Analytical Chemistry. Minors.— Organic Chemistry. Chemical Technology.

IN THE DEPARTMENT OF ENGINEERING.

CANDIDATE FOR THE DEGREE OF CIVIL ENGINEER.
EDWIN JOHN ROSENCRANS, B. S., 1893.

THESIS.— The Structural Features of the Buffalo Savings Bank Building.

IN THE DEPARTMENT OF LAW.

CANDIDATE FOR THE DEGREE OF MASTER OF LAWS.
OSCAR OTTO BADER, LL.B., 1899.

THE TREASURER'S REPORT

FOR THE FISCAL YEAR ENDING JUNE 30, 1900.

To the Finance Committee, Board of Regents, University of Michigan,
    GENTLEMEN: Herewith I submit my annual report for the fiscal year ending June 30, 1900.   Respectfully,   H. SOULE, Treasurer.

RECEIPTS.

From State Treasurer, on acct. ¼ mill tax for General Expenses	$239,438 32	
" " " Accumulation of ¼ mill tax for Special Expenses	42,145 11	
" " " Special Appropriations	12,000 00	
" " " University Interest	28,653 29	
Earnings and Miscellaneous Sources	232,775 48	
Balance overdrawn, June 30, 1900	611 70	$555,623 90

DISBURSEMENTS.

Balance Overdrawn, July 1, 1899	18,764 53	
To Special Fund Accounts, Special Appropriations	8,623 83	
" " " Accumulation of Savings	38,759 22	
" General Fund Accounts, General Expenses	489,476 32	$555,623 90

GENERAL FUND.

RECEIPTS TO THE GENERAL FUND.

From State Treasurer, acct. University Interest	$ 28,653 29	
" " " Mill Tax	239,438 32	
" Interest on Deposits	1,015 85	
" University Hospital Earnings	20,952 37	
" Homœopathic Hospital Earnings	10,218 32	
" Dental Operating Room Earnings	4,299 76	
" Engineering Shops Earnings	570 75	
" Miscellaneous Sources	2,528 02	$307,676 68
From Students' Fees:		
Literary Department	$52,065 00	
Summer School Literary Department	2,725 00	
Engineering Department	12,350 00	
Medical "	22,765 00	
Law "	41,525 00	
Summer School Law Department	1,384 00	
Dental Department	10,890 00	
Homœopathic Medical College	2,945 00	
Pharmacy Department	3,660 00	
Chemical Laboratory	13,013 36	
Hygienic "	2,955 00	
Botanical "	566 00	
Zoological "	802 00	
Physiological "	57 00	
Pathological "	1,630 00	
Histological "	1,834 00	
Anatomical "	2,290 00	
Mechanical "	2,080 00	
Pharmacological "	5 00	
Electrotherapeutical Laboratory	872 00	
Dental Laboratory	723 00	
Medical Demonstrations	4,220 00	
Electrical Engineering (Physics)	529 00	
Key Deposits	198 00	

— 28 —

Drawing Boards	150 00		
Waterman Gymnasium	2,648 00		
Women's Gymnasium	508 00		
Diplomas	7,650 00	$193,048 36	$193,048 36
Fees, Total	193,048 36		
Fees, Refunded	7,698 05		
Fees, Net	185,350 31		
Balance Overdrawn, June 30, 1900			$9,574 53
			510,299 57

DISBURSEMENTS FROM THE GENERAL FUND.

Balance Overdrawn, July 1, 1899			$20,823 25
General Pay Roll	$156,553 75		
Summer School Literary Pay Roll	4,975 00	$161,528 75	
Summer School Current Expenses		360 46	
Law Department Pay Roll	34,312 02		
Summer School Law "	1,013 20	35,325 22	
" " Law Expenses		142 78	
Law Library Books		1,997 02	
" Department Expenses		803 10	
Medical Department Pay Roll	39,610 06	39,610 06	
" " Expenses		516 33	
" " Books		2,159 37	
Pharmacy Department and Chemical Pay Rolls	24,140 02	24,140 02	
" " Expenses		11,306 30	
Homœopathic College Pay Roll	5,500 00	5,500 00	
" " Expenses		407 50	
" " Books		127 39	
Dental College Pay Roll	12,667 47	12,667 47	
" " Expenses		6,131 78	
" " Books		80 98	
Engineering Department Pay Roll	33,523 62	33,523 62	
" " Expenses		907 30	
University Hospital Pay Roll	8,565 04	8,565 04	
" " Expenses		18,876 48	
Homœopathic Hospital Pay Roll	3,168 63	3,168 63	
" " Expenses		10,012 54	
Book Bindery Pay Roll	640 10	640 10	

Amount of Salaries Paid from the General Fund $324,668 91

Contingent Account	5,979 39
" " Real Estate	14,000 00
Repairs "	10,063 86
Fuel "	15,565 70
Lights "	2,242 58
Books for General Library	13,064 51
Current Expenses for General Library	989 51
Materia Medica	380 51
Postage	2,264 56
Advertising and Printing	1,456 01
Museum	1,029 47
Botanical Laboratory	876 76
Botanical Gardens	288 59
Histology	645 11
Hygiene	1,567 66
Zoology	909 37
Engineering Shops	2,515 57
Civil Engineering	208 86
School Inspection	505 93
Observatory	293 32
Practical Anatomy	2,231 66
Physics	780 47
Physiology	248 63
Surgical Demonstrations	188 39
Surgical Clinic	74 65
Pathology	510 97
Electrotherapeutics	464 92
Nervous Diseases	139 06
Insurance	3,079 65
Waterman Gymnasium	512 84
Barbour Gymnasium	174 12
Students' Fees Refunded	7,698 05
Women's Building	4,328 66
Teams	1,133 57

Carpenter Shop	29 71	
Philosophy	417 46	
Geology	127 05	
Electric Supplies	674 32	
Ophthalmology	34 24	
News Letter	74 72	
Latin	151 83	
Music	200 00	
New Homœopathic Hospital	105 91	
Artesian Well	5,009 40	
Appointment Committee	147 71	
General Catalogue	1,051 78	
Heating Supplies	615 78	
Commencement Expenses	866 74	
Gynæcology	27 86	
Theory and Practice	235 62	
Diseases of Women and Children	45	
Dermatology	21 30	
State Pathologist	162 62	
Mineralogy	10 00	
Diplomas	1,289 85	
Water Supply	1,860 81	
New Law Building	537 50	
Alumni Association	600 00	
Mathematics	275 23	
Philology	94	
English	16 34	$489,476 32
		$510,299 57

SPECIAL FUND ACCOUNTS.

Homœopathic Medical College.

Receipts.

Balance in Treasury, July 1, 1899		$ 9 48	
From State Treasurer		6,000 00	$6,009 48

Disbursements.

Vouchers Paid, Pay Rolls		$5,500 00	
Vouchers Paid, Current Expenses		123 83	
Balance in Treasury, June 30, 1900		385 65	$6,009 48

Electric Light Plant.

Receipts.

Earnings		$142 05	
Balance Overdrawn, June 30, 1900		239 88	$381 93

Disbursements.

Balance Overdrawn, July 1, 1899		$381 93	$381 93

Summer Hospitals.

Receipts.

From State Treasurer		$6,000 00	$6,000 00

Disbursements.

Vouchers Paid		$3,000 00	
Balance in Treasury, June 30, 1900		3,000 00	$6,000 00

Accumulation of Savings, Law Building.

Receipts.

Balance in Treasury, July 1, 1899		$498 39	$498 39

Disbursements.

Vouchers Paid		$485 88	
Balance in Treasury, June 30, 1900		12 51	$498 39

Accumulation of Savings, Extension to Foundry.

Receipts.

Balance in Treasury, July 1, 1899		$42 55	$42 55

Disbursements.

Vouchers Paid		$42 55	$42 55

— 30 —

Accumulation of Savings, Repairs on University Hospital.
Receipts.

Balance in Treasury, July 1, 1899	$299 00	$299 00

Disbursements.

Vouchers Paid	$ 51 30	
Balance in Treasury, June 30, 1900	247 70	$299 00

Accumulation of Savings, New Science Building.
Receipts.

Balance Overdrawn, June 30, 1900	$500 00	$500 00

Disbursements.

Vouchers Paid	$500 00	$500 00

Accumulation of Savings, Addition to General Library.
Receipts.

Balance in Treasury, July 1, 1899	$ 988 73	
From State Treasurer	2,145 11	$3,133 84

Disbursements.

Vouchers Paid	$3,133 84	$3,133 84

Accumulation of Savings, Addition to Homœopathic Hospital.
Receipts.

Balance in Treasury, July 1, 1899	$551 36	$551 36

Disbursements.

Balance in Treasury, June 30, 1900	$551 36	$551 36

Accumulation of Savings, Addition to Heating Plant.
Receipts.

Balance in Treasury, July 1, 1899	$18 48	$18 48

Disbursements.

Vouchers Paid	$18 48	$18 48

Accumulation of Savings, University Hospital Laundry.
Receipts.

Balance in Treasury, July 1, 1899	$32 66	$32 66

Disbursements.

Vouchers Paid	$32 66	$32 66

Accumulation of Savings, New Homœopathic Hospital.
Receipts.

From State Treasurer	$40,000 00	$40,000 00

Disbursements.

Vouchers Paid	34,494 51	
Balance in Treasury, June 30, 1900	5,505 49	$40,000 00

SPECIAL FUNDS.
Summary of Balances, June 30, 1900.
Overdrafts.

Electric Light Plant	$239 88	
New Science Building	500 00	$739 88

Balances in Treasury.

Homœopathic Medical College	$ 385 65	
New Law Building	12 51	
Addition to Homœopathic Hospital	551 36	
Repairs to University Hospital	247 70	
New Homœopathic Hospital	5,505 49	
Maintenance of Summer Hospitals	3,000 00	
	$9,702 71	
Net Balance after deducting Overdrafts		$8,962 83
		$9,702 71

GIFTS AND TRUST FUNDS.

Under this head are included gifts and other funds which the Regents have received from time to time from benefactors for special purposes. The new accounts which have been opened by your treasurer during the year are as follows: The Students' Lecture Association Fund (Lecture Board of 1899); The Newton Van der Veer Loan Fund; The James W. Scott Classical Fellowship Fund; American School at Rome; Class of Ninety-nine Memorial Fund; Detroit Archæological Fund; Liquid Air Plant; which accounts are fully detailed in this report.

Philo Parsons Fund.

Receipts.

Balance in Treasury, July 1, 1899	$99 14	
Interest	2 99	$102 13

Disbursements.

Balance in Treasury, June 30, 1900	$102 13	$102 13

Goethe Fund.

Receipts.

Balance in Treasury, July 1, 1899	$203 10	
Interest	5 94	$209 04

Disbursements.

Vouchers Paid	$12 56	
Balance in Treasury, June 30, 1900	196 48	$209 04

Elisha Jones Classical Fellowship Fund.

Receipts.

Balance in Treasury, July 1, 1899	$8 29	
Interest	24	$8 53

Disbursements.

Balance in Treasury, June 30, 1900	$8 53	$8 53

Women's Gymnasium.

Receipts.

Balance in Treasury, July 1, 1899	$4,370 54	
Interest	22 52	
Balance Overdrawn, June 30, 1900	375 92	$4,768 98

Disbursements.

Vouchers Paid	$4,768 98	$4,768 98

Coyl Collection.

Receipts.

Balance in Treasury, July 1, 1899	$11,187 24	
Interest	660 21	$11,847 45

Disbursements.

Balance in Treasury, June 30, 1900	$11,847 45	$11,847 45

Buhl Law Library Fund.

Receipts.

Balance in Treasury, July 1, 1899	$1,581 42	
Interest	44 37	$1,625 79

Disbursements.

Vouchers Paid	$372 00	
Balance in Treasury, June 30, 1900	$1,253 79	$1,625 79

Seth Harrison Scholarship Fund.

Receipts.

Balance in Treasury, July 1, 1899	$27,044 96	
Interest	997 20	$28,042 16

Disbursements.

Vouchers Paid	$867 00	
Balance in Treasury, June 30, 1900	$27,175 16	$28,042 16

Class of Ninety-Four Scholarship Fund.

Receipts.

Balance in Treasury, July 1, 1899	$1,229 12	
Interest	46 97	
Subscriptions Paid	102 45	$1,378 54

Disbursements.

Balance in Treasury, June 30, 1900	$1,378 54	$1,378 54

Ford Messer Fund.
Receipts.

Balance in Treasury, July 1, 1899	$22,626 03	
Interest	962 60	
Balance of Bequest	1,500 00	$25,088 63

Disbursements

Vouchers Paid	$ 280 73	
Balance in Treasury, June 30, 1900	24,807 90	$25,088 63

The Phillips Scholarships Fund.
Receipts.

Balance in Treasury, July 1, 1899	$384 55	
From the Estate	100 26	
Interest	11 03	$495 84

Disbursements.

Balance in Treasury, June 30, 1900	$495 84	$495 84

Music Hall Fund.
Receipts.

Balance in Treasury, July 1, 1899	$1,193 20	
Interest	59 83	$1,253 03

Disbursements.

Balance in Treasury, June 30, 1900	$1,253 03	$1,253 03

Class of Ninety-Six Memorial Fund.
Receipts.

Balance in Treasury, July 1, 1899	$6 12	
Interest	09	$6 21

Disbursements.

Vouchers Paid	$6 16	
Transferred to Library of Early Christian Literature	05	$6 21

Class of Ninety-Seven Scholarship Fund.
Receipts.

Balance in Treasury, July 1, 1899	$141 91	
Interest	8 33	$150 24

Disbursements.

Balance in Treasury, June 30, 1900	$150 24	$150 24

Class of Ninety-Eight Scholarship Fund.
Receipts.

Balance in Treasury, July 1, 1899	$262 85	
Interest	8 00	$270 85

Disbursements.

Balance in Treasury, June 30, 1900	$270 85	$270 85

American School at Rome.
Receipts.

From Donation	$10 00	$10 00

Disbursements.

Balance in Treasury, June 30, 1900	$10 00	$10 00

Parke, Davis & Co. Fund.
Receipts.

Balance in Treasury, July 1, 1899	$ 12 12	
Interest	1 11	
Donation	500 00	$513 23

Disbursements.

Vouchers Paid	$400 00	
Balance in Treasury, June 30, 1900	113 23	$513 23

Stearns Pharmacy Fellowship Fund.
Receipts.

Balance in Treasury, July 1, 1899	$ 78	
Interest	78	
Donation	350 00	$351 56

Disbursements.

Vouchers Paid	$350 00	
Balance in Treasury, June 30, 1900	1 56	$351 56

Library of Early Christian Literature.
Receipts.

Donation	$240 00	
Transfer from Class of Ninety-Six Memorial Fund	05	
Interest	13	$240 18

Disbursements.

Vouchers Paid	$227 37	
Balance in Treasury, June 30, 1900	12 81	$240 18

Frieze Memorial Fund.
Receipts.

Balance in Treasury, July 1, 1899	$357 13	
Subscriptions Paid	65 75	
Interest	8 52	$431 40

Disbursements.

Vouchers Paid	$431 00	
Balance in Treasury, June 30, 1900	40	$431 40

United States Pharmacopœia Fund.
Receipts.

Balance in Treasury, July 1, 1899	$ 50 00	
Contribution	833 33	
Interest	43	$883 76

Disbursements.

Vouchers Paid	$883 76	$883 76

Special Latin Fund.
Receipts.

Balance in Treasury, July 1, 1899	$150 51	
Subscriptions	567 65	
Interest	2 06	$720 22

Disbursements.

Vouchers Paid	$679 28	
Balance in Treasury, June 30, 1900	40 94	$720 22

Good Government Club.
Receipts.

Balance in Treasury, July 1, 1899	$500 00	
Interest	15 33	$515 33

Disbursements.

Balance in Treasury, June 30, 1900	$515 33	$515 33

Peter White Fellowship.
Receipts.

Balance in Treasury, July 1, 1899	$400 00	
Donation	400 00	
Interest	12 47	$812 47

Disbursements.

Vouchers Paid	$400 00	
Balance in Treasury, June 30, 1900	412 47	$812 47

Woman's Professorship Fund.
Receipts.

Balance in Treasury, July 1, 1899	$10,000 00	$10,000 00

Disbursements.

Balance in Treasury, June 30, 1900	$10,000 00	$10,000 00

Ninety-Nine Law Class Scholarship Fund.
Receipts.

Balance in Treasury, July 1, 1899	$25 00	
Interest	5 68	$30 68

Disbursements.

Balance in Treasury, June 30, 1900	$30 68	$30 68

Biological Laboratory Fund.
Receipts.

Donation	$50 00	$50 00

Disbursements.

Vouchers Paid	$50 00	$50 00

Williams Professorship Fund.

The care of the Williams Professorship Fund has been partly in the hands of the Treasurer and partly in the hands of Hon. Levi L. Barbour, of Detroit. A summary of the report of Mr. Barbour is given in an appendix to the present report (see Appendix A). The report on the portion in the hands of the Treasurer is as follows: —

Receipts.

Balance in Treasury, July 1, 1899	$4,899 38	
Interest	132 75	
Interest Credited by Error and Subsequently Returned	60 00	$5,092 13

Disbursements.

Vouchers Paid for Expenses	$75 00	
Vouchers Paid for Interest Returned	60 00	
Cash to Mr. Barbour for Investment	1,000 00	
Balance in Treasury, June 30, 1900	3,957 13	$5,092 13

Morris Alumni Fund.
Receipts.

Balance in Treasury, July 1, 1899	$2,377 01	
Interest	98 17	$2,475 18

Disbursements.

Vouchers Paid	$2 35	
Balance in Treasury, June 30, 1900	2,472 83	$2,475 18

Bates Professorship Fund.
Receipts.

On Account of Principal (See Reg. Proc., April 18, 1900, page 495)

Real Estate, estimated value	$39,000 00		
Mortgages, face value	71,500 00		
Cash	22,804 65	$133,304 65	
Interest and Collections		4,038 87	$137,432 52

Disbursements.

Balance Overdrawn, July 1, 1899	$1,177 10	
Vouchers Paid	3,656 55	
Balance	132,509 87	$137,343 52

D. M. Ferry Botanical Fund.
Receipts.

Donation	$400 00	
Balance Overdrawn, June 30, 1900	50 00	$450 00

Disbursements.

Vouchers Paid	$450 00	$450 00

Class of Ninety-Nine Memorial Fund.
Receipts.

Donation	$6 35	$6 35

Disbursements.

Balance in Treasury, June 30, 1900	$6 35	$6 35

Detroit Archæological Fund.
Receipts.

Subscriptions	$360 66	
Interest	08	$360 74

Disbursements.

Vouchers Paid	$357 00	
Balance in Treasury, June 30, 1900	3 84	$360 74

— 35 —

Newton Van der Veer Loan Fund.
Receipts.

Donations	$100 00	
Interest	1 25	$101 25

Disbursements.

Balance in Treasury, June 30, 1900	$101 25	$101 25

Students' Lecture Association Fund.
Receipts.

From the Lecture Board of 1899	$740 00	
Interest	$16 59	$756 59

Disbursements.

Balance in Treasury, June 30, 1900	$756 59	$756 59

Liquid Air Plant.
Receipts.

Donation	$1,090 64	
Interest	3 83	$1,094 47

Disbursements.

Vouchers Paid	$1,040 03	
Balance in Treasury, June 30, 1900	$54 44	$1,094 47

James W. Scott Classical Fellowship Fund.
Receipts.

Donation	$500 00	
Interest	3 75	$503 75

Disbursements.

Balance in Treasury, June 30, 1900	$503 75	$503 75

SUMMARY OF TRUST FUND BALANCES.

	CASH IN BANK	INVESTED IN LOANS OR REAL ESTATE	TOTAL
Philo Parsons Fund	$ 102 13		$ 102 13
Goethe Fund	196 48		196 48
Elisha Jones Classical Fellowship Fund	8 53		8 53
Coyl Collection "	2,847 45	$ 9,000 00	11,847 45
Buhl Law Library "	1,253 79		1,253 79
Seth Harrison Scholarship "	2,375 16	24,800 00	27,175 16
'94 Scholarship "	1,378 54		1,378 54
Ford Messer Library "	16,307 90	8,500 00	24,807 90
Phillips Scholarships "	495 84		495 84
Music Hall "	1,253 03		1,253 03
'97 Class Scholarship "	36 24	114 00	150 24
'98 Class Scholarship "	270 85		270 85
'99 Class Memorial "	6 35		6 35
Parke, Davis & Co. "	113 23		113 23
Stearns Pharmacy Fellowship "	1 56		1 56
Library of Early Christian Literature Fund	12 81		12 81
Frieze Memorial Fund "	40		40
Special Latin "	40 94		40 94
Good Government Club Fund	515 33		515 33
Peter White Fellowship "	412 47		412 47
Woman's Professorship "		10,000 00	10,000 00
'99 Law Class Scholarship Fund	30 68		30 68
Williams Professorship "	3,957 13		
Williams Professorship in hands of L. L. Barbour	138 98	11,653 46	15,749 57
Morris Alumni Fund	1,322 83	1,150 00	2,472 83
Bates Professorship	27,409 87	66,100 00	
Bates Professorship, Real Estate		39,000 00	132,509 87
Detroit Archæological Fund	2 84		2 84
American School at Rome Fund	10 00		10 00
Newton Van der Veer "	101 25		101 25
Students' Lecture Association "	556 59	200 00	756 59
Liquid Air Plant "	54 44		54 44
James W. Scott Fellowship "	503 75		503 75
	$61,717 39	$170,517 46	$232,234 85
Less Overdrafts,			
Women's Gymnasium	$375 92		
Ferry Botanical Fund	50 00	425 92	425 92
	$61,291 47	$170,517 46	$231,808 93

APPENDICES.

APPENDIX A.

WILLIAMS PROFESSORSHIP FUND.

In July, 1898, by order of the Board of Regents, a portion of the property belonging to the Williams Professorship Fund was placed in the hands of Hon. Levi L. Barbour, of Detroit, for management. According to the schedule made at that time the value (partly estimated) of the property entrusted to Mr. Barbour was as follows:

Mortgage Securities,	$7,077 44	
Other Property,	3,0153 68	$10,231 12

The following statement is a condensed summary of the reports of Mr. Barbour covering the time from July, 1898, to June 30, 1900:

Receipts.

On account of Principal of Mortgages	$2,200 00	
" " " Interest collected	810 60	
" " " Land Contracts	189 60	
" " " Rents	55 00	
" " " Sales	174 58	
From H. Soule, Treasurer, for Investment	1,000 00	$4,429 78

Disbursements.

Investment in Mortgages	$4,000 00	
Taxes	232 60	
Insurance	12 30	
Foreclosure Expenses	27 70	
Commissions	4 48	
Recording Mortgages, etc.	7 52	
Postage, Express, Stationery, and Sundries	6 20	
Cash in bank, June 30, 1900	138 98	$4,429 78

The value of the property in the hands of Mr. Barbour, June 30, 1900 (partly estimated), is given as follows:

Cash in Bank	$ 138 98	
Real Estate Mortgages	7,452 00	
Land Contracts	1,330 00	
Real Estate, Cost	2,584 83	
Claim vs. Fred E. King	286 63	$11,792 44

APPENDIX B.

Contributors to the Ninety-Four Class Scholarship Fund during the year ending June 30, 1900:

Delia Sophia Bailey Cobb	$ 5 00
Lelia Brouillette	5 00
Henry Oliver Chapoton	10 00
Alvick Alfonso Pearson	21 20
Stuart Hoffman Perry	28 00
Adrian John Pieters	5 15
Fred Anson Sager	5 00
Samuel Archibald Smith	6 00
Eugene Cornelius Sullivan	17 10
	$102 45

UNIVERSITY OF MICHIGAN

THE PRESIDENT'S REPORT

TO THE

BOARD OF REGENTS

FOR THE ACADEMIC YEAR

ENDING SEPTEMBER 30, 1901

FINANCIAL STATEMENT

FOR THE FISCAL YEAR

ENDING JUNE 30, 1901

ANN ARBOR, MICH.,
PUBLISHED BY THE UNIVERSITY
1901

THE PRESIDENT'S REPORT

To the Honorable Board of Regents:
I hereby present to you my Annual Report for the year ending Sept. 30, 1901.

The University has sustained heavy losses by death.

On May 20, 1901, Regent William J. Cocker died after a very brief illness in this city, where he had just been attending a meeting of the Board. The son of Dr. Benjamin F. Cocker, who filled the chair of Philosophy in this Institution for several years, a graduate of the Literary Department in 1869, most of the years of his boyhood and early manhood were spent in this city. After graduation he was for some years engaged in teaching, and later in the business of banking. His experience thus fitted him in a peculiar manner for the duties of Regent. His counsels concerning our educational work and concerning our financial affairs were equally valuable. His devotion to his Alma Mater was complete. He grudged no expenditure of his labor or of his time in her service. His conciliatory and winsome spirit made him a most agreeable companion to us in the arduous and sometimes perplexing duties which fall to this Board. He had served one full term of eight years, and was on the third year of his second term.

On Nov. 29, 1900, Burke Aaron Hinsdale, Professor of the Science and the Art of Teaching in this University since February, 1888, died at Atlanta, Ga., where he had gone in quest of health. Before coming to us, Mr. Hinsdale had filled the offices of Professor and of President of Hiram College, and of Superintendent of Schools of Cleveland, Ohio. A more devoted and laborious teacher has never held a place in our Faculty. Having a strong natural bent for history as well as for pedagogy, his instruction naturally laid great emphasis on the history and development of educational ideas and systems. By his ample learning, his weight of personality, and his warm sympathy with students, he made a deep impression on his classes. By his marvelous industry he found time to produce a volume of high merit on a historical or an educational subject nearly every year of his connection with us. Few scholars are so well read in American history as he was. He was scrupulously faithful in the discharge of all the University duties which fell to him outside of his strictly professional work. He was one of the wisest counselors on all questions of general University administration and policy, and his opinions justly carried great weight in the deliberations of the Faculty.

During the last vacation Carroll Dunham Jones, Instructor in Electrical Engineering, died in the Adirondacks, where he had been sent by his physicians to combat pulmonary troubles. He graduated here in 1893, and took his second degree, that of Electrical Engineer, in 1897. His early death cuts short a career which gave marked promise of success.

The Assistant Librarian, in charge of the Law Library, Joseph Hardcastle Vance, LL.B., died on Dec. 23, 1900, after a brief illness. No officer now in the University had so early a connection with it as he. After serving in a clerical capacity for some time, he was made Librarian in 1854, and continued in that office two years. He was graduated from the Law Department in 1861. In 1883 he was appointed to the position which he held at the time of his decease. He was faithful in the discharge of his duties, and was very helpful to the law students in their use of the library.

The attendance of students continues to increase year by year. The number, not counting those in the Summer School, was during the past year 3,482, an increase of 179 over the preceding year. Including the students in the Summer School of 1901, the total attendance was 3,710. As in the previous year there was a gain in every department except that of Pharmacy. The largest gain was in the Department of Engineering, 79; although in the Department of Medicine and Surgery there was a gain of 63, and in that of Law, a gain of 36.

The increase in the number of students from Michigan, which

has been noticeable during the last few years, is still worthy of attention, it being 138 this year as compared with the preceding year. The whole number of Michigan students was 2,144. Taking the enumeration of the last census, it appears that we have one student for 1,129 of the inhabitants. If we add to the Michigan students in the University, the number in the Agricultural College, the Mining School, and in Olivet, Albion, Kalamazoo, Hillsdale, and Alma Colleges, say 1,035, and add one hundred for Michigan students in colleges and universities outside of the State,— and that number is nearly correct,— it appears that the proportion of students receiving collegiate or university education to the whole population of the State is just about one to 738. Evidently Michigan believes in higher education.

The number of students in all the larger universities and colleges of the West steadily and rapidly increases. Each of those institutions has its own constituency which furnishes it a constant supply of pupils. When a new and strong university, like the University of Chicago, is established, it creates its own constituency and flourishes without diminishing the attendance upon the others. The truth is, the population of these Northern Central States, the number of parents who in the general prosperity are able to send their children to college, and the number of high schools prepared to fit pupils for college work, are increasing at such a pace, that the resources of all the better institutions of higher education in those States are taxed to the utmost to meet the multiplying demands upon them. Especially is this true of the co-educational institutions, since the proportion of girls to boys, who are seeking collegiate education, is increasing year by year.

In partial illustration of what is said above it may be observed that while the roll of students in the stronger institutions in the States near us is enlarging, there is no decline here in the number of representatives from several of those States. For instance, Illinois sent us this year 353, an increase of 9; Ohio 247, an increase of 32; Indiana 138, an increase of 9; New York 137, an increase of 40; and several other States a similar increase. We had students from every State except Delaware and Louisana, from every Territory, from the Hawaiian Islands

(4), from Porto Rico (11), from the Philippine Islands (2), and from the following countries and provinces, Ontario (25), New Brunswick, Jamaica, Egypt, South Africa, Mexico, Switzerland, Germany, China, Japan. We have long been prepared to expect some falling off in the number of students from other States where the colleges and universities have been multiplying their attractions. But the number of such students, 1,568, is greater than ever before.

The number of women in the University last year was as follows: —

Department of Literature, Science, and the Arts	650
Department of Medicine and Surgery	41
Department of Law	5
Department of Pharmacy	8
Homœopathic Medical College	6
Department of Dental Surgery	10
	720

The preceding year the total number was 714. The increase in the Literary Department was 15. There was a slight decline in the aggregate attendance of women in the Professional Schools. There was scarcely any change in the proportion of women to men in the whole University.

Some important changes were made in the Literary Department during the year.

In the first place, instead of giving four kinds of Bachelors' degrees, namely, Bachelor of Arts, Bachelor of Philosophy, Bachelor of Science, and Bachelor of Letters, the degree of Bachelor of Arts was conferred at the last Commencement, and is to be conferred hereafter on persons who have completed one hundred and twenty hours of such work as would have won any one of the four degrees under our old statutes.

The proposition to make this important change in our degrees has been under consideration for a long time. It was resisted mainly on the ground that the degree of Bachelor of Arts was by long usage understood to indicate attainments in the ancient classics, and that it was presumptuous, if not unjust to the holders of that degree, for one institution to attempt to deprive it of its historical significance. The change has been advocated on the ground that the ancient classics are no longer entitled to a more honorable recognition than the other branches of knowledge that are taught in colleges and universities, and that it is not just or expedient to foster the pursuit of the ancient classics by offering a special premium for the study of them in the form of a distinctive diploma to be regarded as of higher value than the other diplomas. Those who opposed the change have been obliged to admit that the historic argument has lost much of its force through the action of several of our prominent colleges and universities, which no longer require the study of Latin or Greek as a requisite to the attainment of the degree of Bachelor of Arts. The movement in that direction is so strong that it may reasonably be expected that most of our higher institutions will before long yield to it, though for some time many of the holders of the old diploma of Bachelor of Arts will doubtless regret and criticise the change.

In the second place, the requirements for the attainment of the Bachelor's degree have been modified by offering to the student a somewhat larger liberty of election than he before enjoyed. His liberty is restricted only by the following provisions. He must take six hours of English, three hours in each semester of the first year, unless for exceptional reasons a postponement of this work is allowed by the committee on electives. In addition to this work the first year student must choose the remainder of his studies from the courses offered from three of the following subjects: Greek, Latin, French, German, History, Mathematics, Physics, Chemistry, Biology, including in this last Botany and Zoology.

A careful study of the elections made under the rules heretofore in force showed that with few exceptions the choices have been made so wisely that the Faculty have felt themselves justified in granting this larger liberty. In general, the elections show a distinct and well-conceived plan with no serious abuses from taking a preponderance of "soft snaps" or easy studies. The Committee who made a thorough inspection of the election blanks for last year, reported that it was very doubtful if any committee of the Faculty could on the whole have made better choice for the students. The great mass of our students are here with an earnest purpose and aim to secure the best results from their college course. The regulations may wisely be made to further their ends. The few who lack such purpose will not accomplish much under any restrictive rules. At any rate, it is not fair to the earnest students to hamper them with rules devised, and generally in vain, to get profitable work out of the indolent and wayward. These last, if retained at all, may properly receive special treatment. College discipline deemed needful for these has too often been made applicable to those who not only do not need it, but are hindered by it from reaping the best fruitage from their college life.

The courses which were established last year for giving instruction in higher commercial education and administrative law have attracted much attention. They have been highly commended in the public press, and have deeply interested some of our most earnest students. The organization of the work was necessarily tentative and experimental. A number of eminent specialists assisted us by brief courses of lectures. We have now added to our Faculty Dr. E. D. Jones, formerly of the University of Wisconsin, as Assistant Professor of Commerce and Industry. We shall also have again the aid of some special lecturers. The almost simultaneous establishment of similar courses of work in several of the leading colleges and universities shows that there is a widespread demand for them. Fortunately for us, we had in our various departments a large force of teachers whose work, properly co-ordinated, was easily made tributary to the ends sought by the establishment of these new courses. In our special Announcement, the names of no less than twenty-five teachers appear.

We have also made a new departure in the appointment of an instructor in Forestry. We have taken this action in the hope that we may render in due time some valuable service to the State of Michigan. Large tracts have been stripped of their pine forests, and are left as useless barrens. The problems of the treatment of such lands are of the highest importance. Can they be made productive in any way? Can the pine forests be reproduced? The forests of hardwood are rapidly falling before the woodman's ax. Every one admits that there has been reckless waste in the treatment of the forests of the State, and that there is an urgent need without further delay of taking up in a scientific way the forestry problems now pressing upon us. Though beginning its work in a modest way, the University wishes by its action to announce its desire to contribute its part toward the solution of the problems. It hopes that with proper co-operation by the authorities of the State it may be able, sooner or later, to accomplish something of value. The State of New York has shown its deep interest in the forestry problems by enabling Cornell University to undertake some important experiments in the Adirondack forests. A handsome bequest has been made to Yale University for work in forestry. The American has too long treated trees as his natural enemies to be utterly destroyed with the utmost dispatch. But we are now coming to the point, long ago reached by the European countries, where it is apparent that the care and preservation of forests require the most careful consideration of the State.

At the Observatory the series of observations on Polaris with the meridian circle for the determination of the aberration constant was continued till last February. Professor Hall has been engaged in this work for some years. The reductions are nearly completed. It is desirable that the results be published.

It is intended to take up the determination of the places of a list of stars in the northern sky, the observation of which has been requested by the German Astronomical Society, and which are to serve as fundamental stars.

The number of graduate students was 108, a gain of eighteen over the previous year. Parke, Davis & Co., Frederick Stearns & Co., Hon. D. M. Ferry, Nelson, Baker & Co., all of Detroit, and Hon. Peter White, of Marquette, continued last year the support of the Fellowships which they had previously carried, and Mrs. James W. Scott, of Chicago, supported a classical Fellowship for the year. The Pilgrim Publishing Co., of Battle Creek, has established for the coming year a Fellowship for the method of teaching English. These temporary endowments of Fellowships are very helpful and encouraging. We still await the endowment of a few permanent scholarships.

The number of those who have received degrees during the year is as follows:—

ORDINARY DEGREES.

Bachelor of Letters	3
Bachelor of Science	1
Bachelor of Science (Electrical Engineering)	5
Bachelor of Science (Mechanical Engineering)	25
Bachelor of Science (Civil Engineering)	15
Bachelor of Science (Pharmacy)	1
Bachelor of Philosophy	6
Bachelor of Arts	231
Master of Science	1
Master of Arts	41
Doctor of Philosophy	6
Mechanical Engineer	2
Civil Engineer	6
Doctor of Medicine (Department of Medicine and Surgery)	78
Bachelor of Laws	223
Master of Laws	4
Pharmaceutical Chemist	27
Doctor of Medicine (Homœopathic Medical College)	16
Doctor of Dental Surgery	76
Doctor of Dental Science	1
	768

HONORARY DEGREES.

Bachelor of Arts	1
Master of Arts	3
Doctor of Laws	3

Total, 775

The Engineering Department has received a larger accession of students than any other Department. It is only a few years since a decline in the attendance of Engineering Schools was observed. But the great prosperity which the country has recently enjoyed has given a great stimulus to engineering in all its branches. It is also interesting to note that apparently a change has taken place in the opinions of the conductors of great engineering and manufacturing enterprises concerning the relative value of young men who have and those who have not been trained in some good school. It is found that the former as a rule prove much more capable of assuming, at an early period in their career, posts of responsibility. Consequently there is a demand greater than the supply for graduates of the better engineering schools in the country. We were unable to meet the calls made on us last summer for graduates whom we could recommend.

Our work in Marine Engineering is attracting attention, and students are turning to the pursuit of that branch. We confidently hope to train men who shall prove of service to the shipyards, on lakes, and on sea, and so contribute to the development of our commerce.

The Department of Medicine and Surgery, notwithstanding its elevation of the standard of admission or perhaps partly because of that, has had a larger attendance than was ever before known in its history. The Faculty with the approbation of the Regents have now called for higher attainments, especially in mathematics and in languages, for admission and for graduation. A reading knowledge of French or German is henceforth insisted on. If not attained before admission, it must be afterward in the college classes. This knowledge is deemed essential, since so much of the best medical literature is now presented to the world in either German or French. One who has to learn a modern language after admission must expect to take five years to complete his medical course. It is hoped that a requirement for a knowledge of both French and German may before long be wisely made. In addition to Geometry, Plane Trigonometry is now asked, in order that the student may do proper work in advanced Physics.

It is a cause for congratulation that the laboratory facilities for this Department are to be so largely improved by the erection of the new medical building, for medical instruction is now mainly given by laboratory and clinical methods.

It is with gratification that we have been informed that two of the ten Fellowships established by John D. Rockefeller for advanced medical research, have been awarded to our Department of Medicine and Surgery. These Fellowships have been assigned to a limited number of the most prominent Medical schools in the country.

The Law Department continues its steady growth. It is much the largest in the country. This growth has come in the face of, or in consequence of, constantly increasing requirements for admission and for graduation. It has rendered necessary an enlargement of the Faculty. It is gratifying to observe that an increasing proportion of the students are graduates of some college. The course of instruction is strenuous and exacting. The Practice Court has proved to be a most valuable feature, and has been imitated in other important Law schools.

The Homœopathic Medical College pursues the even tenor

of its way with about the same number of students from year to year. There appears to be no ground for expecting soon a very considerable increase. The attendance seems to be a fair proportion of the total number of homœopathic medical students in the country, and the high standard of preparation and study perhaps places the college at some disadvantage in competition for numbers with homœopathic schools with less exacting requirements. But it is hoped that its high standard may prove in the end to be its strength and attraction as has been the case with our other professional schools. Its new hospital has proved most satisfactory.

The Pharmacy Department scarcely holds its own in attendance. Probably the establishment of great laboratories or manufactories for the preparation of many standard medicines, antitoxins, etc., as well as of so-called proprietary medicines, somewhat narrows the field for pharmacists who dispense medicines under physicians' prescriptions at the drug stores. On the other hand, owing to this cause, there is a field for a certain number of thoroughly trained pharmaceutical chemists in these great establishments, and a distinct and emphatic call for such research work in pharmacy as is done by the holders of Fellowships endowed for the purpose. So if the students are somewhat less numerous, the range of the work attempted is higher than it was formerly.

The Dental College has continued to grow with a rapidity which is rather embarrassing. Our rooms appropriated to it have become altogether inadequate for the service. By raising the requirements for admission we had expected to restrict the number of students within manageable limits. But here as in other Departments the elevation of the standard has thus far been followed by an increase, rather than by a diminution, in the attendance. But as several of the stronger Dental schools which have promised to extend their course to four years, have not done so, while we have already adopted the policy which they have commended, there will undoubtedly be a temporary falling off in our numbers. Still as we have heretofore led the way in lengthening and strengthening the course in Dentistry, we shall do so now regardless of any shrinkage in attendance. We are confident that the men with the best aspirations will come to us, and also that the other principal schools will soon follow our example.

It is clear that at no distant date we must furnish the college with a new and suitable building in place of the present building, which is not only too small, but which, having been built twenty-six years ago for temporary use as a hospital, is really worn out.

The Hospitals have been filled to overflowing during the past year. In the University Hospital 2,012 patients were treated, among them representatives from seventy-five counties of this State. It is interesting to observe that farmers and their wives formed by far the largest class. They numbered 425. Among the patients were persons from almost every calling and condition in life.

In the Homœopathic Hospital 1,612 patients were received, representing seventy-seven counties of this State, and also a great variety of vocations.

The people of the State are showing a juster appreciation of the usefulness of these Hospitals as a public charity. This was to be expected as the beneficent results of their establishment became more fully known through the treatment of patients from all parts of the State. When our citizens see, as they have seen this year, a man who was born blind taken from the Asylum for the Blind at the age of twenty-one, and by surgery enabled to see as well as any of us, and numerous other cases of men who, owing to accident or disease, were a public charge upon the counties, and who at the Hospitals were restored to productive activity and the power of self-support, it is reasonable that they should regard with favor the maintenance of the Hospitals at what is really a trifling expense to the State. The continuance of them is justified on economic grounds as well as on the grounds of humanity.

While the University authorities rejoice in this beneficent and humane result of the work in the Hospitals, yet it will be remembered that we hold prominently in mind the usefulness of the Hospitals to the students of Medicine. When we established them, it was predicted by many that we should accomplish little, because we could not obtain interesting cases or, indeed, any considerable number of patients of any kind in this small city. The prediction has proved erroneous in both particulars. It is now coming to be seen that in some respects medical students obtain more advantage from our Hospitals which are conducted with special reference to the instruction of students than they do from such access as is allowed to them in the hospitals in larger cities, which are managed so as to accommodate students only incidentally. Our students are allowed privileges in our Hospitals which it is not practicable to offer in the great city hospitals. It is an interesting fact that some of the more important schools in the country are now seeking to build hospitals which, like ours, shall be under their own control, and the plan is meeting the warm commendation of prominent physicians.

Three Departments have shared in the work of the Summer School, the Literary and the Law Departments as in previous years, and for the first time the Department of Medicine and Surgery. The number in attendance was as follows: Literary Department, 303; Law Department, 59; Medical Department, 56. Total 418. Of these 190 were students already enrolled in some Department of the University. The new names were therefore 228.

The librarian reports that during the year there has been an increase in our libraries of 10,045 volumes. The total number on June 30 last was 155,524. The recorded circulation in the General Library was 153,193 volumes. The use of books of which no record could be made, which last year was estimated at one half of the actual use has, in the opinion of the librarian, been relatively much greater this year than last. This is accounted for by the fact that more books are now on the shelves, to which there is free access, and also by the fact that there have been very many more temporary admissions to the bookroom.

Frederick Stearns, Esq., has during his recent visit to Europe made important and most valuable additions to the Stearns Collection of musical instruments. It now stands in the front rank of such collections in America.

Mrs. Adah Z. Treadwell, who died in this city, bequeathed to us the sum of $2,000 to be deposited in the State Treasury, to be known as the Treadwell Fund, the interest of which shall be expended annually for the support of a free bed in the University Hospital for some poor and deserving patient. This bequest is the first gift which has come to us under the provision of the law, requiring the State Treasury, on request of the donor, to receive funds presented to us and to pay us interest on them. The State pays us merely the interest it receives on deposits in the banks. This arrangement furnishes absolute security for the funds, though at present we can receive only two or two and a half per cent income from them.

Mrs. Love M. Palmer, widow of Dr. Alonzo B. Palmer, who was for thirty-five years a member of the Faculty of the Department of Medicine and Surgery and for many years its Dean, has bequeathed to us the sum of twenty thousand dollars for the erection of a ward in connection with the University Hospital and fifteen thousand dollars for the endowment of it. Special interest attaches to this gift, as the ward is to be a memorial to Dr. Palmer, who by his long and eminent services contributed so conspicuously to the upbuilding of the Department.

By the generous provision of the Legislature in appropriating fifty thousand dollars for the purpose, a Psychopathic ward is to be erected in connection with the University Hospital. It is found that not a few persons are afflicted with insanity or abnormal states of mind caused by some disease which may be cured or alleviated through treatment by specialists. The disease being thus partially or wholly cured, the insanity disappears. It is proposed that persons who may be adjudged by competent medical authority in a condition to be properly benefited by special treatment in the Psychopathic ward may be received there. If the treatment proves successful in a reasonable time, the patients will escape the necessity of resorting to an asylum for the insane. It is hoped that in this manner a good number may be restored to health, and that thus in some degree the heavy demands now made upon our State Asylums may be relieved. In this ward opportunity will be furnished to our medical students to study some of the problems of alienism. This is a consideration of much importance, as we are always furnishing, from our graduates, assistants and physicians for asylums for the insane.

The continuous growth of the University, and a sense of our

duty to improve our methods of instruction so far as we can, constrain me to call attention briefly to certain pressing needs, which require early consideration.

1. We must have as soon as possible an addition to our electric-light plant. The buildings we have recently erected, and the others which we must soon erect, call at once for the duplication of our present supply of electricity. Until the plant is enlarged, we may be forced to cut out a portion of the lights in our buildings. It need not be added that such a step would be attended with much inconvenience.

2. An enlargement of the physical laboratory so as to furnish in addition to other needed accommodations another large lecture room, is absolutely necessary. This is required because the literary and engineering classes in Physics are larger than they ever were before, and because the medical classes now receive their instruction in that subject in the laboratory building. The projected removal of the Laboratory of Hygiene and Bacteriology from the third floor to the new Medical Building does not leave provision for the needed lecture room.

3. The Engineering Department, which is receiving this year a third more students than it had last year must have more room at once, especially room for the accommodation of students in drawing. That can be furnished only by the enlargement or reconstruction of some of the buildings occupied by that Department, or by the addition of a new building.

4. The laboratories of Botany, Zoology, and Psychology greatly need larger and better rooms. These can be furnished only by a new building.

5. The Literary Department taken as a whole is greatly in need of more recitation rooms and lecture rooms and of better ventilation and better regulation of temperature in all the present rooms. It will be remembered that since Tappan Hall, the last building erected (in 1894) for the Literary Department, was completed, the number of students in that Department has increased some 400 or more, a number equal or superior to the total attendance in many a reputable college. It may readily be seen that the space, which was adequate then is far from adequate now. Some of the rooms are uncomfortably crowded, and many of them are so continuously occupied that with no means

of ventilation available except by the opening of windows and doors, the health of the occupants is endangered. There is also a pressing need of one or two lecture rooms, each of which will accommodate four hundred students.

6. There is urgent need of important repairs in the Library Building and of the addition to it of commodious and spacious seminary rooms. The present provisions for ventilation and regulation of heat in the winter are very imperfect. The number of students has increased nearly threefold since the erection of the Library Building, and the methods of instruction now followed in several branches of study compel the constant use of the books by a larger proportion of our students than formerly. We are seriously lacking in adequate accommodations for the advanced students, both undergraduates and graduates, in carrying on what is known as seminary work, in which immediate access to a considerable number of selected books, and the supply of rooms for the meeting of small sections for conference and discussion in proximity to the books, are necessary.' Few innovations in the method of University instruction have been more fruitful of good results than the introduction of the seminary method, which has found its way into all the best institutions in the country. It is believed that is was introduced here earlier than at any other American University. We should not fall behind other institutions in reaping the largest results from it.

7. Of the need of a new home for the Dental College I have spoken elsewhere.

8. The heating plant for the University Hospital is now in the basement of the Nurses' House. This arrangement is not entirely safe, and is in other respects undesirable. It would be far better to construct a boiler house on the hillside below the Hospital, into which a short spur from the Michigan Central Railway track could run. The coal could thus be unloaded directly from the cars.

All these needs are real and most of them very urgent. If the University is to accomplish with success the work, to which the State has called it, to develop and instruct the minds of the students committed to its care, and to have a due regard for their health and their comfort, while they are here, these needs should be met at the earliest practicable date.

JAMES B. ANGELL.

APPENDICES.

APPENDIX A.

APPOINTMENTS, REAPPOINTMENTS, RESIGNATIONS, ETC., DURING THE YEAR ENDING SEPTEMBER 30, 1901.

Resignations:

At the meeting of February 21, 1901, the resignations of James N. Martin, Ph.M., M.D., Bates Professor of the Diseases of Women and Children, and James G. Lynds, M.D., Demonstrator of Obstetrics and Diseases of Women, to take effect October 1, 1901, were presented and accepted.

At the meeting of April 17, 1901, the resignation of Elias F. Johnson, B.S., LL.M., Professor of Law and Secretary of the Law Faculty, was presented and accepted.

At the meeting of June 7, 1901, the resignation of Benjamin P. Bourland, Ph.D., Assistant Professor of French, was presented and accepted.

At the meeting of August 2, 1901, the resignations of Ernst H. Mensel, Ph.D., Assistant Professor of German, and George L. Grimes, B.S., Instructor in Mechanical Engineering, were presented and accepted.

Leave of Absence:

At the meeting of February 21, 1901, Instructor Carroll D. Jones, E.E., was granted leave of absence for the remainder of the academic year.

At the meeting of April 17, 1901, Professor J. Playfair McMurrich, Ph.D., was granted leave of absence from May 28 to the end of the academic year; Professor Warren P. Lombard, A.B., M.D., was granted leave of absence from September 25 to October 10; Professor Robert M. Wenley, Sc.D., D.Phil., was granted leave of absence from May 20 to the end of the academic year; and the leave of absence previously granted Instructor Arthur G. Hall, B.S., was extended to cover the year 1901–02.

At the meeting of June 7, 1901, Professor Isaac N. Demmon, LL.D., was granted leave of absence from June 12 for the remainder of the academic year, and Professor Paul C. Freer, Ph.D., M.D., was granted leave of absence for one year from October 1, 1901, with the privilege of extending the leave to eighteen months, if found necessary.

At the meeting of June 18, 1901, Instructor John S. P. Tatlock, A.M., was granted leave of absence for the year 1901–02.

Change of Title, etc.:

At the meeting of October 17, 1900, the title of Mr. Keene Fitzpatrick was changed to Director of the Waterman Gymnasium, and the title of Alice G. Snyder, M.D., was changed to Instructor in the Barbour Gymnasium.

At the meeting of January 17, 1901, a portion of the work of the late Professor B. A. Hinsdale was temporarily assigned to Assistant Professor Rebec.

At the meeting of May 16, 1901, the title of George W. Patterson, Jr., Ph.D., was changed to Junior Professor of Electrical Engineering.

At the meeting of June 7, 1901, the title of Alice G. Snyder, M.D., was changed to Associate Director of the Barbour Gymnasium.

At the meeting of June 18, 1901, the title of William F. Breakey, M.D., was changed to Lecturer on Dermatology and Syphilology, and the title of Junior Professor Fred N. Scott, Ph.D., was changed to Professor of Rhetoric.

Special Resident Lecturers and Instructors:

In the Department of Literature, Science, and the Arts, Resident Instructors were appointed for the Summer Session of the year 1901 as follows:

At the meeting of February 21, 1901.

Wooster W. Beman, A.M., Mathematics.
Thomas C. Trueblood, A.M., Elocution.
John C. Rolfe, Ph.D., Latin.
William H. Payne, LL.D., the Science and the Art of Teaching.
Fred M. Taylor, Ph.D., Political Economy.
George W. Patterson, Jr., Ph.D., Physics.
John O. Reed, Ph.D., Physics, Chairman of Executive Committee.
Joseph H. Drake, Ph.D., Latin.
Joseph L. Markley, Ph.D., Mathematics.
Moritz Levi, Ph.D., Spanish and Italian.
Ernst H. Mensel, Ph.D., German, Secretary of the Executive Committee.
Moses Gomberg, Sc.D., Chemistry.
Walter B. Pillsbury, Ph.D., Psychology.
David M. Lichty, M.S., Chemistry.
Tobias Diekhoff, Ph.D., German.
James W. Glover, Ph.D., Mathematics.
Louis A. Strauss, Ph.D., English and Rhetoric.
Herbert J. Goulding, B.S., Drawing.
Victor E. François, French.
Perry F. Trowbridge, Ph.B., Chemistry.
Herbert H. Waite, A.B., Bacteriology.
John S. P. Tatlock, A.M., English and Rhetoric.
James B. Pollock, Sc.D., Botany.
Eugene C. Sullivan, Ph.D., Chemistry.
Henry C. Anderson, M.E., Mechanical Engineering.

Jonathan A. C. Hildner, Ph.D., German.
Duane R. Stuart, A.B., Greek.
Frederick L. Dunlap, Ph.D., Chemistry.
Charles M. Williams, Physical Training.
Charles L. Bliss, B.S., Physiological Chemistry.
John W. Slaughter, A.B., B.D., Philosophy.
Harrison M. Randall, Ph.M., Physics.

At the meeting of April 17, 1901.

Clarence L. Meader, Ph.D., Latin.

At the meeting of June 18, 1901.

George P. Burns, Ph.D., Botany.

At the meeting of July 10, 1901.

George Rebec, Ph.D., Pedagogy.

In the Department of Medicine and Surgery, Special Lecturers were appointed for the year 1901–02 as follows:

At the meeting of June 18, 1901.

Harry B. Hutchins, LL.D., Medical Jurisprudence.
Walter B. Pillsbury, Ph.D., Physiological Psychology.

In the Department of Law Special Lecturers were appointed for the year 1901–02 as follows:

At the meeting of June 18, 1901.

Victor C. Vaughan, M.D., LL.D., Toxicology in its Legal Relations.
Henry C. Adams, LL.D., The Railroad Problem.
Andrew C. McLaughlin, A.M., LL.B., Constitutional Law and Constitutional History.
Richard Hudson, A.M., Comparative Constitutional Law.
William J. Herdman, M.D., LL.D., Neurology, Electrology, and Railway Injuries.

Non-resident Lecturers and Instructors:

In the Department of Literature, Science, and the Arts, Non-resident Instructors were appointed for the Summer Session of the year 1901 as follows:

At the meeting of February 21, 1901.

Charles A. Davis, A.M., Geology.
William H. Munson, B.S., Zoology.
Charles B. Scott, A.M., Nature Study.
James A. Woodburn, Ph.D., History.

In the Department of Medicine and Surgery, Non-resident Lecturers were appointed for the year 1901-02 as follows:

At the meeting of June 18, 1901.

William M. Edwards, M.D., Insanity.
Edmund A. Christian, A.B., M.D., Insanity.
James D. Munson, M.D., Insanity.
Henry B. Baker, A.M., M.D., Administration of Health Laws.
George L. Chamberlain, M.D., Insanity.
Cressy L. Wilbur, M.D., Vital Statistics.

In the Department of Law, Non-resident Lecturers were appointed for the year 1901-02 as follows:

At the meeting of June 18, 1901.

John B. Clayberg, LL.B., Mining Law.
Melville M. Bigelow, LL.D., Insurance.
Henry H. Swan, A.M., Admiralty.
Frank H. Reed, A.B., Copyright Law and Law of Trademarks.
Albert H. Walker, LL.B., Patent Law.
Dallas Boudeman, M.S., Michigan Statute Law and Statutory Construction.
Harlow P. Davock, C.E., M.S., Practice under Bankruptcy Law.

In the Homœopathic Medical College, Non-resident Lecturers were appointed for the year 1900-01, as follows:

At the meeting of October 17, 1900.

Oscar R. Long, M.D., Mental Diseases.
William A. Polglase, M.D., Nervous Diseases.

Other Appointments and Reappointments:

Appointments and reappointments were made in the several departments as indicated in the lists given below. The names of persons appointed as Assistants or, with a few exceptions, to other positions of lower grade than Instructor, are not included. Professors and Junior Professors were appointed for unlimited time, Assistant Professors for three years, and Instructors for one year, except in cases where a different period of service is mentioned.

At the meeting of October 17, 1900.

Carl F. A. Lange, A.M., Instructor in German.
Fred M. Green, B.S., Instructor in Civil Engineering.
Walter B. Ford, A.M., Instructor in Mathematics.

At the meeting of December 21, 1900.

William H. Payne, LL.D., Professor of the Science and the Art of Teaching.

Charles Baird, A.B., Director of Outdoor Athletics.

At the meeting of February 21, 1901.

Dean T. Smith, A.M., M.D., Acting Professor of Surgery in the Homœopathic Medical College for the remainder of the academic year.

At the meeting of April 17, 1901.

Reuben Peterson, A.B., M.D., Bates Professor of the Diseases of Women and Children in the Department of Medicine and Surgery, the appointment to date from October 1, 1901.

Dean T. Smith, A.M., M.D., Professor of Surgery and Clinical Surgery in the Homœopathic Medical College, the appointment to date from October 1, 1901.

Edwin C. Goddard, Ph.B., LL.B., Secretary of the Law Faculty for the remainder of the academic year.

At the meeting of May 16, 1901.

Vernon J. Willey, B.S., Instructor in Electrotherapeutics for the second semester, 1900–01.

At the meeting of June 7, 1901.

S. Lawrence Bigelow, Ph.D., Assistant Professor of General Chemistry, in charge of the Laboratory of General Chemistry, for one year.

At the meeting of June 18, 1901.

John W. Dwyer, LL.M., Instructor in Law.
John R. Rood, LL.B., Instructor in Law.
Edson R. Sunderland, A.M., Instructor in Law.
Robert E. Bunker, A.M., LL.B., Professor of Law.
Frederick L. Dunlap, Ph.D., Instructor in Analytical Chemistry.
James R. Arneill, A.B., M.D., Instructor in Internal Medicine.
Vernon J. Willey, B.S., Instructor in Electrotherapeutics.
Robert C. Bourland, A.B., M.D., Instructor in Anatomy.
John S. P. Tatlock, A.M., Instructor in English for three years.
Louis A. Strauss, Ph.D., Instructor in English for three years.
Alviso B. Stevens, Ph.C., Assistant Professor of Pharmacy.
Edward D. Jones, Ph.D., Assistant Professor of Commerce and Industry.
John R. Effinger, Jr., Ph.D., Assistant Professor of French.
Arthur G. Hall, B.S., Instructor in Mathematics for three years.
James W. Glover, Ph.D., Instructor in Mathematics for three years.
Herbert J. Goulding, B.S., Instructor in Descriptive Geometry and Drawing for three years.
William H. Wait, Ph.D., Instructor in German for three years.
Warren W. Florer, Ph.D., Instructor in German for three years.

Alfred H. White, A.B., Instructor in Chemical Technology for three years.
James B. Pollock, Sc.D., Instructor in Botany for three years.
Ewald Boucke, Ph.D., Instructor in German for three years.
Hugo P. Thieme, Ph.D., Instructor in French for three years.
George L. Grimes, B.S., Instructor in Mechanical Engineering for three years.
Jonathan A. C. Hildner, Ph.D., Instructor in German for three years.
William L. Miggett, B.S., Superintendent of Engineering Shops for one year.
Eugene C. Sullivan, Ph.D., Instructor in Analytical Chemistry.
Henry C. Anderson, M.E., Instructor in Mechanical Engineering.
Arthur L. Cross, Ph.D., Instructor in History.
George A. Hulett, Ph.D., Instructor in General Chemistry.
Samuel J. Holmes, Ph.D., Instructor in Zoology.
John Dieterle, A.B., Instructor in German.
Alice L. Hunt, Instructor in Drawing.
Edward B. Escott, M.S., Instructor in Mathematics.
William Marshall, M.S., Instructor in Mathematics.
Herbert D. Carrington, Ph.D., Instructor in German.
Carl F. A. Lange, A.M., Instructor in German (half time).
Fred M. Green, B.S., Instructor in Civil Engineering.
Colman D. Frank, Ph.B., Instructor in French and Spanish.
George K. Burgess, B.S., Instructor in Physics.
Durand W. Springer, B.S., Lecturer on Accounts.

At the meeting of July 10, 1901.

Herbert S. Jennings, Ph.D., Assistant Professor of Zoology.
Charles A. Davis, A.M., Instructor in Forestry.
John A. Fairlie, Ph.D., Assistant Professor of Administrative Law for one year.
Walter B. Ford, A.M., Instructor in Mathematics.
Harrison M. Randall, Ph.M., Instructor in Physics.
Joseph M. Thomas, Ph.B., Instructor in English.
William E. Bohn, A.M., Instructor in English.
Royal A. Abbott, Ph.B., Instructor in English.
Winthrop H. Chenery, A.M., Instructor in French.
Benjamin F. Bailey, A.M., Instructor in Electrical Engineering.
Clarence B. Morrill, B.L., Instructor in English.
Alphonso M. Clover, B.S., Acting Instructor in General Chemistry.

At the meeting of September 4, 1901.

Carl E. Eggert, Ph.D., Instructor in German.

APPENDIX B.

SUMMARY OF STUDENTS

For the Academic Year, September 24, 1900, to September 23, 1901.

DEPARTMENT OF LITERATURE, SCIENCE, AND THE ARTS.

Holders of Fellowships:
- Resident 2
- Non-Resident 1

Resident Graduates 101
Candidate for an Advanced Degree, enrolled in the Department of Law 1
Graduates Studying *in Absentia* 3
Undergraduates:
- Candidates for a Degree 1106
- Students not Candidates for a Degree . . . . 155—1369

DEPARTMENT OF ENGINEERING.

Holder of Fellowship 1
Resident Graduates 2
Graduates Studying *in Absentia* 7
Undergraduates . . . . 349— 359

DEPARTMENT OF MEDICINE AND SURGERY.

Resident Graduates 7
Fourth Year Students 81
Third Year Students 117
Second Year Students 132
First Year Students 193
Enrolled in other Departments of the University:
- Third Year Student in Medicine 1
- Second Year Students in Medicine 11
- First Year Students in Medicine . . . . . 21— 563

DEPARTMENT OF LAW.

Resident Graduates 5
Third Year Students 228
Second Year Students 289
First Year Students 266
Special Students 42
Enrolled in the Department of Literature, Science, and the Arts . . . . 43— 873

SCHOOL OF PHARMACY.

Holder of Fellowship 1
Resident Graduates 4
Enrolled in the Department of Literature, Science, and the Arts 1
Undergraduates:
- Candidates for a Degree 58
- Students not Candidates for a Degree 7
Enrolled in the Department of Law . . . . . 1— 72

HOMŒOPATHIC MEDICAL COLLEGE.

Resident Graduates 4
Fourth Year Students 16

Third Year Students	8	
Second Year Students	18	
First Year Students	25—	71

COLLEGE OF DENTAL SURGERY.

Resident Graduate	1	
Seniors	85	
Juniors	87	
Freshmen	99	
Enrolled in the Department of Literature, Science, and the Arts	1—	273
	3580	
Deduct for names counted more than once		98
Total, exclusive of Summer Session		3482

SUMMER SESSION OF 1901.

In Department of Literature, Science, and the Arts	303	
In Department of Medicine and Surgery	59	
In Department of Law	56—	418
Deduct for students enrolled in 1900-01 in some department of the University	190—	228
Grand total		3710

APPENDIX C.

Examinations for higher degrees were held as follows during the year 1900-01:

IN THE DEPARTMENT OF LITERATURE, SCIENCE, AND THE ARTS.

CANDIDATES FOR THE DEGREE OF DOCTOR OF PHILOSOPHY.

CARL HERBERT COOPER, A.B., *Upper Iowa University*, 1895, A.M., 1897.

THESIS.— The economic aspects of the alcohol industry in Germany. Subjects for examination: Major.— Political Economy. Minors.— Finance. History.

JOHN WILLIS SLAUGHTER, A.B., *Lombard University*, 1898, B.D., *ibid.*, 1898.

THESIS.— A study of the theory of natural selection, with a view to ascertaining the fundamental concepts on which it is based. Subjects for examination: Major.— Metaphysics. Minors.— Psychology. Sociology.

LOUIS A. STRAUSS, B.L., 1893, Ph.M., 1894.

THESIS.— The Ethical Character of the English Novel, from Lilly to Richardson. Subjects for examination: Major.— English Literature. Minors.— Rhetoric. History.

DUANE REED STUART, A.B., 1896.

THESIS.— The epigraphic sources of Dion Cassius. Subjects for examination: Major.— Greek. Minors.— Latin. Classical Archæology.

CANDIDATES FOR THE DEGREE OF MASTER OF ARTS.

JOSEPH ELLET ANTRAM, A.B., *Mount Union College,* 1897.
Subjects for examination: Major.— Latin. Minors.— History. Hellenistic Greek.

JOSEPH HERSHEY BAIR, Ph.B., *Grove City College,* 1899, Ph.B., 1900.
Subjects for examination: Major.— Psychology. Minors.— Political Economy. Sociology.

GRACE GRIFFITH BEGLE, Ph.B., 1900.
Subjects for examination: Major.— Latin. Minors.— Roman Political Antiquities. Rhetoric.

WINIFRED ERNESTINE BEMAN, A.B., 1899.
Subjects for examination: Major.— American History. Minors.— European History. Sociology.

WINIFRED BOGLE, A.B., 1900.
Subjects for examination: Major.— Greek. Minors.— Latin. German.

HAROLD MARTIN BOWMAN, LL.B., 1899, B.L., 1900.
Subjects for examination: Major.— Finance. Minors.— Comparative Constitutional Law. History.

FRANK EGBERT BRYANT, B.L., 1899.
Subjects for examination: Major.— Rhetoric. Minors.— English Philology. Aesthetics.

CHARLES WILLIAM BURROWS, A.B., 1898.
Subjects for examination: Major.— Physics. Minors.— Mathematical Physics. Mathematics.

ORMA FITCH BUTLER, A.B., 1897.
Subjects for examination: Major.— Latin. Minors.— Roman Political Antiquities. English Literature.

MARGARET SPRAGUE CARHART, Ph.B., 1899.
Subjects for Examination: Major.— History. Minors.— Rhetoric. German.

ELISHA WARNER CASE, B.S., 1900.
Subjects for examination: Major.— Organic Chemistry. Minors.— Chemical Technology. General Chemistry.

CLARENCE LUTHER CATHERMAN, Ph.B., *Hillsdale College,* 1897.
Subjects for examination: Major.— Pedagogy. Minors.— Sociology. English Literature.

VERA CHAMBERLIN, Ph.B., 1900.
Subjects for examination: Major.— English Literature. Minors.— German. Rhetoric.

MINNA CAROLINE DENTON, B.S., 1900.
Subjects for examination: Major.— Botany. Minors.— Plant Physiology. Ecology.

JOHN DIETERLE, A.B., 1898.
Subjects for examination: Major.— Germanic Philology. Minors.— Germanic Literature. Philosophy of Religion.

OREN SAMUEL FLANEGAN, A.B., *Kalamazoo College,* 1892.
Subjects for examination: Major.— European History. Minors.— American History. Pedagogy.

VICTORIA MARGARET FOHEY, Ph.B., 1900.
Subjects for examination: Major.— English Literature. Minors.— Rhetoric. French.

CLARENCE JOHN FOREMAN, B.S., *Michigan Agricultural College*, 1894, M.S., *ibid.*, 1896.
Subjects for examination: Major.— History. Minors.— Political Economy. Pedagogy.

FREDERICK RUSSELL GORTON, B.S., 1900.
Subjects for examination: Major.— Physics. Minors.— General Chemistry. Mechanics.

FRANCES KATHERINE GOULD, B.L., 1892.
Subjects for examination: Major.— English Literature. Minors.— American Literature. Rhetoric.

MARTHA NATHALIE GREINER, Ph.B., 1900.
Subjects for examination: Major.— German Literature. Minors.— French Literature. Latin.

CONSTANS ALEXIS HEMBORG, A.B., *Augustana College*, 1899, Ph.B., 1900.
Subjects for examination: Major.— Latin. Minors.— Roman Archæology. English Literature.

MILDRED HANNAH KEITH, A.B., 1900.
Subjects for examination: Major.— Greek. Minors.— Latin. History.

RAE HARMAN KITELEY, A.B., 1899.
Subjects for examination: Major.— History. Minors.— Administrative Law. Pedagogy.

ELANA GODDARD KNOTT, A.B., *University of Cincinnati*, 1900.
Subjects for examination: Major.— English Literature. Minors.— Rhetoric. Latin.

WILLY LEHNARTZ, B.S., 1900.
Subjects for examination: Major.— Mathematics. Minors.— Physics. Applied Mechanics.

JOHN SEYMOUR McELLIGOTT, Ph.B., 1900.
Subjects for examination: Major.— Political Economy. Minors.— Sociology. Industrial History.

SEBERN SYLVESTER McVAY, Ph.B., 1899.
Subjects for examination: Major.— Mathematics. Minors.— Physics. Astronomy.

KRISTINE MANN, A.B., *Smith College*, 1895.
Subjects for examination: Major.— Rhetoric. Minors.— English Literature. Philosophy.

JOHN JAY MARSHALL, Ph.B., *Albion College*, 1893.
Subjects for examination: Major.— General Chemistry. Minors.— Physical Chemistry. Physics.

LETTIE JEANNETTE POE, B.L., 1900.
Subjects for examination: Major.— Mathematics. Minors.— Physics. Pedagogy.

GILBERT JEREMIAH ROBERTS, A.B., *Penn College*, 1892, A.M., *ibid.*, 1899.
Subjects for examination: Major.— Latin. Minors.— Greek. Roman Archæology.

JESSIE MAY ROBERTSON, Ph.B., 1900.
Subjects for examination: Major.— Latin. Minors.— German. Pedagogy.

ALICE ELEANORE ROTHMANN, Ph.B., 1896.
Subjects for examination: Major.— Germanic Philology. Minors.— German Literature. English Literature.

DANIEL CORNELIUS SCHAFFNER, A.B., *College of Emporia*, 1898.
Subjects for examination: Major.— Geology. Minors.— Mineralogy. Zoology.

THOMAS HALL SHASTID, M.D., *University of Vermont*, 1888, A.B., *Harvard University*, 1893.
Subjects for examination: Major.— English Literature. Minors.— English Philology. Rhetoric.

LA MONTE TAYLOR, A.B., *University of Kansas*. 1899.
Subjects for examination: Major.— Rhetoric. Minors.— Greek. Pedagogy.

JENNIE PATTERSON WHITE, Ph.B., 1897.
Subjects for examination: Major.— Rhetoric. Minors.— Aesthetics. German.

HERBERT WILLIAM WHITTEN, A.B., 1898.
Subjects for examination: Major.— Greek. Minors.— Latin. Latin Philology.

ERNEST PAUL WILES, A.B., *Indiana University*, 1898.
Subjects for examination: Major.— English Literature. Minors.— Rhetoric. American History.

THERESA GERTRUDE WILLIAMSON, B.S., 1897.
Subjects for examination: Major.— Botany. Minors.— Plant Morphology. General Chemistry.

CANDIDATE FOR THE DEGREE OF MASTER OF SCIENCE.

WILBUR PARDON BOWEN, B.S., 1900.
Subjects for examination: Major.— Physiology. Minors.— Physiological Chemistry. Vertebrate Histology.

IN THE DEPARTMENT OF ENGINEERING.

CANDIDATES FOR THE DEGREE OF CIVIL ENGINEER.

MORTIMER GRANT BARNES, B.S., 1896.
Thesis.— A discussion of the proposed movable dam in connection with the Illinois and Mississippi Canal Feeder at Sterling, Illinois.

ERNEST PAYSON GOODRICH, B.S., 1898.
Thesis.— The Supporting Power of Piles.

ALEXANDER EDWARD KASTL, B.S., 1885.
Thesis.— A Method of Driving Long Sheet Piling with Water Jet.

RALPH EELLS NEWTON, B.S., 1898.
Thesis.— Development of Waterpower of Rainbow Falls, Missouri River.

CANDIDATES FOR THE DEGREE OF MECHANICAL ENGINEER.

ELMER HARTSON NEFF, B.S., 1890.
Thesis.— Design for a Surface Grinding Machine.

GEORGE BINGHAM WILLCOX, B.S., 1895.
Thesis.— Design for a Triple-Expansion Marine Engine.

IN THE DEPARTMENT OF LAW.

CANDIDATES FOR THE DEGREE OF MASTER OF LAWS.

FREDERIC WARREN BIGELOW, LL.B., 1900.
Thesis.— Was the case of Handley *v.* Stutz, 139 U. S., 417 (1890), correctly decided?

LEWIS FISHER, LL.B., 1900.

THESIS.— Who can complain, in what way, and with what effect, of an executed *ultra vires* purchase of land by a corporation?

JOSEPH LEWIS HARTER, A.B., *Indiana University*, 1894, LL.B., 1900.

THESIS.— What is the liability of a corporation to exemplary damages for the malicious torts of its servants?

RUSSELL GRUBY SCHULDER, LL.B., 1900.

THESIS.— The liabilities of stockholders in mining corporations on their unpaid stock in the United States.

IN THE COLLEGE OF DENTAL SURGERY.

CANDIDATE FOR THE DEGREE OF DOCTOR OF DENTAL SCIENCE.

BYRON LINZIE KESLER, D.D.S., 1897.

THESIS.— A study of dental antiseptics and disinfectants.

Financial Statement.

For several years past it has been the practice to print, in connection with the President's Annual Report, the full itemized report of the Treasurer. This year, in place of the Treasurer's report, the Regents present a statement concerning the receipts and expenditures of the University and the condition of its finances and accounts in different form, as follows:

Under the direction of the Board the books and vouchers of the Treasurer, covering the financial transactions for the fiscal year ending June 30, 1901, have been examined in detail. The many thousands of book entries have been checked and compared with registration tickets, laboratory tickets, expenditure vouchers, and other records of various kinds that were available as aids in establishing the accuracy of the books, the abstracts, and the classification of accounts. In the course of this examination, a few clerical errors of minor importance, not affecting the correctness of the final balances, were detected and corrected; and the Treasurer's report is accepted as an accurate and complete accounting for all University moneys received or disbursed by him during the year. His report, which comprises a large number of items, is to be printed in full in the Proceedings of the Board. There is also on file with the Secretary of the Board a detailed report by the assistant employed in the examination of the books. The present statement is, in large measure, compiled from these two reports.

In recent years the University has received from generous friends a considerable number of gifts of money and other forms of property, to be held in trust for the specific objects named in each case. These trust funds are not merged with the general fund of the University, but are cared for independently; an individual account is kept with each fund, and separate reports upon these accounts are made by the Treasurer in connection with his annual report. In the present statement, also, they will be treated by themselves, after a description of the ordinary transactions of the year has been given.

I. GENERAL ACCOUNT.

I. Disregarding, then, for the present, the condition of the trust funds and taking no account of the balances at the beginning and the end of the year, it appears that the receipts amounted in the aggregate to $588,423.15, and the disbursements to $565,953,54; thus showing an apparent gain of $22,469.61. But that this is not an indication of any real improvement in the condition of the funds will be clearly recognized, when attention is called to the fact that, at the close of the previous fiscal year, June 30, 1900, the University had received from the State Treasurer only six tenths of the proceeds of the quarter-mill tax for the year 1900, while, on the 30th of June, 1901, seven tenths of the tax for 1901 had been received, thus abnormally increasing the receipts by the sum of $27,627.50.* Indeed, when the accounts for the year are analyzed and scrutinized with care, it becomes evident that only by the exercise of strict economy and by postponing outlay for many needed improvements has it been possible to keep the expenditures within the income.

In the itemized statement of the sources of income, given below, the net receipts from students for laboratory expenses and other charges of analogous character are given as $34,850.29; but this sum should not be considered as an actual addition to the income of the University, but rather as a reimbursement for the cost of material and special supplies purchased by the University for students' use. Neither should the Hospital receipts be treated as earnings of the University, for they are made up of payments by patients for board, medicines, and special nursing, the cost of which appears on the other side of the account in the large items of Hospital expenses. The services of the Faculties are gratuitous to patients whose cases are available for clinical instruction. The Hospitals are, in fact, a continual source of large expense, not of income. The receipts from the dental operating room, coming from persons who take advantage of the clinical opportunities there offered, paying only for mate-

---

* $27,627.50 is one tenth of the annual tax on the basis of the valuation of the State as equalized in 1896.

rial used, are also to be regarded as an offset against the expenses of the Department.

The money set aside by the State Treasurer and the Auditor General as a University Building Fund is drawn, under provisions of State laws, from the proceeds of the quarter-mill tax, and can only be used by the Regents in the erection of new buildings or for extraordinary repairs. From this fund there was expended during the past year sums as follows:

On the New Homœopathic Hospital	$45,811 99
On Addition to Old Homœopathic Hospital	551 36
On Repairs to University Hospital	247 70
	$46,611 05

The amount standing to the credit of this fund on the 30th of June, 1901, will be exhausted by the time the new medical building now under way, is completed. It is expected that the new building will be ready for occupancy in 1902.

The pay rolls for the year amounted in the aggregate to $350,345.32, constituting the largest item of expenditure. As the University is organized, it is not easy to apportion with exactness the aggregate sum among the several Departments; but a close approximation is reached by preparing a separate pay roll for each Department (excepting the Department of Literature, Science, and the Arts), and placing upon it the names of all the officers whose duties lie wholly, or chiefly, in such Department. (The portion of salaries paid to the Bates Professor of the Diseases of Women and Children, and his assistants, in the Department of Medicine and Surgery, amounting to $2,310.00, which was drawn from the income of the Bates Fund, is not here included.)

The pay roll of the Department of Literature, Science, and the Arts is included in what is designated below as the General Pay Roll. This comprises in addition to the salaries of professors and other instructors, the salaries of the administrative officers of the University, with their necessary assistants and clerks, and of the whole body of permanent employees, of whatever grade, who are paid by the year or month and are not included in the department rolls. The pay rolls of laborers employed for short periods and paid weekly are charged to the contingent account, the repairs account, or otherwise, according to the nature of the service rendered.

In the summary of expenditures given below, the classification is intended to show, as clearly as may be, the relative cost of the different departments of the University and of the different lines of work it is carrying on, without entering into undesirably minute details. No attempt, for example, is made to distribute *pro rata* among the departments the cost of general administration, heating and lighting, care of buildings and grounds, etc., nor the expenses of the gymnasium and the laboratories in which students from more than one department receive instruction at the same time; and some of the minor expenditures provided for in the annual budget are here grouped under some more comprehensive heading. A minute account of all these matters is given by the Treasurer in his report to the Regents.

Summary of Receipts, showing sources of income, for the fiscal year ending June 30, 1901:

A. FROM THE STATE TREASURY:
  For Current Expenses:
    From quarter-mill tax for the year 1900 (two tenths)$ 55,255 00
    From quarter-mill tax for the year 1901 (seven tenths) 193,392 50
    From special appropriation for Homœopathic College 6,000 00
    From University Interest Fund.................. 38,436 32
  For Building Fund................................. 36,048 35

        Total from State Treasury...................$329,132 17

B. FROM STUDENTS' FEES AND DEPOSITS:
  (1) Matriculation Fees and Annual Fees:
    Department of Literature, Science, and the Arts... $53,470 00
    Department of Engineering...................... 15,720 00
    Department of Medicine and Surgery............ 24,640 00
    Department of Law............................. 40,887 50
    School of Pharmacy............................ 3,250 00
    Homœopathic Medical College................... 3,085 00
    College of Dental Surgery...................... 12,580 00
    Summer Schools:
      Literary Department........................ 8,166 00
      Medical Department........................ 615 00
      Law Department 1,745 00

                                                $164,158 50

Less amounts refunded to students under the regulations of the Regents.................. ...... 3,850 00

Net receipts from matriculation fees and annual fees $160,308 50
(2) Diploma Fees........................$7,710 00
    Less sums refunded................... 80 00 $ 7,630 00
(3) Payments and deposits on account of laboratory courses, rent of gymnasium lockers, use of drawing boards, and the like...........................$ 37,892 27
    Less sums returned to students on settlement...... 3,041 98

    Net receipts from this source, as previously stated...$ 34,850 29

C. Receipts from Miscellaneous Sources:
  From University Hospital.............................$ 28,625 11
  From Homœopathic Hospital.......................... 10,169 91
  From Dental Operating Room........................ 5,434 33
  From Engineering Shops............................ 418 95
  From Interest on Bank Deposits..................... 1,281 61
  From return of premium on canceled insurance policies.. 1,305 46
  Unclassified 2,294 84

    Total Miscellaneous Receipts................$ 49,530 21

Recapitulation:
  From State Treasury.............................$329,132 17
  From Students' Fees and Deposits (gross receipts)... 209,760 77
  From Miscellaneous Sources....................... 49,530 21

    Total receipts, as previously stated...............$588,423 15

Summary of Expenditures for the fiscal year ending June 30, 1901.

A. Pay Rolls:
  General Pay Roll....................................$165,575 46
  Department of Engineering............................ 38,676 87
  Department of Medicine and Surgery.................. 38,220 00
    University Hospital 10,273 72
  Department of Law................................. 35,362 00
  School of Pharmacy and Chemical Laboratory......... 24,006 80
  Homœopathic Medical College....................... 10,900 00
    Homœopathic Hospital........................... 3,616 35
  College of Dental Surgery........................... 12,875 00
  Bindery 2,435 50
  Summer Schools:
    Literary 7,075 00
    Law ....,..... 1,328 62

    Total, as previously stated..................$350,345 32

B. Expenses for Laboratories, Shops, Demonstration Courses, etc.:
Botanical Laboratory and Garden	$1,058 51
Zoological Laboratory	621 54
Chemical Laboratory	11,242 42
Physical Laboratory	2,447 66
Engineering Laboratories and Shops	2,914 66
Histological Laboratory	482 41
Hygienic Laboratory	1,078 09
Anatomical Laboratory, material and supplies	1,950 43
Physiological Laboratory	367 00
Surgical Demonstrations, etc.	366 99
Pathological Laboratory	762 03
Electrotherapeutical Laboratory	521 82
Dental Operating Room (including incidental expenses of the College of Dental Surgery)	6,109 97
	$ 29,923 56

C. Libraries:
Book Purchases (not including purchases from trust funds):
General Library	$ 10,842 76
Medical Library	1,212 43
Law Library	1,560 53
Homœopathic Library	242 44
Dental Library	90 26
Incidental Expenses, assistants, cataloguing, etc.	1,481 55
	$ 15,429 97

D. Departmental Expenses:
Department of Literature, Science, and the Arts (Appointment Committee, English, Geology, German, Greek, Latin, Mineralogy, Music, Philosophy, Semitics)	$ 1,327 67
Department of Engineering	614 81
Department of Medicine and Surgery (Asylum Pathologist, Dermatology, Gynæcology, Materia Medica, Nervous Diseases, Ophthalmology, Theory and Practice, Incidentals)	1,970 70
Department of Law	930 44
Homœopathic Medical College	212 92

Summer Schools:
Literary Department	483 37
Law Department	91 38

Hospitals:
University Hospital	24,016 17
Homœopathic Hospital	13,482 88
Laundry Account	2,777 76
	$ 45,908 10

E. New Buildings and Extraordinary Repairs:
New Homœopathic Hospital................$	45,811 99
Addition to Engineering Laboratory...................	9,899 77
Alterations and Repairs at the Hospitals.............	7,934 94
	$ 63,646 70

F. Miscellaneous Current Expenses:
Contingent Account ....$	6,432 51
Ordinary Repairs	8,750 53
Fuel and Lights.......................................	22,878 14
Water Supply	1,760 77
Supplies for Electrical and Heating Plants............	3,447 80
Care of Teams..	922 24
Carpenter Shop, Material............................	169 46
Advertising and Printing.............................	2,415 84
Postage	1,276 92
General Catalogue	1,323 17
Diplomas	1,135 23
School Inspection	586 84
Museum	468 08
Astronomical Observatory	98 52
Commencement Expenses	779 14
Gymnasiums and Athletic Field......................	1,081 82
Artesian Well, Completion...........................	200 90
Return of Students' Fees and Deposits...............	6,971 98
	$ 60,699 89

Recapitulation:
Pay Rolls ....$	350,345 32
Laboratories, etc.	29,923 56
Libraries	15,429 97
Departmental Expenses (including hospital accounts)..	45,908 10
New Buildings and Extraordinary Repairs............	63,646 70
Miscellaneous Expenses (heating, lighting, repairs, etc.).	60,699 89
Total, as previously stated...................$	565,953 54

II. TRUST FUNDS.

II. The changes in the trust funds during the year may be summarized as follows:

Balance reported by Treasurer, June 30, 1900..............		$231,808 93
Received during the year as gifts and contributions.........		11,235 94
Income (interest, rents, etc.).............................		10,508 75
		$253,553 62
Paid for expenses and the specific objects of the several funds $9,408 65		
Shrinkage from estimated value on sale of property belonging to the Williams Fund........	254 36	9,663 01
Balance, June 30, 1901.......................		$243,890 61

This sum is represented by property as follows:

Cash in Bank	$ 91,117 03
Investments and Securities	119,896 00
Real Estate (book-value)	32,877 58
	$243,890 61

At the beginning of the year there were thirty-three separate trust accounts on the books of the Treasurer. During the year three of these accounts were closed, and eight new accounts were opened.

The purposes for which these funds were established, and these accounts were opened, have been quite various in character:

(1) It frequently happens that sums of money, of larger or smaller amount, are offered by individuals, or are obtained by solicitation by the heads of departments most closely interested, to enable the University to procure an expensive piece of apparatus or to meet some specially urgent call for an expenditure which the Regents are unable to make from the funds under their control. Gifts of this kind are available for immediate use; but it is often desirable, or even necessary, to spread the expenditure over some considerable period of time, and it is sometimes the case that additional aid is asked for. Such accounts are essentially temporary in character, and the balances reported by the Treasurer from time to time are no just measure of the value of the gifts or the generosity of the givers. As belonging to this category, the following funds and accounts may be enumerated:

1. The Philo Parsons Fund for the increase and enlargement of the Parsons Library.

2. The Buhl Fund for the purchase of books for the Law Library.

3. The fund contributed for the purchase of books relating to early Christian literature.

4. The fund for the purchase of material to illustrate the instruction in Latin, known as the Special Latin Fund.

5. The fund contributed by persons in Detroit for the purchase of material illustrative of archæology.

6. The fund given for the purchase of apparatus for experimenting with liquid air.

7. The fund for the purchase of chemical apparatus.

8. The moneys given toward the cost of construction of the Women's Gymnasium.

9. The contribution toward a fund for the construction of a music hall.

10. The contribution in aid of the American School at Rome, with which Professor F. W. Kelsey was connected in the year 1900–01.

11. The contribution for a Class Memorial from members of the Literary Class of 1899.

12. The contributions for the Frieze Memorial in honor of the late Professor Henry S. Frieze.

13. The bequest of the late Mrs. Love M. Palmer for the erection of a hospital ward in memory of her husband, Alonzo Benjamin Palmer, who for many years was Dean of the Department of Medicine and Surgery. The proceeds of this bequest have not yet reached the hands of the Treasurer.

14. The Warner Deposit the ultimate disposition of which has not yet been determined.

(2) In a second class of cases the Treasurer of the University simply serves as a medium of communication between the supporters and the holders of scholarships and fellowships. He has nothing to do with the management or disposition of the principal sum of a permanent endowment; and though in this connection, during the past few years, many thousands of dollars have passed through his hands, from donors to beneficiaries, the amount of money in his possession at any one time has been comparatively small.

In the following list the funds of this class are named. Some of them have been maintained for several years in succession by the generosity of individual givers or associations.

1. The Elisha Jones Classical Fellowship.
2. The Parke, Davis & Co. Fellowship in Chemistry.
3. The Stearns Pharmacy Fellowship.
4. The Peter White Fellowship in American History.
5. The D. M. Ferry Botanical Fellowship.
6. The James W. Scott Classical Fellowship.
7. The Pilgrim Publishing Company Fellowship in Rhetoric.
8. The Michigan Gas Association Fellowship for "special post-graduate work in the line of gas engineering."

9. International Club Scholarships, for the support of three Philippine students in the University; the fund to be administered according to instructions accompanying the draft sent by the club.

10. Nelson, Baker & Co. Fellowship in Pharmaceutical Research.

11. Biological Laboratory Scholarship.

(3) In a third class of cases the University has accepted moneys or other property in trust for the formation of loan funds, or of funds the income of which only is to be expended for scholarships, fellowships, or prizes. In this class of cases the trusts are usually subject to certain conditions or limitations. Some of these conditions are mentioned in the descriptions that follow:

1. The Seth Harrison Scholarship Fund was established, in memory of her father, by Mrs. Clara Harrison Stranahan, of Brooklyn, New York. The income is to be used for the benefit of descendants of Seth Harrison who may be pursuing studies in the Department of Literature, Science, and the Arts of the University of Michigan, whenever applicants properly qualified present themselves. Provision is made, however, for applying the income of the fund to scholarships for other persons, "if at any time there shall be a period of seven years during which there are no qualified applicants," descendants of Seth Harrison. There is also a condition to the effect that "if the income . . . provides a surplus for any year, . . . such surplus shall be held for a period of three years to meet the needs occurring when a larger number of beneficiaries present themselves. But at intervals of three years any unexpended portion of the income shall be added to the principal."

2. The Phillips Scholarships Fund was established, under the conditions of the bequest, for the maintenance of scholarships, to be open only to candidates for the degree of Bachelor of Arts, who excel in the Greek and Latin studies required for admission to the University. As an endowment for this fund Mr. Phillips set aside certain pieces of real estate in the city of Philadelphia, which are still held by the University. This property has no valuation assigned it on the books of the University, but it yields a small income each year, and this is accounted for by the Treasurer in his reports.

3. In September, 1897, at the request of the Alumni Asso-

ciation of the University, the Regents assumed the management of moneys contributed toward a fund for the maintenance of fellowships, the first of which, when established, to be named in memory of the late Prof. George Sylvester Morris. The income of the fund which is as yet insufficient for the proper support of the fellowship, is added yearly to the principal.

4. In July, 1900, certain pieces of real estate were conveyed by deeds to the University, subject to the life-interests of persons named therein. Upon this foundation, after the termination of the life-interests, the Charles James Hunt Fellowships and the Margaret Smith Hunt Scholarships are to be established. For the present no valuation is assigned to these funds on the books of the Treasurer.

5. The Class of 1894 established a fund, which now amounts to $1,450.67, " to be used as a loan fund for the benefit of needy and worthy undergraduates in the Literary Department " of the University.

6, 7, 8. The Classes of 1897 and 1898, and the Law Class of 1899, have also laid the foundations of funds to be used under certain conditions for loans or for scholarships.

9. The Newton Van der Veer Loan Fund is to be used to aid " needy students in such amounts and under such conditions as the executive head of the University may deem proper and wise."

10. In the year 1899, and again in 1900, the Directors of the Students' Lecture Association placed in the hands of the Regents a portion of the profits of the year's entertainments, to be used as a loan fund under certain specified conditions.

11. The Good Government Club, an organization of students, has presented to the Regents the proceeds of courses of lectures, the income from which is available as a prize " for the best essay on some theme connected with the subject of good government."

(4) A fourth group of funds includes those intended to provide for some special want of the University, though the Regents are restricted in their expenditures to the income derived from them. To this group the following funds belong.

1. The Goethe Library Fund was established in the year 1886 by contributions solicited by Prof. Calvin Thomas. The

records show that the sum of $1,318.00 was received from contributors, of which $1,000.00 was available for immediate use. It was also provided that "all money above the said $1,000.00 which is in or may come into this fund, shall be invested, . . . and only the interest thereon . . . be expended." By an oversight the principal sum has become impaired, and, in consequence, the expenditure of income is temporarily suspended.

2. In the year 1894, the University received a bequest of $10,000.00 for the benefit of the General Library, under the will of Miss Jean L. Coyl, of Detroit. By the terms of the will the "income is to be devoted to the purchase of . . . books, . . . and the books thus purchased are to be named after my deceased brother, Col. William Henry Coyl, the Coyl Collection."

3. The late Professor Corydon La Ford left by will to the University the sum of $20,000.00 for the purchase of books for the General Library, the condition being attached that the books thus purchased shall bear a label reading — "Bought with the income of the Ford-Messer Fund."

4. The Williams Professorship. In March, 1887, at the request of the Society of the Alumni of the Department of Literature, Science, and the Arts, the Regents established the Williams Professorship, as an *Emeritus* Professorship, the incumbent to be appointed in accordance with the terms of a resolution adopted at that time. For several years the fund raised by subscription among the alumni remained in charge of the Society of the Alumni or its agents; but in 1897 the property constituting the fund was transferred by the Society to the custody of the Regents, and entered upon the books of the University at its face value, though doubt existed as to the real value of some of the items. The condition of the fund is thought to be much better at present than for several years past.

5. The Bates Professorship. By the will of the late Elizabeth H. Bates the University came into possession of money, real estate, and securities of various kinds, with which to found a professorship according to conditions named in the will. In the settlement with the executors of the will the property was accepted by the Regents at a valuation approved by the proper

court. On the basis of this settlement the Regents, in April, 1900, placed the value of the principal sum of the fund at $133,304.65. It is possible, however, that a revaluation of some of the property may be needed, and the sum above named is to be regarded as the closest approximation to the real value now attainable.

6. In the spring of 1899 the Regents accepted a gift of $10,-000.00 to be applied toward the endowment of a woman's professorship. As the income of this sum would be insufficient for the salary of the professor, no appointment to the position has yet been made, and for the present the interest is to be added annually to the principal.

7. During the year just closed the University has received the proceeds of the bequest of the late Hannah E. Davis for the benefit of the Hospital under the charge of the Faculty of the Department of Medicine and Surgery (described in the will as the Allopathic Hospital and, therefore, so designated in the title of the account on the Treasurer's books).

8. The Treadwell Fund. Under the provisions of the will of the late Adah Z. Treadwell, and in accordance with the state law governing such deposits, the sum of $2,000.00 has been placed in the State Treasury, to be known as The Treadwell Fund, the annual income of which is to be used by the Regents for the support of a free bed for some poor and deserving patient in the University Hospital. No income from this source has yet reached the hands of the University Treasurer.

The following table shows the balances in the several trust funds at the beginning and the end of the fiscal year.

June 30, 1900.		June 30, 1901.
$ 102 13	Philo Parsons Fund..........................$	105 27
1,253 79	Buhl Law Library Fund......................	602 42
54 44	Liquid Air Plant Fund.......................	12 40
12 81	Early Christian Literature Fund.............	8 08
40 94	Special Latin Fund..........................	31 99
2 84	Detroit Archæological Fund.................	
	Chemical Apparatus Fund...................	101 00
*375 92	Women's Gymnasium Fund.................	
1,253 03	Music Hall Fund...........................	1,291 58
10 00	Fund in aid of the American School at Rome..	10 00

* Overdrawn.

6 35	Class of 1899 Memorial Fund...............	6 35
40	Frieze Memorial Fund.....................	
8 53	Elisha Jones Classical Fellowship...........	8 95
113 23	Parke, Davis & Co. Fellowship..............	
1 56	Stearns Pharmacy Fellowship................	1 56
412 47	Peter White Fellowship....................	422 14
*50 00	D. M. Ferry Botanical Fellowship...........	
503 75	James W. Scott Classical Fellowship.........	342 91
	Pilgrim Publishing Company Fellowship......	300 00
	Gas Association Fellowsnip..................	43 28
	Nelson, Baker & Co. Fellowship.............	
	Biological Laboratory Scholarship...........	50 00
	International Club Scholarships.............	4,565 00
27,175 16	Seth Harrison Scholarship Fund (original principal, $25,000 00; principal, June 30, 1901, $26,163 59)........................	27,874 15
495 84	Phillips Scholarships Fund.................	651 10
2,472 83	Morris Alumni Fellowship...................	2,590 75
	Charles James Hunt Fellowships.............	
	Margaret Smith Hunt Scholarships...........	
1,378 54	Loan Fund of the Class of 1894.............	1,450 67
150 24	Class Scholarship of 1897...................	160 95
270 85	Class Scholarship of 1898...................	279 14
30 68	Law Class of 1899 Loan Fund..............	31 40
101 25	Newton Van der Veer Loan Fund...........	155 14
756 59	Students' Lecture Association Loan Fund.....	966 94
	Warner Deposit	1 02
515 33	Good Government Club Prize Fund..........	634 71
196 48	Goethe Library Fund (principal, $318 00)....	200 02
11,847 45	The Coyl Collection Fund (principal, $10,000 00)	12,299 20
24,807 90	Ford-Messer Fund (principal, $20,000 00)....	25,424 70
15,749 57	Williams Professorship Fund................	16,170 54
132,509 87	Bates Professorship Fund..................	134,471 66
10,000 00	Woman's Professorship Fund................	10,525 00
	Hannah Elizabeth Davis Allopathic Hospital Fund (principal, $2,054 05).............	2,100 59
	Treadwell Fund (principal, $2,000 00, on deposit with State Treasurer)..............	
$231,808 93†		$243,890 61

For the Regents,

GEORGE A. FARR,
HERMANN KIEFER } *Finance*
ARTHUR HILL,   } *Committee.*
HENRY S. DEAN,

---

* Overdrawn.
† After deducting overdrafts.

UNIVERSITY OF MICHIGAN

THE PRESIDENT'S REPORT

TO THE

BOARD OF REGENTS

FOR THE ACADEMIC YEAR

ENDING SEPTEMBER 30, 1902

FINANCIAL STATEMENT

FOR THE FISCAL YEAR

ENDING JUNE 30, 1902

ANN ARBOR, MICH.,
PUBLISHED BY THE UNIVERSITY
1902

THE PRESIDENT'S REPORT

To the Honorable, the Board of Regents:

I have the honor to present to you my Report for the year ending June 30, 1902.

No important changes have been made in the scope or methods of work during the past twelve months, but the year has been characterized by quiet, orderly, and successful labor. While it is recognized by the public that this University has always been ready, unhampered as it is by too many obstructive traditions, to try with courage and enterprise promising experiments in education, yet it has tried to be wise and conservative enough not to introduce innovations rashly, merely for the sake of being thought progressive. There must be a certain degree of steadiness in the policy of an institution like this, if it is to command the confidence of serious men and to secure the best results for its students. If, therefore, its record for the year presents little that is exceptional or eventful, we are not to draw an unfavorable inference, but rather to conclude that the fact is one for congratulation, and that steady and undisturbed work has earned its legitimate harvest.

The completion of the General Catalogue has enabled us to gather some interesting facts, which are given in detail in Appendix E (page 26). The following may be noted here. Degrees have been conferred in the several departments, down to 1901, as follows:

Department of Literature, Science, and the Arts	4,553
Department of Engineering	786
Department of Medicine and Surgery	3,523
Department of Law	6,657
School of Pharmacy	840
Homœopathic Medical College	372
College of Dental Surgery	1,005
Honorary Degrees	151
	17,887

Deducting 703, the number of persons who have received degrees in more than one department, we have the total number of persons who have received degrees, namely, 17,184. Of these 1,835 were women.

The number of deaths recorded in our books being 2,186, the number of graduates supposed to be living at the date of printing this report, November 15, 1902, is 14,998.

The number of graduates for each of the last five years has been: 1898, 708; 1899, 722; 1900, 777; 1901, 766; 1902, 823.

The number of persons, matriculated prior to the beginning of the year 1897-98, who have pursued studies in some department, but have not graduated, is 12,623, of whom 2,145 are known to be deceased.

It thus appears that the General Catalogue contains the names of 29,728 persons (excluding recipients of honorary degrees), who had, for a longer or a shorter time, been enrolled in the University. Of these it is probable that about 25,000 are now living.

These simple figures must impress one deeply with the extent of the work which the University has accomplished in its comparatively brief life. Its children are found engaged in honorable and useful pursuits in all parts of the earth. It has made the name of Michigan known and respected throughout the civilized world. Yet the total cost to the State of its support of the University has been less than the cost to the nation of a first-class battleship.

Owing to our increased requirements for admission and for graduation, there was a slight falling off in the attendance on the Schools of Medicine, Law, and Dentistry last year. On the other hand, there was a slight increase (31) in the Literary Department, and a large increase (130) in the Engineering Department. The total attendance, exclusive of that in the Summer Session, was 3,508, a gain of 26 over that of the preceding year. Including the Summer Session, the aggregate attendance was 3,709. The year previous it was 3,712.

The students from Michigan numbered 2,156, or 12 more than in the preceding year. The number from other States still continues large; for example, from Illinois, 326; Ohio, 246; Indiana, 144; New York, 144; Pennsylvania, 102; Iowa, 84;

Missouri, 58. Every State, save Delaware and Louisiana, and our new possessions, the Hawaiian Islands, Porto Rico, and the Philippines, and every Territory, except Alaska, are represented. So, also, are Ontario, Quebec, British Columbia, South Africa, Jamaica, Japan, Turkey, England, Bulgaria, China, Egypt, and Mexico. The cosmopolitan feature, which has so long characterized our student population, is thus still conspicuous.

The attendance of women (not counting that in the Summer School) was as follows:

Department of Literature, Science, and the Arts	668
Department of Medicine and Surgery	35
Department of Law	5
School of Pharmacy	3
Homœopathic Medical College	7
College of Dental Surgery	7
	725

In the year preceding, the number was 720. There has, therefore, been no appreciable change in the relative number of women and of men. The women form twenty per cent of the total attendance, and forty-seven and seven tenths per cent of the attendance in the Literary Department.

Last year we allowed the first year students in the Literary Department a larger liberty of election of studies than had been permitted before. They were required to take three hours of English in each semester, and were asked to choose the remaining studies from a list of nine specified branches. The elections were scrutinized by a committee of the Faculty, which was charged with the duty of seeing that the rule was complied with, but which had the power to grant some modifications of the rule in certain cases, and also of advising the students in making their elections.

On the whole, the elections seem to have been wisely made. There was less deviation from the elections made under our previous requirements than was generally expected. The largest losses were sustained, as was anticipated, by Greek (about 45 per cent), Latin (33 per cent), and Mathematics (about 55 per cent). The largest gains were in German and History. The Languages, History, and Mathematics mainly absorbed the attention of the class.

The increase in the number of students in the Engineering Department is making heavy demands on us. It has compelled us to enter on the erection of a large building. The call for our engineering graduates is greater than we can meet. Our best men speedily gain important and remunerative positions. Some of our most important industrial establishments have filed with us requests to send them at any time the names of our most promising graduates, whom they desire to put in the path to highly responsible positions. Our provisions for instruction in the construction of vessels are attracting much attention. We have deemed it wise to establish the degree of Bachelor of Science in Marine Engineering.

So large training in the sciences and their application is now needed to fit men for conspicuous service in the various departments of engineering, that we have found the four years' curriculum scarcely adequate to furnish it. We have, therefore, decided that the engineering students must give six weeks of the summer at the end of the third year of their course to special work, the students in civil engineering to surveying and field work; in mechanical engineering to a course in dynamo-electrical machinery and in designs of boilers and engines; in electrical engineering to foundry work and the designing of boilers and engines; and in chemical engineering to a course in dynamo-electrical machinery. We furnish the instruction without additional cost to the students.

It may be questioned whether there has been greater improvement in any department of education during the last twenty years than in medical education. To no department have recent scientific discoveries been more directly useful. In the methods of instruction in none have they compelled greater changes. The laboratory methods have, to a great extent, superseded the communication of knowledge by lecturing. This fact has called for the large additional expense in the provisions made by all the strong medical schools. Our school, which was one of the first in the country to be furnished with a chemical laboratory for medical students, has long been conspicuous for its laboratory work in other sciences than chemistry. The completion of our new and spacious building for medical laboratories adds greatly to our facilities for such instruction. We have every reason to expect that the Department of Medicine and Surgery will continue to maintain the high rank it has so long held among the leading medical schools of the country. The scientific researches of members of its Faculty have given it a position which is recognized abroad as well as in our own land.

Although law schools of good standing are multiplying in the West, our school still continues to lead all others in the country in the number of its students. The demands made upon them by the course of instruction grow more exacting every year. We have not deemed it necessary or wise to require a collegiate training as the condition precedent to entering upon the study of the law, though we encourage those who can procure such training to avail themselves of their opportunity to do so. We are glad to observe that the proportion of those who bring college diplomas at their entrance is increasing.

The Law Faculty have given a signal proof of their devotion to the interests of the school by establishing a law journal, which most creditably represents the Department. Although heavily burdened by their regular work as teachers, they have undertaken this task without any compensation. The proceeds of the Journal are to be appropriated to the increase of the Law Library. It is to be hoped that our Law Alumni will heartily co-operate with them in the maintenance of this magazine.

The Homœopathic Medical College is pursuing the even tenor of its way, and receiving as large a share of patronage as can perhaps be expected for a school which holds higher standards of attainment for admission and graduation than most of the Homœopathic schools in the country. Its students reap the advantages of instruction in most of the scientific laboratories of the Department of Medicine and Surgery.

The School of Pharmacy shows no tendency to growth in numbers, but meets an increasing demand for advanced instruction for a limited number of students.

The Dental School, having led the way in lengthening its course to four years, fell off somewhat in numbers, as was anticipated. But we do not regret that fact. Other strong schools are finding themselves compelled to follow our example. We have no solicitude about the attendance, if we can only see our way clear to the erection of a suitable building for the accommodation of the School.

The attendance of students in the Summer Session of six weeks in 1902 was as follows:

Department of Literature, Science, and the Arts..................349
Department of Medicine and Surgery........................... 70
Department of Law... 44

Total 463

Of these 189 were regularly connected with some department. The number of new students was, therefore, 274. Though the Summer Session causes us some expense, the usefulness of it, especially to teachers, is so great that it seems to be our duty to continue it.

The hospitals still have their capacity tested by applicants for medical and surgical attention. In the University Hospital, 2,307 patients were treated, and in the Homœopathic Hospital, 1,857. About one fourth of the patients were farmers or farmers' wives. Representatives from seventy-six counties were received and cared for, and not a few persons who were supported at the public expense were restored to health, and thus enabled to earn their own living.

From the Librarian's Report it appears that we had, on June 30, 1902, in all the libraries, 165,000 volumes. The number added during the year is 9,539. The periodicals regularly received number 1,000. The recorded circulation of books, estimated not to exceed one half of the actual use, was 167,949 volumes.

We have for some years had reason to suspect that diplomas, especially our medical diplomas, had occasionally been fraudulently obtained. It happens, of course, that now and then a diploma is either lost in the transportation of baggage or destroyed by fire. For some years we issued a duplicate diploma on the simple request by letter of the holder of the original. Of late years we have required the applicant to send us an affidavit, swearing to the loss of the diploma and to the circumstances of the loss. We write the word "duplicate" in red ink on the new diploma. But even these precautions do not furnish an absolute safeguard against fraud. This very year we found that a woman, who had an undesirable reputation as a practitioner, was exhibiting one of our diplomas bearing the name of one of our graduates, which she had assumed. She had procured the diploma by writing to our offices under this assumed name, and asking for it on the ground that her old one had been destroyed. We have deemed it our duty to protect our genuine diplomas by bringing her into court and securing her punishment. Fortunately, we were able to secure the presence in court of the woman whose name she had borrowed.

The services of the Faculty Committee of Appointment, which aids students in finding suitable positions as teachers, are proving of greater and greater value, both to students and to schools. The school boards who are in quest of competent teachers in many cases come directly to our Committee, who strive to make the best selection to meet the particular conditions in each school. The labor and responsibility thrown upon the Committee are very considerable.

I take pleasure in recognizing the great value of the services rendered by the Student's Christian Association, the Young Men's Christian Association, and the Women's League in aiding new students in finding suitable homes and also employment, by which they can earn something toward their support. The great body of our students have very limited means, and many of them are glad of the opportunity to gain something by honorable toil, however menial.

In accordance with the wise policy recently adopted of purchasing, when our means were adequate, some desirable pieces of land adjacent to our campus, the Regents embraced the opportunity presented to them to buy the school building and grounds opposite the University, on State Street. That is a good site for a fine building, which may be erected when needed. Meantime, the school building can at once be made available for relieving the overcrowded state of the rooms in University Hall. We have given to the building the name of West Hall, and classes in English, in the Modern Languages, and in Forestry have already been assigned quarters there.

We have had in hand an unprecedented amount of work in

repairs and construction, much of which is still unfinished. The continued growth of the University for years has been making these demands for reconstruction and enlargement. But not until now have we had the means to meet the demands. Happily, the recent addition to our income has enabled us to attempt to erect some, though not all, of the buildings we greatly need.

1. We have completed the Barbour Gymnasium for Women, an act which was not only desirable in itself, but which was necessary to comply with the conditions of some of the private subscriptions through which the building was erected.

2. We have constructed a new floor in the Reading Room and the Librarian's rooms in the General Library, and have so arranged the seating of the Reading Room as to accommodate a half more students than before. We have also improved the ventilation of those rooms. These steps were of pressing necessity for the comfort and even for the health of the readers.

3. We have begun the construction of a new boiler house and laundry for the University Hospital. We shall remove the boilers from the basement of the Nurses' Home, where an explosion would have caused great loss of property and life. This change is costly, but deemed absolutely necessary.

4. We have erected a building for the accommodation of the following laboratories of the Department of Medicine and Surgery: Hygiene, Physiological Chemistry, Anatomy, Bacteriology, and Pathology. The accommodations for these in our old buildings were inadequate, and the space they occupied was, for the most part, urgently needed for other purposes. For instance, the laboratories of Hygiene and Bacteriology were in the upper story of the Physical Laboratory, every inch of which was needed by the Department of Physics.

5. The Palmer Ward, built primarily for the care of children in the University Hospital, we owe to the generous bequest of Mrs. Love M. Palmer, who gave it and an endowment fund as a monument to her husband, the late Professor Palmer. It will soon be ready for occupancy.

6. The Psychopathic Ward, now in process of erection, is built by a special appropriation of the Legislature, to care for patients suffering from nervous ailments akin to insanity. It is hoped that great benefits may accrue to them from the treat-

ment here, and that thus the pressure upon our asylums for the insane may be somewhat relieved.

7. The Engineering Building will be the most costly of our new structures. The growth of the Engineering Department for the last few years has been so extraordinary that we were compelled to provide larger and better accommodations for it. We deemed it wise to make our new building large enough to meet our needs for some few years to come, though the demand for thoroughly trained engineers is so great that it will not be surprising if before many years still ampler room will be needed.

It will be remembered that Mr. Charles J. Hunt (A.B., 1846) and his wife, Margaret E. Hunt, have already deeded to us a large tract of valuable timber land in California. Mrs. Hunt has now deeded to the Regents in trust another large tract of timber land, situated in Humboldt County, California, for the endowment, after the termination of certain life interests, of scholarships in the Literary Department. One of them is to be named for her husband's father, James B. Hunt, who was formerly a representative in Congress from this State.

Our thanks are again due to Hon. D. M. Ferry, Parke, Davis & Co., Frederick Stearns & Co., Nelson, Baker & Co., and Mr. Theodore Buhl, of Detroit, Hon. Peter White, of Marquette, and the Michigan Gas Association, for the continuance of graduate fellowships which they have been supporting for the last few years; and to the Rockefeller Research Fund for two new fellowships in Bacteriology. We are still looking with hope for the permanent endowment of at least a few fellowships for graduates.

We have also to thank Hon. D. M. Ferry for presenting us with a tract of land, some seventeen acres, adjacent to our athletic field. This furnishes a spacious field, in which not only the ball teams can have their practice, but in which the great body of students can simultaneously have outdoor exercise. No gift could be more acceptable or more useful to the students generally. Previously the advantages of the field were for the most part limited to the comparatively small number of students who composed the teams. Our well-equipped gymnasiums and the large field, embracing nearly thirty acres, now afford every facility for physical training.

Notwithstanding the welcome addition which has been made to our buildings, certain of the pressing wants mentioned in my last Report are still unprovided for; namely, an enlargement of the Library Building, furnishing seminary rooms for advanced students and more book room; a suitable building for the Dental School, which is now badly housed; an enlargement of the Physical Laboratory; and the erection of a laboratory building for the work in Zoology and Botany, and perhaps of Psychology. An endowment for a certain number of fellowships for graduate students is also greatly needed. These should yield an income of four hundred or five hundred dollars a year for each fellowship.

If our present income is not curtailed, we hope, by careful economy, to be able in due time to supply most of these lacking buildings, although most of the larger universities in the country, even those which have fewer students than we, are conducted at an expense from fifty to sixty per cent greater than this institution, while Harvard annually expends just about double our income. We are constantly threatened with the loss of some of our ablest professors, because our scale of salaries is below that of several other universities. We have indeed suffered some such losses. It is owing to the loyalty and devotion to us of some of our best men that alluring temptations to go elsewhere have been resisted by them. We enter upon the work of another year with the confident hope that the people of the State, for whose welfare the University was founded and is conducted, will continue to cherish pride in its success and to furnish it their hearty support.

JAMES B. ANGELL.

APPENDICES

APPENDIX A
APPOINTMENTS, REAPPOINTMENTS, RESIGNATIONS, ETC., DURING THE YEAR ENDING SEPTEMBER 30, 1902.*

Resignations:

At the meeting of December 20, 1901, the resignation of Perry F. Trowbridge, Ph.B., Instructor in Organic Chemistry, was presented and accepted.

At the meeting of May 15, 1902, the resignation of Eliza M. Mosher, M.D., Professor of Hygiene and Women's Dean, was presented and accepted.

At the meeting of June 17, 1902, the resignations of William H. Dorrance, D.D.S., Professor of Prosthetic Dentistry and Dental Metallurgy, and John C. Rolfe, Ph.D., Professor of Latin, were presented and accepted.

Leave of Absence:

At the meeting of January 24, 1902, Professor Volney M. Spalding, Ph.D., was granted leave of absence from February 10 to April 11.

At the meeting of February 27, 1902, Professor John A. Watling, D.D.S., was granted leave of absence for four weeks.

At the meeting of May 15, 1902, Assistant Professor Walter B. Pillsbury, Ph.D., was granted leave of absence from June 2 to the close of the academic year; and the leave of absence previously granted Instructor John S. P. Tatlock, A.M., was extended to cover the year 1902-03.

Change of Title, etc.:

At the meeting of December 20, 1901, the title of Charles S. Denison, M.S., C.E., was changed to Professor of Stereotomy, Mechanism, and Drawing.

At the meeting of January 24, 1902, the title of Joseph H. Drake, Ph.D., was changed to Junior Professor of Latin and Roman Law.

At the meeting of May 15, 1902, the title of Junior Professor Edward D. Campbell, B.S., was changed to Professor of Chemical Engineering; the title of Instructor Tobias Diekhoff, Ph.D., was changed to Assistant Professor of German; the title of Assistant Professor Moritz Levi, A.B., was changed to Junior Professor of French; the title of Junior Professor Allen S. Whitney, A.B., was changed to Professor

*The names of Assistants and of persons holding positions of grade lower than the grade of Instructor are, with a few exceptions, not included in the lists given.

of Pedagogy and Inspector of Schools; the title of Acting Professor Max Winkler, Ph.D., was changed to Professor of the German Language and Literature; and the title of Instructor Clarence G. Wrentmore, M.S., was changed to Assistant Professor of Descriptive Geometry and Drawing.

At the meeting of June 17, 1902, the title of Professor Edward D. Campbell, B.S., was changed to Professor of Chemical Engineering and Analytical Chemistry; the title of Assistant Professor Earle W. Dow, A.B., was changed to Junior Professor of History; the title of Instructor Henry A. Sanders, Ph.D., was changed to Assistant Professor of Latin; the title of Alice G. Snyder, M.D., was changed to Director of the Barbour Gymnasium; and the title of Assistant Professor Aldred S. Warthin, Ph.D., M.D., was changed to Junior Professor of Pathology in the Department of Medicine and Surgery.

Special Resident Lecturers and Instructors:

In the Department of Literature, Science, and the Arts, Resident Instructors were appointed for the Summer Session of the year 1902 as follows:

At the meeting of February 27, 1902.

Wooster W. Beman, A.M., Mathematics.
George P. Burns, Ph.D., Botany.
Isaac N. Demmon, LL.D., English Literature.
Tobias Diekhoff, Ph.D., German.
Joseph H. Drake, Ph.D., Latin.
Frederick L. Dunlap, Sc.D., Chemistry.
John R. Effinger, Ph.D., French.
Warren W. Florer, Ph.D., German.
James W. Glover, Ph.D., Mathematics.
Moses Gomberg, Sc.D., Chemistry.
Herbert J. Goulding, B.S., Drawing.
Karl E. Guthe, Ph.D., Physics.
George O. Higley, M.S., Chemistry.
Jonathan A. C. Hildner, Ph.D., German.
Moritz Levi, A.B., Spanish and Italian.
David M. Lichty, M.S., Chemistry.
Joseph L. Markley, Ph.D., Mathematics.
Clarence L. Meader, Ph.D., Latin.
William H. Payne, LL.D., D.Litt., Pedagogy.
Harrison M. Randall, Ph.M., Physics.
George Rebec, Ph.D., Psychology.
John O. Reed, Ph.D., Physics.
John C. Rolfe, Ph.D., Latin.
Henry A. Sanders, Ph.D., Greek.

Volney M. Spalding, Ph.D., Botany.
Eugene C. Sullivan, Ph.D., Chemistry.
Fred M. Taylor, Ph.D., Political Economy.
Joseph M. Thomas, Ph.B., English.
John C. Thorpe, B.S., Mechanical Engineering.
Thomas C. Trueblood, A.M., Elocution and Oratory.
Robert M. Wenley, Sc.D., LL.D., Philosophy.
Allen S. Whitney, A.B., Pedagogy.

In the Department of Medicine and Surgery, a Special Lecturer was appointed for the year 1902–03 as follows:

At the meeting of June 17, 1902.

Walter B. Pillsbury, Ph.D., Physiological Psychology.

In the Department of Law, Special Lecturers were appointed for the year 1902–03 as follows:

At the meeting of June 17, 1902.

Henry C. Adams, LL.D., The Railroad Problem.
Joseph H. Drake, Ph.D., Roman Law.
William J. Herdman, M.D., LL.D., Neurology, Electrology, and Railway Injuries.
Richard Hudson, LL.D., Comparative Constitutional Law.
Andrew C. McLaughlin, A.M., LL.B., Constitutional Law and Constitutional History.
Victor C. Vaughan, M.D., LL.D., Toxicology in its Legal Relations.

Non-resident Lecturers and Instructors:

In the Department of Literature, Science, and the Arts, Non-resident Instructors were appointed for the Summer Session of the year 1902 as follows:

At the meeting of February 27, 1902.

William H. Munson, B.S., Zoology.
William H. Sherzer, Ph.D., Geology and Physical Geography.
Clayton T. Teetzel LL.B., Physical Training.
James A. Woodburn, Ph.D., History.

In the Department of Medicine and Surgery, Non-resident Lecturers were appointed as follows:

At the meeting of December 20, 1901.

Elijah M. Houghton, Ph.C., M.D., The Manufacture and Preparation of Medicines (for the year 1901–02).

At the meeting of June 17, 1902 (for the year 1902–03).

Henry B. Baker, A.M., M.D., The Administration of Health Laws.
George L. Chamberlain, M.D., Insanity.
Edmund A. Christian, A.B., M.D., Insanity.
William M. Edwards, M.D., Insanity.
Elijah M. Houghton, Ph.C., M.D., The Preparation of Medicines.
James D. Munson, M.D., Insanity.
Cressy L. Wilbur, M.D., Vital Statistics.

In the Department of Law, Non-resident Lecturers were appointed for the year 1902–03 as follows:

At the meeting of June 17, 1902.

Melville M. Bigelow, LL.D., Insurance.
Dallas Boudeman, M.S., Michigan Statute Law and Statutory Construction.
John B. Clayberg, LL.B., Mining Law.
Harlow P. Davock, C.E., M.S., Practice under Bankruptcy Law.
Frank H. Reed, A.B., Copyright Law and Law of Trademarks.
Henry H. Swan, A.M., Admiralty.
Alfred H. Walker, LL.B., Patent Law.

In the Homœopathic Medical College, Non-resident Lecturers were appointed for the year 1902–03 as follows:

At the meeting of June 17, 1902.

Oscar R. Long, M.D., Mental Diseases.
Rollin C. Olin, M.D., Theory and Practice.
William A. Polglase, M.D., Nervous Diseases.

Other Appointments and Reappointments:

Appointments and reappointments were made in the several departments as indicated in the lists given below. Professors and Junior Professors were appointed for unlimited time, Assistant Professors for three years, and Instructors for one year, except in cases where a different period of service is mentioned.

At the meeting of October 16, 1901.

Carl F. A. Lange, A.M., Instructor in German (full time).
Homer J. Parker, M.E., Instructor in Mechanical Engineering.
John W. Scholl, A.B., Instructor in German (quarter time).

At the meeting of November 26, 1901.

George A. May, M.D., Instructor in the Waterman Gymnasium.

At the meeting of December 20, 1901.

Charles Baird, A.B., Director of Outdoor Athletics.

John R. Effinger, Ph.D., Secretary of the Executive Committee of the Summer Session of the Department of Literature, Science, and the Arts.

Edward Lucas, Dispensing Accountant in the Chemical Laboratory.

John O. Reed, Ph.D., Chairman of the Executive Committee of the Summer Session of the Department of Literature, Science, and the Arts.

At the meeting of January 24, 1902.

John C. Thorpe, B.S., Instructor in Mechanical Engineering.

At the meeting of February 27, 1902.

Guy M. Winslow, M.D., Instructor in Anatomy.

At the meeting of May 15, 1902.

Royal A. Abbott, Ph.B., Instructor in English.

Henry C. Anderson, M.E., Instructor in Mechanical Engineering for three years.

S. Lawrence Bigelow, Ph.D., Assistant Professor of General Chemistry until the return of Professor Freer.

William E. Bohn, A.M., Instructor in English.

Herbert D. Carrington, Ph.D., Instructor in German.

Winthrop H. Chenery, A.M., Instructor in French.

Charles H. Cooley, Ph.D., Assistant Professor of Sociology.

Arthur L. Cross, Ph.D., Instructor in History for three years.

Charles A. Davis, A.M., Instructor in Forestry.

John Dieterle, A.B., Instructor in German.

Earle W. Dow, A.B., Assistant Professor of History.

Frederick L. Dunlap, Sc.D., Instructor in Analytical Chemistry.

Carl E. Eggert, Ph.D., Instructor in German.

Edward B. Escott, M.S., Instructor in Mathematics.

John A. Fairlie, Ph.D., Assistant Professor of Administrative Law.

Colman D. Frank, Ph.B., Instructor in French and Spanish. .

Moses Gomberg, Sc.D., Assistant Professor of Organic Chemistry.

Fred M. Green, B.S., Instructor in Civil Engineering.

Arthur G. Hall, Ph.D., Instructor in Mathematics for three years.

Samuel J. Holmes, Ph.D., Instructor in Zoology.

George A. Hulett, Ph.D., Instructor in General Chemistry for three years.

Alice L. Hunt, Instructor in Drawing.

Carl F. A. Lange, A.M., Instructor in German.

Joseph L. Markley, Ph.D., Assistant Professor of Mathematics.

William Marshall, M.S., Instructor in Mathematics.

Clarence L. Meader, Ph.D., Instructor in Latin for three years.

William L. Miggett, B.S., Superintendent of Engineering Shops for one year.
Clarence B. Morrill, B.L., Instructor in English.
Raymond Pearl, A.B., Instructor in Zoology.
Harrison M. Randall, Ph.M., Instructor in Physics.
Julius O. Schlotterbeck, Ph.D., Assistant Professor of Pharmacognosy and Botany.
John W. Scholl, A.B., Instructor in German.
Durand W. Springer, B.S., Lecturer on Accounts.
Duane R. Stuart, Ph.D., Instructor in Greek and Latin.
Eugene C. Sullivan, Ph.D., Instructor in Analytical Chemistry for three years.
Joseph M. Thomas, Ph.B., Instructor in English.
John C. Thorpe, B.S., Instructor in Mechanical Engineering.

At the meeting of June 17, 1902.

James R. Arneill, A.B., M.D., Instructor in Internal Medicine.
Benjamin F. Bailey, A.M., Instructor in Electrical Engineering.
George P. Burns, Ph.D., Instructor in Botany.
Kenyon L. Butterfield, A.M., Instructor in Rural Sociology.
Alphonso M. Clover, B.S., Instructor in General Chemistry.
Cyrenus G. Darling, M.D., Lecturer on Genito-Urinary and Minor Surgery.
Walter Dennison, Ph.D., Junior Professor of Latin.
Lydia M. De Witt, B.S., M.D., Instructor in Histology.
John W. Dwyer, LL.M., Instructor in Law.
Walter B. Ford, A.M., Instructor in Mathematics.
Hermann Kiefer, M.D., Professor *Emeritus* of the Practice of Medicine in the Department of Medicine and Surgery.
Lyman F. Morehouse, B.S., Instructor in Physics.
John R. Rood, LL.B., Instructor in Law.
Vernon J. Willey, B.S., Instructor in Electrotherapeutics.
Frederick C. Wilson, B.S., Instructor in Descriptive Geometry and Drawing.

At the meeting of June 26, 1902.

Myra Beach Jordan, Women's Dean in the Department of Literature, Science, and the Arts for one year.

At the meeting of July 17, 1902.

Charles M. Briggs, D.D.S., Instructor in Clinical Dentistry.
Cyrenus G. Darling, M.D., Lecturer on Oral Pathology and Surgery in the College of Dental Surgery.
Robert Brown Howell, D.D.S., Instructor in Prosthetic Technics and Comparative Odontology in the College of Dental Surgery.

Frank Lincoln Sage, B.S., LL.B., Assistant Professor of Law.
Edson R. Sunderland, A.M., LL.B., Instructor in Law.
William G. Smeaton, A.B., Instructor in Chemical Engineering.

At the meeting of September 10, 1902.

Fred G. Frink, B.S., Instructor in Civil Engineering.
Louis P. Hall, D.D.S., Assistant Professor of Dental Anatomy, Operative Technique, and Clinical Operative Dentistry.

APPENDIX B

Degrees were conferred as follows during the year from October 1, 1901, to September 30, 1902:

ORDINARY DEGREES

Bachelor of Arts	272
Bachelor of Laws	261
Bachelor of Science (in Chemical Engineering)	1
Bachelor of Science (in Civil Engineering)	8
Bachelor of Science (in Electrical Engineering)	9
Bachelor of Science (in Marine Engineering)	1
Bachelor of Science (in Mechanical Engineering)	16
Bachelor of Science (in Pharmacy)	3
Civil Engineer	2
Doctor of Dental Surgery	69
Doctor of Medicine (Department of Medicine and Surgery)	86
Doctor of Medicine (Homœopathic Medical College)	7
Doctor of Philosophy	10
Doctor of Science	1
Master of Arts	36
Master of Laws	1
Master of Science (Department of Engineering)	1
Pharmaceutical Chemist	15
	799

HONORARY DEGREES.

Master of Arts	3
Doctor of Laws	4
Doctor of Medicine	1
Total	807

APPENDIX C
SUMMARY OF STUDENTS
For the Academic Year, September 24, 1901, to September 22, 1902.

DEPARTMENT OF LITERATURE, SCIENCE, AND THE ARTS

Graduates:
  Resident 105
  Studying *in Absentia*............................... 2
Undergraduates:
  Candidates for a Degree.............................. 1,178
  Students not Candidates for a Degree............... 115—1,400

DEPARTMENT OF ENGINEERING

Resident Graduates...................................... 3
Graduates Studying *in Absentia*....................... 2
Undergraduates .... 484— 489

DEPARTMENT OF MEDICINE AND SURGERY

Resident Graduates...................................... 3
Fourth Year Students................................... 92
Third Year Students.................................... 116
Second Year Students................................... 159
First Year Students.................................... 105
Enrolled in other Departments of the University:
  Second Year Students in Medicine.................... 18
  First Year Students in Medicine..................... 20— 513

DEPARTMENT OF LAW

Resident Graduates...................................... 3
Third Year Students.................................... 276
Second Year Students................................... 246
First Year Students.................................... 250
Special Students....................................... 52
Enrolled in the Department of Literature, Science, and the
  Arts .... 27— 854

SCHOOL OF PHARMACY

Resident Graduates...................................... 9
Undergraduates:
  Candidates for a Degree............................. 51
  Students not Candidates for a Degree................ 8— 68

HOMŒOPATHIC MEDICAL COLLEGE

Resident Graduates...................................... 5
Fourth Year Students................................... 8
Third Year Students.................................... 13
Second Year Students................................... 16
First Year Students.................................... 18— 60

COLLEGE OF DENTAL SURGERY

Seniors		84
Juniors		77
Sophomores		10
Freshmen	32—	203
		3,587
Deduct for names counted more than once		79
Total, exclusive of Summer Session		3,508

SUMMER SESSION OF 1902

In Department of Literature, Science, and the Arts	349	
In Department of Medicine and Surgery	70	
In Department of Law	44—	463
Deduct for duplicates and for students enrolled in 1901-02 in some department of the University		189—274
Grand Total		3,782

APPENDIX D

Examinations for higher degrees were held as follows during the year 1901-02:

IN THE DEPARTMENT OF LITERATURE, SCIENCE, AND THE ARTS.

CANDIDATE FOR THE DEGREE OF DOCTOR OF SCIENCE

JOSEPH WILLIAM TELL DUVEL, B.S., *Ohio State University*, 1897.

THESIS.— Conditions influencing Vitality and Germination of Seeds.

Subjects for examination: Major — Botany; Minors — Vegetable Physiology, Organic Chemistry.

CANDIDATES FOR THE DEGREE OF DOCTOR OF PHILOSOPHY

EDWIN NEWTON BROWN, A.B., 1883, A.M., 1884, LL.B., 1887.

THESIS.— The Pedagogical Significance of the Imagination.

Subjects for examination: Major — Pedagogy; Minors — History of Philosophy, Psychology.

GEORGE DEPUE HADZSITS, A.B., 1895, A.M., 1896.

THESIS.— Ethical Conditions in Greece in the First Century of the Christian Era.

Subjects for examination: Major — Greek; Minors — Latin, Philosophy.

WALTER DAVID HADZSITS, A.B., 1898, A.M., 1899.

THESIS.— The Apotheosis of Augustus.

Subjects for examination: Major — Latin; Minors — Greek, Philosophy.

OTTO EDWARD LESSING, A.B., 1895.
THESIS.— Ueber Schillers Einfluss auf Grillparzer: Ein Beitrag zur Kenntnis des oesterreichischen Klassikers.
Subjects for examination: Major — German Literature; Minors — German Philology, General Linguistics.

CHARLES EDWARD MARSHALL, PH.B., 1895.
THESIS.— The Aëration of Milk.
Subjects for examination: Major — Bacteriology; Minors — Hygiene, Organic Chemistry.

YOSHINAGA MIKAMI, *Keio College*, 1897.
THESIS.— A Critical Examination of Clark's Theory of Distribution.
Subjects for examination: Major — Political Economy; Minors — History, International Law.

AURA MAUD MILLER, B.L., 1890, A.M., 1897.
THESIS.— The Text of Hamlet.
Subjects for examination: Major — English Literature; Minors — English Philology, Pedagogy.

RAYMOND PEARL, A.B., *Dartmouth College*, 1899.
THESIS.— The Movements and Reactions of Fresh-water Planarians.
Subjects for examination: Major — Zoology; Minors — Plant Physiology, Psychology.

HARLOW STAFFORD PERSON, PH.B., 1899, A.M., 1900.
THESIS.— The Physical Factors of Production and the Theory of Political Economy.
Subjects for examination: Major — Economic Geography; Minors — Economic Theory, Sociology.

RAYMOND HAINES POND, B.S., *Kansas Agricultural College*, 1898, M.S., *ibid*, 1899.
THESIS.— The Biological Relations of Aquatic Plants to the Substratum.
Subjects for examination: Major — Botany; Minors — Plant Physiology, Organic Chemistry.

HARRISON McALLESTER RANDALL, PH.B., 1893, PH.M., 1894.
THESIS.— The Determination of the Coefficients of Expansion of Nickel and Quartz at High Temperatures.
Subjects for examination: Major — Physics; Minors — Mathematics, General Chemistry.

WILLIAM HITTELL SHERZER, B.S., 1889, M.S., 1890.
THESIS.— The Geology of Monroe County, Michigan.
Subjects for examination: Major — Geology; Minors — Zoology, Palæontology.

CANDIDATES FOR THE DEGREE OF MASTER OF ARTS

PAUL AGNEW, B.L., *Hillsdale College*, 1901.
Subjects for examination: Major — Astronomy; Minors — Mathematics, Physics.

ROBERT EARLE ANTHONY, AB., *Southwestern Baptist University*, 1901.
Subjects for examination: Major — Latin; Minors — Greek, Roman Political Institutions.

HENRY HERBERT ARMSTRONG, A.B., 1901.
Subjects for examination: Major — Latin; Minors — Greek, Roman Archæology.

LOIS LeBARON AVERY, B.L., 1898.
Subjects for examination: Major — Rhetoric; Minors — American History, English Literature.

SAMUEL BAUMAN, B.L., *German Wallace College*, 1889.
Subjects for examination: Major — German; Minors — English Literature, Rhetoric.

MARY ELLA BENNETT, Ph.B., 1895.
Subjects for examination: Major — Botany; Minors — Plant Physiology, Invertebrate Zoology.

JOHN KNIGHT MUNRO BERRY, A.B., 1901.
Subjects for examination: Major — German; Minors — Latin, Roman Political Antiquities.

KENYON LEECH BUTTERFIELD, B.S., *Michigan Agricultural College*, 1891.
Subjects for examination: Major — Political Economy; Minors — Sociology, History of Education.

ALVIN NELSON CODY, B.S., *Albion College*, 1901.
Subjects for examination: Major — Botany; Minors — Plant Physiology, Pedagogy.

RUIE ANN CONNOR, Ph.B., 1899.
Subjects for examination: Major — Latin; Minors — Philosophy, Hygiene.

ALBERT ROBINSON CRITTENDEN, A.B., 1894.
Subjects for examination: Major — Latin; Minors — Greek, Roman Political Institutions.

DAVID D. CULLER, Ph.B., *De Pauw University*, 1896.
Subjects for examination: Major — English Literature; Minors — German, Pedagogy.

WINIFRED CAMPBELL DABOLL, A.B., 1900.
Subjects for examination: Major — Latin; Minors — Roman Political Antiquities, English Literature.

COLMAN DUDLEY FRANK, Ph.B., 1897.
Subjects for examination: Major — French; Minors — German, Spanish.

FRED FULLERTON, B.S., *Alma College*, 1896, M.S., *ibid*, 1897.
Subjects for examination: Major — Theoretical Astronomy; Minors — Practical Astronomy, Mathematics.

IDA AUGUSTA GREEN, Ph.B., *Oberlin College*, 1890.
Subjects for examination: Major — American History; Minors — English Literature, Sociology.

ARTHUR JOSEPH HOARE, A.B., 1900.
Subjects for examination: Major — Latin; Minors — Mathematics, Pedagogy.

IRVING BENJAMIN HUNTER, A.B., 1901.
Subjects for examination: Major — Latin; Minors — Greek, Roman Political Antiquities.

MARY OLIVE HUNTING, A.B., *Alma College,* 1893.
Subjects for examination: Major — Latin; Minors — Greek, Roman Political Antiquities.

JESSIE GERTRUDE JENNINGS, A.B., 1901.
Subjects for examination: Major — Latin; Minors — Greek, German.

HARRY EDWIN KING, B.L., 1891.
Subjects for examination: Major — History; Minors — International Law, Political Institutions.

OTTO CHARLES MARCKWARDT, A.B., 1901.
Subjects for examination: Major — German Literature; Minors — English Literature, Rhetoric.

FELICITAS MARECK, B.L., *University of Minnesota,* 1900.
Subjects for examination: Major — English Philology; Minors — German, Scandinavian.

JOHN CASTELAR PARKER, B.S., 1901.
Subjects for examination: Major — Physics; Minors — Mathematics, Applied Mechanics.

JULIA MAGRUDER PHILLIPS, A.B., 1901.
Subjects for examination: Major — Political Economy; Minors — Sociology, English Philology.

LINDLEY PYLE, A.B., 1901.
Subjects for examination: Major — Physics; Minors — Mathematics, General Chemistry.

HELEN MAY ST. JOHN, Ph.B., 1899.
Subjects for examination: Major — Rhetoric; Minors — American History, American Literature.

JOHN WILLIAM SCHOLL, A.B., 1901.
Subjects for examination: Major — German Literature; Minors — German Philology, French.

MARVIN MANAM SHERRICK, A.B., *Coe College,* 1896.
Subjects for examination: Major — German; Minors — English Philology, Pedagogy.

FLORA ANN SIGEL, Ph.B., 1898.
Subjects for examination: Major — American History; Minors — European History, English Literature.

MABEL ALICE STEWARD, A.B., *Bates College,* 1895.
Subjects for examination: Major — English Philology; Minors — German, English Literature.

MARY COURTLAND VANDERBEEK, A.B., *Smith College,* 1893.

Subjects for examination: Major — Latin; Minors — Pedagogy, Roman Political Antiquities.

ELIZABETH MAY VICKERS, A.B., *University of Kansas*, 1899.
Subjects for examination: Major — Rhetoric; Minors — Anglo-Saxon, General Linguistics.

LAWRENCE ROOT WALDRON, B.S., *North Dakota Agricultural College*, 1899.
THESIS.— The Development of the Genital Ducts in Amia.
Subjects for examination: Major — Zoology; Minors — Embryology, Botany.

AGNES WEGENER, A.B., *Northwestern University*, 1901.
Subjects for examination: Major — Mathematics; Minors — German, Physics.

LEWIS HART WELD, A.B., *University of Rochester*, 1900.
Subjects for examination: Major — Zoology; Minors — Plant Morphology, Plant Physiology.

MARY BESSIE WILEY, A.B., *Antioch College*, 1897.
Subjects for examination: English Literature; Minors — Latin, Pedagogy.

VERNON JUSTIN WILLEY, B.S., *Michigan Agricultural College*, 1893.
Subjects for examination: Major — Physics; Minors — General Chemistry, Mathematics.

JANE E. WORK, B.L., 1895.
Subjects for examination: Major — English Literature; Minors — American Literature, German.

THEOPHIL JOHN ZIMMERMAN, A.B., 1901.
Subjects for examination: Major — American History; Minors — European History, Sociology.

IN THE DEPARTMENT OF ENGINEERING

CANDIDATE FOR THE DEGREE OF MASTER OF SCIENCE

HARRY J. SPROAT, B.S., 1901.

CANDIDATES FOR THE DEGREE OF CIVIL ENGINEER

CLARENCE WARREN NOBLE, B.S., 1899.
THESIS.— Design for a Steel Rampant Arch.
CLARENCE GEORGE WRENTMORE, B.S., 1893, M.S., 1898.

IN THE DEPARTMENT OF LAW

CANDIDATE FOR THE DEGREE OF MASTER OF LAWS

STONEWALL JACKSON DODSON, LL.B., *Cumberland University*, 1891, LL.B., 1901.
THESIS.— The Liability of Directors of a Corporation to its Creditors for Negligence in Management of Corporate Property.

APPENDIX E.

The following Tables and Summaries exhibit, in statistical form, items of information regarding the University, believed to be of general interest. They have been compiled from the recently published General Catalogue of the University, and have been revised, in some respects, down to date of publication, November 15, 1902. Similar tables would have appeared with that catalogue, had not pressure of other duties delayed their preparation.

SUMMARY OF GRADUATES
1845-1901

DEPARTMENT OF LITERATURE, SCIENCE, AND THE ARTS: —
    Ordinary Degrees conferred . . . — 4,402
        Deduct for cases where two degrees
        were conferred on the same person . — 14 . 4,388

    Higher Degrees conferred on examination — 484
        Deduct for cases where two degrees
        were conferred on the same person . 33
        Deduct for cases where the graduate received his bachelor's degree in this
        Department 286   319   165   4,553

    Higher Degrees conferred in course (1849-1877), 476

DEPARTMENT OF ENGINEERING: —
    Ordinary Degrees conferred . . . — 800
        Deduct for cases where two degrees
        were conferred on the same person . — 16   784

    Higher Degrees conferred on examination — 36
        Deduct for cases where the graduate received his first degree in this Department . . . . — 34   2   786

    Higher Degrees conferred in course (1869-1872), 3

DEPARTMENT OF MEDICINE AND SURGERY: —
    Degree of Doctor of Medicine . . — — — 3,523

DEPARTMENT OF LAW: —
    Degree of Bachelor of Laws . . . — — 6,636
    Degree of Master of Laws . . . — 130
        Deduct for cases where the degree was conferred on graduates of this Department . . . . . . — 109   21   6,657

SCHOOL OF PHARMACY: —
    Degree of Pharmaceutical Chemist . . — 839
    Degree of Master of Pharmacy . . — 5
    Degree of Bachelor of Science in Pharmacy — 9 853

Deduct for cases where two degrees were conferred on the same person . — — 13 840

HOMOEOPATHIC MEDICAL COLLEGE: —
Degree of Doctor of Medicine . . — — — 372
COLLEGE OF DENTAL SURGERY: —
Degree of Doctor of Dental Surgery . — 1,005
Degree of Doctor of Dental Science . — 8 1,013

Deduct for cases where two degrees were conferred on the same person . — — 8 1,005

HONORARY DEGREES: —
Degree of Master of Arts . . . — 49
Degree of Master of Science . . . — 5
Degree of Doctor of Philosophy . . — 12
Degree of Civil Engineer . . . — 2
Degree of Mechanical Engineer . . — 1
Degree of Doctor of Medicine . . . — 7
Degree of Master of Laws . . . — 1
Degree of Bachelor of Science in Pharmacy — 1
Degree of Master of Pharmacy . . . — 3
Degree of Doctor of Dental Surgery . — 1
Degree of Doctor of Laws . . . — 72
Degree of Doctor of Science . . — 1 155

Deduct for cases where two degrees were conferred on the same person . — — 4 151

17,887

From the above total (17,887) there should be further deducted for cases where persons have taken degrees in more than one Department of the University, as follows: —

Graduates of the Department of Literature, Science, and the Arts who have also received —
    A Degree in the Department of Engineering 29
    A Degree in the Department of Medicine and Surgery . . 146
    A Degree in the Department of Law 316
    A Degree in the School of Pharmacy 27
    A Degree in the Homœopathic Medical College . . . 12

> A Degree in the College of Dental Surgery 4
> An Honorary Degree . . 31   565

Graduates of the Department of Engineering (not counted above) who have also received —
> A Degree in the Department of Medicine and Surgery . . 2
> A Degree in the Department of Law 8
> A Degree in the College of Dental Surgery 2
> An Honorary Degree . . 8   20

Graduates of the Department of Medicine and Surgery (not counted above) who have also received —
> A Degree in the Department of Law 6
> A Degree in the School of Pharmacy 78
> A Degree in the Homœopathic Medical College . . . 1
> A Degree in the College of Dental Surgery 15
> An Honorary Degree . . 7   107

Graduates of the Department of Law (not counted above) who have also received —
> A Degree in the College of Dental Surgery 2
> An Honorary Degree . . 4   6

Graduates of the School of Pharmacy (not counted above) who have also received —
> A Degree in the Homœopathic Medical College . . . 2
> A Degree in the College of Dental Surgery 1
> An Honorary Degree . . 2   5   703

Total Number of persons who have received degrees   17,184

NUMBER OF GRADUATES WHOSE DEATHS HAVE BEEN RECORDED [*]: —
    In the Department of Literature, Science,
        and the Arts 546
    In the Department of Engineering . . 59
    In the Department of Medicine and Surgery 731
    In the Department of Law . . . 705
    In the School of Pharmacy . . . 90
    In the Homœopathic Medical College . 36
    In the College of Dental Surgery . . 53
    Recipients of Honorary Degrees . . 50 2,270

    Deduct for cases where the deceased
      had received degrees in more than
      one Department of the University . 84   2,186

NUMBER OF GRADUATES SUPPOSED TO BE STILL LIVING . . 14,998

SUMMARY OF DEGREES CONFERRED ON WOMEN
1871–1901

DEPARTMENT OF LITERATURE, SCIENCE, AND THE ARTS: —
    Ordinary Degrees conferred . . . — 1,203
    Deduct for cases where two degrees
      were conferred on the same person . — 2 1,201

    Higher Degrees conferred on examination . — 145
    Deduct for cases where two degrees
      were conferred on the same person . 6
    Deduct for cases where the graduate re-
      ceived her bachelor's degree in this De-
      partment 94 100 45 1,246

    Higher Degrees conferred in course (1877), 2
DEPARTMENT OF ENGINEERING . . . . — — — 1
DEPARTMENT OF MEDICINE AND SURGERY . . — — — 398
DEPARTMENT OF LAW: —
    Degree of Bachelor of Laws . — 41
    Degree of Master of Laws . . — 2 43

    Deduct for cases where the Master's de-
      gree was conferred on a graduate of
      this Department . . . . . — — 2 41
SCHOOL OF PHARMACY . . . . . . — — — 40
HOMŒOPATHIC MEDICAL COLLEGE . . . — — — 86
COLLEGE OF DENTAL SURGERY: —
    Degree of Doctor of Dental Surgery . . — 44

[*] Including deaths known to have occurred down to date of publication, November 15, 1902.

Degree of Doctor of Dental Science . . —	2	46	
Deduct for cases where the higher degree was conferred on a graduate of this College . . . . —	—	2	44
HONORARY DEGREES . . . —	—	—	4
			1,860

From the above total (1,860) there should be further deducted for cases where women have received degrees in more than one Department of the University, as follows: —

Graduates of the Department of Literature, Science, and the Arts, who have also received —
  A Degree in the Department of Medicine and Surgery . . . — 13
  A Degree in the Department of Law — 4
  A Degree in the School of Pharmacy — 1
  A Degree in the Homœopathic Medical College . . . . — 1
  An Honorary Degree . . . — 2   21

Graduates of the Department of Medicine and Surgery (not counted above) who have also received —
  A Degree in the School of Pharmacy — — 3
Graduate of the School of Pharmacy (not counted above) who has also received —
  A Degree in the College of Dental Surgery . . . . . — — 1   25

Total number of women who have received degrees . . . 1,835

SUMMARY OF NON-GRADUATES.

The list of non-graduates in the General Catalogue was intended to include the names of all persons who matriculated in any Department of the University, prior to the beginning of the academic year 1897–98, and who had not taken a degree. The list also includes the names of a few persons, who matriculated subsequent to that date, and are not now living.

The total number of names recorded in this way is 12,623. Of these, 2,145 are known to have died, and 10,478 are supposed to be living.

TABLE I.

Tabular Summary of Degrees Conferred in the Department of Literature, Science, and the Arts since the Organization of the University. — 1845-1901.

Year	A. B.	A. M. without previous A. B.	Ph. B.	Ph. M. without previous Ph. B.	B. S. (General)	B. S. (Chemistry)	B. S. (Biology)	B. L.	M. L. without previous B.	A. M.	Ph. M.	M. S.	A. M.	Ph. M.	M. S.	M. L.	Ph. D.	Sc. D.	Total
1845	12																		12
1846	17																		17
1847	12																		12
1848	16																		16
1849	24									2									26
1850	12									5									17
1851	10									4									14
1852	9	1								7									17
1853	11									4									15
1854	21									18									39
1855	15																		17
1856	20				2					4									24
1857	28				7					8									43
1858	30				20					9									59
1859	27				12					13			1			1			54
1860	21				13					25	2								61
1861	37				16					17	3		2						75
1862	37				11					15	4		1		2				70
1863	23				6					8	1		3						41
1864	22				3					12	5		1						43
1865	22				5					28	6				1				62
1866	32				6					19	5								62
1867	26				10					5	5		1						47
1868	37				5					14	2								58
1869	23				9					16	1		1						50
1870	41	1	7		16					21	4		1						91
1871	36		6		8					17	1		1						69
1872	58		7		12					10	1		1						93
1873	40		15		13					18	8		1						95
1874	35		14		13					18	2		2						84
1875	42		21		18					27	2	4	3		1				118
1876	38		13		14					31	6	7			1		2		112
1877	40		19		11					23	3	2	2	1	1				102
1878	41		9		5								2	1			1		59
1879	36		11		4								4	1	1		1		62
1880	33	6	16		2			3					1	2			1		64
1881	54	5	15		5			2					4				1		87
1882	40		19	1	6			8	1				4		3		2		84
1883	51	2	18	1	2			3	1				8	1	3	1			91
1884	52	5	14	1	2			10					8		3		2		97
1885	37	2	17		7			11	1				4		1				80
1886	50		13		7	3	2	5					4				3		87
1887	44		18		9			10					6	1	2		2		92
1888	54		19		8	4	1	18					6	2			3		115
1889	35		28		7		1	15					4		2	1	2	1	96
1890	51		29		10	3	1	20					10	2	3		3	1	133
1891	54		35		11	8	2	19					10	4	3		4		150
1892	62		35		11	6	6	26					5	2	4		7		164
1893	74		53		16	5	8	30					12	5	4	2	1		210
1894	60		44		18	11	5	31					16	9	4	3	5	1	207
1895	66		54		18	5	7	47					6	3	8	3	1		218
1896	58		53		11	4	8	45					11	5	4	3	1		203
1897	63		49		18	9	14	41					18	7	7	1	3	2	232
1898	79		61		26	7	10	59					13	4	11	3	6		279
1899	62		65		37	6	5	54					15	1	4	2	4		255
1900	64		80		51			58					29		4		7		293
1901	241												42			1	5		289
Total	2335	26	857	4	521	71	70	515	3	398	11	67	263	51	79	19	67	5	5362

NOTE.— When the number of ordinary degrees conferred in any year exceeds the number of graduates in the corresponding class-list in the General Catalogue, the difference is due to the fact that, in the class lists, the name of a graduate is not repeated, though he may have taken more than one ordinary degree.

TABLE II.

Tabular Summary of Degrees Conferred in the Department of Engineering since the Organization of the University:—1860-1901.

Year	Ordinary Degrees							Higher Degrees in Course		Higher Degrees on Examination					Total
	Civil Engineering	B. S. (Civ. Eng.)	Mining Eng.	B. S. (Min. Eng.)	B. S. (Mech. Eng.)	B. S. (Elec. Eng.)	B. S. (Chem. Eng.)	A. M.	M. S.	Civ. Eng.	Min. Eng.	Mech. E.	Elec. Eng.	M. S.	
1860	2														2
1861	3														3
1862	1														1
1863	5														5
1864	1														1
1865	6														6
1866	7														7
1867	6		2												8
1868	11		6												17
1869	10		7												18
1870	12		3					1							15
1871	16		1												17
1872	11		1							2					14
1873	11														11
1874	14														14
1875	21														21
1876	11														11
1877	6														6
1878	14		4												18
1879	5		3												8
1880	4		3												7
1881	9														9
1882		3													3
1883		6			1										7
1884		5													5
1885		6			1									1	8
1886		10		2	1										13
1887		10		1	6										17
1888		13		1	7										21
1889		9		4	6										19
1890		12		1	4	3				1	1				22
1891		11			4	3				2					20
1892		9		2	5	5									21
1893		14		2	13	14				1					44
1894		11			15	5				2	1				34
1895		21			11	16				1				1	50
1896		26		1	21	26				1		2	1	1	78
1897		8			16	20				2		1	1	4	48
1898		19			14	23				2				2	60
1899		9			17	22				4				1	53
1900		19			20	9				1					49
1901		10			25	5	1			4		2			47
Total	186	231	30	14	187	151	1	1	2	21	2	6	2	5	839

Note.—Compare Note to Table I.

TABLE III.

Tabular Summary of Degrees Conferred by the University Since Its Organization, arranged by Years and by Departments:—1845-1901.

Year	Dept. of Lit., Sci., and Arts - Ordinary Degrees	Higher Degrees in course	Higher Degrees on Examination	Dept. of Engineering - Ordinary Degrees	Higher Degrees in Course	Higher Deg. on Ex	Degree of M.D. Medicine and Surgery	Dept. of Law - Degree of LL.B.	Degree of LL.M.	School of Pharmacy - Degree of Ph.C.	B.S. (Phar.)	Deg. of Phar. M.	Homœopathic Medical Col. - Degree of M.D.	College of Dental Surg'y - Degree of D.D.S	Deg. of D.D.Sc.	Honorary Degrees	Total
1845	12																12
1846	17																17
1847	12																12
1848	16																16
1849	24	2															26
1850	12	5															17
1851	10	4					6										20
1852	10	7					27									2	46
1853	11	4					34										49
1854	21	18					41										80
1855	17						23										40
1856	20	4					30										54
1857	35	8					27										70
1858	30	9					29										68
1859	39	13	2				24										78
1860	34	27		2			22	24									109
1861	53	20	2	3			43	44									165
1862	48	19	3	1			41	44									156
1863	29	9	3	5			32	48					1				126
1864	25	17	1	1			50	71									165
1865	27	34	1	6			71	81								1	221
1866	38	24		7			74	109								2	254
1867	36	10	1	8			83	146								1	285
1868	42	16		17			81	152								4	312
1869	32	17	1	17	1		97	129		23						3	320
1870	65	25	1	15			86	120		28						3	343
1871	50	18	1	17			82	117		21						2	308
1872	77	15	1	12	2		89	142		5						3	346
1873	68	20	1	11			91	123		9						2	331
1874	62	20	2	14			71	127		20						1	317
1875	81	33	4	21			79	136		18						2	374
1876	65	44	3	11			93	159		31				9			415
1877	70	28		6			84	122		28			13	10		1	366
1878	55		4	18			98	148		22			22	14		1	382
1879	55		7	8			104	193		25			25	15		5	437
1880	60		4	7			92	175		24			19	34		3	418
1881	82		5	9			101	145		33			23	37		7	442
1882	75		9	3			91	170		40			16	32		4	440
1883	78		13	7			117	155		37			17	26		5	455
1884	84		13	5			85	134		38			20	25		2	406
1885	75		5	7	1		80	136		26			6	28		4	368
1886	80		7	13			83	116		23			17	30		4	373
1887	81		11	17			81	154		29		1	13	27		19	433
1888	104		11	21			65	146		23			13	38		3	424
1889	86		10	19			82	147		41			21	34		3	443
1890	114		19	20	2		89	212	6	33			22	38		5	560
1891	129		21	18	2		102	266	15	31		1	18	29		4	636
1892	146		18	21			116	294	20	29		1	18	39		2	704
1893	186		24	43	1		47	327	18	22		1	20	54		4	747
1894	169		38	31	3		64	278	21	22			9	65	1	6	708
1895	197		21	48	2		69	301	9	19			1	45	2	7	721
1896	179		24	74	4		52	324	20	23			6	60		6	772
1897	194		38	44	5		67	52	10	23	3		5	54		8	503
1898	242		37	56	4		70	204	4	19	2		9	55	2	4	708
1899	229		26	48	5		88	219	2	24			10	65	2	4	722
1900	253		40	48	5		93	222	1	24	3		13	67		12	777
1901	241		48	41	6		77	224	4	26	1		16	75	1	6	766
Total	4402	476	484	800	3	36	3523	6636	130	839	9	5	372	1005	8	155	18883

NOTE.—Compare Note to Table I.

TABLE IV.

Table Showing the Number of Degrees That Have Been Conferred on Women; —1871-1901.

Year	A.B.	A.M. no previous A.B.	Ph.B.	B.S. (General)	B.S. (Chemistry)	B.S. (Biology)	B.L.	M.L. no previous B.L.	Ph.M. in Course	A.M.	Ph.M.	M.S.	M.L.	Ph.D.	R.S. (C.E.) Dep't of Engineering	M.D., Dep't of Med. and Surgery	LL.B.	LL.M.	Ph.C., School of Pharmacy	M.D., Homeopathic Med. College	College of Dental Surgery D.D.S.	D.D.Sc.	Honorary Degrees	Total
1871																1	1		2					4
1872	1			1												7	1							10
1873			1													12	2							15
1874	4		3	1												10	2		2					23
1875	4		3	2						1						14	2							27
1876	6		4	2						2		1				15	1		1					30
1877	7		6	1							1	1				16	1		2	2				38
1878	8								1							9	1		1	5				25
1879	4		2	1												16				5				28
1880	4	1	4				1									15	2		1	6	1			34
1881	8	1	1							1						10	1		2	1				26
1882	3		6	1			1									12	1		3	3	4		2	35
1883	8		6	1			2					1				17	2		1	4				42
1884	14		2				3			2						15			1	4	1			42
1885	5		6	2			7	1		1						11	1		1	1	3			39
1886	7		6	2			1			1				1		19	2		1	6	4			50
1887	12		4	3			5			4						15	4		1	6	1			55
1888	15		4			1	6			2	2			1		17	1		1	7	3			60
1889	12		8				8			2						12			1	6				49
1890	15		11	1			8			5	1	1				18	2		1	8	3		1	75
1891	15		17	2			9			1	2				1	16			1	5	1			70
1892	17		16	3		2	11			2	2			2		13	1		2	4	4			78
1893	25		22	5	1	3	17			3	2	1	2			14	2	1	2	3	2	1		104
1894	14		21	8	2		13			3	4		2			6			2	3	3			87
1895	26		28	9		4	17			2	2	2	2		1	10	2			2		1		106
1896	19		34	2	1	4	28			4	2					14	1				1			110
1897	24		28	6		5	14			7	7	2	1	1		13			5	1	2			116
1898	36		30	4			30			6	1	2	2	2		13	3		2	1	1	1		134
1899	33		32	14			25			3		1	2	1		13	1		1	1	1		1	129
1900	31		46	17			34			14						17	1		1	3	5			169
1901	121									19						6	1		6	1	2			156
Total	498	2	351	88	4	19	240	1	2	89	24	11	12	9	1	398	41	2	40	86	44	2	4	1968

NOTE—Compare Note to Table I.

FINANCIAL STATEMENT

The annual report of the University Treasurer, as printed in full in the Proceedings of the Board of Regents, gives a detailed account of the receipts and disbursements of his office for the fiscal year ending June 30, 1902. Under the direction of the Board, this report has been subjected to a careful examination, and has been compared with the books and vouchers in the Treasurer's office. It has been found to be a correct record of the transactions of the year. There is also on file with the Secretary of the Board a full report by the assistant employed in the examination of the books. From the two reports the present summarized statement is, in large measure, compiled.

For several years the University has been receiving from generous friends gifts of money and other forms of property to be held in trust for specific objects named in each case. These gifts are not merged with the general fund of the University, but are cared for independently. An individual account is kept with each fund, and a report of its condition is made by the Treasurer annually. In the present statement, also, these funds will be treated by themselves, after a description of the ordinary transactions of the year.

I. GENERAL ACCOUNT

Leaving out of consideration the balances at the beginning and the end of the year, the Treasurer reports the receipt of $719,251.58, and disbursements amounting to $690,063.36. In this connection, however, attention is called to the fact that the sum of $42,082.30, included by the Treasurer in his receipts, was returned, in June, to the State Treasury for transfer from the general fund to the special accumulating fund for buildings, and that, in consequence, the figures, on both sides of the account are larger by the sum named than they otherwise would be.

Receipts.— In the itemized statement of the sources of income given below, the net receipts from students for laboratory expenses and other charges of analogous character are given as $32,341.26; but this sum should not be considered as an actual addition to the income of the University, but rather as a reimbursement for the cost of material and special supplies purchased by the University for students' use. Neither should the hospital receipts be treated as earnings of the University, for they are made up of payments by patients for board, medicines, and special nursing, the cost of which appears on the other side of the account in the large items of hospital expenses. The services of the faculties are gratuitous to patients whose cases are available for clinical instruction. The hospitals are, in fact, a continual source of large expense, not of income. The receipts from the dental operating room, coming from persons who take advantage of the clinical opportunities there offered, paying only for material used, are also to be regarded as an offset against the expenses of the Department.

Building Fund.— The money set aside by the State Treasurer and the Auditor General as a University Building Fund is drawn, under provisions of State laws, from the proceeds of the quarter-mill tax, and can only be used by the Regents in the erection of new buildings or for extraordinary repairs. The amount received from the State during the year was $71,298.35. The expenditures were as follows:

On the New Medical Building	$76,187 22
On the Science Building	700 00
On the Barbour Gymnasium	469 98
On the New Engineering Building	24 70
On the Law Building	12 51
	$77,394 41

The condition of the building fund, June 30, 1902, was as follows:

Amount in hands of State Treasurer		$187,959 80
Less Overdrafts on books of University Treasurer:		
Electric Light Plant	$ 184 54	
New Engineering Building	24 70	
Barbour Gymnasium	469 98	
New Medical Building	9,147 02	9,826 24
Net Balance		$178,133 56

The whole of the amount standing to the credit of the building fund on the 30th of June, 1902, has been set aside by the Board and by the State Treasurer for use in the construction of the new medical and engineering buildings and in the completion of the Barbour gymnasium; and no part of it is available for other purposes.

General Expenses.— As the University is organized, it is not possible to apportion with accuracy among the several departments the total sum expended during the year; but, in the classification of expenditures given below, an attempt is made to show as clearly as may be the more important facts without entering into minute details. No attempt is made to distribute *pro rata* among the departments the cost of general administration, heating and lighting, care of buildings and grounds, etc., nor the expenses of the gymnasium and the laboratories in which students from more than one department receive instruction at the same time; and some of the minor expenditures provided for in the annual budget are grouped under some comprehensive heading.

In making up the monthly pay rolls, a separate roll is prepared for each department (except the Department of Literature, Science, and the Arts), upon which are placed the names of all the officers whose duties lie wholly, or chiefly, in the department. (The salaries of the Bates Professor of the Diseases of Women and Children, and his assistants, in the Department of Medicine and Surgery, being drawn from the income of the Bates Fund, are not here included.)

The pay roll of the Department of Literature, Science, and the Arts is included in what is designated below as the General Pay Roll. This comprises, in addition to the pay of professors and other instructors in the department, the salaries of the administrative officers of the University, with their necessary assistants and clerks, and of the whole body of permanent employees, of whatever grade, who are paid by the year or month, and are not elsewhere included. The pay rolls of laborers employed for short periods, and paid accordingly, are charged to the contingent account, the repairs account, or otherwise, according to the nature of the service rendered.

Summary of Receipts, Showing Sources of Income, for the Fiscal Year Ending June 30, 1902

A. From the State Treasury:
  For Current Expenses:
    Proceeds of quarter-mill tax for the year 1901 (two
      tenths, on the basis of the valuation of 1896)..$ 55,255 00
    Proceeds of quarter-mill tax for the year 1902 (seven
      tenths, on the basis of the valuation of 1901).. 276,167 50

Special Appropriation for Homœopathic Medical
  College ....$ 6,000 00
Special Appropriation for Summer Hospitals...... 3,000 00
University Interest.............................. 38,285 47
For Buildings and Extraordinary Repairs............ 71,298 35

  Total from State Treasury...................$450,006 32

B. FROM STUDENTS' FEES AND DEPOSITS:

  (1) Matriculation Fees and Annual Fees:
    Department of Literature, Science, and
      the Arts......................$ 55,180 00
    Department of Engineering......... 21,365 00
    Department of Medicine and Surgery. 20,995 00
    Department of Law................. 40,195 00
    School of Pharmacy................ 3,225 00
    Homœopathic Medical College....... 2,820 00
    College of Dental Surgery.......... 8,335 00
    Summer Sessions:
      Literary Department............ 5,115 00
      Medical Department............. 1,150 00
      Law Department................. 1,158 00
                                      $159,538 00
    Less amounts refunded to students un-
      der the regulations of the Regents 3,600 00 $155,938 00

  (2) Diploma Fees..................... $8,240 00
      Less sums refunded...............   95 00   8,145 00

  (3) Payments and deposits on account of
      laboratory or demonstration courses,
      rent of gymnasium lockers, use of
      keys and drawing boards, and the
      like $35,519 25
      Less sums returned to students on
        settlement of accounts......... 3,177 99   32,341 26

    Net Receipts from Students' Fees and Deposits....$196,424 26

C. RECEIPTS FROM MISCELLANEOUS SOURCES:
    From University Hospital.............$ 39,204 33
    From Homœopathic Hospital............ 14,942 71
    From Dental Operating Room...........   5,027 66
    From Engineering Shops...............   661 83
    From Interest on Bank Deposits.......   898 73
    Unclassified 5,212 75 $65,948 01

RECAPITULATION:
- From State Treasury..............................$450,006 32
- From Students' Fees and Deposits (gross receipts)..... 203,297 25
- From Miscellaneous Sources.......................   65,948 01

  Total receipts, as previously stated...............$719,251 58

Summary of Expenditures for the Fiscal Year Ending June 30, 1902

A. PAY ROLLS:
- General Pay Roll................................$176,579 44
- Department of Engineering........................   42,686 38
- Department of Medicine and Surgery................   38,785 00
  - University Hospital............................   12,791 83
- Department of Law...............................   39,184 00
- School of Pharmacy and Chemical Laboratory.........   24,453 26
- Homœopathic Medical College.....................   11,000 65
  - Homœopathic Hospital..........................   4,337 09
- College of Dental Surgery...........................   13,240 00
- Summer Schools:
  - Literary 6,545 00
  - Medical 803 75
  - Law 1,556 00

  $371,962 40

B. EXPENSES FOR LABORATORIES, SHOPS, DEMONSTRATION COURSES, ETC.:
- Anatomical Laboratory, material and supplies......... $ 2,094 98
- Botanical Laboratory and Garden....................   965 58
- Chemical Laboratory...............................   12,055 64
- Dental Operating Room (including incidental expenses of the College of Dental Surgery)................   6,038 29
- Electrotherapeutical Laboratory.......................   433 09
- Engineering Laboratory and Shops....................   5,825 48
- Histological Laboratory.............................   742 71
- Hygienic Laboratory...............................   3,123 19
- Pathological Laboratory............................   557 04
- Physical Laboratory...............................   1,222 44
- Physiological Laboratory............................   509 04
- Surgical Clinics and Demonstrations.................   299 16
- Zoological Laboratory.............................   997 04

  $34,863 68

C. LIBRARIES:
Book Purchases (not including purchases from trust funds):
  General Library................................. $8,580 69

Medical Library	$ 2,124 31
Law Library	2,135 77
Homœopathic Library	218 38
Dental Library	364 33
Bindery Pay Roll	2,152 10
Incidental Expenses, assistants, cataloguing, etc.	1,134 30
	$16,709 88

D. DEPARTMENTAL CURRENT EXPENSES:

Department of Literature, Science, and the Arts (Appointment Committee, English, French, Geology, German, Greek, History, Latin, Mineralogy, Music, Philosophy, Semitics)	$ 1,532 96
Department of Engineering (Civil Engineering, Incidentals, Naval Architecture)	1,021 58
Department of Medicine and Surgery (Asylum Pathologist, Dermatology, Incidentals, Materia Medica, Nervous Diseases, Ophthalmology, Theory and Practice)	1,506 81
Department of Law	805 82
Homœopathic Medical College	454 24
Summer Schools:	
Literary	372 77
Medical	31 75
Law	81 28
Hospitals:	
University Hospital	22,624 52
Summer Expenses	1,995 35
Homœopathic Hospital	14,534 94
Summer Expenses	1,004 65
Laundry	4,556 80
	$50,523 57

E. MISCELLANEOUS CURRENT EXPENSES:

Contingent (including purchase of real estate)	$ 9,501 14
Ordinary Repairs	11,120 15
Fuel and Lights	21,937 95
Water Supply	1,858 57
Electrical and Heating Plants (supplies and pay rolls)	3,355 73
Carpenter Shop (material) and Care of Teams	2,306 25
Diplomas and Commencement Expenses	2,513 90
Advertising and Printing	2,302 34
Postage	1,672 17
News Letter and Alumni Association	1,400 00
General Catalogue	2,920 26
Michigan Law Review	300 00
Gymnasiums	993 04

Museum	$ 451	35
Observatory	216	91
Inspection of Schools	644	51
Return of Students' Fees and Deposits	6,872	99
	$70,367	26

F. NEW BUILDINGS AND EXTRAORDINARY REPAIRS:

On account of New Law Building	$ 12	51
On account of Psychopathic Ward	24	60
On account of Engineering Building	24	70
On account of Barbour Gymnasium	469	98
On account of Science Building	700	00
On account of Addition to Heating Plant	26,135	26
On account of Medical Building	76,187	22
	$103,554	27

G. RETURNED TO STATE TREASURY:

For Transfer to Special Building Fund............... $42,082 30

RECAPITULATION:

Pay Rolls	$371,962	40
Laboratories, etc.	34,863	68
Libraries	16,709	88
Departmental Current Expenses (including hospital accounts)	50,523	57
Miscellaneous Current Expenses (heating, lighting, ordinary repairs, refunds to students, etc.)	70,367	26
New Buildings and Extraordinary Repairs	103,554	27
Refund to State Treasury for Transfer to Building Fund	42,082	30
Total, as previously stated	$690,063	36

II. TRUST FUNDS

The changes in the trust funds during the year may be summarized as follows:

Balance reported by Treasurer, June 30, 1901	$243,890	61
Received during the year as gifts and contributions	23,824	36
Proceeds of sale of real estate in Detroit (Walter Crane Fund)	1,165	60
Gain over book value on sale of property belonging to the Williams Fund	46	24
Income (interest, rents, etc.)	12,435	43
	$281,362	24

Paid for expenses and the specific objects of the several funds	$ 20,449 06		
Shrinkage from estimated value on sale of property belonging to the Bates Fund	325 00	$20,774	06
Balance, June 30, 1902		$260,588	18

The foregoing sum is represented by property as follows:

Cash in hands of University Treasurer...	$103,630 29	
Investments and Securities (not including those belonging to the Williams Fund)	114,785 00	
Real Estate belonging to the Bates Fund (estimated value)..................	29,423 43	
		$247,838 72
Williams Fund (portion not included above):		
Cash in hands of Mr. Field......... $	487 36	
Investments and Securities..........	10,495 00	
Real Estate (book value)..........	1,767 10	12,749 46
		$260,588 18

At the beginning of the year there were thirty-eight trust accounts on the books of the Treasurer, though in three of them (the Parke, Davis & Co. Fellowship, the D. M. Ferry Botanical Fellowship, and the Nelson, Baker & Co. Fellowship) there was temporarily no balance of cash on hand. During the year one account was closed (the Pilgrim Publishing Company Fellowship), and three new accounts were opened (the Palmer Memorial, the Buhl Classical Fellowship, and the Walter Crane Fund).

In February, 1902, Mrs. Margaret Smith Hunt conveyed to the Board of Regents, in trust, the title to a certain tract of land, subject to certain life interests therein and to other conditions named in the deed. The purpose of this gift was to establish two new scholarships, the James B. Hunt Scholarship and the Charles J. Hunt Scholarship, and to provide a larger endowment for the Margaret Smith Hunt Scholarships, established in 1900. No valuation has been assigned to this real estate on the Treasurer's books, and, as no income has yet been derived therefrom, no account has been opened with the fund.

The purposes for which the several funds were established, and accounts were opened, have been quite various in character:

Funds Available for Immediate Use.— It frequently happens that money is given, or funds are raised, to procure an expensive piece of apparatus, or to provide for an expenditure which the Regents are unable to make from other funds under their control. Gifts of this kind are available for immediate use, and the accounts are essentially temporary in character. But it is often necessary to keep an account open for a considerable time, and the balances reported by the Treasurer are no just measure of the value of the gifts or the generosity of the givers. The following funds and accounts belong in this category:

1. The Philo Parsons Fund for the increase and enlargement of the Parsons Library.
2. The Buhl Fund for the purchase of books for the Law Library.
3. The fund contributed for the purchase of books relating to early Christian literature.
4. The fund for the purchase of material to illustrate the instruction in Latin, known as the Special Latin Fund.
5. The fund given for the purchase of apparatus for experimenting with liquid air.
6. The fund for the purchase of chemical apparatus.
7. The contribution toward a fund for the construction of a music hall.
8. The contribution in aid of the American School at Rome, with which Professor F. W. Kelsey was connected in the year 1900-01.
9. The contribution for a Class Memorial from members of the Literary Class of 1899.
10. The bequest of the late Mrs. Love M. Palmer for the erection of a hospital ward in memory of her husband, Alonzo Benjamin Palmer, who for many years was Dean of the Department of Medicine and Surgery.
11, 12. The Warner Deposit and the Walter Crane Fund, the ultimate disposition of which has not yet been determined.

Fellowships and Scholarships Supported by Individuals or Associations.— In a second class of cases the Treasurer of the University simply serves as a medium of communication between the supporters and the holders of scholarships and fellowships. He has nothing to do with the management or disposition of the principal sum of a permanent endowment; and though, in this connection, during the past few years, many thousands of dollars have passed through his hands, from donors to beneficiaries, the amount of money in his possession at any one time has been comparatively small.

In the following list the funds of this class are named. Some of them have been maintained for several years in succession by the generosity of individual givers or associations.

1. The Elisha Jones Classical Fellowship.
2. The Parke, Davis & Co. Fellowship in Chemistry.
3. The Stearns Pharmacy Fellowship.

4. The Peter White Fellowship in American History.
5. The D. M. Ferry Botanical Fellowship.
6. The James W. Scott Classical Fellowship.
7. The Michigan Gas Association Fellowship for "special post-graduate work in the line of gas engineering."
8. The International Club Scholarships, for the support of three Philippine students in the University; the fund to be administered according to instructions accompanying the draft sent by the club.
9. The Nelson, Baker & Co. Fellowship in Pharmaceutical Research.
10. The Biological Laboratory Scholarship.
11. The Buhl Classical Fellowship.

Endowed Fellowships, Etc.— In a third class of cases the University has accepted moneys or other property in trust for the formation of loan funds, or of funds the income of which only is to be expended for scholarships, fellowships, or prizes. In this class of cases the trusts are usually subject to certain conditions or limitations. Some of these conditions are mentioned in the descriptions that follow:

1. The Seth Harrison Scholarship Fund was established, in memory of her father, by Mrs. Clara Harrison Stranahan, of Brooklyn, New York. The income is to be used for the benefit of descendants of Seth Harrison who may be pursuing studies in the Department of Literature, Science, and the Arts of the University of Michigan, whenever applicants properly qualified present themselves. Provision is made, however, for applying the income of the fund to scholarships for other persons, "if at any time there shall be a period of seven years during which there are no qualified applicants," descendants of Seth Harrison. There is also a condition to the effect that "if the income . . . provides a surplus for any year, . . . such surplus shall be held for a period of three years to meet the needs occurring when a larger number of beneficiaries present themselves. But at intervals of three years any unexpended portion of the income shall be added to the principal."

2. The Phillips Scholarships Fund was established, under the conditions of the bequest, for the maintenance of scholarships, to be open only to candidates for the degree of Bachelor of Arts, who excel in the Greek and Latin studies required for admission to the University. As an endowment for this fund Mr. Phillips set aside certain pieces of real estate in the

city of Philadelphia, which are still held by the University.
This property has no valuation assigned it on the books of the
University, but it yields a small income each year, and this is
accounted for by the Treasurer in his reports.

3. In September, 1897, at the request of the Alumni Association of the University, the Regents assumed the management
of moneys contributed toward a fund for the maintenance of
fellowships, the first of which, when established, to be named
in memory of the late Prof. George Sylvester Morris. The
income of the fund, which is as yet insufficient for the proper
support of the fellowship, is added yearly to the principal.

4. In July, 1900, certain pieces of real estate were conveyed
by deeds to the University, subject to the life-interests of persons named therein; and again in February, 1902, other conveyances of similar character were made. Upon these foundations,
after the termination of the life-interests, the Charles James
Hunt Fellowships, the Charles James Hunt Scholarship, the
James B. Hunt Scholarship, and the Margaret Smith Hunt
Scholarships are to be established. For the present no valuation is assigned to these funds, and no accounts with them have
been opened on the books of the Treasurer.

5. The Class of 1894 established a fund, which now amounts
to $1,526.41, "to be used as a loan fund for the benefit of needy
and worthy undergraduates in the Literary Department" of the
University.

6, 7, 8. The Classes of 1897 and 1898, and the Law Class
of 1899, have also laid the foundations of funds to be used under
certain conditions for loans or for scholarships.

9. The Newton Van der Veer Loan Fund is to be used to
aid "needy students in such amounts and under such conditions
as the executive head of the University may deem proper and
wise."

10. In the year 1899, and again in 1900, the Directors of
the Students' Lecture Association placed in the hands of the
Regents a portion of the profits of the year's entertainments,
to be used as a loan fund under certain specified conditions.

11. The Good Government Club, an organization of students, has presented to the Regents the proceeds of courses of
lectures, the income from which is available as a prize "for the
best essay on some theme connected with the subject of good
government."

Other Endowments.—A fourth group of funds includes those

intended to provide for some special want of the University, though the Regents are restricted in their expenditures to the income derived from them. To this group belong the funds described below:

1. The Goethe Library Fund was established in the year 1886 by contributions solicited by Prof. Calvin Thomas. The records show that the sum of $1,318.00 was received from contributors, of which $1,000.00 was available for immediate use. It was also provided that "all money above the said $1,000.00 which is in or may come into this fund, shall be invested, . . . and only the interest thereon . . . be expended." By an oversight the principal sum has become impaired, and, in consequence, the expenditure of income is temporarily suspended.

2. In the year 1894, the University received a bequest of $10,000.00 for the benefit of the General Library, under the will of Miss Jean L. Coyl, of Detroit. By the terms of the will the "income is to be devoted to the purchase of . . . books, . . . and the books thus purchased are to be named after my deceased brother, Col. William Henry Coyl, the Coyl Collection."

3. The late Professor Corydon La Ford left by will to the University the sum of $20,000.00 for the purchase of books for the General Library, the condition being attached that the books thus purchased shall bear a label reading — "Bought with the income of the Ford-Messer Fund."

4. The Williams Professorship. In March, 1887, at the request of the Society of the Alumni of the Department of Literature, Science, and the Arts, the Regents established the Williams Professorship, as an *Emeritus* Professorship, the incumbent to be appointed in accordance with the terms of a resolution adopted at that time. For several years the fund raised by subscription among the alumni remained in charge of the Society of the Alumni or its agents; but in 1897 the property constituting the fund was transferred by the Society to the custody of the Regents, and entered upon the books of the University at its face value, though doubt existed as to the real value of some of the items. The condition of the fund is thought to be much better at present than for several years past.

5. The Bates Professorship. By the will of the late Elizabeth H. Bates, the University came into possession of money, real estate, and securities of various kinds, with which to found a professorship according to conditions named in the will. In

the settlement with the executors of the will the property was accepted by the Regents at a valuation approved by the proper court. On the basis of this settlement, the Regents, in April, 1900, placed the value of the principal sum of the fund at $133,304.65. It is possible, however, that a revaluation of some of the property may be needed, and the sum above named is to be regarded as a close approximation to the true value, though subject to future revision.

6. In the spring of 1899, the Regents accepted a gift of $10,000.00 to be applied toward the endowment of a woman's professorship. As the income of this sum would be insufficient for the salary of the professor, no appointment to the position has yet been made, and for the present the interest is to be added annually to the principal.

7. The Allopathic Hospital Fund was established in conformity with the bequest of the late Hannah E. Davis for the benefit of the Hospital under the charge of the Faculty of the Department of Medicine and Surgery (described in the will as the Allopathic Hospital, and, therefore, so designated in the title of the account on the University's books).

8. The Treadwell Fund. Under the provisions of the will of the late Adah Z. Treadwell, the sum of $2,000.00 has been placed in the State Treasury, to be known as The Treadwell Fund, the annual income of which is to be used by the Regents for the support of a free bed for some poor and deserving patient in the University Hospital. No income from this source has yet reached the hands of the University Treasurer, and no account has been opened on his books.

Tabular statement of the balances in the several trust accounts on the books of the Treasurer at the beginning and at the end of the fiscal year (including the portion of the Williams Fund in charge of Mr. George S. Field, of Detroit). For the Hunt Fellowships and Scholarships and the Treadwell Fund, no accounts have yet been opened, as has been stated above.

Balance, June 30, 1901.	DESIGNATION OF FUND.	Balance, June 30, 1902.
$ 105 27	Philo Parsons.............................$	108 46
602 42	Buhl Law Library.........................	542 75
12 40	Liquid Air Plant..........................	12 49
8 08	Early Christian Literature.................	8 20

31 99	Special Latin	$ 2 32
101 00	Chemical Apparatus	107 67
1,291 58	Music Hall	1,330 76
10 00	American School at Rome	11
6 35	Class of 1899 Memorial	6 35
	Palmer Ward	17,932 30
1 02	Warner Deposit	1 05
	Walter Crane (principal, $1,165.60)	1,168 60
8 95	Elisha Jones Classical Fellowship	9 16
	Parke, Davis & Co. Fellowship	
1 56	Stearns Pharmacy Fellowship	1 56
422 14	Peter White Fellowship	437 94
	D. M. Ferry Botanical Fellowship	
342 91	James W. Scott Classical Fellowship	16 93
300 00	Pilgrim Publishing Co. Fellowship	
43 28	Gas Association Fellowship........*Overdrawn*	[42 43]
	Nelson, Baker & Co. Fellowship	
	Buhl Classical Fellowship	
50 00	Biological Laboratory Scholarship	50 00
4,565 00	International Club Scholarships	3,526 25
27,874 15	Seth Harrison Scholarships (original principal, $25,000.00; accumulated principal, $26,939.96)	29,052 31
651 10	Phillips Scholarships	550 55
2,590 75	Morris Alumni Fellowship	2,718 67
1,450 67	Loan Fund of the Class of 1894	1,526 41
160 95	Class Scholarship of 1897	177 53
279 14	Class Scholarship of 1898	286 70
31 40	Law Class of 1899 Loan Fund	32 12
155 14	Newton Van der Veer Loan Fund	210 59
966 94	Students' Lecture Association Loan Fund	1,005 33
634 71	Good Government Club Prize Fund	653 89
200 02	Goethe Library (principal, $318.00)	206 09
12,299 20	Coyl Collection (principal, $10,000.00)	12,659 38
25,424 70	Ford-Messer (principal, $20,000.00)	24,375 77
16,170 54	Williams Professorship	16,849 00
134,471 66	Bates Professorship	131,677 12
10,525 00	Woman's Professorship	11,221 95
2,100 59	Hannah Elizabeth Davis Allopathic Hospital (principal, $2,054.05)	2,164 30
$243,890 61		*$260,588 18

*After deducting overdraft of $42.43 in the Gas Association Fellowship Fund.

For the Regents,
GEORGE A. FARR,
ARTHUR HILL,
Finance Committee.

www.ingramcontent.com/pod-product-compliance
Lightning Source LLC
Chambersburg PA
CBHW030403230426
43664CB00007BB/719